THE DIVINE VISION OF DANTE'S *PARADISO*

In Canto XVIII of the *Paradiso*, Dante sees thirty-five letters of Scripture – LOVE JUSTICE, YOU WHO RULE THE EARTH – "painted" one after the other in the sky. It is an epiphany that encapsulates the *Paradiso*, staging its ultimate goal – the divine vision. This book offers a fresh, intensive reading of this extraordinary passage at the heart of the third canticle of the *Divine Comedy*. While adapting in novel ways the methods of the traditional *lectura Dantis*, William Franke meditates independently on the philosophical, theological, political, ethical, and aesthetic ideas that Dante's text so provocatively projects into a multiplicity of disciplinary contexts. This book demands that we question not only what Dante may have meant by his representations, but also what they mean for us today in the broad horizon of our intellectual traditions and cultural heritage.

WILLIAM FRANKE is Professor of Comparative Literature and Religious Studies at Vanderbilt University and Visiting Professor of Philosophy at the University of Navarra. He is a research fellow of the Alexander von Humboldt-Stiftung and has been Fulbright-University of Salzburg Distinguished Chair in Intercultural Theology and Study of Religions. His books include *Dante's Interpretive Journey* (1996), *On What Cannot Be Said* (2007), *Poetry and Apocalypse* (2009), *Dante and the Sense of Transgression* (2013), *A Philosophy of the Unsayable* (2014), *The Revelation of Imagination: From the Bible and Homer through Virgil and Augustine to Dante* (2015), *Secular Scriptures: Modern Theological Poetics in the Wake of Dante* (2016), *A Theology of Literature* (2017), and *On the Universality of What Is Not: The Apophatic Turn in Critical Thinking* (2020).

THE DIVINE VISION
OF DANTE'S *PARADISO*

The Metaphysics of Representation

WILLIAM FRANKE

CAMBRIDGE
UNIVERSITY PRESS

Shaftesbury Road, Cambridge CB2 8EA, United Kingdom

One Liberty Plaza, 20th Floor, New York, NY 10006, USA

477 Williamstown Road, Port Melbourne, VIC 3207, Australia

314–321, 3rd Floor, Plot 3, Splendor Forum, Jasola District Centre, New Delhi – 110025, India

103 Penang Road, #05–06/07, Visioncrest Commercial, Singapore 238467

Cambridge University Press is part of Cambridge University Press & Assessment, a department of the University of Cambridge.

We share the University's mission to contribute to society through the pursuit of education, learning and research at the highest international levels of excellence.

www.cambridge.org
Information on this title: www.cambridge.org/9781009016919

DOI: 10.1017/9781009037839

First published 2021
First paperback edition 2023

A catalogue record for this publication is available from the British Library

Library of Congress Cataloging-in-Publication data
NAMES: Franke, William, author.
TITLE: The divine vision of Dante's Paradiso : the metaphysics of representation / William Franke.
DESCRIPTION: Cambridge, United Kingdom ; New York, NY : Cambridge University Press, 2021. | Includes bibliographical references and index.
IDENTIFIERS: LCCN 2021010782 (print) | LCCN 2021010783 (ebook) | ISBN 9781316517024 (hardback) | ISBN 9781009037839 (ebook)
SUBJECTS: LCSH: Dante Alighieri, 1265–1321. Paradiso. Canto 18. | Revelation in literature. | LCGFT: Literary criticism.
CLASSIFICATION: LCC PQ4454 .F73 2021 (print) | LCC PQ4454 (ebook) | DDC 851/.1–dc23
LC record available at https://lccn.loc.gov/2021010782
LC ebook record available at https://lccn.loc.gov/2021010783

ISBN   978-1-316-51702-4   Hardback
ISBN   978-1-009-01691-9   Paperback

Contents

Figures

Prologue

Subject and Scope of the Work

This book offers a sharply focused reading of one of the most extraordinary passages at the heart of Dante's *Paradiso*. In Canto XVIII, Dante sees thirty-five letters of Scripture – DILIGITE IUSTITIAM / QUI IUDICATIS TERRAM – "painted" ("dipinto") one after the other in the sky. After a dazzling song and dance, each of the incandescent letters breaks up into its component sparks, each spark a blessed soul. These soul-sparks then regroup to form the next letter in the series. The last letter, M, finally metamorphoses into a figure – the emblematic sign of the Roman Imperial Eagle outlined in its head and wings. Considered specifically from a literary-theoretical point of view, this scene is arguably the most challenging and intriguing in the poem. In some vertiginous regards, this epiphany encapsulates the *Paradiso* as a whole by staging its ultimate goal – the divine vision – self-reflexively in a *mise-en-abîme* as an instance of the writing of letters.

In this cosmic staging of letters from Holy Scripture, the inner, spiritual experience of Dante's *visio Dei* takes on an external, aesthetic form as a written figure. Words and letters that are revealed from heaven show forth also as a consummate poetic creation. In teasing ways, this extraordinary revelation of Scripture constitutes an exception within a poem in which the divine vision as such tends to withdraw behind the veil of ineffability that is tirelessly evoked from beginning to end. This exception, in which God is directly envisioned in the letters of Scripture, each one being individually contemplated as a divine Name, serves to reveal the enabling condition of the entire poem, namely, writing, since the poem in the end is made up of nothing but writing. The divine vision is displayed here as revealed in the poem's material means – writing – which is itself then broken down into its own basic building blocks, *viz.*, letters. These letters, furthermore, dissolve into what appear to be random sparks, though actually they are providentially guided soul-lights forming, as if by a miracle, into the intelligible shapes of letters and even spelling out a verse from Scripture, hence the divine Word.

The monograph in hand presents a reading of this particularly provocative passage near the climax of Dante's complete oeuvre. At the same time, such an exegetical exercise also furnishes the occasion for investigating some fundamental theoretical issues concerning, notably, the metaphysics of representation, particularly with respect to God. The scene probes the epistemological conditions of possibility of a vision of theological transcendence. For this purpose, Dante employs poetic modes as his indispensable means. Dante's text raises key questions regarding representation in language of the ultimately real, questions that are decisive today for criticism throughout the humanities and social sciences and even more broadly across the entire spectrum of discursive disciplines. These questions and their analogues are inseparably literary-critical, philosophical, and theological, and they infiltrate the domains of the ethical and the political as well.

The book, accordingly, aims to interpret Dante's paradisiacal vision of writing in terms opening it up to philosophical analysis and, furthermore, to speculative contemplation that is simultaneously aesthetic and spiritual in nature. The Heaven of Jupiter (or Jove, "Giove," as this heaven is christened explicitly in XVIII. 95) is, in crucial respects, the metaliterary pivot-point where the poem probes most searchingly its own creative source springs and the poeticological methods that make it materially feasible as a linguistic performance. In the passage placed under scrutiny (*Paradiso* XVIII. 71–136), the poem reflects upon itself both in its theological underpinnings and in its literary techniques. It turns attention specifically to the material substrate and scriptural medium comprised by its own representational apparatus as the vehicles and pragmatic instruments for its actualization of a mystical experience.

In following up Dante's literary visions with philosophical reflections, I am continuing a procedure already at least implicit within the poem itself. I intend, furthermore, that the book should be useful to many diverse readers looking to find in Dante something answering to their own interests and quests. It aims to interest researchers, for example, investigating the relation between word and image in art history and aesthetic theory, as well as those sounding the materialities of signification in media studies. But the consequences for these and for other disciplines are left largely to be drawn by scholars working in those fields.

The book offers a kind of *lectura Dantis* focused on one heaven of the *Paradiso*, yet it also enfolds in embryo a philosophical interpretation of modernity as it emerges from the intellectual and spiritual matrices that Dante discloses in this astonishing and perspicuous epiphany. This interpretation is extended to other passages of the *Paradiso* in a companion work titled *Dante's* Paradiso *and the Origins of Modern Thought: Toward a Speculative Philosophy of Self-Reflection* (Routledge, 2021). Here, in contrast, I remain focused on a single – albeit superlatively significant – juncture of the poem.

Unlike the traditional *lectura Dantis*, the present work proposes not only to "read" the text as accurately as possible, adhering strictly to Dante's own views, but also to meditate independently on the philosophical, theological, political, ethical, and aesthetic ideas that Dante's text so audaciously projects onto a multiplicity of disciplinary backgrounds. The question is not only what Dante may have meant by his representations, but also what they can mean for us today in the broad horizon of our intellectual traditions and cultural heritage.

Thus, like my previous books on Dante, this book, too, is a work of philosophical reflection. It interprets Dante's text as disclosing to us the nature of a fundamental idea in philosophy, namely, that of mediation. This idea evolves in the course of intellectual history. Mediation of supersensible ideas by their sensible instantiations through metaphysical "participation," as laid out in Plato's philosophy, eventually turns, particularly with Hegel's thinking, into dialectical mediation of material and ideal phenomena dynamically by their negations. These mediations make up the course of world history, with its triumphant progression and tragic struggles. Mediation, as an overarching trope connecting the universe together in this culminating Hegelian paradigm, is subsequently dismantled by the deconstruction of representation through writing – or *écriture* – with Hegel's postmodern heirs, signally Jacques Derrida.

This entire trajectory, with its divergent possibilities, is prefigured by Dante's poetics aiming at a kind of comprehensive theological revelation of the relation of all reality to its ungraspable Ground, which must be imagined as both necessary and impossible. Ultimately, this is a *negative-theological* revelation – and thus also a withdrawal from revelation – since Dante's vision suggests that revelation as mediation takes place essentially in the gaps opened up by ruptures in the chain of rationally demonstrable links between divinity and its material manifestations. At its most intense and climactic moments in its "figuration of Paradise," the "sacred poem" must "jump, like someone who finds their path cut off" ("e così, figurando il paradiso, / convien saltar lo sacrato poema, / come chi trova suo cammin reciso," XXIII. 61–63).

Dante's text, moreover, displays how these gaps can be filled in by the "revelatory" work of the imagination operating in a state of ecstasy. Dante's imagining of the Empyrean, where God governs directly and without any means of mediation ("dove Dio sanza mezzo governa," XXX. 122) purports to convey a kind of unmediated vision. This is where Dante sees the face of Beatrice "without admixture of any medium" ("ché sua effige / non discendea a me per mezzo mista," XXXI. 77–78). And yet, the scene of letters flashing in the Heaven of Jupiter contemplates how the medium of writing is itself intrinsic to the vision – how Dante's vision of God is an irreducibly *written* vision. In the end, this theophany of letters in *Paradiso* XVIII graphically shows that the medium itself is what Dante immediately views. In this scene, Dante totally mediates the divine Absolute with his vision's own *literary* medium. His vision of God is literally a written vision and is hardly imaginable apart from this written form. Such are among the consequences of his Christian understanding of the revelation of God as Incarnate Word apprehended in and through Scripture. The incarnation of the Word specifically in writing reveals another face of this doctrine, one that poetry alone can expound and explore.

For the record, the original and working title for the manuscript of this book throughout the course of its elaboration was "The Written Vision: Scripture as Theophany in Dante's Heaven of Jupiter." Publishing has its own exigencies and imposes them now especially in determining books' titles as they go on the market, but the seed of the work's conception preserved in its original title is worth bearing in mind. This title is a (re) source that makes it possible to grasp the internal coherence of the book and that accurately expresses the essential insight from which it springs in all of its overflowing implications.

Method of Inquiry and Bifocal Structure

In order to accommodate the different purposes of primarily literary readers together with those who are more philosophically minded, I have capped the extent to which the philosophical inquiry is pursued in the main chapters by moving a substantial amount of material to Excursuses. This allows the reader to focus on the book's critical interpretation of the passage from the *Paradiso* without being unduly sidetracked by its philosophical ramifications. As a result, the "Excursuses" are something more than what this expedient rubric might suggest. They are integral to the philosophical reflection proposed by the book, but they are supplementary with respect to its literary-critical agenda. The successive subsections in each main chapter already tend in this speculative direction, so I do not mean to suggest anything like a neat division between criticism and philosophy – or between exegesis and theoretical reflection. Quite the contrary. In the course of the more exegetical segments, I have always already adumbrated the paths that speculative inquiry would pursue, even where the further development of such connections is deferred to the Excursuses.

Nonetheless, the structure of the book, as articulated into two parts, mirrors its hybrid nature and inflects its contents in a way meant to assist different sorts of readers in finding their way to what interests them most. Relegating the further pursuit of the theoretical arguments to separate Excursuses enables the reader to ponder the reading of the primary poetic text – *Paradiso* XVIII. 70–136, followed by cantos XIX and XX, all of which together comprise the Heaven of Jupiter – through to the end without examining in all their details the more far-reaching ideas concerning language that come up along the way. Nevertheless, both of these registers are fully intertwined in Dante's overall vision and, consequently, in the conception of the book.

Although wide-ranging theoretical issues are raised by the poetic text and its interpretation as it unfolds in the discussion in the chapters, there are limits as to how much of this material can be absorbed and supported by a unified structure of continuous exposition. Giving a coherent reading of the Heaven of Jove is wedded here to a broader enterprise of following up and working out the intellectual implications and speculative suggestions of Dante's scene in terms engaging philosophical and theological thought and literary theory in our own time. The scene's representation of an apotheosis of letters of Scripture flickers with insights for elucidating the nature and origins of language considered as originary theological revelation. This speculative *élan* is not only my own penchant: it belongs also intrinsically to Dante's project itself. The text calls to be read as a synthesis, if not a summa, of ideas that probe perennial philosophical and theological questions concerning language, its origins, its seemingly miraculous capacities, and its limits – especially as a vehicle of divine revelation.

My expository division between the literary vision and pertinent philosophical reflections is thus merely heuristic and highly porous. It is not even fully consistent, since it applies only in a reduced degree to the first chapter, where I feel the need to outline in some detail the theoretical issues that are central to the book as a whole. In any case, this method distinguishes exegetical and speculative moments not in order ultimately to separate them but rather to articulate their synergisms more effectively.

Dante's vernacular masterpiece opens itself to the dynamism of language and life: it relinquishes the static ideal of an unchanging law and linguistic norm. This has generally been viewed as a mark of Dante's modernity and can even be taken as representing a decisive break with a medieval transcendental theological viewpoint in favor of a more secular outlook. Still, it is important to see that the sources of this insight are, nevertheless, theological in nature. I intend by this close – and, at the same time, also distant – reading of a particular text by Dante to illustrate more broadly the theological inspiration of some of the most path-breaking insights of the modern world. My reading of Dante thus views him in his historical context designedly from the distance of our own.[1]

This, then, is an example of how the study of Dante can be pursued not exclusively for the sake of a more accurate understanding of his text alone, but also as a means of deepening our knowledge of certain pivotal topics in the humanities and of their high degree of relevance to human concerns generally. This book endeavors to link the extraordinary insight into language opened up by Dante's inventions in the *Paradiso* to some of the most challenging thinking about language in contemporary thought, especially in linguistically oriented philosophies.

The *Paradiso* comprises something of a poetic encyclopedia or compendium of theories of language, and the book in hand touches on a considerable range of them. In terms of contemporary forms and equivalents, it privileges post-structuralist theories of language for their affinity with Dante's premodern poetic adventure specifically in the *Paradiso*. This affinity owes much to the negative-theological matrix within which crucial aspects of Dante's culminating work are embedded. The French thinking of "difference" figures prominently in this approach, just as it figures prominently in the theoretical debates concerning critical theory in recent decades. However, the present work places this French deconstructive theoretical background into an integrated frame with the German hermeneutical tradition. These two broad currents in theory – the German hermeneutic and the French deconstructive – informed, respectively, my previous two monographs dedicated entirely to Dante: *Dante's Interpretive Journey* (1996) and *Dante and the Sense of Transgression*: *"The Trespass of the Sign"* (2013). The present book brings these strands together – by leading

---

[1] The paradigm of "distant reading" refers especially to Franco Moretti, *La letteratura vista da lontano* (Turin: Einaudi, 2005). In English, see Franco Moretti, *Distant Reading* (London: Verso, 2013).

them both back to their common origins and interests in phenomenology broadly conceived. It therewith brings to Dante's poem a more unified view of contemporary theory, employing a fuller range of its resources and directly exploiting them for detailed exegesis of specific passages of the poem.

Of course, some other recent developments within the ambit of theory, such as iconology and media studies, with their focus on the materialities of culture, are also rife with resources for illuminating Dante's text. They, too, have an appreciable impact on the interpretations offered here in the wake of art-historical and cultural theorists such as Hans Belting, Georges Didi-Huberman, Jean-Claude Schmitt, and Friedrich Kittler. These authors' studies have shown the dialectic of presence and absence in the image to be key to evoking otherworldly experience and to representing communication with the gods or the divine – generally viewed from an anthropological perspective. The complex interplays of word and image, of painting and writing, of visibility and legibility, have been analyzed in ways that can brilliantly illuminate Dante's poetic representations of writing as a visual epiphany in the form of Scripture. These resources help us to work out the reasons why divine presence, however pictorial and positive, is experienced necessarily in a negative mode. Even the "presencing" of the divine in incarnate forms of flesh, or in material images, remains "writing" in the sense of the presencing of an absence.

Kittler's *Die Wahrheit der technischen Welt: Essays zur Genealogie der Gegenwart* (2013) furnishes a broad historical background reflecting on some of the more technical and even technological aspects of the representation of presence and of truth in images, and this treatment casts new light useful for interpreting Dante's technically self-reflective vision of God in and through writing in heaven. In *Das Nahen der Götter vorbereiten* (2011), Kittler directs his thinking to the implications of mediality specifically for representing and for "preparing for" the "nearing of the gods." His interpretation of Wagnerian opera, furthermore, enables us to find refracted there one possible, suggestive destiny of Dante's spectacle in the Heaven of Jupiter, which likewise fuses sound and light, *son et lumière*, in a synaesthetic, dramatic, and lyrical *Gesamtkunstwerk* revealing divinity.

Several of my literary-critical books allude to more detailed readings of texts from Dante's *Paradiso*. They reference a few journal articles, but for the most part this referral has been in the mode of promise. Much of my theoretical reflection on the *Paradiso* has gone into print in advance of extended critical reading of relevant texts. The present volume intends to make good on these promises and to show in more detail what I am talking

about in terms of the specifics of Dante's text when I write about theological transcendence through language and the apotheosis of lyric in the
Paradiso as Dante's final testament. There is a certain limit to what
philosophical interpretation of Dante's text can achieve. Beyond that
limit, only very specific attention to the detail of his textual performances
can take our understanding further. A degree of penetration can be gained
by conceptualizations such as "mediation," but this can go only so far
before it is necessary to return to Dante's own images and the singular
experience that they embody in order to follow his thought. Only so does
this thought release its store of seeds and sparks and make manifest its
uniquely fecund insights. Image and concept emerge into clarity only
through their reciprocal interaction and thoroughgoing interpenetration.

Hence the book's distinctive bifocal structure, which requires still
a further word of explanation. The Excursuses sometimes summarily
restate theses of the chapters in order to bring out further connections,
moving in directions complementary to those taken by the expositions in
the main text. The Excursuses are aligned loosely with the respective
chapters (Chapter 1 with Excursus I, and so forth), supplementing their
arguments with further reflections. However, their relevance spills over
into other chapters as well. Most importantly, the Excursuses are linked
together so as to enable them to be read most profitably in series after the
main body of the chapters. Their diverse considerations follow coherently
upon one another. They consist largely in philosophical elaborations that
are not strictly necessary in order to follow the principal reflection proposed in the corresponding chapters from beginning to end. Some of these
elaborations engage philosophical traditions and resources that are not
necessarily familiar to readers of Dante. The excursus-structure enables
them to be explored on an elective basis by removing them from the
principal axis of the argument. This strategic division between what is
indispensable and what is enhancement aims to make the work readable for
all and yet rewarding also for the keenest and most initiated, in spite of its
wide interdisciplinary stretch.

The ambition of the book is not only to elucidate a crucial passage in the
Divine Comedy but also to think through the status of language as an event
of revelation in terms spanning from the theological outlook of Dante to
the phenomenological methods of Heidegger, Levinas, Merleau-Ponty,
and contemporary theological thinkers in their wake. This book makes
an original contribution to understanding some of the most fundamental
and perennial questions of philosophy and theology, as well as of literature.
As just mentioned, the book is designed to accommodate various types of

readers whose disciplinary competences may not encompass the whole range of fields involved. Still, that such an overarching interdisciplinary and speculative project be undertaken is proposed as one way of answering to Dante's own veiled challenge, expressed in his ardent desire to "spark" what he imagines as a glorious burst of light for human culture. As *Paradiso* I. 34, with false modesty, attests: "A great flame may follow a little spark" ("poca favilla gran fiamma seconda"). In evoking Jesus's promise of the sending of the Holy Spirit in order to accompany his disciples and their acts after his departure (John 14:15–18), Dante intimates that his own work takes root and bears fruit only in the answering works that it is able to spark. He is echoing, most exactly, the Epistle of St. James 3:5: "Behold, how great a matter a little fire kindleth!" ("Ecce quantus ignis quam magnam silvam incendit!") in his transmission of the sparks of Scripture to future literary lights and poetic beacons.

Acknowledgments

A first sketch of my interpretation of Dante's Heaven of Jove appears in "Scripture as Theophany in Dante's *Paradiso*," *Religion and Literature* 39/2 (Spring 2007): 1–32. This paper was delivered as the 2006 Annual Lecture in Religion and Literature at the University of Notre Dame at the invitation of James Dougherty, Donald Werge, and Kevin Hart. I presented a different, complementary approach to the topic in "Schrift als Theophanie in Dantes *Paradiso:* Das Medium als Metapher für die göttliche Unmittelbarkeit" in the context of a comparative literature conference that brought this work into dialogue with media studies: "Schrift und Graphisches im Vergleich," XVII. Tagung der DGAVL (Deutsche Gesellschaft für Vergleichende und Allgemeine Literaturwissenschaft), at the University of Bochum, Germany, 2017. A fragment adapted from Chapter 1 of this book appears in German, together with other papers from the conference, in *Schrift und Graphisches im Vergleich: Beiträge zur XVII. Tagung der DGAVL in Bochum vom 06. bis 09. Juni 2017*, eds. Monika Schmitz-Emans, Linda Simonis, and Simone Sauer-Kretschmer (Bielefeld: Aisthesis, 2019), 59–70. Another extract from the first section of Chapter 4 was adapted for publication as "The Vision of Language in *Paradiso* XVIII in Light of Speculative Grammar" in *Miscellanea in onore di Antonio Lanza*, vol. 2, eds. Marcellina Troncarelli and Marta Ceci (Rome: Serra, 2020), 215–25.

I also gratefully acknowledge the helpful recommendations of the anonymous readers for the Press.

Note on Translations and Primary Source Editions

All translations not otherwise attributed are my own. The default reference throughout is to Dante's *Paradiso* cited by canto and verse from Dante Alighieri, *La Divina Commedia secondo l'antica vulgata*, ed. Giorgio Petrocchi, 4 vols. (Milan: Mondadori, 1966–67). Dante's "minor" works are cited from *Opere minori*, 2 vols., eds. A. Frugoni, F. Brugnoli, et al. (Milan: Ricciardi, 1979–88).

Bible quotations are from the Authorized King James Version (1611) checked against and corrected, where necessary, by the *Bibliorum Sacrorum iuxta Vulgatam Clementinam Nova Editio* (Vatican: Typis Polyglottis, 1959) and *The Greek New Testament*, 2nd ed. (New York: United Bible Societies, 1968).

PART I

The Literary Vision

CHAPTER I

Writing as Theophany: The Medium as Metaphor for Immediacy

In Canto XVIII of the *Paradiso*, in the sphere of Jupiter, Dante's revelatory journey to God features a special kind of vision, a vision of written characters. Thirty-five letters written in the sky make up a sentence: DILIGITE IUSTITIAM QUI IUDICATIS TERRAM, the *incipit* of the Book of Wisdom. This is a "vision," in other words, that coincides with reading, for its object is an instance of writing. Yet, by their conspicuous visibility, the letters at the same time absorb interest and rivet attention as immediate presences. They loom large as visual spectacles appearing one at a time in series. The effect of the scene as a whole is that of a spectacular fireworks in the firmament. Enhancing their aesthetic value for the sense of sight, Dante describes the letters metaphorically as a "painting" ("dipinto"). By a suggestion vested in the visionary power and intensity of the poetry, this experience of direct vision of the "literal" as revealed to Dante is made to stand, at least provisionally and proleptically, for the vision of God that the whole poem builds up to and is based on. The implication we are teased with is that something of the divine vision (*visio Dei*) itself may be directly glimpsed in these letters.

The letters seen displayed in the heaven of Jupiter are letters specifically of Scripture – hence, the Word of God. Even more intimately revealing of divinity, the letters are readable specifically as Names of God, and as such they are identifiable in biblical mystic and theurgic tradition with God's Attributes. The mystical contemplation of the Names of God is a peculiarly privileged way of contemplating the divine essence or being. Such contemplation is most readily associated with the Jewish mysticism of the Kabbalah, but it has long traditions of influence in Christian and Islamic theologies as well. It is typically mixed with Neo-Platonic philosophical speculation on the divine Names. Such speculation originates in Plato's *Parmenides* and its reflections on predicates such as Changeless, Unmoving, Indivisible, Impassible, etc., as names for the Unnamable One. The tradition of commentary on Plato's text can be followed from Plotinus and Porphyry, through Proclus and Damascius, to Latin Scholasticism and Sufi mysticism.[1] The canonical model in Christian circles is Dionysius the Areopagite's *Divine Names* (*De divinis nominibus*). The speculation on abstract attributes or predicates as divine names becomes entangled with the letter mysticism that depends especially on Hebrew sources. This latter approach was transmitted to Dante by Isidore of Seville, among others, and its methods were developed to their highest pitch of sophistication in the Jewish Kabbalah.[2]

Indeed, all letters of the alphabet could be and, in central strands of this tradition, were considered to be Names of God. But this is especially evident in the case of the first three letters of the first word, DILIGITE, which Dante singles out for separate mention in a preliminary description of his vision, when he first relates how the sparking souls in the heaven formed "now *D*, now *I*, now *L* in its figures" ("or D, or I, or L in sue figure," XVIII. 73–78). Each of these letters is peculiarly recognizable as a name of God: "L," or its equivalent, when pronounced aloud, "El," is a name for God in the Hebrew tongue. "I," according to Dante, was the name that Adam first called God in Paradise before descending to Limbo, as Adam himself explains in *Paradiso* XXVI. 133–36. And "D," finally, reads as abbreviating "Deus," the name of God in a yet younger sacred language, the Latin of the Vulgate, not to mention "Dio" in Dante's own vernacular, the language of his "sacred poem" ("poema sacro," XXV. 1).

The pronouncement from Adam's own lips in *Paradiso* XXVI that he first called God by the single vocalic syllable "I" revises Dante's statement in *De vulgari eloquentia* that "God ... that is, *El*" ("Deus ... scilicet *El*") had been the syllable uttered by Adam ("prius vox primi loquentis," I. iv. 4). At the time he wrote *De vulgari eloquentia*, and following Patristic precedents, notably Jerome and Isidore, Dante held the original language of Adam to have been Hebrew, and he believed the Hebrew word "El" to have been Adam's original name for God.[3] Taken together, these positions, although incompatible, confirm the status of "L," along with "I," as letters peculiarly apt to serve as Names of God. It is also surely significant for Dante that "I," taken as a Roman numeral, equals the first integer, the

---

[1] William Franke, ed., *On What Cannot Be Said: Apophatic Discourses in Philosophy, Religion, Literature, and the Arts* (Notre Dame: University of Notre Dame Press, 2007), vol. 1, charts this trajectory.

[2] Enrico Castelli, ed., *L'analyse du langage théologique: Le nom de Dieu* (Paris: Aubier, 1969) probes the theology of the divine Names from these and a wide spectrum of confessional and disciplinary angles.

[3] Jerome, *Epistle* 25, 2; Isidore, *Etymologiarum* VII, 1, 3. See also Augustine, *De civitate Dei* XVI, 11; Rabanus Maurus, *Commentarium in Genesis* II, 11.

number 1, "from which all numbers are measured" ("sicut in numero cuncta mensurantur uno," *De vulgari eloquentia*, XVI. 2) and therewith stands for the supreme, the ineffable One of Neo-Platonic mysticism, as well as for the one God of biblical monotheism.[4]

This reading of the letters highlighted here by Dante – D, I, and L – as Names of God is meant only to suggest some ways of accounting for the pervasive, even if elusive, sense that Dante's poetic *presencing* of Scripture in this heaven demands to be understood as a theophany. Taking them as Names of God is especially conducive to elucidating how the visual display of letters that Dante discerns and contemplates in the Heaven of Jupiter is, in fact, a revelation of the Being and Essence of God, albeit in a metaphorical and even a pictorial guise.

Dante may wish subliminally to evoke this theology of the divine Names on account of its embodying the idea of access through language, and more specifically through the letter, to God's being and essence. Yet the vision strains in every detail to go beyond a merely nominal and abstractly linguistic approach and to apprehend divinity in concrete, phenomenal form. The divine presence is intimated not just by a cryptic code of Kabbalistic letters for the unutterable, transcendent Name. Instead, this presence is displayed openly in rich, gothic detail to Dante's sense of sight. Dante's understanding of the revelation of God as incarnate in the Word seeks full realization in the words and images of his poetry. Concordantly, the externality and objective, thing-like character of the letters is here thrown flamboyantly into relief.

The dramatic force of Dante's vision of Scripture in the Heaven of Jove evidently resides in the fascination of the immediately visible presence of the letters on which he gazes. The phenomenalization of the letters on the backdrop of the heaven in a vividly representational space and time is elaborated with extravagant precision and detail. There is a touch of sensationalism here that is hard to overlook. The scene is likely to appear to readers today as cinematographic. More exactly and literally, the visual concreteness and the *painting*-like quality of the writing Dante sees lend it an objective density that induces critics to invoke the theoretically suggestive moment of words and letters becoming perceptible as things. This motif is, in fact, invoked by Lino Pertile, who describes the reified words as "citation things": "a biblical citation become citation-thing, sign and

---

[4] Corrado Calenda, "Canto XVIII," in *Lectura Dantis Romana: Cento canti per cento anni*, eds. Enrico Malato and Andrea Mazzuchi (Rome: Salerno, 2013), 548n34, among others, further observes that numerologically D (500), I (1), and L (50) form an anagram of 515, the number of the one "sent by God" ("messo di Dio") as an apocalyptic figure in *Purgatorio* XXXIII. 43–44.

referent at the same time; in sum, the signifier triumphs ..." ("una citazione biblica divenuta citazione-cosa, segno e referente allo stesso tempo; trionfa insomma il significante ...").[5] Numerous commentators draw out felicitously the visual and pictorial quality of the letters. Some of them emphasize that the painted letters issue in the image of the lily garlanding the last letter, M, which then, finally, metamorphoses into the fully figurative emblem of the eagle. "From writing that is already painted we move on to an emblem that is living figure" ("Dalla scrittura che è già dipinta, passiamo a un emblema che è figura viva").[6]

The drawing of attention to the sensible form of the signifier is perhaps not for Dante the defining characteristic of poetic language, as it was for Roman Jakobson.[7] Nevertheless, such self-referentiality evidently belongs to Dante's sense, too, of the peculiar capabilities of such language, capabilities that he exploits in this instance to extraordinary effect. Like Jakobson – and in opposition to St. Augustine's strictures warning against being distracted by the senses – Dante throws into relief the immediately perceptible and concretely present component of these signs as used in his poetic language. Beyond Jakobson, moreover, Dante confronts us with the further challenge of understanding this important feature whereby poetic language highlights the signifier not just formally and structurally, but also in terms of language's innermost meaning. This meaning is manifest paradigmatically in Scripture. Dante forces us to understand the letters scripturally and theologically, that is, as bound up with the vision's status as written and perhaps even as *revealed*. The vision of letters is understood as mediating a manifestation to the senses of the divine essence – of the presence of God. In other words, this is an indirect manner of saying that the vision is a theophany – an appearing of God.

Of course, all that Dante sees in Paradise, as well as all that he sees throughout the other world, is in some sense a theophany. In different ways, the visions of each of the heavens stand for and embody ultimately the divine vision, the *visio Dei*, the goal of the entire journey: they anticipate and preliminarily enact it. Even the terrestrial world, when seen in the allegorical perspective of Dante's theological poem and of medieval symbolism generally, is theophany. Every aspect of the Creation, to the extent that it bears the image or imprint of its Creator, makes God manifest. This commonplace in various religious traditions is

[5] Lino Pertile, "*Paradiso* XVIII tra autobiografia e scrittura sacra," *Dante Studies* 109 (1991): 38.
[6] Gaetano Marcovaldi, *Il Canto XVIII del Paradiso* (Turin: SEI, 1964), 19–37.
[7] Roman Jakobson, "Linguistics and Poetics: Closing Statement," in *Style in Language*, ed. T. Sebeok (Cambridge: MIT Press, 1960), 350–77.

grandly elaborated by Augustine and Bonaventure (to name just two of Dante's principal sources and authorities) in their theologies of Creation as consisting in the *vestigia Dei*. It is popularly expressed in the widely circulated medieval jingle: "Omnis mundi creatura / quasi liber et figura / nobis est et speculum" ("Every creature in the world / is like a book and figure / and a mirror for us"), variously attributed to Nicholas of Lyre or Alain of Lille.

Thus, the whole of the universe is a theophany in an inclusive sense. And, since it is forged in the Creation's image, so too is the whole of the *Divine Comedy*. But the *Paradiso* in particular is theophantic in a more specific sense, one that is intimately and mysteriously related to its scriptural medium. Precisely this is what Dante foregrounds thematically in the heaven of Jupiter, where the scriptural medium itself is projected into spectacular relief. Throughout the poem, writing is the medium by which Dante conveys his vision, and the problematic of language's and especially of writing's capacities and incapacities to manifest divinity is diffusely present. But in the heaven of Jupiter in particular, with its thematic focus on a given instance of writing taken from Holy Writ, the question specifically of what its written form and mode mean for Dante's vision of God – with its claim to be theological revelation in a strong sense – becomes exceptionally acute.

In principle, of course, writing is only the means by which Dante conveys his experience of seeing God. Writing cannot normally be conflated with the divine itself as the object of that experience. Yet, notoriously in the case of the *Paradiso*, and more generally in the case of perhaps all the most linguistically innovative and challenging poetry, language becomes something of a revelation in its own right. The linguistic and scriptural means of representation become indissociable from the matters for which they serve as vehicle. The means itself – written language – in telling ways, tends to become the object of the vision. Here, in the heaven of Jove, by imaginatively objectifying what is *prima facie* only the material condition of his craft, Dante explicitly represents a vision that is not only conveyed *by* writing, but is itself a vision *of* writing. In this manner, beyond being just its necessary means, writing becomes also the immediate theme and content of Dante's poetic contemplation of a purportedly divine presence.

Ostensibly, it is in its quality as something directly visible that writing assumes such importance for Dante in this scene insinuating the status of his poem as theophany. Writing's own immediately visible presence to the sense of sight epitomizes the kind of direct vision of God that professedly the whole poem is striving to achieve in its repeatedly outlined trajectory toward a personal apocalypse – an unveiling of the divine to Dante. This immediate presence of language in the form of the written and visible signifier – the letter – comes to stand metaphorically for the unmediated presence and vision of God. In this way, writing becomes the essential metaphor for theophany – at least here in the heaven of Jove.

Writing is a medium, to be sure, and its essential function is mediation, but at this juncture in Jove it takes on importance for Dante also as a metaphor for the immediacy of his sought-for vision of God. It does so thanks to the immediacy of vision that it realizes by virtue of its own literally visible medium. The material markings of any actually written letter, with all their sensory qualities, are immediately visible. Dante often harps on or plays up such qualities of specifically poetic language, but he does so especially here in Canto XVIII and in the ensuing cantos of this heaven. The fully externalized, visible form of the letter is exalted by Dante's presentation of the vision as a divine display and "painting" in the heaven. Through the explicit metaphor of painting (XVIII. 92, 109), Dante intensively meditates on writing in a palpably material sense. His intensively visual focus identifies writing with its own directly perceptible, visible, viscous medium. In fact, a written or printed letter, just like any painted image, is composed of relatively opaque shapes and traits or marks that are perceived in the phenomenal space of a visual field.

Of course, the metaphor of writing for the *visio Dei* also signals the *impossibility* of realizing direct vision of anything such as the Divine Essence. The *sense* or *meaning* of writing, by its very nature, remains invisible – its fully manifest written *form* notwithstanding. Written signs are understood as conveying a reference beyond themselves to something that is absent and deferred, or in any case not present as such in the letter that can be seen displayed on the page (or other surface). Writing is a medium made up of referential signs. It offers sensible substitutes or ciphers in lieu of the presence of what it signifies. That precisely writing should be featured here as the means of realizing the divine presence in Dante's theophany, thus, at the same time, indirectly indicates this theophany's inherent limitations and even "impossibility."

What Dante implicitly admits by presenting this theophany in the form of a vision of writing is that seeing God – or God's direct self-revelation in a blaze of light and glory – could only be a phenomenon of "writing," that is, of the differential play of signifiers, which can signify divinity only indirectly. Whatever one might see of the divine would still be in need of being *read*, that is, of being deciphered according to its divine significance, and the presence of God would, accordingly, still only be signified rather than being simply, immediately, plainly present, or directly laid open to view. Whatever could appear directly as an object before human eyes or intellect could not be God per se in a simple or absolute presence. Even another human being is never revealed in the direct way that only an object of purely visual perception, a shape or line or color, can be exhaustively revealed. *Persons* always infinitely transcend any of their immediate, concrete manifestations. Built into the metaphor of writing used for the divine vision is a recognition of this unsurpassable barrier. Writing reminds us indirectly, by means of its signifying function, of a certain transcendence beyond the visible that belongs to the very structure of meaning, not to mention of any possible encounter with other persons or with God alike.

As in the Troubadour tradition of *trobar clus* or "closed form," so also in philosophical tradition, specifically that of Plato's *Phaedrus*, writing is normally – or at least very often – considered to be an opaque medium that can, at best, convey the mind's intentions only indirectly and inadequately. It is removed one relay further than speech from the reality that it is supposed to represent. Thus, it is not only in our own day, with "deconstruction," that writing has become recognized as an emblem of the impossibility of realizing presence, whether of persons or meaning, in any pure, objective form, let alone as the absolute of "divine presence."[8] The medieval world was well aware of writing as a medium inevitably devoid of the concrete presence of the objects that it means or represents. Such a principle was rendered commonplace by Augustine's theory of signs erected on the fundamental distinction between *res* and *signum*, thing and sign.

The constitutive absence of the object designated by the linguistic sign is compounded in the *written* sign or letter by the removal of any actual manifestation of voice in which intention or meaning – the presence of the mind and its thought – could be directly embodied. This structural absence is implicitly recognized, for example, by Isidore of Seville at the beginning of his encyclopedia: "But letters are indexes of things, signs of words, and they have such power that, when said to us, they speak without voice of absent things" ("Litterae autem sunt indices rerum, signa verborum, quibus tanta vis est, ut nobis dicta absentium sine voce

---

[8] The works of Jacques Derrida, particularly *De la grammatologie* (Paris: Minuit, 1967) and *L'écriture et la différence* (Paris: Seuil, 1968), have led the way in showing how writing supposedly renders vain the philosophical ambition of discursively realizing the full "presence" of "truth" or "being," in a "parousia." This originally Greek term is used in Christian theology for Christ's return to preside in person over the Last Judgment.

loquantur").[9] In another strand of this tradition, Thomas Aquinas explains writing as necessary to man living in society because of his need to be able to abstract from the here and now.[10] Thus, *prima facie*, writing communicates and conveys *anything but* immediacy and presence.

There is, then, in this regard, a provocative irony and a bold revisionary gesture in Dante's singling out writing as the medium for his realization of a vision of divine presence. He not only relies on writing out of practical necessity (as the means necessary to write his work): he also elevates it to a position of spectacular thematic relief in this segment of his poem. To be present in this manner, through being signified by written characters, is a very ambiguous way of being present indeed. It means being present in a form that, at the same time, emblematically signifies the absence of what is represented. God is made present and visible in writing, which, ironically, is constituted by the absence of what it signifies. The idea of seeing God, and *a fortiori* that of being spoken to by him, connote a strong sense of immediacy and presence, whereas writing is widely recognized as the medium of absence and deferral.

The impossibility of capturing the divine presence in any representation whatever is made explicit and programmatic in Dante's writing throughout the *Paradiso* by his continual recourse to the ineffability topos. It is already astonishing that writing, as a form of signifying a *res* in its absence, should turn out to be the concrete basis for Dante's poem's manifestation of a divine presence. But this, in reality, is only a special case of the general paradox that its very ineffability should prove to be integral to Dante's poetic expression of the divine revelation he lays claim to in the *Divine Comedy* as his *poema sacro* and particularly in the *Paradiso*. The same paradox applies to all the linguistic, rhetorical, and material means of expression employed by Dante in the poem. All can be epitomized as, in an extended sense, "writing."

Concentrated meditation on the (theo)logical limits inherent in writing as a medium is what, at the same time, makes the miracle of divine vision possible and even makes it come to pass. For writing happens to be just what Dante's poem is made out of and, in an immediate sense, *is*. Writing is also what the poem directly manifests itself *as* to the physical sense of sight. Dante, in this manner, portrays himself as intensely aware of writing as integral to his achieving in his poem a purportedly unmediated

---

[9] Sancti Isidori, *Etymologarium*, in *Patrologia Latina*, LXXXII. 314, ed. J.-P. Minge (Turnhout: Brepols, 1858), 74–75.

[10] Aristotle, *On Interpretation, Commentary by St. Thomas and Cajetan*, trans. Jean T. Oesterle (Pittsboro: InteLex, 1992), Lesson II. 2–5.

experience of divinity. In fact, Dante's acute sensitivity to and concentration on his scriptural medium shows itself throughout the *Paradiso* to be fundamental to his whole imaginative conception of the possibility of envisioning God and of experiencing the divine presence.

Whereas vision in a literal sense posits a unique object, writing is a differential system. To see the divine vision as writing is not to doubt or deny its authenticity but rather to redefine it in terms of relations within a web of significances – a text. The *visio Dei*, Dante's text suggests, is such a writing, whatever else it may be. God manifests himself not as a discrete object, but rather as a play of significances, as a signifying. In some sense, throughout the *Paradiso*, the vision *is* the poem, the written text itself – although "text" here must be understood to be not just a material artifact but also a mysterious and inexhaustible inter-animation of significances. In the heaven of Jove, the vision's content itself, a written text, peculiarly and conspicuously thematizes this astonishing equivalence of the vision and the text.

Another, and a final, acknowledgment that envisioning God cannot but be tantamount to a totalized vision of the emblematic medium – namely, writing – comes as part of the final vision of God at the end of the whole poem. It is a vision of a book, in fact, a vision of the whole world *as* a book – all substances and accidents and their interaction throughout the universe conflated together ("sustanze e accidenti e lor costume / quasi conflati insieme") in a single volume ("in un volume," XXXIII. 85–90). The experience of the world itself, if read as an all-encompassing book, is divine revelation and can identify itself with the experience of the *visio Dei* – of all reality as seen by God.

The *Commedia* may, in the end, offer no other – and certainly no more direct – way to experience God. Although Dante retains, at least at the levels of myth and metaphor, the quest for a direct ("sanza mezzo") intuition of the divine essence, what he concretely realizes in his poem is vision of a wholly different kind, vision that is, in effect, writing – a written vision. The verbal and scriptural mediations themselves, in their sensuously perceptible forms, *become* the divine vision. These mediations, and not the perception of a discrete essence of divinity to be isolated as an object of intellection, constitute the essential vision of the poem. Dante pictorially says as much through the final vision of divinity as the total writing of the universe in a book "bound by love" ("legato con amore in un volume," XXXIII. 86).

Its *writtenness* is one index of the "secularity," literally the "worldliness," of Dante's revolutionary vision. In this regard, Dante concurs with

Thomas Aquinas that human knowledge of God is indirect. For Aquinas, God is known, at least by us in this life (*in hanc vitam*), only from his creation, from creatures, not by intellectual intuition. Aquinas proves this proposition in *Summa Theologica* Ia, Quaestio 12: "Quomodo Deus a nobis cognoscitur." For his part, Dante, taking this cue, denies the possibility of direct intellectual intuition of divinity, as of any immaterial substance, in *Convivio* III. iv. 9 on the "defect" of "our intellect" ("nostro intelletto, per difetto ..."). Yet, failing an intellectual intuition of the divine essence, poetry can provide a sensuously mediated type of intuition or "vision" of divinity. Nevertheless, divinity is seen still as a dynamic interaction of signs or traces rather than as a discrete form or particular object.

Taken to the zero-degree, writing is concentrated directly on the presentation of itself in its sheer immediacy – and does not primarily serve as a medium of some content other than itself. This immediacy can be achieved through poetry, with all its resources for visual and sensuous realization of experience. Poetry, and particularly its incarnation in writing, Dante seems to suggest, may be able to exceed, or at least to displace, the epistemological barriers of signification that are written into logical semantics, as well as into dogmatic theology. Poetry thereby makes it possible for the impossible to come to pass. The potentiality for realizing the divine in the immediate presence of the medium of writing is played out by poetry, especially by virtue of its propensity for sensuous expression and concrete creation. Dante focuses so intensely and exclusively on the medium of writing that it disappears *as* medium or mediation and becomes present in its immediacy. Writing serves Dante to enact an experience of sheer immediacy – of God. This is possible because, considered most rigorously, Dante's writing in the *Paradiso* has no object. What it mediates cannot be objectified. By definition, God is something or someone who exceeds every possibility of objectification and finite expression.[II]

Language, or the Unlimited Presence of the Medium

By representing mediation par excellence, indeed divine self-revelation to humans in Scripture, through the immediacy of the medium of writing – its visible presence – Dante sets up the paradox upon which the scene in the heaven of Jupiter (and indeed the whole poem) pivots: Mediation itself

---

[II] Key excerpts from Patristic and Scholastic traditions of negative theology articulating these reasons for God's unrepresentability or "ineffability" are gathered in Franke, ed., *On What Cannot Be Said*, vol. I: "Classic Formulations."

becomes immediate and absolute. In this case, where vision is supposedly of God, there can be no object to be represented. The Absolute and Infinite can be comprehended in no finite object of representation. Instead, the infinity and absoluteness of the medium itself serve to intimate divinity as an unrepresentable *non*-object. By taking *itself* as object, language fulfills its irrepressible formal propensity to represent, or at least intend, some object. Yet still it designates no object external to itself that could delimit it. Not as any represented thing, but rather in its own inherent and *unlimited* molten *potency* for representing, language *is* infinite.[12] Language thus makes a good metaphor for – and even constitutes a concrete, sensuous manifestation of – the unrepresentable infinity of divinity.

Language, as the medium of representation, is never fully present as such or as a whole in the form of a separate, discrete object, yet indirectly it is *in* everything that *is* represented, and it is present in these representations as an indivisible whole. Such an infinite medium is present everywhere, like God sustaining the very being of all that is, albeit nowhere discretely to be seized as an object, nowhere able to be contained.[13] Just as God is wholly present in all beings (otherwise they would not be), but even the whole of being does not contain God, similarly language is wholly present in every word and utterance (otherwise they would not be language) yet is always infinitely more than any actual word or phrase. This suggests why Dante's metaphors for God are fundamentally metaphors of language all the way to the "final" vision of the book ("volume") bound with love ("legato con amore") in *Paradiso* XXXIII. 85–93.

Language is the paradigmatic medium, indeed the medium of mediums. It is the very nature of language as a system of interconnected differences to be active and impinging all at once on any given instance or unit of language. The medium itself and as a whole is necessarily present in all representations within that medium. In fact, the medium is what is most immediately present therein. Just as language or writing, taken as medium,

---

[12] The potential infinity inhering in language was to be developed much later in linguistic terms of hermeneutic theory in the Romantic period by Wilhelm von Humboldt (1767–1835) and Friedrich Schleiermacher (1768–1834). Its theoretical and historical roots, nevertheless, reach back to Dante's Italian tradition of linguistic humanism, as demonstrated by Karl-Otto Apel, *Die Idee der Sprache in der Tradition des Humanismus von Dante bis Vico* (Bonn: Bouvier, 1980).

[13] The medieval Latin source text *Liber* XXIV *Philosophorum* conveys the image of God as an infinite sphere whose center is everywhere but whose circumference is nowhere (Proposition 2). This is the sort of metaphysical language used of God also in Neo-Platonic sources such as the *Liber de causis*, which Dante repeatedly cites or paraphrases in the *Convivio*. The Neo-Platonic metaphysics of the divine light radiating throughout the universe, as rehearsed by Dante, for instance, in *Convivio* III. xiv. 3–6, articulates this outlook, which appears pervasively throughout the *Paradiso*, starting from its very first verses.

is present in everything written, so the presence of God is at least diffusely apprehended as a grounding presence of the infinite in every finite being. Dante's description of the essence of God in letters makes vivid and visible how, in the case of the experience of God in language, the medium, in its inexhaustible, tangible plenitude, is the most present element or aspect of all that is experienced. Such a metaphysical analogy contributes to making language, and specifically writing, the privileged metaphor for Dante's poetic representations of the vision and presence of God.

It is ultimately the question of how (by what means) God's presence can be experienced, or of how God can be "seen" – a question subtending the whole project of the *Paradiso* – that is brought to a particularly sharp and self-reflexive focus by Dante in a programmatic way in the Heaven of Jupiter through its thematization of writing. The way in which the medium can – and perhaps must – merge with, and itself become, the revelation of God lies at the heart of Dante's projection of writing as his visionary and, we cannot but say, mystical object in this heaven.

Dante is an artist for whom his medium becomes paramount in its own right. This is, of course, not the same as the obsession of many modern artists, for whom the artwork has no reference to any reality beyond itself.[14] In some respects, it is close to the opposite: Dante's medium becomes paramount for its capability of signifying what is absolutely *other* than – or beyond and above – it. Nonetheless, the unlimited importance of the medium itself in realizing the transcendent world and meaning, the goal towards which it is a means, begins to assert itself. With the acknowledged precedent of experiments such as those of Arnaut Daniel, Dante begins to move writing as a medium into the foreground as a principal preoccupation and theme. We can see this especially well in the way that the Heaven of Jupiter highlights its own status as written. This heaven, in Dante's exposition, reflects intensively on itself as linguistic event and specifically as scriptural revelation.[15]

Thus Dante's vision of God via poetic writing might be hailed as a distinct linguistico-mystical way to divine vision. It is different from

---

[14] The "intransitivity" of modern literary writing is brought out with panache by Roland Barthes, *Le plaisir du texte* (Paris: Seuil, 1973).

[15] Dante may actually be closer to the creative revolutionaries of modern poetry and poetics than can be appreciated until one is disabused of glib critical slogans about the latter's elimination of reference. The oversimplification of Mallarmé's poetics as flatly "non-referential" by a certain dominant line of literary theorists following Hugo Friedrich is effectively refuted already by Paul De Man, in "Lyric and Modernity," in *Forms of Lyric*, ed. Reuben A. Brower (New York: Columbia University Press, 1970), 151–76. Bertrand Marchal, *La religion de Mallarmé: Poésie, mythologie et religion* (Paris: J. Corti, 1988) provides a persuasive recasting of the issue.

that of the pure, wordless contemplation practiced by ascetic mystics. It might also be differentiated from the philosophical path of mysticism as purely intellectual illumination through the dialectic of negative theology pioneered by Neo-Platonist philosophers and church fathers and pursued further, in their wake, by Scholastic theologians. Imagination and verbal expression harbor positive resources of their own to be exploited in the quest for the vision of God.[16] Dante is one of the most original explorers in a genealogical line of prophetic poets including Milton and Blake, Klopstock, Hölderlin, Novalis, and Victor Hugo, and leading to the likes of Hugo Ball, alias Dionysius DADA Areopagita, among avant-garde experimental writers of the twentieth century. Ball was in quest of "a theory of language, image, and symbol grounded in theological revelation" ("eine offenbarungstheologische begründete Sprach-, Bild-, und Symboltheorie").[17] Dante should also be counted as a crucial figure in the pursuit of poetry as ecstatic visionary experience that flourishes in traditions since antiquity traversing Indo-European, Hebrew, Persian, Nahuatl (Meso-American), and other cultures (Scandinavian, Celtic, Buddhist, etc.).[18] These disparate references indicate some of the wider ramifications of analogues with Dante's revelatory use of language highlighted in the letter mysticism of his vision in the Heaven of Jove.

The significance of the self-reflexive mirror-view of writing that turns on itself as object in this heaven concerns the very nature of its status as a medium and, indeed, the essence of mediation as such. Mediation operates ambiguously as both a bridge and a barrier to relation with the absolutely other and the ultimately real. I maintain that Dante's text embodies a radically Incarnational (and equally radical Trinitarian) rethinking of the very notions of the medium and of mediation in an optics of theological revelation. This thinking enfolds a Christian understanding of theological transcendence that is paradoxical to classical philosophical paradigms and logic in ways that recent postmodern turns of thought have prepared us to re-inherit. Mediation of transcendence, as it is at work in the language of the poem, will bear comparison not only with

---

[16] The aesthetic consciousness of language may actually have more importance in the Scholastic Middle Ages and particularly in Thomas Aquinas than it is usually accorded. This thesis is developed at length by Olivier-Thomas Venard in *Thomas d'Aquin, poète théologien, vol. 2: La langue de l'ineffable* (Paris: Ad Solem, 2004).

[17] Bernd Wacker, ed., *Dionysius DADA Areopagita: Hugo Ball und die Kritik der Moderne* (Paderborn: Schöningh, 1996), 8. In this volume, medievalist Kurt Flasch brings to focus the continuity of Dada's critique of German rationalism with Dionysius the Areopagite's mysticism.

[18] D. J. Moores, *The Ecstatic Poetic Tradition: A Critical Study from the Ancients through Rumi, Wordsworth, Whitman, Dickinson and Tagore* (Jefferson: McFarland, 2014).

medieval paradigms, such as the writings of St. Augustine, but also with modern thinking, particularly Hegel's, along with that of certain "postmoderns" in his wake.[19] Both a premodern Dante and a certain postmodern "Hegel," in their different ways, carry Christian Logos-based thinking to a limit where all possible being that can be revealed or experienced is shown to be determined fundamentally by the essence of language as mediation. For Dante, furthermore, as for a number of postmodern, post-Hegelian writers today (notoriously, Žižek, Agamben, Badiou), this means that experience and its sense stand necessarily in relation to what transcends them.

Dante's vision of writing, in effect, dismantles the opposition between immanence and transcendence by its concentration on the medium as *itself* revelation rather than only its means. Dante thereby presents us with a seemingly impossible experience of transcendence *in* and *of* the medium. In this way, he is proposing the idea that divinity is at least ambiguously present in the letter, the very medium of absence. He does so by decomposing this medium (as will be demonstrated in Chapter 3), for its very breakdown as a medium is what transforms it into an immediacy such as God, or the divine vision, is traditionally conceived to be. Similarly – according to the ultimately negative-theological conception of God in Christian theology from Gregory of Nyssa to Pseudo-Dionysius to Thomas Aquinas and Bonaventure – transcendent divinity is graspable only negatively, precisely as the negation of every possible mediation. In this deconstructive logic of mediation, immediacy, or more exactly the negation of mediation – im/mediacy – is indirectly realized in the breakdown of language.

This dialectic is worked out by Dante concretely in terms of time and eternity, with language as their constitutive medium. Just as meaning collapses into its linguistic medium, so eternity is affirmed precisely in the radical experience of its mediation by time – and of the collapse of this mediation *as* mediation. This collapse opens to the abyss of divinity. Similarly, mystics experience eternity in the immediacy of the *now*, but often only as a rupture of temporal mediation, thus as *im-mediate*. The unlimited presence of the "now" is experienced as outside of sequential time and all its mediations.

---

[19] Intended here are especially Levinas, Derrida, and Blanchot, whose understanding of Hegel was shaped by Jean Hyppolite's lectures at the Collège de France in the late 1960s, as well as Bataille and Lacan, who were galvanized by Alexandre Kojève's Hegel lectures in the 1930s. All are brought into dialogue with Dante's *Paradiso* in my *Dante and the Sense of Transgression: "The Trespass of the Sign"* (London: Bloomsbury, 2012).

The impossibility of God's becoming a visual object, or indeed an object at all, will force Dante to resort to reading signs of God's presence. And yet, it is not as if these mere signs are empty of the real presence of God, which would then be something else. Dante will minimize the difference between sign and presence to the point of letting it disappear altogether. In this manner, he performs a deconstruction of the sign. This is, in fact, a way of conceptualizing what incarnation, or more generally sacraments, are supposed to achieve: the signifier becomes the real presence of what it signifies.[20] The Eastern Orthodox theory and cult of the icon and the Roman Catholic rite and sacrament of the Eucharist, each in their different ways, incarnate this intuition and experience with spiritual profundity. In the text of the heaven of Jove, this total mediation between signifier and signified is achieved precisely in and through writing exalted to the status of "scripture." Writing here is modeled on Holy Scripture. Writing attenuates and elides, or absorbs into itself, its very status as mediation, until it becomes sensibly present as embodied divine Word. This attenuation or absorption of the means of mediation as mere means is pursued all the way to the point at which writing per se becomes revelation.

The vision of Dante's poem is a vision in and of writing, not a sighting of some discrete object, but a tracing of significances in and through a series of verbal signifiers. Divinity, such as it can be present in the poem, is present in the process of signifying. Just this is said in the opening lines of the Heaven of Jupiter, with their reference to the "love that was there." This love is God, as Scripture itself makes explicit in I John 4:8: *Deus caritas est.* This love is the divine presence that is seen by Dante to "signify our language to my eyes" ("segnare a li occhi miei nostra favella," XVIII. 72).

Language for the eyes, in this case, is writing. It is described here as an act of signifying. In this signifying *itself,* more than in any*thing* signified, God is directly present: he is "the love that was there" ("l'amor che lì era," XVII. 71). Yet, as such, God's presence – like writing itself – is compounded of absence. Since God cannot be present as a particular object of experience, it is only in the process of signifying that God can be concretely experienced at all by the poet and his readers. God is immanently present: God is just as immanent and present as the medium itself. Language, or the letter, is no longer just a cipher for an object outside and beyond itself that it would refer to or *re*present. The medium itself, in its immediate presence,

---

[20] Such terms of sacramental theology are applied to the reading of Dante, for example, by Sheila J. Nayar, *Dante's Sacred Poem: Flesh and the Centrality of the Eucharist to the "Divine Comedy"* (London: Bloomsbury, 2014).

embodies the all-encompassing infinity of divinity. Divinity is experienced concretely as writing, that is, as an open field of significances projected by love or desire that is there in its unlimited *signifyingness*.

This infinity is perhaps best conceived of as an infinite degree of intensity. Dante in the *Convivio* (IV. xix–xxi) adopts, or at least parallels, the vocabulary of "degrees of intensity," which had been newly forged in Scholastic philosophy at this time by Duns Scotus.[21] This vocabulary was to be developed further in modern thought and reaches, especially through Spinoza, to Gilles Deleuze.[22] We have already noticed how Dante exalts the signifier in something like the way that Roland Barthes analyzes as the degree-zero of writing.[23] However, it is also clear that in focusing on the significance inhering in the signifier itself, Dante at no point in the *Paradiso* simply gives up on preserving a perfectly clear objective conceptual sense for his statements.

The *Paradiso* is full of information about Trinitarian dogma and Neo-Platonic theology, the heavens and their hierarchy or "angelology," cos-mology, meteorology, ethical and political philosophy, and even the earth and its history – its topographies and geographies, its monastic orders and princely dynasties, etc. The *Paradiso* also abounds in chronicles detailing daily life, especially in Dante's own native city, Florence (particularly in Cantos XV–XVI). The intimate secrets surrounding its emblematic figures widen out into the history of the Holy Roman Empire as a whole and even to far-flung territories outside its precincts. The poem purports to deliver authoritative truths, as if from a bird's-eye view in heaven. All this, however, is projected onto another order of significance as reflecting the unfathomable reality of the divine. Its true sense is beyond what can be signified, even though this transcending is effected by statements that have a perfectly clear conceptual significance. In relation to "God," as the poem's object – or rather its "ultimate concern" – this first-order level of signification is negated.

In effect, each of the heavens, with their visual symbols and emblematic representations, offers a kind of writing in which the vision of God, the divine presence, is dynamically realized. The *Paradiso* in general is a writing of the divine vision that the poem as a whole promises and claims to realize. If the divine vision is realized at all, it is realized in the form of writing, the

[21] I describe "Scotus's Discovery of a New Path for Metaphysics: Intensities of Being" in *Dante's Paradiso and the Origins of Modern Thought: Toward a Speculative Philosophy of Self-Reflection* (New York: Routledge, 2021), part II, section 21.
[22] Gilles Deleuze, *Spinoza et le problème de l'expression* (Paris: Minuit, 1968).
[23] Roland Barthes, *Le degré zéro de l'écriture* (Paris: Seuil, 1953).

writing that the poem itself *is.* The literal claim of an actual intuition of the divine essence is certainly not excluded, but it remains rather hypothetical and optative with respect to what is literally and literarily realized before our very eyes in the writing, or verbal animation, of the poem that we hold in our hands. We realize this meaning performatively in our reading by following the poem's cues for imagining its narrative scenarios and meditating on its variegated images and reflections. Dante's penchant for secularizing, for realizing otherworldly, purely spiritual idealities in concrete, worldly terms, finds a crowning exemplification in this performance in Canto XVIII of the *Paradiso* as a decidedly *written* vision.

I hasten to emphasize, however, that Dante's secularizing rendition of divine and holy idealities as visible script is not meant to destroy or discard their spiritual reality. It is rather intended as a way of exalting their prophetic claims and of concretely realizing their imperishable truth. It *does* involve a kind of deconstruction of typically mythologizing and objectifying interpretations of concepts like divinity, truth, and other such abstractions. Dante (at a certain level) liberates his vision's meaning from rigidly dogmatic and naively or superstitiously reifying views that actually obscure their spiritual significance even in attempting to affirm and establish it. A subtler, "negative" or "apophatic" theo-logic is necessary to make sense of the divine vision, and this is what is enacted and embodied in Dante's scene of writing. Such an a/logic is worked out theologically all through Christian tradition, starting from Saint Paul and his exaltation of the "foolishness of God" that is "wiser than men" (I Corinthians 1:25). It attains to great speculative heights in Gregory of Nyssa (fourth century) and Dionysius the Areopagite (fifth–sixth centuries) and still with utmost intensity in Dante's own time, with Aquinas and Eckhart, at the culmination of a great age of apophatic theology in the Middle Ages.[24] Running parallel with Christian tradition is the Jewish mysticism of the Kabbalah. Kabbalah is itself a powerful source of negative-theological imagination. It, too, bears affinities with Dante's vision that demand to be sounded.

Dante is one of the chief inventors and inaugurators – or at least innovators – of a specifically literary method of mystic vision and ascent. Especially in the vision of writing in *Paradiso* XVIII, he creates a language mysticism akin to the contemplation of God through letters in the Kabbalah and in some forms of Sufism. Both of these mysticisms flourish

---

[24] Pierre Hadot, "Apophatisme et théologie négative," in *Exercices spirituels et philosophie antique* (Paris: Études Augustiniennes, 1981), 185–93, concisely expounds the historical emergence of this negative logic from Neo-Platonic abstraction (*aphaeresis*) and Christian language mysticism. For a synopsis of this history, see my *On What Cannot Be Said*, vol. 1.

and peak in precisely the formative period of Dante's own life at the end of
the thirteenth century, with Moses of Léon (1240–1305), the presumable
author of the *Zohar*, and Ibn al-Arabi (1165–1240), who prepares the way
for the great Persian mystic poet of Islamic inspiration Jalal al-Din Rumi
(1207–1273). According to Michael Sells, "The 150-year period from the
mid-twelfth to the beginning of the fourteenth century constitutes the
flowering of apophatic mysticism."[25]

The experience of poetic language, with its focus on language as mediation turning into immediacy, itself becomes mystical experience par
excellence. Living at the height of Catholic medieval religiosity, with its
sophisticated sense of hierarchy as a necessary mediation of the
Transcendent, Dante was well positioned to apprehend religious experience as essentially a matter of *mediation* of the Absolute. The creaturely can
itself become a manifestation of God, and language embodies the very
essence of this mediation – eminently in theological poetry. Medieval
Catholic tradition is, at its heart, about such a mediation of divinity. At
the same time, Dante synthesizes this sense of mediation with proto-
Protestant urgings of a new impulse to immediacy of the individual "I"
in relation to the divine. In his exemplary experience, linguistic and
specifically literary mediation turn, paradoxically, into theological revelation of an im-mediate presence of the divine in the experience of an
emergent modern subject. I designate this experience as "im-mediate" in
order to emphasize its inevitable negativity in relation to the infinite and
absolute – its grounding in the apophatic experience of what God *is not*.

Letter Mysticism (Kabbalah): The Magic in the Means

Dante's vision of the letters of Scripture scintillating in the heavens is not
without precedents in the religious and mystical literature of his time,
signally in the Jewish Kabbalah. The Kabbalah, too, is a language-based
mysticism. It understands reality fundamentally in linguistic terms. This
makes it akin to Dante's poetic vision, especially as expressed in the Heaven
of Jupiter. Flourishing in the thirteenth century in Spain, and reaching one
of its peaks with Abraham Abulafia (1240–1292) in Rome about Dante's
own time, the Kabbalah furnishes suggestive models and parallels for
Dante's vision. According to Gershom Scholem, this was the time of the
appearance of the *Zohar*, the fundamental text of Jewish Kabbalah: "While
in the years after 1275 Abraham Abulafia established his teaching of the

---

[25] Michael A. Sells, *Mystical Languages of Unsaying* (Chicago: University of Chicago Press, 1994), 5.

prophetic Kabbalah in Italy, somewhere in the heart of Castile a book was written that was fated to surpass all other documents of Kabbalistic literature in fame and success and rising influence, namely, the *Zohar*, the Book of Splendor."[26] So the Kabbalah was blossoming in the last quarter of the thirteenth century, contemporaneously with Dante, and in Italy, too.[27] What might it have offered Dante?

Most pertinently, the Kabbalah presents a highly evolved repertoire of theophanies in the letters of Holy Scripture understood doctrinely as Names of God. For Kabbalists, "... every individual letter by itself represents a Name [of God]" ("schon jeder einzelne Buchstabe für sich selber einen Namen darstellt").[28] God's Name is at once the shortest and the longest name, identical with every letter, but also with the Torah as a whole. "The whole of the Torah is the Name of the Holy One" (*Zohar*, Yithro 87a).[29]

The Kabbalah and specifically its seminal work, the *Zohar*, commonly called *The Book of Splendor*, features visionary scenes of letters sparkling in the heavens that are teasingly similar to Dante's Scriptural letters in the Heaven of Jupiter, embossing its silver with their gold. In one celestial vision, the characters of the Torah feature as flying and flaming letters flashing up and down and all around in space.

> Now they came forth, these carved, flaming letters
> flashing like gold when it dazzles.
>
> All of Israel saw the letters
> flying through space in every direction,
> engraving themselves on the tablets of stone.[30]

According to the Kabbalah's outlook, the real is constituted fundamentally by linguistic modes of signification. Symbolically, all Creation

[26] Gershom Scholem, *Die jüdische Mystik in ihren Hauptströmungen* (Frankfurt am Main: Suhrkamp, 1957), 171: "Während in den Jahren nach 1275 Abraham Abulafia seine Lehre der prophetischen Kabbala in Italien aufstellte, wurde irgendwo im Herzen Kastiliens ein Buch geschrieben, das dazu bestimmt war, alle anderen Dokumente der kabbalistischen Literatur an Erfolg und Ruhm, sowie an steigendem Einfluß zu überflügeln; das war das *Sefer ha-sohar*. Oder 'Das Buch des Glanzes'."

[27] Illuminating reflections on the probable place of Hebrew mysticism in Dante's culture, especially as mediated by the ambience of the University of Bologna, are offered by Alessandro Raffi, *La Gloria del volgare: Ontologia e semiotica in Dante dal "Convivio" al "De vulgari eloquenta"* (Catanzaro: Rubettino, 2004), 156–60.

[28] Gershom Scholem, "Der Name Gottes und die Sprachtheorie der Kabbala," *Eranus Jahrbuch* 39 (1970): 270.

[29] Geoffrey H. Hartman, "Midrash as Law and Literature," *Journal of Religion* 74/3 (1994): 338–55. Citation, 345.

[30] *Zohar: The Book of Enlightenment*, trans. Daniel Chanan Matt (New York: Paulist Press, 1983), 119–20.

proceeds from the letter, which remains its essential nature. The Letter is
the Law of Creation. Divinity is, ever after, present in the universe in the
form of signs and eminently of letters. In such a conception, language is
a self-revelation of God. Creation and revelation in Scripture are both
understood as God's self-manifestation in which the infinity of the
Godhead is symbolically – and linguistically – communicated, even
while remaining in its own proper nature ineffable. God's incommensur-
ability with any finite, perceptible or intuitable, object makes any direct,
unsymbolic presentation impossible.

On the basis of Kabbalah wisdom, and from a linguistic-theoretical
perspective, Gershom Scholem defines the symbolic character of language
in such a way as makes it inherently a kind of reaching towards the
ineffable:

> In the definition of the symbolic, the language theories of the mystics are
> often in disaccord; that, however, something here in language is communi-
> cated that reaches far beyond the sphere of what is susceptible of expression
> and form; that something expressionless, which shows itself only in symbols,
> moves in each expression, underlies it and, so to speak, shines through the
> cracks of the world of expression, is the common ground of all language
> mysticism and at the same time the experience out of which it in every
> generation, our own not excepted, is nourished and renewed.[31]

The Inexpressible is revealed in the letter especially by a kind of logic of the
fragment. We will see in Chapter 4 how Dante makes use of this logic in
breaking the Scriptural text down by grammatical parsing ("Grammatical
Shattering of Wholeness").

This "symbolic" character of language, whereby something else alien
from the order of beings and representation is mediated by it, makes
language peculiarly the medium of God's self-revelation in and to finite
creatures. For this symbolic dimension of language, paradoxically, conveys
what cannot be expressed or communicated.[32] Dante has a very strong

---

[31] I translate from Scholem's "Der Name Gottes und die Sprachtheorie der Kabbala," 244: "In der
Bestimmung dieses Symbolischen gehen die Sprachtheorien der Mystiker nicht selten auseinander;
dass aber sich hier in der Sprache etwas mitteilt, was weit über die Sphäre hinausreicht, die Ausdruck
und Gestaltung gestattet; dass ein Ausdrucksloses, das sich nur in Symbolen zeigt, in allem Ausdruck
mitschwingt, ihm zugrunde liegt und, wenn ich so sagen darf, durch die Ritzen der Ausdruckswelt
hindurchscheint, das ist der gemeinsame Grund aller Sprachmystik und ist zugleich die Erfahrung,
aus der sie sich noch in jeder Generation, die unsere nicht ausgeschlossen, genährt und erneuert hat."

[32] Such a mystical conception of language is not remote even from contemporary theorizations such as
Walter Benjamin's 1916 essay "Über Sprache überhaupt und über die Sprache des Menschen" ("On
Language as such and on the Language of Humans"), in *Gesammelte Schriften* II. I (Frankfurt am
Main: Suhrkamp, 1977), 140–56.

sense of language as symbolic in just this sense. Paradise, as represented in the poem, and as itself a created realm that manifests God's presence in spite of his transcendence, can only be "symbolic," as Dante so perfectly understands in giving his Paradise its special non-objective, metaphorical status.[33] The phenomena Dante sees are there only "in order to make a sign" ("per far segno") specially for him and accommodated to human faculties of knowing, as explained by Beatrice in Canto IV. 28–48. The *symbolon* (Greek σύμβολον), in general, is a manifestation of what nevertheless remains at least partly absent. In Scholem's special sense, a symbol is the signification of something that nevertheless remains ineffable. Dante heightens and infinitizes this symbolic dimension of language through his poetry, even while, at the same time, pursuing the rational understanding of language newly advanced by Scholastic philosophy in his day.

In the theophany of the script of the Book of Wisdom in *Paradiso* XVIII, God is present in letters – which is to say that he is absent, but is signified. However, God is also present in the letters' action of *signifying* – at least, if we accept that not Dante, but God (or God more fundamentally than Dante) is originally the author of the *Paradiso*'s verbal fireworks – those specifically that blow up the *incipit* of the Book of Wisdom. We observed at the outset that each of the letters of Dante's vision (starting with D, I, L) is in some way a Name of God.[34] We can now add some analytic reasons to the traditional associations previously adduced.

In L or "El," differentiation between vowel (e) and consonant (l) embodies the principle of difference that Dante is aware produces linguistic significance in historical language as we know it. "El" contrasts with the undifferentiated, single, simple sound of the mystical name "I," which Adam originally used for God (XXVI. 134). "I" curiously functions as both consonant and vowel, notably in words like "Iustinian" and "Iehovah," commonly written also as "Justinian" and "Jehova," to cite examples from what were sacred languages for Dante.[35] In the Italian name for God,

---

[33] The Letter to Can Grande (*Epistole* XIII) relates the type of representation characteristic of *Paradiso* to Plato's use of metaphors ("assumptionem metaphorismorum," 29.84).

[34] Silvio Pasquazi, "Il Canto XIX del *Paradiso*," in *All'eterno dal tempo*, 2nd ed. (Florence: Le Monnier, 1972), 235–59, suggests some mystic significances inhering in these individual letters. Each in some way signifies a name for God, and taken together they form "a sort of invitation to contemplate and adore God in the multiplicity of his names" ("una sorta d'invito a contemplare e adorare Dio nella molteplicità dei suoi nomi," 241). Cf. also Piero Scazzoso, "I nomi di Dio nella 'Divina Commedia' e il 'de Divinis Nominibus' dello Pseudo-Dionigi," *La scuola cattolica* 86 (1958): 198–213.

[35] YHWH (Yodh, He, Waw, He) is the more correct transliteration from Hebrew, but the Latinate form Jehova beginning with I is documented in Ubertino of Casale and John of Garland. See Domenico Guerri, "Il nome adamatico di Dio," in *La Commedìa: Nuovo testo critico secondo i più antichi manoscritti fiorentini*, ed. Antonio Lanza (Anzio [Rome]: De Rubeis, 1995), 63 and 69.

"Dio," however, this very phoneme "i" (/eɪ/) is included between a consonant and a vowel and so is made perceptible, just as it happily stands in the middle of the sequence D, I, L that Dante quotes from the text of the Book of Wisdom. The three-letter Latinate sequence, so presented, appears as an image of the Trinitarian God – of God, that is, according to the economy in which he reveals himself to humankind. In a kabbalistic spirit, it might be pointed out that "I" counts as the initial letter of JHWH, the Old Testament Father in heaven, whereas the L of *Logos* stands for the Son, while D is a cue for the *divinitas* of disseminating Spirit.

Umberto Eco observes that "for Abulafia, the atomic elements of the text, its letters, have a significance for themselves to such an extent that every letter of the name YHVH is already a divine name and thus even just Yod alone is a name of God" ("per Abulafia gli elementi atomici del testo, le lettere, hanno significato di per se stesse, al punto tale che ogni lettera del nome di YHVH è già un nome divino e quindi è nome di Dio anche la sola Yod").[36] Eco suggests that the status of "I" as a name for God in Dante could have been determined by transliteration as "I" of the "Y" in YHVH ("Traslitteriamo, come Dante poteva fare, la Yod come 'I'") (55). Others have pointed out that by coinciding with the Roman numeral I – just as Hebrew letters also coincide with and are numbers, a fact exploited by the Kabbalists – the uniqueness or oneness of God is appropriately signified, and so his essence is named.[37]

The absolutely simple, single-stroke letter or number – "I" – signifies a recuperation of unity and eternity from among the multifaceted forms of history. It encloses, hidden within itself, the unity before or beyond the split into difference of consonant and vowel. Certainly, more specific historical explanations could further illuminate this choice, which, according to Eco, "no commentator has succeeded in explaining adequately" ("nessun commentatore è riuscito a spiegare in modo soddisfacente").[38] The literary-theoretical perspective, however, gives this letter and the others with which it combines in Trinitarian formation a powerful motivation on the level of very basic theosophical considerations concerning language. By beginning a recitation with the first three letters (D, I, L) in a series that is continued ("DILIGITE IUSTITIAM, etc."), Dante gives the impression that perhaps every letter has potentially the significance of

---

[36] Umberto Eco, *La Ricerca della lingua perfetta nella cultura europea* (Rome: Laterza, 1993), 55.
[37] Angelo Penna, "El," in *Encyclopedia Dantesca* (Rome: Treccani, 1970–1975), vol. 2, 647.
[38] Eco, *La Ricerca della lingua perfetta*, 55.

naming God and of containing immanently all things in itself. This accords with Scholem's previously noted statement that "God, one may perhaps say, is for the Kabbalists at once the shortest and the longest name. The shortest because *every single letter already by itself represents a name.* The longest because only in the sum total of the Tora is it exhaustively expressed" ("Der Name Gottes," 270).

What interests us more than trying to pin down Dante's specific sources are the general concept and the dramatic gesture of letter mysticism as it is employed in and performed by Dante's text. Nervertheless, in order to make this connection convincing, it is worth noticing briefly some of the details of Dante's incipient Christian Kabbalism. Eco, rounding out his chapter on Dante's conception of a perfect language with a section on "Dante and Abulafia," reminds us of how Christian exegesis typically sought to individuate a latent content in texts, but without altering their form of expression through anatomization and permutation of letters. Kabbalistic letter mysticism, in contrast, was wont to reshuffle this form on the linguistic surface in accordance with the three basic techniques of *notariqon, gematria,* and *temurah.*

All three of these techniques, nevertheless, happen to be rather prominently exhibited in Dante's description of letters in the heaven of Jove. The first, *notariqon,* is acrostic. Dante conspicuously weaves an acrostic into this very heaven with the verse-head anaphoras at the beginning of consecutive tercets spelling LUE ("plague") as an embroidery on the roster of unjust princes in Canto XIX. 115–41. The third technique, *temurah,* the art of anagram, is exploited by Dante in multifarious ways in these cantos, as throughout the poem, but here most strikingly perhaps in the hidden occurrences of the names of God, as already reviewed.

The possible cues for anagrammatic reading of Dante's texts are rife. At the end of Canto XVIII, Dante addresses Pope John XXII with contempt as "you, who write only in order to erase" ("che sol per cancellare scrivi," XVIII. 130) and puts these words into his mouth: "'I' have my desire set on him who willed to live alone" ("I' ho fermo 'l disio / sì a colui che volle viver solo," XVIII. 133–34). The pope's desire fixed upon "the one who lived alone" – at a first level of interpretation, John the Baptist – can be heard also as a twisted wish to be God, the One and only. With the first-person pronoun shortened to simply "I," this utterance can be read as a usurpation of the identity of God: "I" for "io" confounds the first-person pronoun with a name for God that we have discovered in the vision of *Paradiso* XVIII. 77, especially in light of Adam's originally naming God "I" ("I s'appellava in terra il sommo bene," XXVI. 134).

The interpretive detachment of a letter from its syntagmatic insertion in the word, in order to speculate on its possible significance on its own, or in a reconstructed sequence, is elicited, furthermore, by a deformation of Paul's name – Paolo – to "Polo," in the speech attributed to John XXII (1316–1334), the second Avignonian pope, born Jacques Duèze in Cahors, France, in 1244. Dante ingeniously captures the inadvertant difference of his Gallic pronunciation of the apostle's name "Polo." Disrespect for others is unwittingly conveyed through his garbling the orthography, or orthophony, of this name. At bottom, this spells a lack of respect for the principle of difference that is already encapsulated in Pope John's wishing his own "io" to be the one and only. And yet he writes not in order to create but only to cancel ("sol per cancellare scrivi," 130). In these terms, his writing is contrasted implicitly with the act of God, who creates the world by making fundamental distinctions between heaven and earth, by separating the waters that are above the firmament from those below it and the dry land from the sea, etc. (Genesis 1:4–10).

While the possible influence of the Kabbalah for the passage in question is not perhaps integral, neither can it be confined to just a few isolated details.[39] Finally, we must add that numerical symbolism (*gematria*) is also present and prominent here (as in so many places in the *Commedia*), most obviously in the breakdown of the letters sighted in Jove into $5 \times 7 = 35$. This number can count as a Christological cipher, since Dante holds Christ to have died just before reaching his thirty-fifth birthday and therewith at the peak of the seventy-year arc of human life (see Excursus III). The Kabbalah exploited to the full multiple procedures of converting letters and words to their numerical equivalents in order to detect in them arcane symbolic meanings.

Gematria is based on the numbers as which Hebrew letters double, and, although quite different, Dante's attention to the numerical quantity of his letters, five times seven, becomes the more significant when ranged together with such rabbinical techniques of mystical reading. Dante, in fact, uses letters as numbers again, somewhat in the manner of Kabbalistic uses of Hebrew letters, shortly hereafter in Canto XIX. 127–29, where "I" stands for 1 and M for 1,000 in reckoning the merits and demerits respectively of the nefarious "Ciotto of Jerusalem." This is Dante's sarcastic

---

[39] Sandra De Benedetti Stow demonstrates this in "La mistica ebraica come chiave per l'apertura del livello anagogico del testo dantesco," in *Lectura Dantis 2002–2009: Omaggio a Vincenzo Placella per i suoi settanta anni*, ed. A. Cerbo (Naples: L'università Orientale, 2011), vol. IV, 1205–30, particularly 1226–29 on the *DIL* and *M*, and more extensively in her *Dante e la mistica ebraica* (Florence: Giuntina, 2004).

title for the "Cripple (morally speaking) of IerusaleM," Charles II of
Anjou, named after an empty honorific left him by his father, who had
accompanied Saint Louis on the Seventh Crusade (1248-54) in the attempt
to regain Jerusalem after its fall in 1244.

Dante's interpretive practice and its application in poetic representation
is, of course, based on Christian exegesis. But that does not prevent him
from being open to influence from directions such as those of the letter
mysticism more fully developed and exploited in the Kabbalah. He would
not be alone among Christian writers in evincing this receptivity. One
thinks of Pico della Mirandola later in the Italian Renaissance, with his vast
project of translation of Hebrew esoterism, but kindred interests are in
evidence also well before Dante. Much letter mysticism can be learned
already from Isidore of Seville's *Etymologiarum sive Originum libri XX*.
Book I of this work begins its discussion of grammar with the derivation of
all Greek and Latin letters from Hebrew ("Litterae Latinae et Graecae ab
Hebraeis videntur," I. iii. 4), while Book VII, chapter I lays out and
interprets ten Hebrew names for God.[40]

A certain Hebrew letter mysticism, transformed by coming into contact
with Christian Logos theology of the Incarnation, may well have found its
way by such a route into the heart of Dante's reflections on his poetic medium
as writing. We are reminded that Dante, in *De vulgari eloquentia* I. vi. 7,
considered Hebrew to have been the original language of humankind,
a situation supposed to have remained intact down to the disaster at Babel
recorded in Genesis 11:1–9. And in the broader midrashic tradition of Jewish
thought following Genesis 1, the Word of God is already the agent of Creation
and history. The letters of the Torah, in their visible iconic form, are at the
origin of the world and of all that happens in it. Dante envisions such
normative power in the letters from the Word of God, the Book of
Wisdom, displayed in the Heaven of Jupiter, the Heaven of Justice. He sees
the ultimately just order of things as emanating from, or at least as signified by,
these letters. All order of any kind in the world is, in fact, but an image of this
template of order – the incarnate Logos. And Dante has contrived, by using
techniques analogous to those of kabbalistic writings, to indicate that the
order he discerns is indeed a manifestation precisely of Christ (Excursus III).

These tantalizingly suggestive specifics notwithstanding, Dante's sense of
divine revelation in the letter probably rests not so much on interpretations of
specific letters as on the theological status of the letter as such. This would

---

[40] Roger Dragonetti, *Dante pèlerin à la Sacre Face* (Ghent: Romanica Gadensia, 1968) offers an
extensive reading of Dante based largely on Isidore.

correspond to the character of his interest as a poet, as an artisan working with letters. He refashions all the traditions that he eclectically assimilates. The letter mysticism of Joachim of Flores in his *Liber Figurarum* has also been plausibly linked with Dante's vision in this heaven.[41] The outlook on language and reality developed in existing language mysticisms is appropriated by Dante and fused with his own syncretistic vision.[42]

In any event, the kabbalistic side of Dante's presentation of letters of Scripture in *Paradiso* XVIII should not be considered to be restricted to quaint, outdated notions of mysticism and myth that might still be taken seriously and even be believed only in the Middle Ages. They have perennial appeal and find their counterparts even among modern poets in fully secularized settings, for example, in Mallarmé's notion of the Book as a "total expansion of the letter" ("Le livre, expansion totale de la lettre").[43] Fascination with the letter taken in itself induced Saussure to raise the anagram to the level of a ubiquitous principle of poetry.[44] Some of these resources have been tapped specifically for reading Dante by Philippe Sollers in the post-structuralist current of culture that renewed interest in *écriture* as quasi-magical and, at any rate, as much more than just a tool or technique at the disposal of a human subject.[45]

In some way, a kabbalistic background must certainly be felt to bear on the exaltation of the letter in this heaven. Scholem explains that Kabbalistic speculation really begins in the *Sefer Jezira*, probably from the third or fourth century of our era, with "speculation on the godly Sophia as divine Wisdom, in which all creation is grounded" ("Der Name Gottes," 256). *Sophia*, Wisdom, the name of the Book whose *incipit* Dante quotes as the *Leitmotif* of this heaven, had a central role in Gnostic and in Kabbalistic thinking such as Dante also accords it in his contemplation of writing.[46]

---

[41] Marjorie Reeves and Beatrice Hirsch-Reich, *The Figurae of Joachim of Fiore* (Oxford: Clarendon Press 1972), 320–22, explore the influence of this book upon Dante's visual imagination, deriving the skywriting of *Paradiso* XVIII. 94–108 from the *Liber Figurarum*. See, further, Leone Tondelli, *Il Libro delle Figure dell'abate Gioachino da Fiore* (Turin: SEI, 1940), 205–11: "La M che si trasforma in aquila. L'ingigliarsi all'M."

[42] Franz Dornseiff, *Das Alphabet in Mystik und Magie* (Leipzig: Teubner, 1922) offers a comprehensive treatment of numerous relevant backgrounds.

[43] Stéphane Mallarmé, "Le livre, instrument spirituel," in *Œuvres complètes* (Paris: Pleiades, 1945), 380.

[44] Ferdinand de Saussure, *Anagrammes homériques*, ed. Pierre-Yves Testenoire (Paris: Lambert-Lucas, 2013); Jean Starobinski, *Les mots sous les mots: Les anagrammes de Ferdinand de Saussure* (Paris: Gallimard, 1971).

[45] Philippe Sollers, "Dante et la traversée de l'écriture," *Tel Quel* 23 (1965): 12–25.

[46] This figure, Sophia, in biblical tradition has been richly mined in relation to Dante by Paola Nasti, *Favole d'amore e "saver profondo": La tradizione salamonica in Dante* (Ravenna: Longo, 2007); and Antonio Rossini, *Il Dante sapienziale: Dionigi e la bellezza di Beatrice* (Pisa: Fabrizio Serra, 2009). See, further, Jaroslav Pelikan, "Wisdom as *Sophia* and *Sapienza*," in *Eternal Feminines: Three*

Dante's choice of the Book of Wisdom as his text of reference in this
heaven gains in motivation thanks to the foundational role Wisdom plays
in this tradition concerning the mystical significance of letters. Wisdom
inheres in letters ("ist die Weisheit in den Buchstaben"), according to these
original sources, as Scholem shows, and the writing of the letters that
Dante sees is central to the wisdom he seeks and to the drama he represents
in Jove.

Nevertheless, speculation concerning sources is not the central object of
concern in the present interpretation of Dante's scene of writing in the
heaven of Jove. If we wish to appreciate Dante's poetry as fully as possible,
it is advisable not to aim to find the master key to this passage in any system
of cultural referents outside the poetic structures of his text itself and their
own dynamics. Dante's letter mysticism in this passage is not exactly what
one finds in the Kabbalah or anywhere else: it is, rather, in important ways,
his own creation. Even more significant than the traditional doctrines
Dante evokes is the speculatively theoretical insight he opens into the
essentially poetic nature of language and the potential that resides therein
for apprehending language as theophany. Such is the central reflection
I wish now to continue developing, after this detour into the more arcane
speculations of the Kabbalah on the threshold of opening further paths
into fundamental aspects of Dante's vision in the following chapters. Yet
one strong thread of connection to hold on to, one that will be extended
further in Chapter 3, is an emphasis in Kabbalistic tradition on the
"*absolute* randomness" of language. This emphasis surprisingly hangs
together with the Kabbalah's "magical theory of all language" as "overdetermined," which has been suggestively compared to "deconstructive"
theories and their "linguistic nihilism."[47]

Mediation as Signification and as Incarnation

Writing taken thus as a medium that reveals – and that becomes itself,
metaphorically, revelation, Word of God – harbors the same sort of
paradox as is enshrined in the doctrine of the Incarnation, namely, the
coinciding of what is in principle ungraspably transcendent with the sheer
immanence of a medium. In Dante's vision of writing, a phenomenon

Theological Allegories in Dante's Paradiso (New Brunswick: Rutgers University Press, 1990), 123–35.
Umberto Eco also notes that "the Torah was identified with Wisdom and in many passages with
a world of forms, a universe of archetypes" (*La Ricerca della lingua perfetta*, 37).

[47] Harold Bloom, "The Breaking of Form," in *Deconstruction and Criticism*, ed. Harold Bloom
(New York: Seabury Press, 1979), 4.

that, considered in itself, would appear contingent, merely material and external, folds into – and is practically identified with – the transcendent being or sense that it mediates. What Dante sees written in the heaven of Jove is literally Scripture, the Word of God, and this also means the second Person of the Trinity. This remarkable phenomenon is presented in such a way as to suggest that the words and letters Dante sees are the real presence of Divinity. Beyond simply signifying God by absence, they can concretely manifest him in a perceptible medium. They render him, in some miraculous manner, visually perceptible and "present." Their mysterious ability to do this has something to do essentially with the nature of writing and, more particularly, with *Scriptural* revelation.

The strategy of the poet is to represent himself contemplating the transcendent sense or "meaning" of the divine Word, or even the transcendent presence of God, in fully objectified form. He can do so by identifying the medium – namely, writing, and particularly the visible marks or letters in which it consists – poetically and metaphorically with what it mediates. This does not mean that God is metamorphosed into the form of written characters but rather that the divine Being is directly revealed as present in this medium, which is thereby, in this instance, divinized. The medium – writing – becomes in some sense an incarnation of God, without God's being changed into it. Such are the radical incarnational implications of this theophany. God has no finite objective being that could be transformed, but the finite objective being of the written character can be transfigured into the divine by being broken open to an ungraspable, infinite dimension that can be found absconding in its mysterious depths.

The paradoxes involved here are those inherent in the theology of the Incarnation as Word of God become flesh. Incarnation here means not God's metamorphosis into matter so much as his full self-expression in the medium of history and of sensuous humanity. Incarnation of the Word, in this sense, is to be understood, in the first place, in terms of semiology rather than of physiology or chemistry. It presupposes understanding reality, at the most fundamental level, not as reified matter but rather as semiological in nature. Its substance is literally communication of itself. In a perspective determined by biblical theology and anthropology rather than by Greek substance metaphysics, phenomena of speech, of naming and being addressed, are ontologically prior to the existence of substances. God speaks things into existence in Genesis 1. Experience, accordingly, is, in its origins, not experience of objects so primordially as experience of *others* as communicated in speech.

An important modern transmission and rendering of this essentially biblical ontological framework of the real as constituted in its essence by the word is Martin Buber's *I and Thou*. Its implications for an alternative to substance-based ontologies deriving from Greek philosophical tradition are developed further by Franz Rosenzweig and Emmanuel Levinas.[48] Such a linguistic ontology, moreover, is conceived incarnationally by Christian theologians, notably Karl Rahner. In Rahner's philosophical theology, "hearing the Word" becomes the very foundation of Christian existence.[49]

Hans-Georg Gadamer brings to focus, in its far-reaching significance for the whole history of Western thought concerning language, the radical difference of the Christian conception of the *Verbum* from Greek thinking of the *Logos*. According to Gadamer, the thought of the Incarnation of the Word is much more adequate to the *being* of language than is anything in Greek thought. The latter (in the metaphysical form it assumed in the tradition) was responsible, instead, for a pervasive *forgetfulness* of language in the philosophical thinking of the West.[50] This thesis was powerfully advocated by Gadamer's teacher Martin Heidegger.

Something like a semiological or linguistic-ontological outlook on human, as well as divine, reality is presupposed and applied by Dante throughout his works. We have already called it his "linguistic humanism." In *De vulgari eloquentia*, Adam's first act of consciousness articulates itself as a proferring of God's name. Adam expresses his joy in being, and this joy itself is the Name of God: "and since no joy is external to God, but wholly within God and God himself is totally joy, it follows that the first speaker said 'God' before all else" ("et cum nullem gaudium sit extra Deum, sed totum in Deo, et ipse Deus totus sit gaudium, consequens est quod primus loquens primo et ante omnia dixisset 'Deus'," I. iv. 4). This embryonic phenomenology of the origins of human consciousness suggests that primordial experiential reality is a reality of signs and discourse. These signs, however, are intrinsically structured as pointing towards a God who infinitely transcends them.

---

[48] Through historical and hermeneutic reflection, Graziano Ripanti skillfully draws these luminaries of modern Jewish thought together into a Christian theological framework in *Le parole della metafisica*, 2nd ed. (Urbino: QuattroVenti, 1993) and *Parola e ascolto* (Brescia: Morcelliana, 1993).

[49] Karl Rahner, *Hörer des Wortes: Zur Grundlegung einer Religionsphilosophie* (Munich: Kösel: 1963), trans. Joseph Donceel as *Hearer of the Word* (New York: Continuum, 1994).

[50] See discussion of "die Sprachvergessenheit des abendländischen Denkens," in subsection III, 2, b, "Sprache und Verbum," of Hans-Georg Gadamer, *Wahrheit und Methode* (Tübingen: Mohr, 1960), 422, trans. Joel Weinsheimer and Donald G. Marshall as *Truth and Method*, 2nd rev. ed. (New York: Continuum, 2004), 418. Excursus VI takes up and follows these threads.

In relation to the Incarnation, this perspective implies a subtle view of identity, one different from the scientific, naturalist view of the hylo-morphic unity of form and matter in the physical thing. As marked by the semiological metaphor of the word that incarnates thought, the material in question is one to which significance is intrinsic and which, therefore, cannot be understood in purely material terms, but only in terms of an event of sense. And when the revelation of divinity in the Word is understood semiologically in this way, its incarnational logic applies as much to Scriptural revelation in word and letter as to God's becoming a human being.

In the Christian conception, the Incarnation of the Word in human flesh in Christ makes explicit and concrete what is already realized in a different way in Scripture – in the Divine Word rendered intelligible in human language. Saint Augustine describes the eternal divine Word as without extension or succession in the bosom of the Father and as electing to be created in a verbal body in the syllables of time – and this is Scripture. Thus, the divine Word becomes human language in the Scriptures even before it becomes flesh in the humanity of Jesus of Nazareth. In Augustine's pithy formula: the Word was made word (*Verbum verbum factum est*).[51] For Augustine, the Incarnation and the Bible are parallel channels of revelation through which God continues to speak with man even after the Fall.[52]

This analogy between the incarnate Word, God become man, and Scripture as an outward, visible expression of the divine Word is also intimated by Pseudo-Dionysius the Areopagite. Dionysius considers the Incarnation as an "instance of differentiation" of the divine Name that Scripture likewise serves to articulate.[53] This is why the Word must now be distinguished as He exists in Scripture and in human flesh. And Dante would simply be extending this idea if, as Marsha Colish suggests, he is proposing his *Commedia* as "the poetic corollary of the Incarnation."[54]

---

[51] Augustine, in *Ps.* 101, 4, 1. See discussion of Graziano Ripanti, "Ermeneutica della fede e filosofia della religione," in *Filosofia della religione: Storia e problemi*, ed. Piergiorgio Grassi (Brescia: Queriniana, 1988), 9–37.

[52] Cf. G. R. Evans, *The Language and Logic of the Bible: The Earlier Middle Ages* (Cambridge: Cambridge University Press, 1991 [1984]), 1. John M. Fyler, *Language and the Declining World in Chaucer, Dante, and Jean de Meun* (Cambridge: Cambridge University Press, 2007) reminds us to keep constantly in view that *our* language, together with all its names, is fallen (124).

[53] Pseudo-Dionysius the Areopagite, *De divinis nominibus* 644C and 648A. On this head, see Andrew Louth, *Denys the Areopagite* (Wilton: Morehouse-Barlow, 1989), 90.

[54] Marcia L. Colish, *The Mirror of Language: A Study in the Medieval Theory of Knowledge*, rev. ed. (Lincoln: University of Nebraska Press, 1983), 225. This idea of Dante's poetry as incarnation of divinity lies at the core also of Guy P. Raffa's *Divine Dialectic: Dante's Incarnational Poetry* (Toronto: University of Toronto Press, 2000).

Of course, it is important to avoid simply conflating the Incarnation of God in the flesh as Christ with Scriptural revelation. Yet the continuity and implicit unity of both manifestations of God's Word cannot but influence the Christian's sense of Scripture's relation to God and of Scripture's mediation of God's Being and presence. The inner unity of Scriptural revelation with the Incarnation, so deep-seated in the Christian vision, is expressed nearer to Dante's own times, for example, by Hugh of St. Victor: "The matter of all of divine Scripture is the incarnate Word with all its 'sacraments' or manifestations, as much those preceeding the beginning of the world as those that are futural until the end of the world" ("Materia divinae Scripturae est Verbum incarnatum cum omnibus sacramentis suis, tam praecedentibus a principio mundi quam futuris usque ad finem saeculi").[55]

Incarnation of the divine Word occurs eminently, but not exclusively, in the event of Christ in Jesus of Nazareth. Hugh's thought of the "three words" is based on an apprehension of the threefold unity of "the word of man, the word of God spoken in creation, and the uncreated Word of God."[56] The mimetic continuity between the divine Word and human words such as Scripture necessarily employs as both essentially outward manifestations of an inner essence was formulated authoritatively by Augustine in his teaching of the inner word ("verbum interioris"). This teaching became a commonplace of medieval thought. It appears, for example, quite explicitly in Vincent of Beauvais (d. 1264): "Man, in uttering a word, is incarnating the word of his mind in order that it may be made manifest to human senses, just as the Word of God was made flesh in order that He might be made manifest to human senses."[57]

This parallel between verbal expression and the Incarnation of the Word becomes an interpenetration (or, more technically, a "circuminsession") that in Christian theology displaces the very logical basis for understanding the roots of being, as well as for understanding language as the mediation of being, and indeed for understanding the notion of mediation in general. In the world-historical event of the Incarnation, logic has left its abstractness behind in order to become the Logos in person. A supra-logic of the

---

[55] Hugh of St. Victor, *De scripturis et scriptoribus sacris*, chapter XVII (*Patrologia Latina* 175 24).

[56] Hugh of St. Victor, *De arca Noe morali* 2.13, "De tribus verbis." For further elucidation, see Margaret F. Nims, "*Translatio*: 'Difficult Statement' in Medieval Poetic Theory," *University of Toronto Quarterly* 43 (1974): 229n17.

[57] "Ita enim verbum nostrum vox quoddamodo corporis fit, assumendo eam in qua manifestetur sensibus hominum; sicut Verbum Dei caro factum est, assumendo eam in qua et ipsum manifestetur sensibus hominum." *Speculum naturale* 27.6.1921b. The translation follows Nims, "*Translatio*," 221.

medium operates paradigmatically in the absolute paradox of the Incarnation. For the Incarnation of divinity realizes the material, temporal medium – a human existence in the flesh – as absolute.

Such a paradox must be faced in any attempt to define the status of the flesh of God, and it becomes especially acute in any specifically Christian claim concerning the ability of human language to attain to prophetic or divine status. In this paradigm, a material form that, semiotically considered, would be no more than a vehicle or sign of the immaterial is affirmed as incorporating concretely the very person of the transcendent God. This is a logic that could never have been produced by the schools, but somehow it captures a truth of religious experience lived in relation to the Christ, a truth that exceeds and confounds every formalizable rationality.[58]

Christians from Tertullian to Kierkegaard have borne witness to this miracle in so many absolute paradoxes. In the medieval age, Alain de Lille in his *Rythmus de Incarnatione et de septem Artibus* expresses such a paradox in describing the impotence of grammar to comprehend the Incarnation: "In hac verbi copula / Stupet omnis regula" ("In this copula of the Word / Every rule is stupefied").[59] A poetic rationality, instead, is necessary, in which seemingly contradictory truths can coexist. Dante's image, in *Paradiso* XIII. 37–51, of mutually exclusive points on the circumference of a circle being reconciled at its center ("nel vero farsi come centro in tondo") schematically suggests some such possibility of mediation between the rational and the transcendent.

As Joan Ferrante aptly notes at the outset of her article on the *Paradiso*'s exceptional language, "In the *Paradiso*, Dante attempts and achieves the impossible. . . . Dante conveys the essence of his vision by stretching his medium to its limits, by using words that do not exist, images that contradict each other, by distorting sequential and logical order, and by ignoring the boundaries of separate languages." It is by such means that "his language and imagery reflect the nature of the divine."[60]

---

[58] Paul Tillich's understanding of revelation as the depth of reason in "Reason and the Quest for Revelation," in *Systematic Theology*, 3 vols. (Chicago: University of Chicago Press, 1967), vol. 1, 79–81 suggests how such a view can itself be "rational" in an enlarged sense.

[59] Alanus Insulis, *Patrologia Latina* 210. Emmanuel Falque, *Dieu, la chair et l'autre: D'Irénée à Duns Scot* (Paris: Presses Universitaires de France, 2008), trans. William Christian Hackett as *God, The Flesh, and the Other: From Irenaeus to Duns Scotus* (Evanston: Northwestern University Press, 2015), shows these paradoxes connected with divine flesh in the Incarnation to be very much alive both in medieval and in contemporary phenomenological theologies of the Incarnation.

[60] Joan M. Ferrante, "Words and Images in the *Paradiso*: Reflections of the Divine," in *Dante, Petrarch, Boccaccio: Studies in the Italian Trecento in Honor of Charles S. Singleton*, eds. Aldo

Incarnate revelation requires escaping from the classical Aristotelian logic of non-contradiction in a direction that will be developed and eventually lead all the way to Hegel's dialectical logic, which is itself conceived to a very considerable extent on the basis of Christian, particularly Lutheran, religious experience centered in the humanity of God.[61] Such broadening of the notion of reason to the point where it comprehends what is analytically contradictory can be found in embryo even in Thomas Aquinas.[62] As reflected in Christian theological speculation, this is a logic of the Logos as a whole, as complete and "eternal," yet also as living and concrete.

These paradoxes of the theology of the Incarnation – as metaphorically converting or "transuming" (see the final section of Chapter 5) the pagan phenomenon of metamorphosis, which also fascinates Dante, with specific reference to Ovid, all the way through the *Paradiso* – give Christianity its peculiar outlook on language as revelation of an unspeakably transcendent divinity. Crucial resources for pursuing them further include St. Augustine's discussion of the interior Word in *De trinitate*, Book XV, and St. Athanasius's *De incarnatione verbi*.

We will consider later (in Excursus III) just how the Incarnation is actually ciphered into the crux of Dante's vision in the heaven of Jove, specifically in the number of the letters, thirty-five, which turns out to be a figure for Christ's life on earth in its attaining to exactly the apex of the arc of human life (*Convivio* IV. xxiii. 10). At the present juncture, the main point is simply that Incarnation serves as an overarching theological paradigm for the presentation of Scripture as theophany in the form of conspicuously visible (and even audible) letters in Dante's vision in the heaven of Jove. Incarnation impinges on the divine vision of the whole poem – culminating in the human effigy ("nostra effige") inscribed within the Trinitarian deity in the final vision of the last canto (XXXIII. 131). However, a subtle linguistic logic of sensuous incarnation of divinity has been anticipated by the pyrotechnic lights forming visible/audible letters and gaily

S. Bernardo and Anthony L. Pellegrini (Binghamton: Medieval and Renaissance Texts and Studies, 1983), 115.

[61] Beyond the pivotal place given to religion in his *Phenomenology* and *Encyclopedia*, Hegel's early development as a theological thinker, as charted in *G. W. F. Hegel: Theologian of the Spirit*, ed. Peter Hodgson (Minneapolis: Fortress Press, 1997), maps out this trajectory.

[62] Denis Turner portrays such an Aquinas in *God, Mystery, and Mystification* (Notre Dame: University of Notre Dame Press, 2019), chapter 2: "One with God as to the Unknown: Prayer and the Darkness of God."

sparking across the heaven of Jove in the vision of Scripture in Canto XVIII.

Corollary on Incarnation and Semiology in Radical Orthodoxy

The creative power of the word has been rediscovered in recent decades by theoretical investigations that have enabled theology to regain access to its own deepest understanding of being after the hiatus of a modern age dominated by dogmas of secularism. Exemplary with regard to the semiological perspective sketched in the last section is the contemporary rethinking of incarnational theology by the so-called Radical Orthodoxy theologians. This movement, in fact, turns on just the kind of theologico-semiological insight that we have been exploring here at the threshold between the medieval and the modern worlds. This rethinking refocuses the originating power of signs as illuminated by the theological discourse of the creative Word.

John Milbank traces the routes by which orthodox Christian thinkers ever since Gregory of Nyssa and Augustine have undermined substance metaphysics by a Trinitarian understanding of reality in semiotic terms. Modern, and especially postmodern, thought has achieved something similar through its own linguistic turn, which revolutionizes the traditional problems of philosophy by thinking them through from a linguistic point of view that turns against substance metaphysics. However, whereas in the modern, secular age everything tends to be reduced to mere language as a production of the human mind, for Dante and a medieval theologico-symbolic outlook, language is in itself the revelation of another world and even of a divine reality.

For Dante, language is inherently theological, and theology is a discourse inherently attuned to the transcendent. Theology is predicated on transcendence of itself and of (human) discourse per se. Milbank argues that theology alone avoids erasing the difference between the Absolute and its revelation in immanence through created things: "For theology, and theology alone, difference remains real difference since it is not subordinate to immanent univocal process or the fate of a necessary suppression."[63]

Of course, Dante takes a giant step toward secularizing language in *Paradiso* XXVI. 130-32, where Adam says that the *manner* of human

---

[63] John Milbank, "The Linguistic Turn as a Theological Turn," in *The Word Made Strange: Theology, Language, Culture* (Oxford: Wiley-Blackwell, 1997), 113. See also "Only Theology Overcomes Metaphysics" in the same volume.

speaking is a matter of free choice ("secondo che v'abbella"). Nonetheless, the faculty of speech itself is God-given as inherent to human nature ("Opera natural è ch'uom favella"), and this is enough to preserve the absolute difference of language as transcendent gift, like being and life, from any humanly produced techniques or capabilities.

The problem with secular culture, for Milbank, is that it loses all sense of any possible difference from its own comprehensive system of nature and history: everything that is at all possible is subjected to human categories.[64] The real is thus reduced to what we can fathom and conceive. Radical Orthodoxy, by contrast, understands universal linguistic mediation not as a reduction to the same, but as a passage to the absolutely Other.[65] It finds resources in Christian thinkers, ancient and modern, focused on transcendent divinity as alone preserving real difference that cannot be reduced to an immanent system. The immanent system of language remains an allegory for a transcendent Word. In "The Linguistic Turn as a Theological Turn," Milbank concentrates on eighteenth-century thinkers including Robert Lowth, Johann Georg Hamann, George Berkeley, Giambattista Vico, and Johann Gottfried Herder, who accord the status and capability of divine revelation to language, even in recognizing its semiological arbitrariness. But we might just as well take Dante for such a focus at a much earlier moment in theological and intellectual history.

Signs emerge, in the tradition that Milbank outlines, as mediations of the real as absolute and as theological. In fact, there is the mediation of signs in all our knowledge, which consists never simply in direct possession and presence. All our knowledge is semiologically mediated to the extent that its object is the real and not merely the supposed "things themselves" that we forge through our abstract schemas and concepts. This fundamental acknowledgment is undercut by Kant's (and earlier by Scotus's) epistemological subjectivism, which makes the sign merely arbitrary and makes all our knowledge to be only "transcendentally" related to things themselves through the subject who employs signs.[66] The corresponding "transcendent" correlate of the sign is made irrelevant to human symbolic-noetic activity: it becomes for Kant a fideistic hypothesis of things-in-themselves

---

[64] See especially John Milbank's *Beyond Secular Order: The Representation of Being and the Representation of the People* (Oxford: Blackwell, 2013), but the critique was already trenchant with his *Theology and Social Theory: Beyond Secular Reason* (Oxford: Blackwell, 1991).

[65] Incisive avenues are broached in Phillip Blond, ed., *Post-secular Philosophy: Between Philosophy and Theology* (London: Routledge, 1998), 2.

[66] In Kant's vocabulary, the "transcendental" concerns the conditions of the possiblity of knowing, whereas the "transcendent" regards a noumenal realm beyond human knowing.

(*Dinge an sich*) with only practical, not theoretical import. Milbank proposes, instead, a realist metaphysics, or a theological ontology, that does not need to be overcome. With reference to a theory of George Berkeley's, he makes the general point that *semiosis* involves real relations, substitutionary transitions which, though inscrutable, are more than arbitrary; the signifying relation becomes also symbolic ("The Linguistic Turn," 103). This recaptures the sense of "symbolic" elicited earlier from Scholem's remarks in relation to the ineffable.

In an essay on "Christological Poetics" likewise in *The Word Made Strange*, Milbank's emphasis again falls on signs as real mediations of the divine nature, but also on their interruption. He stresses how the natural life of the sign needs to be negated in order that it open up into a kind of resurrected life. Moreover, this resurrected presence is an invisible image and is evoked by a shattered, broken sign. Through his death, together with the drama of the Last Supper that enframes it, Christ institutes himself and his body as a broken sign ("he took the bread, blessed it and broke it, and gave it to his disciples, and said, take this all of you, and eat of it, for this is my body," Matthew 26:26). This broken sign opens into universal meaning that will be achieved fully only through the subsequent Christian centuries. "The words of Maundy Thursday and the acts of Good Friday together compose a poetic act characterized by an 'overtaking', such that the intention of the sign is only realized in the full outcome of its explication" (138).

Jesus commits himself to "death as the reality of sign *qua* sign," since only as "a *function* of its lifelessness" can the sign become complete and fully defined and thereby totally significant. Milbank's terms prove helpful here for reformulating Christian doctrine on the far side of the post-structuralist critique of the sign: "One paradoxical reason for our recognition of Christ as the true sign is that all the signs he offers us are broken signs that offer their own asymmetry as a testimony to their own inadequacy and to the infinite distance between humanity and God" (137). Milbank thus inscribes the historical breakdown of the sign (declared and diagnosed by "deconstruction") into the Christian mystery of the crucified Logos.

The upshot of these reflections is that Incarnation needs to be thought in semiological – more than just in material or chemical – terms. This means not reducing divinity to the dimensions of the physical universe but rather opening our conception of physical reality to the immeasurable dimension of the infinite and divine. We must conceive the physical per se as the sign of another reality and the Incarnation as the key that enables us to interpret its meaning in terms of the physical phenomena that alone (following the teaching of Thomas Aquinas) we can perceive and experience with our senses.

The Incarnation is not adequately thought of simply as God's making himself accessible to us in worldly terms that we know and understand. The estrangement of this apparently familiar world as more deeply connected with – and as an allusion and prelude to – some other world that we do not comprehend is equally entailed by the idea of the Incarnation. The entry of God into the world estranges *it* from our common understanding. God's entry into it is a sign that the world is not masterable by any laws of physical science. The Incarnation teaches us the mystery of the world.[67] Our "knowledge" of the world, more deeply considered, is an *un*knowing of the divine – and of everything else as well – in its light (and darkness). This is the side of Christian doctrine that has been cast into shadow by too positive – not to say too positivistic – an interpretation of revelation, specifically of the incarnate revelation of Christ in Jesus of Nazareth.

God becomes incarnate in human flesh as an individual person, an incarnate sign of the (w)hol(l)y other. The man, Jesus of Nazareth, was God in the form of human perfection. He wrote nothing. We, however, receive this revelation later through the word of testimony of his witnesses. For us, the experience of his Incarnation is mediated by language, and Dante explores how language can become concretely a vehicle for this incarnate revelation. It requires exploiting the imaginative resources of writing and specifically the sensuous qualities of poetic language. Yet this seeming indirection and distance from the "original" event of Incarnation can help us to realize ourselves anew something of the truly awesome, unfathomable event of the incarnation of the Word.

The linguistic means of this incarnation can themselves become the substance of revelation, especially of the poetic type of revelation that Dante explores so originally. Exploration and rediscovery of the meaning of "incarnation" continues as mediated into ever new contexts. The profound implications for Dante's vision of its written means or medium

---

[67] Eberhard Jüngel, *Gott als Geheimnis der Welt: Zur Begründung der Theologie der Gekreuzigten im Streit zwischen Theismus und Atheismus* (Tübingen: Mohr, 1977), trans. Darrell L. Guder as *God as the Mystery of the World: On the Foundation of the Theology of the Crucified One in the Dispute between Theism and Atheism* (London: Bloomsbury, 2014) offers an evangelical theology of the word based on the ways that God speaks into the world in its radical historicity and finitude. The analogy of worldly phenomena to the divine marks them as uncanny and turns their brokenness into an image of the Crucifixion.

are startlingly illuminated by recent theorization in the field of media studies.

The Significance of Dante's Vision of Scripture in a History-of-Media Perspective

Dante's vision of letters freed from their normal meaning-function and projected into the heaven as visual spectacles in their own right furnishes an outstanding illustration of what Friedrich Kittler describes as a media revolution that prepares for "the nearing of the gods."[68] Kittler centers his own view on Richard Wagner's musical drama as a development that reverses the literary culture of the West dating from Gottfried von Straßburg's thirteenth-century *Tristan und Isolde*, which counts as the first vernacular literary work in German. For Kittler, the significance of Wagner's daring employment of a new range of media in his "music drama" is that it marks the end of an epoch dominated by meaning and exegesis. Wagner's innovations achieve an emancipation from bondage to the letter and to interpretation of its meaning in the syntax of the state-ment. This latter system of meaning and interpretation is what Kittler calls "literature," and he contends that, "The musical drama outstrips all litera-ture" ("Das Musikdrama schlägt alle Literatur," 45). Wagnerian musical drama emancipates images and sensory phenomena from the regime of literature and releases them into a new, revolutionary multi-medial dimen-sion. Data are no longer coded into an alphabet. Instead, they are ampli-fied, intensified, and rendered capable of endless reproduction. These augmented means are exploited not only in synthetic artistic forms such as film, but also eventually in media extravaganzas such as rock concerts and hyper-technologized tele-transmitted sports events and political rallies.

Kittler locates the springboard for this media revolution in the way that Wagner's invisible orchestra (lowered into the pit at Beyreuth) picks up on the words of his text and makes them into rhythm and music that move people unconsciously to rapture and, potentially, even to madness. The *Gesamtkunstwerk* procures this effect without having to pass by way of the usual intellectual channels of sense-making. Dante, too, explores these same phenomenal resources as issuing directly from an immediately ocular and auditory experience of letters. Dante presents the letters in their own internal dynamic as engaged in producing the sensory phenomena of a multimedia spectacle. Yet he deploys these supra- or ultra-literary

---

[68] Friedrich A. Kittler, *Das Nahen der Götter vorbereiten* (Munich: Fink, 2012).

functions and capacities in order to effect an apotheosis of the letter rather than as rebounding back against literature and annulling it.

Kittler gives a different ideological twist to essentially the same – or at least analogous – sorts of phenomena. According to Kittler, Wagner returns from the literary system of codified signification to pure sound and spectacle, reversing the system of communication that reigns supreme from Gottfried in the thirteenth century to Gutenberg in the fifteenth and eventually even to Goethe in the early nineteenth century. Dante, with his visionary letters, similarly sets into motion a regressive system that returns from intellectually signified meaning to physical form and movement of the concrete, sensory means of literary communication. He focuses particularly on the material marks that constitute the letters. The letters are blown up and explode into combustible sparks that then regroup and reconstitute themselves into visual spectacles rather like letter- and figure-forming fireworks. Dante's purpose, however, is not to circumvent the intellect but rather to achieve a higher and deeper immediacy of intellectual apprehension.

The "Orchestergraben," literally the "orchestral grave," out of which the music issues in Wagner's drama serves symbolically as the body of the earth in its endless depth. It represents the materiality of the body as the physical source of breath and life and therewith of every possibility of meaning. Wagner held that music is the "breath of language" ("Atmen der Sprache," Kittler, *Das Nahen der Götter vorbereiten*, 43–44). This allegorization finds its counterpart in the corpus of Dante's *singing* letters. For all their spiritual in*spir*ation by the intelligence of love, the letters remain rooted in an inarticulable sensuousness of sparks and of musical notes ("note") that are "sung" ("cantavan" XVIII. 76–81). Dante's language in the *Paradiso* has its music, too, and aspires to rise thereby from earth to heaven, from the materiality of sound to an ethereal music of silence in the purely intellectual apprehension of God.

Dante's scene of apotheosized letters becoming themselves the object of vision serves well to illustrate Marshall McLuhan's famous dictum that "the medium is the message."[69] This idea is fundamental for Kittler, too. However, Kittler takes a step beyond – dialectically reversing – McLuhan in that he does not simply identify "the medium" with the message or the meaning conveyed by contemporary, technologized forms of communication. He does not supplant what formerly counted as meaning by these

---

[69] Marshall McLuhan, *Understanding Media: The Extensions of Man* (Cambridge: MIT Press, 1994). The catchphrase occurs already in the Contents and in the title of chapter 1.

technical means apprehended merely objectively and taken as positive presences. Instead, he hails a relinquishing of all pure and plain positivity in a more shimmering and equivocal sort of "presence-absence." Kittler thereby opens literature up to an incalculably infinite and indescribable dimension that he figures in the penultimate chapter of *Das Nahen der Götter vorbereiten* as "the gods" and their coming – their eternal returning or "nearing." Kittler – like Dante – turns toward a powerfully productive and elusive image, a traditional image for the presence of transcendence: *viz.*, the "nearing" of the divine. This figure for approaching something asymptotically parallels Dante's trajectory in the last canto as he "was nearing" ("appropinquava") the "end" and "goal" (*fine*) of all (his) desires ("fine di tutt' i disii," XXXIII. 47–48), namely, the vision of God.

Talk, even profane talk, of the gods proves unavoidable for Kittler, too, in describing the ultimate message at stake in media. At the very end, and as the final words, of his essay on "Der Gott der Ohren" ("The God of the Ears"), Kittler quotes Pink Floyd's singer and guitarist Roger Waters: "The medium is not the message, Marshall . . . is it? I mean, it's all in the lap of the fucking gods . . ." (Kittler, *Das Nahen der Götter vorbereiten*, 61). The medium as such is not enough, or at least it is not the All: its inherent message directs us elsewhere to a divine productivity and creativity manifest in fecund images.

Kittler appeals to a mystical dimension that is activated in media events such as rock concerts and operatic musical drama, and he emphasizes their Dionysian potential for inducing ecstasy. Dante has staged such a media event in his own ecstatic vision in terms that anticipate virtually all the elements highlighted by Kittler's theory. The combination of technical means and mystical effect is already at the center of Dante's contemplation of the mystery of the letter broken down in the grammatical terms available in his time for the techniques and mechanics of writing (see Chapter 3). Dante already exposes and exalts the material media and technological infrastructures of his vision through a focus on writing as his means and through an ostentatious display of its spectacular technicity. Dante has boldly anticipated the type of revolution of consciousness inherent in communications media that will break onto the scene so pervasively in our own day.[70] He has also begun implicit theoretical reflection on this transformation in an ingenious vein that media studies are currently

---

[70] Innumerable indices can be culled from Antonella Braida and Luisa Calè, eds., *Dante on View: The Reception of Dante in the Visual and Performing Arts* (Aldershot: Ashgate, 2007); Francesco Tigani Sava, *Dante scrive il cinema: Per una lettura cinematica della "Divina Commedia"* (Catanzaro: Max, 2007), 637–42; and the articles in *Dante e l'arte* 3 (2016): Dante e il cinema 1.

developing further. This speculative penchant, too, makes him highly pertinent to our present and future self-metamorphoses by ever enhanced and ever more self-reflexive technical means.

Popular Culture versus Esoteric Modes of Reception

A codicil to be added here is that highlighting the mediality of Dante's writing and its graphic message has a long tradition behind it that attends to the vision's embeddedness in popular culture.[71] Peter Hawkins inventories the media by which the narrative and culture of the Bible were disseminated in the vernacular among the various classes and components of medieval lay society. He emphasizes the preeminent role of the iconographical programs of cathedrals, sacred drama such as miracle plays, and the preaching of lay sermons, which often included amusing anecdotes and could become entertainment. These media and various others provided supplements to regular practices of biblical recitation and liturgical prayer. "The Bible was far more readily seen and heard than it was ever read."[72]

Hawkins's work approaches my own perspective in developing a vision of Dante's *Commedia* as essentially a rewriting of Scripture that makes it happen over again, anew (15). His highly personal "Prologue" emphasizes the grounds in individual existence of the poem's effects in converting and guiding the lives it touches – and sometimes even shatters and reorganizes. Hawkins's examination, nevertheless, remains largely concentrated on clarifying the contexts and vividly representing what Dante's literary corpus derives from its sources. Further resources can be brought to bear in explicating in detail the verbal action of Dante's poetry and the dynamic event-character of his writing. Hawkins offers illuminating reflections on Holy Scripture as Dante's inspiring source and provides penetrating exegesis of Dante's "Scriptural imagination." However, his pages contain no extended reading of the scene of Scripture actually appearing to Dante in Jupiter – its being written out in all the technicolor splendor of its golden letters on the silver background of the Heaven animated by coruscating sparks.

---

[71] The importance of "Popular Culture" generally in the *Commedia* is discussed by Jan M. Ziolkowski in a homonymous chapter of *Dante in Context*, eds. Zygmunt G. Barański and Lino Pertile (Cambridge: Cambridge University Press, 2015), 389–98. The immediately ensuing chapters of the volume treat visual and performative culture, which are closely related and pertinent backgrounds to Dante's display in this heaven.

[72] Peter S. Hawkins, *Dante's Testaments: Essays in Scriptural Imagination* (Stanford: Stanford University Press, 1999). Citation, 20.

And yet the specific sentence from Scripture that is performed in the Heaven of Jupiter has a powerful and demonstrable iconographical presence in medieval Tuscany. The very verse from Wisdom enjoining justice upon the rulers of the earth is blazoned on a scroll held by the Christ child in a painting (*Maestà*, 1315) by Simone Martini in the Sala del Consiglio of the Palazzo Pubblico in Sienna. Some twenty years after Simone's painting, Ambrogio Lorenzetti painted in the adjacent Sala della Pace a fresco entitled "Good Government" ("Buon Governo," 1338–1340) that similarly displays the same verse of Scripture (*Diligite iustitiam* . . .) and surrounds it with allegorical representations of Sapienza (Wisdom) and Justice.[73] A scene dependent on Simone's was produced also by his brother-in-law Lippo Memmi (*Maestà*, 1317) in the Palazzo Pubblico of San Gimignano. These renderings suggest the role that this Scriptural sentence played in public life as a standing admonishment to the city's rulers.

Rachel Jacoff studies this presence of Wisdom 1:1 in the iconographical program in Sienna and reflects on its importance for the republican ideologies of the city-states.[74] The paintings bear Dante's imprint through inscriptions with *terza rima* verses echoing the poetry of the *Commedia* – as if in answer to this work's own intrinsic demand for visual representation. A proclivity to become pictorial is already patent in Dante's text, with its turning of word into image, notably with the transfiguration of the M of TERRAM into the emblematic image of the lily and then of the heraldic eagle. Jacoff adds vital material for our appreciation of how Dante's text plays out in its historical contexts. Although like Hawkins she does not directly focus on or analyze philosophically the verbal action of the signifiers as they generate phenomena of meaning and truth – and hence of "revelation," in Dante's text – she does significantly gesture in this "metaliterary" direction.

Jacoff follows John Freccero and Lino Pertile in remarking how this divine writing, this "legibile parlare" (readable speech), recalling *Purgatorio*'s "visibile parlare" (X. 95), can miraculously span the otherwise insuperable gap between linguistic signifier and signified thing. It can thereby make language into a more concrete embodiment of truth and meaning. Since Dante poetically creates this language, he, too, seems to

---

[73] Lucia Battaglia Ricci, *Decrittare i segni: A proposito di "Paradiso" XVIII 70–117*, in *Studi di letteratura italiana per Vitilio Masiello*, eds. P. Guaragnella and M. Santagata (Bari: Laterza, 2006), vol. I, 108–9.

[74] Rachel Jacoff, "'Diligite iustitiam': Loving Justice in Siena and Dante's *Paradiso*," *Modern Language Notes*, special issue in honor of John Freccero, Supplement to MLN 124/5 (2009): 81–95.

claim the divinely revelatory powers that he attributes to the divine painter, as suggested by Piero Boitani.[75]

At the other end of the spectrum from the focus on popular culture and civic contexts for reading Dante's vision of Scripture, many interpreters seek Dante's sources, instead, in esoteric traditions. Readers in the esoteric vein have long been fascinated by Dante's letter magic and mysticism. Such phenomena can be deciphered according to presumable alchemical correspondences and clues. Secret languages and numerological codes, along with sacred astronomy and geometry, find much to work with in this scene. The eagle emblem is exceptionally rich in esoteric connotations.[76]

Despite its many seductive suggestions, this interest has generally been focused on unlocking these cantos' supposedly hidden symbolism rather than on interpreting the play of signifiers that is written right onto the surface of the text and which can be put on display and enacted by its "performance" in reading. We lack certain keys for understanding this passage if we do not enter fully into the performative dimension of the text.[77] We remain, instead, somewhat mesmerized by Dante's sources, attempting to reconstruct the contextual conditions that surround and impinge on, but do not constitute, his inspiration as such. All pre-existing contexts and contents are surpassed by the verbal, prophetic action of the letters that dance and sing, sparking their incomprehensible joy into the open abyss of the Heaven. This has long been realized, even if most often only subliminally. My present purpose is to develop in full, with the interdisciplinary resources available to us today, the revelation and revolution (in poetic language) that are in act in Dante's vision of writing.

General Introduction to the Heaven of Jupiter and Its Contemporary Interpretation

Having begun with an intensive focus on the vision itself at the outset of the Heaven of Jove, I will now offer a few words of general introduction to this heaven as a whole and to its contemporary interpretion. This will serve

---

[75] Piero Boitani, *Winged Words: Flight in Poetry and History* (Chicago: University of Chicago Press, 2007), 142.

[76] René Guénon, L'esoterisme de Dante (Paris: Gallimard, 1925) builds especially on the nineteenth-century projects of Eugène Aroux and Gabriele Rossetti. This branch of interpretation flourished, with a focus particularly on the eagle, notably in Luigi Valli's *La chiave della Divina Commedia: Sintesi del simbolismo della croce e dell'aquila* (Bologna: Zanichelli, 1925).

[77] Albert Russell Ascoli, "Performing Salvation in Dante's *Commedia*," *Dante Studies* 135 (2017): 74–106 draws attention to the performance aspect of poetry in the *Purgatorio*.

to orient readers and to organize the following chapters. The vision of the
letters spelling the Scriptural sentence ending in TERRAM features the
final gothic M (Figure 1(a)) composed of soul-lights and adorned by other
souls descending directly from the Empyrean onto its tip ("Vidi scender
altre luci dove / era il colmo de l'emme," 98–99). The latter shape
themselves into the form of a lily ("ingigliarsi a l'emme," 113; Figure 1
(b)). We are reminded here of the lilies of the field ("lilia agri") that neither
sow nor spin and yet are attired more magnificently than Solomon in all his
glory ("nec Salomon in omni gloria sua coopertus est sicut unum ex istis").
In Jesus's Sermon on the Mount, these lilies stand for those who seek first
the kingdom of God and his righteousness ("quarite ... primum regnum
Dei et iustitiam eius," Matthew 6:28–33).[78]

The M, so adorned, then morphs into the emblem of the eagle (Figure 1
(c)), and all this unequivocally reveals to Dante that justice is being prepared
for here on earth, even though we cannot see or understand it. As already in
Justinian's discourse in *Paradiso* VI, the eagle is the standard-bearer for
imperial justice. The M arguably stands for "Monarchia," Dante's preferred
word for Empire (as in his treatise on that subject), which he deems to be
divinely ordained for the governance of the world. The lily has been linked
with Mary and thence with mercy (*Misericordia*), which is necessary to
divine justice in Dante's view, but it might also symbolize Florence.[79] The
lily is the image on the verso of the city's golden coin, the florin, which is
ambiguously also a symbol of earthly corruption in *Inferno* XXX. 73–74.

The lily as *fleur-de-lys* is also often associated with the French monarchy,
particularly with the Angevins.[80] However, the momentary lily formation
on the M yields without resistance to further figures, and the souls in it are
seen to be "content" ("d'ingigliarsi a l'emme contenta / pareva"). It
therefore signals more plausibly than a corrupt dynasty the virtue that is
ideally united with power to rule, earthly power serving divine providence,
as in the iconography of Solomon (a Christ figure) represented with lilied
scepter or with a lily in one hand and a scepter in the other.[81]

---

[78] Compare Lucia Battaglia Ricci, "*Con parole e con segni*. Lettura del Canto XVIII del *Paradiso*,"
L'Alighieri 36/6 (1995): 7–28, 23n25.
[79] Michelangelo Picone, "Canto XVIII," in *Lectura Dantis Turicensis: "Paradiso"*, eds.
Georges Güntert and M. Picone (Florence: Franco Cesati, 2002), 277–78.
[80] Ernesto Giacomo Parodi, "Il giglio d'oro nel c. XVIII del 'Paradiso'," *Arte e scienza* 1 (1903): 5–14.
This thesis is defended more recently by Edoardo Fumagalli, "*Par*. XVIII, 88–114, l'enigma del giglio
e la sapienza di re Salomone," *L'Alighieri*, n.s. 26 (2005): 111–25.
[81] Gian Roberto Sarolli, "Ingigliarsi a l'emme (Par. XVIII, 113): Archetipo di poliunivoca concor-
danza," in *Atti del Congresso Internazionale di Studi Danteschi (20–27 aprile 1965)*, vol. II (Florence:
Sansoni, 1966), 237–254 table I. Cf. Battaglia Ricci, "*Con parole e con segni*," 19.

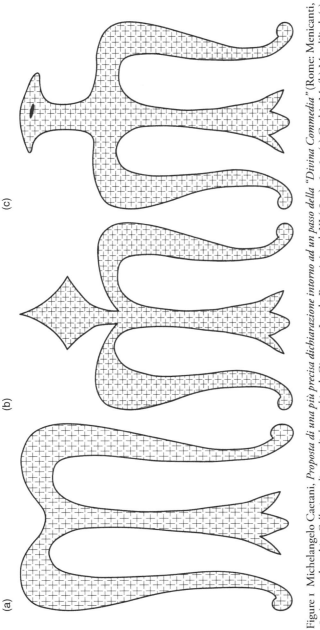

Figure 1 Michelangelo Caetani, *Proposta di una più precisa dichiarazione intorno ad un passo della "Divina Commedia"* (Rome: Menicanti, 1852), reproduced in *Collezione di opuscoli danteschi*, ed. Giuseppe Lando Passerini, vol. XI (1894), 61–63. (a) Gothic M. (b) M enlilied. (c) M as eagle. Graphics by Jessica Topart www.jgraph.fr

Figure 2 Francesco Scaramuzza (1803–1886), Just Spirits of the Sky of Jupiter, *Paradiso* 18, Biblioteca del Centro Studi Danteschi, Ravenna. Photo ©Fine Art Images/Heritage Images

The possible symbols and allegorizations here are many and debatable and, in any event, not the most immediate meaning of the vision. We, too, by being made to share in Dante's vision, presumably experience this revelation, like him, through the sheer power and majesty, not to mention the mystery, of the spectacle placed before us. The inimitable sublimity of its very artifice speaks to us of something increate and absolute.

The writing in the heaven is divine, but it is also Dante's artifact. John Ahern sees the parallel between God's writing the Scriptural sentence in the "star" ("stella," XVIII. 115) and Dante's writing on the page of his book as asserting "Dante's claim that his poem is a sacred and inspired text."[82] Ahern avowedly echoes kindred claims made by Robert Hollander and Peter Dronke. He supplies rich classical and biblical backgrounds for reading stars as letters painted in the sky and for understanding their movement as divine speech (9). These precedents set the stage for Dante's dramatic presentation of the divine Word's becoming a revelatory event in the form of writing in the sky of this heaven – and in his poem.

The Heaven of Jupiter turns on the question of justice, specifically on the discrepancy between divine justice revealed to Dante from this heavenly height and the deplorable state of the earth below, which is full to overflowing with *in*justice perpetrated, above all, by its rulers.[83] The revelation thus encompasses also the unrightousness reigning in human history. Following the vision of Scriptural writing in XVIII. 88–117, Dante turns in conclusion to the malfeasance of the popes (especially John XXII), which wreaks havoc on earth (XVIII. 118–36). He prays to God (118–23) for just chastisement and to the saintly souls ("O milizia del ciel cu'io contemplo," 124–26) to protect a misguided humanity. Cantos XIX and XX, comprising the balance of the heaven, then pursue the issue of divine justice and its jarring dissonance with worldly wrongs.

The scene in XVIII, as developed in XIX, with the eagle answering Dante's unspoken doubts about divine justice, is reminiscent of the Book of Job. In this biblical precedent, the Vision out of the Whirlwind staggers and confounds Job, browbeating him into tacit assent without exactly answering his questions and objections (Job 38–42). Job is overpowered by the majesty of the Creation, to which he cannot but submit in awe and reverence. Dante, too, is told that God's will cannot be questioned and that whatever conforms to it is right ("Cotanto è giusto quanto a lei consuona," XIX. 88). In Dante's case, however, the sublimity of the vision satisfies his longing to know rather than simply silencing him. His long and great

---

[82] John Ahern, "Dante's Last Word: The *Comedy* as a *liber coelestis*," *Dante Studies* 102 (1984): 1–14. Citation, 9
[83] Fausto Montanari, "L'aquila di Giove," *Critica letteraria* 5 (1977): 211–20, effectively introduces the heaven in these terms.

hunger ("gran digiuno"), which found no food on earth (XIX. 25–27), is appeased. Going well beyond Job's repentant acknowledgment confessing his abhorrence of his own presumption (42:2–6), Dante exultantly exclaims that he now sees sweet justice finally vindicated in the universe (XVIII. 115–17).

In the two cantos dominated by its speeches (XIX and XX), the Eagle stresses the fallibility of human judgment, warning us not to presume to be able to judge concerning the salvation of souls (as already in *Paradiso* XIII. 130–42), since God's just judgment remains wholly beyond our fathoming. This admonition is developed at length in discourses in XIX. 40–90 and XIX. 97–114 and is reiterated at the conclusion of Canto XX in the apostrophe to mortals ("E voi mortali, tenetevi stretti," 130–38) called on to recognize their shortsightedness. This warning is issued not without a twinge of indignation on the part of the Eagle that the Almighty's justice should be questioned by a mere mortal. This scenario clearly adheres to biblical models.

The image of God creating the universe with his compass ("Colui che volse il sesto / a lo stremo del mondo," XIX. 40–41) recalls a famous biblical vision of God founding and circumscribing the world in Proverbs 8:27–31. The closely kindred image in Job 38:4–12 of God as architect stretching his measuring line over the earth belongs to the arsenal of artillery blasting Job out of his critical posture by overwhelming him with awesome and fear-inspiring spectacles. However, Dante's text performs also a self-subverting movement against this kind of bluster – which, for many readers, runs the risk of turning into bullying with terrifying and hallucinatory phantasms. Dante repeatedly calls into question the efficacy of any image whatsoever to represent the metaphysically distinct and higher reality of God.

The rhetoric of appearing – *parea* from the very first word of XIX – pervades the canto (1, 3, 24, 49, 57, 136) and is complemented by a persistent foregrounding of imagination and images (2, 9, 21, 95) in a context where the divine is said to be in excess of all possible human representation and comprehension. This imagery of appearing, with its projection of myths, is counterpointed by the action of *letters*, Holy *Scripture* being recognized repeatedly as the supreme authority. Scripture is heard in constant echoes from Matthew and Paul warning against the limits and fallacies of human judgment.[84] Divine justice, in its perfection, is hideously perverted by its human imitations or parodies, as Dante

---

[84] Cf. Battaglia Ricci, "*Con parole e con segni.*"

demonstrates through literary devices, with his catalogue of unjust Christian princes (XIX. 115–48) exposed graphically as morally crippled ("Ciotto") through "truncated letters" ("lettere mozze," 134).

Dante's text thus builds a self-deconstructive dynamic into its own unfolding. What it gives in the form of visionary images appearing in heaven is undermined by its status as a text consisting in letters, as is constantly brought out through such explicit metaliterary self-reference. As a medley of letters, the text can scintillate and reflect a meaning not quite within its grasp, a meaning that cannot be delivered as an unequivocal statement of truth in the discourse of (human) reason. This language beneath language, which breaks it down into its component parts – letters – that speak for themselves, calls forth submission to an endless process of self-correction.

Canto XIX. 115–48 organizes its letters into the form of an acrostic: LUE, signifying "pestilence." This indirect statement in writing inscribes the injustice of princes in an iconic form that is present on the page. In communicating iconically, Dante's text runs parallel to the divine writing in the sky at the outset of the heaven. Four instances, furthermore, where "Cristo" occurs three times rhyming only with itself, establish a cruciform pattern through the repetition "Cristo, Cristo" in the middle line (XIX. 100–8).[85] This constitutes another iconic use of letters sculpting the verses and conferring on them an extra-discursive meaning through their immediately visible form. Such patterns of letters can insinuate another story that can question or even contradict the myths represented at higher levels of discourse. At any rate, they present another register of communication. This redoubling of the letters' communicative function opens a potential gap between heavenly and earthly perspectives on justice. Their splitting apart in our finite perspective is concretely inscribed into Dante's argument for their ultimate alignment in a divine perspective.

Cantos XIX and XX have been read influentially by Andrea Battestini as focused on the limitations and incapacity of human vision to plumb the depths of divine justice as articulated in the discourse of the celestial Eagle. Battestini's *La retorica della salvezza* has done much to highlight the thematic of tension between heavenly and earthly justice in this heaven.[86] The eagle is an apt symbol of the maximum power of vision

---

[85]   Thomas Elwood Hart, "The *Cristo*-Rhymes, the Greek Cross, and Cruciform Geometry in Dante's *Commedia*: 'giunture di quadranti in tondo,'" *Zeitschrift für romanische Philologie* 106/1–2 (1990): 106–24. Research into Dante's intricate use of mathematical proportions in placing certain repeated lexemes within his poem suggests how Dante exploits a geometry inherent in letters.

[86]   Andrea Battestini, *La retorica della salvezza: Studi danteschi* (Bologna: Il Mulino, 2016).

trained on the earth as seen from a great distance. The Eagle, the "sacro-santo segno" celebrated by Justinian (VI. 32), which made the Romans revered the world over (XIX. 101–102), stands ambiguously for both human and divine justice. It is a symbol of their unity and fusion. Both "just and holy" ("giusto e pio" XIX. 13), ideally the eagle would perfectly unite the two justices. Justice is ideally one. Although it is composed of many souls ("we"), the Eagle speaks with one voice ("I," XIX. 10–12), even as one heat is produced from many coals (XIX. 19–21), or one sweet smell from various flowers (22–24).

Recalcitrant to being understood abstractly, this incomprehensible union of incommensurables (divinity and humanity) requires incarnate demonstration. In chapters 10 and 11, on *Paradiso* XIX and XX, respectively, Battestini calls attention to how the abstract theological arguments of XIX concerning generic cases ("un uom nasce") on the banks of the Indus or in Ethiopia or Persia give way in XX to concrete historical instances in the acts of Trajan and Riphaeus. The miraculous salvation of these two pagans celebrated in XX responds with facts to the question left unanswered theologically in XIX. 70–78 of how it can be just to condemn a person born out of hearing of the Gospel, whether geographically (on the Indus) or temporally (*ante* Christo). And yet, although particular explanations for how these singular pagan individuals attained to faith and even baptism are given, the general question remains unanswered and tormenting.

Concerning Riphaeus, Virgil had already protested against the injustice of the gods ("dis aliter visum") in condemning to untimely death such a superlatively righteous man ("iustissimus unum"), one most devoted to justice ("servantissumus aequi," *Aeneid* II. 426–28). Unlike Virgil, Dante can justify his caring Christian God by deferring to an eternal afterlife that will eventually right all apparent wrongs. A future life at least opens further possibilities for rectification. Yet Virgil's case in particular will still haunt the poem all the way to its end. Dante cannot give a comprehensive logical answer but only an emblematic and a literary one relying on letters – with their kenotic fragility, as displayed in this heaven. The triumphalism of the Holy Roman Eagle is itself only a composition of letters.

In XIX and XX, the Eagle replaces human mediators like Beatrice and addresses Dante from a height that emphasizes the unknowability ("l'inconoscibilità") of God's deepest dispositions. For Battestini, this device is "a proceeding that is wholly negative, devoted to deepening the abyss between human limits and divine omnipotence" ("un incedere tutto negativo, votato all'approfondimento dell'abisso tra i limiti dell'uomo e l'onnipotenza divina," 219). In this condition, we would be lost in doubt if Scripture were not above us ("se la Scrittura sovra voi non fosse / da dubitar sarebbe a maraviglia," XIX. 83). But we also need concrete accompaniment on earth. Dante's synaesthetic images, drawn from familiar experiences, work powerfully in this direction.

We noted, following Ahern, that the book in its materiality becomes a concrete allegory for the heavens written with stars. Human and divine writing are thus made self-reflectively to image one another. The letters revealing God's justice offer a sensuous display rather than a logical argument, and they leave Dante still with a doubt, which the Eagle expresses for him in XIX. 70–78. A sort of (non-)answer to the question of justice in XIX, which stresses the incapacity of human reason to comprehend, comes in Canto XX. The unsoundable mysteries of providence are displayed in the saving of the pagans Trajan and Riphaeus by its allowing them to embrace belief in Christ – the one proleptically, over 1,000 years before the Incarnation, and other *post mortem* by the miracle of his soul returning to its body in answer to the fervent prayer of Gregory the Great some four centuries later.

Dante's answer to the excruciating theological question of how it can be just to condemn virtuous pagans thus takes the form of concrete instances of salvation. Battestini underscores how XX answers to XIX and its "sorites" of syllogisms in series, yet without responding in terms of binary *sic et non* logic. There is an anxiousness and even an anxiety in Dante's humanly unanswerable questions concerning justice in XIX. This need not exclude a certain serenity produced by the questioning self's being forced to a different level of awareness, one that is epitomized lyrically in the lark satiated by the ultimate sweetness ("tace contenta / dell'ultima dolcezza che la sazia," XX. 73–78), which relieves Dante's long gnawing hunger (XIX. 25–27).

Dante triumphantly affirms the justice of the supreme ruler of the universe, even though he cannot really understand ("non le intendi") the "notes" ("note," XIX. 98, heard as musical; cf. 39; XVIII. 99) of the eagle's discourse concerning heavenly justice. On the other hand, Dante is prompt to denounce and decry the injustices of the wicked popes and princes of the earth. Still, this knowledge is negative, and it leaves Dante with only a negative understanding of the divine. I submit that this negativity is written into the very logic of sense in literature as based on the letter and its differential, diacritical signifying. Demonstrating in detail how this can open into all the plenitude of the theophantic revelation that Dante proclaims is the burden of much of what follows.

Divine right triumphs, but not without suffering violence ("*Regnum celorum* vïolenza pate*," XX. 94), which it accepts to suffer in order to manifest a truth that cannot be discursively explained but is embodied in Christ and his Passion. Human reason can reach this truth only through a negative dialectic. Reason must be brought up against its limits in order to recognize a principle of truth that is higher than itself. Even though the divinity above humanity is still for Dante eminently rational, there is a break. The break falls between humanity and divinity rather than within reason. The reason that remains intact is not reason as we know it but rather the higher reason that only God can fully fathom – at least until the book of the final Judgment looming in Revelation 20:12 shall be opened ("come vedranno quel volume aperto," XIX. 113).

The issue of justice in this heaven elicits a dialectic of light and darkness ("tenèbra od ombra," XIX. 65–66), of revealed truth and ever resurgent doubt (XX. 79–84), in which God is affirmed to be in control and yet our human experience is admitted to be indelibly troubled. Human reason alone, without the help of faith in the "Sacred Letters" (*Sacris Licteris*) of Scripture (*Monarchia* II. vii. 4), is insufficient to comprehend the justice of the divine judgment that faith in Christ and baptism are necessary for salvation (XIX. 76, 104), even for one who is otherwise perfect in virtue. *Monarchia* II. vii. 4 corroborates the Eagle's speeches on these points of Church doctrine. This leaves an unresolvable tension that is literally *written* into the heaven. The most penetrating answers given in this heaven require a deeper understanding of the implications of writing. And writing is itself to be understood from the paradigm of the revelation of divinity in *Scripture*.

Dante's examination on faith in Canto XXIV confirms that knowledge of profound things ("Le profonde cose") is possible only through faith ("in sola credenza," XXIV. 73). Already in the *Convivio*, faith alone sees perfectly ("perfettamente") what reason glimpses obscurely ("con ombra di oscuritade," II. viii. 15), as through bat's eyelids (II. iv. 17). In *Convivio* III. xv. 6, divine things are seen and believed most certainly ("certissimamente") by faith: otherwise, they cannot be known by us except negatively ("se non cose negando") and by approximation ("si può appressare"). In the *Paradiso*, Dante focuses specifically on Scripture, the "old and new parchments," literally "leathers" ("cuoia"). Writing and its materiality figure most prominently in Dante's sense of revelation as vouchsafed to humans by the generous rain of the Holy Spirit ("larga ploia / de lo Spirito Santo," XXIV. 91–93). Such is the gift of writing through which Dante apprehends Scripture essentially as theophany.

CHAPTER 2

The Presence of Speech in Writing: Speaking as Sparking

Speech versus Writing, or the Dialectic of Art and Unmediated Presence

Dante exposes his vision, from its outset, as consisting radically in writing. Writing appears initially as a medium and, paradoxically, just because it is a medium, it turns into a transcendent *reality* (*res*) in which, purportedly, divinity can be envisioned as present. Divinity here is not just the absent signified: it is actively present in the event of signifying. Dante tells us in the first tercet describing what he saw in the heaven of Jove that it was the Love which was there ("l'amor che lì era") that signified ("segnare") to his eyes "our speech" ("nostra favella"):

> Io vidi in quella giovial facella
> lo sfavillar de l'amor che lì era
> segnare a li occhi miei nostra favella.
>
> (XVIII. 70–72)

> (I saw in that jovial torch
> the sparkling of the love that was there
> signify to my eyes our speech.)

When we ask exactly *what* is present or represented in this heaven, these initial verses of the scene in Jove answer that Dante sees "the sparkling of the love that was there" ("lo sfavillar de l'amor che lì era"). Ultimately, this is a manifestation of the presence of God, who is Love (I John 4:8), or of the souls who receive, reflect, and transmit this Love, or perhaps both – the one in and through the other. In any case, God's loving presence is not a simple presence, as of a particular object, but is rather distributed and dispersed into a complex phenomenon of signifying. To be exact, what this signifying gives Dante to see is not as such the love that is there, but the *sparking* ("lo sfavillar") of this love, a visible display that sparkles and in so doing "signifies" ("segnare"). The love that signifies in this manner manifests itself as letter, and the signifying letter becomes a visual event in Dante's poem. By this means, the love which "was there" in and through its own act of signifying – that is, as a semiological event – takes on externality and appears manifest. It becomes a theophany in the form of the lively sparking of what are later called "living lights" ("vive luci," XX. 10) – the shining souls that constitute the medium of this mode of signification.

These visual signals constitute the presence of the divine, although they do so in a signifying that is an oscillating play between presence and absence, not just the simple presence of a discrete substance. In this play of signifiers, the presence of the divine is not unequivocally localizable. It appears always only in a flash pointing elsewhere and playing off against other signifiers. On theological, or more precisely negative-theological, principles, God's total transcendence means that there will always be something that does not and cannot become manifest in the divine vision. Dante interprets this principle semiologically. He presents the divine vision as a semiological event, a vision of signifying by *writing* that discloses and, at the same time, disguises: it reveals, yet equally *re-veils*, or conceals. Cacciaguida "hidden and appearing by his own smile" ("chiuso e parvente del suo proprio riso," *Paradiso* XVII. 36) in the preceding canto is typical of the idiom Dante uses to express this paradox. The same point is highlighted earlier in the appearing/dis-appearing of Justinian's soul, which is hidden by the very intensity of its joy manifest as light ("per più letizia sì mi si nascose," V. 136). Is speech that is revealed *as writing*, for an analogous reason of hyper-intensity, inevitably concealed or "*re*-veiled"?

We are often led to think of Dante's poem as an artwork in which the divinity that is celebrated becomes embodied in the sensuous media of art. However, the *Paradiso* has a very tense and tenuous relation to the categories of art and the artwork. *Purgatorio* is the place where art reigns supreme and where both human and divine art unite in achieving the highest purposes of aesthetic representation. In the *Paradiso*, Dante, like every artist facing the ultimate possibilities of his art ("come a l'ultimo suo ciascun artista," XXX. 33), pushes up against the limits where art must desist ("or convien che mio seguir desista," 31). The *Paradiso* endeavors in certain ways to move beyond the range of art into a purely spiritual dimension accessible only to mystical experience. Its art tends to convert into anti-art. And yet, ironically, Dante's vision of divinity turns writing back into an aesthetic spectacle. Writing plays the ambiguous role of the in-between or *metaxu* (μεταξύ in Greek) like Eros as a *daimon* moving between gods and humans and mediating between poverty (πενία) and plenitude or resource (πόρος), according to Diotima's description of him in Plato's *Symposium* (203 B–C).

Writing, as a flickering play between presence (of a signifier) and absence (of the intended meaning or object), is more immediately suited to be the *Paradiso*'s medium than are the concrete incarnations of artworks, the "visible speech," such as we see engraved in marble on the ledges of Purgatory. Writing, by virtue of its abstractness, is predisposed to relate us to the invisible, which is what Dante's art in the *Paradiso* aims at all along and finally succeeds in evoking only by transcending the aesthetic register of art.

Karlheinz Stierle aptly suggests that "the *Paradiso* is poetry beyond poetry, which figures a reality beyond reality" ("Das *Paradiso* ist eine Dichtung jenseits der Dichtung, die eine Wirklichkeit jenseits der Wirklichkeit figuriert").[1] This is all the more true in that Purgatory, as a whole, is only a temporary place and state on the way to Paradise, so even its art aims at a fulfillment beyond itself and beyond art. In the bas-reliefs depicting the virtue of humility in *Purgatorio* X, perfect mimetic representation is already marked as being not for its own sake but rather for purposes of edification, of soul-building toward salvation, as the chrysalis aims to become the angelic butterfly.[2]

Paradiso is still a consummate artwork, but it is already aspiring beyond the range of art and the aesthetic, which are based in sensible realizations, toward pure and direct experience of a spiritual reality. And yet, for all his mystical *élan*, guided by medieval religious belief, Dante approaches this spiritual experience as an incorrigible artist: he strives to realize it in and through the medium of art, particularly the art of poetry, whose medium is writing. The *Paradiso* is drawn taut by a great tension between Dante's work as a human artist and his belief in a transcendent, spiritual divinity in relation to whom all such means are, in principle, vain. While striving presumably for the immediacy of transcendent vision, Dante nevertheless takes the detour of expression by artistic means. He deftly employs elaborate artistic methods, all the while chafing against them, spurred by an impulse towards a direct, unmediated, purely spiritual relation with divinity. The categories of art are, in the end, transcended.

In his exalted vision of Holy Scripture in the heaven of Jove, the same utterance that is opaque writing from our human point of view is

---

[1] Karlheinz Stierle, *Das große Meer des Sinns: Hermeneutische Erkundungen in Dantes "Commedia"* (Munich: Fink, 2007), 203.
[2] Cf. my "Reality and Realism in *Purgatorio* X," in *Dante's Interpretive Journey* (Chicago: University of Chicago Press, 1996), 171–76.

transcendent speech from God's divine point of view, and Dante is momentarily able to glimpse the continuity between the two. While writing effects an obvious interruption of the transparency of speech, this transparency is recuperated at another level as a higher immediacy or "vision" represented as a revelation in writing – in a spectacle of letters. Writing does not deflect and dissimulate speech in Dante's vision in this heaven. Instead, speech subsumes writing and turns its underlying chaos into a more translucent order, its externality and opacity into a more interior and immediate visionariness. The concretely present, visible form of the writing of God's "speech" is a metaphor for the immediacy of the vision of God (*visio Dei*) – which means, ultimately, for God's *own* vision of the world and of us. We may be given to participate in this vision, and in this way the *visio Dei* turns out to be our seeing the universe from God's point of view.

This reversal of human by divine perspectives is often enacted in seminal works and sources of negative theology by the likes of Gregory of Nyssa and Meister Eckhart, and it becomes explicit and programmatic in Nicholas of Cusa's *De visione Dei* (1453). Dante's *Paradiso*, seen from within this tradition, instead of delivering a vision of God as object (which is impossible), fundamentally aims to view the fields of history and cosmology, together with all their objects, from a point of view such as God's can only be imagined to be. Naturally speaking, this point of view can *only* be imagined – even with all the divine grace that such an undertaking requires and implores. The separation of human imagining from divine reality is signified by writing as *indicating* something else that it *is not*. And yet, Dante discovers in writing also the resources for mediating, and to some degree overcoming, this gap of separation between the human and the divine. This ambiguity plays out in an oscillation between speech and writing, which become inseparable.

Writing as Speech, Chaos as Occulted Order

A tantalizing question as to the semiological mode of God's presence in this canto's poetic realization or "performance" of Scripture is opened up by the striking fact that the letters signified to Dante's eyes are actually designated not as writing but as "speech." "Io vidi in quella giovial facella / lo sfavillar de l'amor che lì era / segnare a li occhi miei *nostra favela*." ("I saw in that jovial torch / the sparkling of the love that was there / signify to my eyes *our speech*.") "Nostra favella" should probably be taken to mean human speech generally. For Dante sees letters not of his own vernacular idiom, but of Latin, and yet, even so, the love of God that is present in this heaven is signified by a language that is recognizably "ours." The force of the "nostra," to this extent, seems to be to emphasize the mediation of a divine presence or sense into a human form of language. Of course, speech that one *sees* is, in fact, writing. As the immediately following sentence (XVIII. 73–78) unequivocally shows, the "speech" that is envisaged here as seen actually consists in nothing other than written characters, "D," "I," "L," and so forth. But the designation of this communication by letters as "speech" is nonetheless too deliberate and *telling* to be ignored.

The equivalence of the Scriptural letters Dante *sees* with language *spoken* by God, hinting that the writing which Dante sees is really an indirect form of God's *speech*, is confirmed a few lines later. In describing his reception of the vision letter by letter, Dante writes, "I noted the parts thus, as they appeared to me *dictated*" ("io notai / le parti sì, come mi parver *dette*," XVIII. 89–90). Here, while a metaphor of writing or "noting down" is used to denote Dante's own receiving and remembering of the verbal message communicated to him, a metaphor of speech or dictation is used for the divine manifestation itself in the form of written characters. This resort to reciprocal substitution between writing and speech – the one being consistently called in to substitute metaphorically for the other – is an index of Dante's profound apprehension of how speech and writing, with their respective connotations of presence and absence, transparency and opacity, immediacy of spirit versus material mediation, are intrinsically connected and mutually interpenetrating.

What, specifically, does it mean that what Dante perceives is really "speech," even though it presents itself to him manifestly and literally in the form of writing? Dante suggests that God is directly present here as if speaking, his love revealing itself in the transparency of speech, the divine Mind immediately communicating what it intends. Indeed, even their graphic visuality does not, after all, in Dante's view, remove the luminous signs from the nature of speech. On the contrary, this medium is so transparent to intention as to be tantamount to direct speech. The painterly visibility of the letters itself suggests the analogy of a divine Painter, *Deus Pictor,* completely in control of the visual medium he manipulates for the purpose of perfectly executing his divine Will:

> Quei che dipinge lì, non ha chi 'l guidi;
> ma esso guida . . .
>
> (XVIII. 109–11)

He who paints there has no one to guide him;
rather, he guides . . .

The point of the painting image here is to illustrate God's direct and
deliberate command over the manifestation under way in the heaven, as in
general over all of nature. The figure of God as painter, moreover, works as
a metaphorical equivalent for the idea of an author who writes simply at
will, without being conditioned by anything exterior. This author/artist
writes or paints as if he were simply to speak his mind without hindrance or
resistance from any material medium. So, in the end, this emphasis on
God's free self-expression in "painting" the letters – as in creating nature
and controlling it with providential purpose – tends to turn writing back
into "speech" in the sense of the spontaneous and immediate expression of
the mind unencumbered by any extraneous medium.

In philosophical tradition, this verbal condition of speech has often been
figured as the pure transparency of voice to the mind or soul.[3] The medium
becomes so perfectly conformed to the will and intent of the one who uses
it as to utterly disembarrass itself of all status as external and other. In this
case, writing, in effect, becomes speech. Even in becoming a fully external,
visible manifestation, this writing remains fully transparent and obedient
to the mind that it expresses, and to this extent it remains essentially
speech. Despite the implication of absence and indirectness inherent in
the written vision, Dante still reminds us insistently that the visual displays
he perceives are signs coming directly from God. God's Mind is present in
the visible letters given as if they were directly spoken. The letters are the
equivalent of divine speech.

Although in this heaven, if anywhere, the specifically written character
of God's Word, as well as of Dante's written imitation and interpretation
of it, is paramount, nevertheless Dante invites us, even here, to read this
writing as in essence an extension of the *speech* of God. This need not in
itself be so surprising, for God's self-revelation, even as written in
Scripture, is understood traditionally as his *Word – Verbum Dei*. The
phrase from the biblical Book of Wisdom that Dante sees can thus be
qualified as the "Word of God" expressed in "our" ("nostra") speech, in
human language, since this can be said of the Bible itself as a whole and in

---

[3] As noted in Chapter 1, the polarized connotations of speech as immediate transparency or presence of
mind, and of writing as removed from presence, are traced through Western philosophical tradition
since Plato by Derrida, most fully in *De la grammatologie* (Paris: Seuil, 1967). Crucial aspects of this
problematic are articulated also in Derrida's reflection on Plato's *Phaedrus* in "La pharmacie de
Platon," in *La dissémination* (Paris: Seuil, 1972), and on Husserl's phenomenology in *La voix et le
phénomène* (Paris: Presses Universitaires de France, 1967).

all of its parts. It is especially with respect to its unity and source in the divine Mind that Scripture, particularly within a Christian incarnational perspective, is grasped as God's *utterance* of his Being in the Word. And yet, this in no way attenuates the essential *writtenness* – along with the accompanying reified visuality – of the revelation that Dante contemplates. Precisely the written medium is key to achieving the immediacy that eminently characterizes Dante's vision of God and that makes it apt to be called God's "speech." It is by being seen in the directly visible form of writing that the divine presence in language actually shows and makes itself present. It is most emphatically as opaque, spatialized, pictorial phenomena that the letters are depicted as fully in correspondence with the divine intention.

The extraordinary burden of Dante's vision is that it unreservedly embraces the consequences of writing that are most devastating to any purportedly immediate and unified meaning such as speech stands for. Dante fully admits the dependency of speech, even divine speech, on what is in essence written signification, with all its material implication and opacity. Yet, at the same time, he reaffirms his faith ("credo," XVIII. 99) that the writing in heaven and the universe that he sees exemplified here is, after all, the Word of God and, as such, perfectly one with and adequate to God's Intention. This visionary epistemology of the written word, moreover, is inseparable from an apotheosis of Justice. Dante declares his faith that there is an overarching, unified order to the world, even though we are only able to perceive this order essentially as writing, and in writing every putative message or meaning is delivered over to random chaos because it is consigned to an external form and medium.

In ways to be examined in detail in Chapter 3, Dante's vision emphasizes precisely the mincing or breaking up into pieces of writing as a contingent medium that remains external to meaning as constituted by conventional semantics and their regulated sense. Breaking any purported meaning down into chance fragments is apprehended by Dante as the specific liability of writing. It is the very nature of writing as medium to introduce chance and fragmentariness into the message as we apprehend it, even – and especially – when this message is a divine revelation. Indeed, Dante envisions the contingency of writing as intrinsic to its revelatory potential. Dante testifies to a faith that the absolutely unified and simple presence or significance of the divine is itself written into this process of seemingly random chaos to which writing, by its externalized nature, gives rise. This connection is reinforced particularly by the imagery of speech as sparking. Dante's sparks represent a random, material manifestation that turns out to be part of a significant pattern: as such, they are a form – indeed a paradigm – of writing.

Fascinating and most theoretically challenging about the vision of writing in Jove is the way Dante couples his apprehension of writing as a visual display in space and, moreover, in a sensuous, material medium subject to contingency, with his concept of the divine Word and of its *speech* as a direct, uninhibited expression of the divine Mind. As such, this utterance is governed by an unabashedly transcendental intention. In Dante's vision, the full realization of the divine intention and its ideality – what naturally induces to description in terms of speech – takes place conspicuously, deliberately, and programmatically in and through the contingent materiality of the written. Dante's implying that writing, his medium, becomes the speech of God, a direct revelation or theophany, insists on the apparent contingencies built into writing that then unveil themselves as dictated by a transcendent agency, a divine Subject. These contingencies are revealed as immediate manifestations of a divine intent. The fact that this signifying appears to be beyond any humanly calculable intention that could control or account for it is necessary in order that it signify precisely a higher, a transcendent intentionality.

Dante's steady impulse is to see a higher, divine purpose in what to human vision makes no sense. This is clear and explicit in many places in the *Commedia*, for example, in the diatribe in *Purgatorio* VI. 76–151, which anticipates the focus on divine justice in the heaven of Jove. The poet-prophet begins by denouncing "abject Italy" ("Ahi serva Italia," 76), proceeds to take the Emperor to task, and culminates with "O sommo Giove" ("O highest Jove," 116), addressing and protesting against even the supreme Deity. It *seems* that God is simply neglectful of earthly affairs, but Dante wishes and hopes that the seeming chaos and anarchy let loose upon the world are just the effect of our ignorance of how God's hidden counsel and the unsearchable ways of his providence are secretly at work already for the purpose of bringing about final justice. So he asks, concerning the world's disarray:

> O è preparazion che ne l'abisso
>   del tuo consiglio fai per alcun bene
>   in tutto de l'accorger nostro scisso?

(Purgatorio VI. 121–23)

> (Or is it a preparation in the abyss
>   of your counsel made for some good
>   completely removed from our apprehension?)

What providence has in store may be a benefit too deep for us to discern. We see only senseless contingency where actually divine necessity is already working behind the scenes with its design to justify the ways of God in the final analysis.

Figure 3 Gustave Doré (1832–1883), The Eagle, *Paradiso* 19, engraving by Duncan (1890). Getty Images

Bird Formations and Contingency

The theme of contingency in the nature of letters is highlighted right from
the heaven of Jove's second tercet by a simile of far-reaching and practically
systematic significance in the *Commedia*, that of birds in their flight
forming patterns resembling letters. The birds are depicted taking wing
from a riverbank upon which they have fed, jubilant in their mutual
"congratulation":

> E come augelli surti di rivera,
>   quasi congratulando a lor pasture,
>   fanno di sé or tonda or altra schiera ...

(Paradiso XVIII. 73–75)

> (And as birds risen up from banks,
>   as if congratulating one another on their good fare,
>   make of themselves by turns a round or other-shaped swarm ...)

The simile of the birds in flight as letters depicts the miraculous
emergence of order, specifically of the order of speech as established
by the law of the letter, out of apparently irrational, instinctual motions.
The simile thereby brings the order of revelation by means of words to
rest symbolically on what is apparently a chaos of natural contingency.
As it occurs in *Purgatorio* XXIV. 64–66 ("Come li augei che vernan
lungo 'l Nilo ..."), the model for this topos of birds' flight patterns as
letters is a passage in Lucan's *Pharsaglia* (V. 711–13) that depicts specifically cranes forming figures in their flight from the frozen Strymon to the
Nile. "As when cranes by pale fog leave the frozen Strymon and to your
doors, Nile, in their first flight, outline various figures as shown *by
chance* ..." ("Strymona sic gelidum bruma pallente relinquunt /
Poturae te, Nile, grues, primoque volatu / Effingunt varias *casu* mon-
strante figuras ...").[4] Lucan emphasizes that the figures are formed by
chance ("casu"), and in the following lines he describes how, conglom-
erated from random confusion ("Confusos temere inmixtae glomerantur
in orbes") and beaten by the wind, finally the letter is dissolved and the
birds dispersed ("Et turbata perit dispersis littera pinnis"). This mysterious conjunction between legible order and random chance is precisely
the thematic line developed by Dante.

Kenneth Knoespel brings forth examples of texts by Isidore of Seville,
Hugh of Saint Victor, and other authors in the considerable reservoir of

---

[4] Lucan is cited from *M. Annaei Lucani Belli civilis libri X*, ed. A. E. Housman (Cambridge: Harvard
University Press, 1926).

texts from the Middle Ages and Antiquity, that describe perceiving flocks of cranes on the wing as forming the shapes of letters. Such patterns of flight became proverbial for their "ordine litterato," their being ordered as letters or discourse.[5] Knoespel demonstrates particularly the communitarian connotations of the crane topos as it develops against a background of patristic and monastic exegetical literature in which cranes served as a model for orderly community life and conformity on the part of separate and potentially anarchic individuals to the needs of the collectivity. Seen from this angle, the image illuminates Dante's exploration of the socio-political essence of writing and letters. As means of communication and concordance, they are indispensable for human community.

This simile of the birds, serving to describe the flight of the souls that come together to compose the letters of the Scriptural message that Dante reads in the heaven of Jove, forms just the final link in a series of similes in the *Divine Comedy* likening birds to letters. In *Inferno* V. 46–47, the simile of the cranes that form a long line as they go chanting their lays in flight ("E come i gru van cantando lor lai, / faccendo in aere di sé lunga riga") creates what Knoespel calls "only an illusion of order." Similarly, Francesca in that canto masks the madness of her love passion in perfectly turned, courtly verse. In the *Purgatorio*, the letter formation of birds connotes the ordered discipline necessary for moral correction and redemption. In the *Paradiso*, the birds forming themselves into letters reveal the divine order of nature translated to history and expressed in the Scriptural injunction to "Love justice, you who rule the earth."

As it evolves from *Inferno* V, through *Purgatorio* XXIV and XXVI, to its apotheosis in *Paradiso* XVIII, the simile connotes the uncanny fact of order issuing from chaos or intelligible meaning from blind instinct. However, in Paradise, Dante ups the ante of this phenomenon of chance motion resolving into an ordered configuration by adding in the theme of the dispersion of form in time as revealing an *eternal* meaning. The order emerging from seeming chaos is thus made transcendent – it embodies divine Justice.

Since writing, taken as theophany, is made to represent some kind of an opening to an eternal presence and to a transcendent, divine intention, it is quite remarkable and full of challenge that in representing writing Dante should highlight its apparent contingency. Dante's imagery attempts the

---

[5] Kenneth Knoespel, "When the Sky Was Paper: Dante's Cranes and Reading as Migration," in *Lectura Dantis Newberryana* II, ed. P. Cherchi and A. Mastrobuono (Evanston: Northwestern University Press, 1990), 178.

impossible – to represent the unrepresentable, transcendent order of the divine. But it does so negatively – by exposing all manifest order as insufficient, or in other words by giving up on mimetically representing divine order and rather endeavoring to suggest its imperceptibility to humans through the representation of chaos.

This type of strategy has become more explicit and deliberate in our own times in ways that can cast some light retrospectively on Dante's procedure. God is typically approached by postmodern thinkers likewise only through "uncontrollable contingency," through negation of all our human controls: "Radical contingency grounds the truth of an infinite faith beyond our primordial drive and instinct to control all things."[6] Absolute chance often takes on this function as the only representable equivalent of divinity in postmodern negative theologies, whereas modern a/theological thinking was typically equated with the embrace of chance instead of God.[7]

The potential of writing to subvert or distort pure intentions stems principally from its materiality and contingency, which Dante dramatically foregrounds and poetically exploits. At the same time, however, Dante emphasizes this script's ideality and capacity for bearing the transcendency of "sense" inasmuch as it encodes a meaning that is nothing less than the revelation of universal divine justice. It is precisely the theophany's contingent quality that highlights the inadequacy of all our schemas and categories to comprehend it. Transcendence is manifest to us paradoxically through radical contingency – what utterly escapes and exceeds our ability to grasp it rationally. What we cannot account for, what to our perception appears totally random and arbitrary, is used by Dante – in a gesture common to primordial religions the world over[8] – to indicate an act of God.

Thus, Dante uses metaphors of contingency drawn from apparently mindless, chaotic events in nature that he believes to be, in reality, providentially guided. In heaven, their apparent contingency is revealed as in reality divinely programmed. In heaven, Dante sees his faith in an inscrutable providence at work in history confirmed, even if it normally proves humanly impossible to discern any pattern of justice beneath the apparent chaos of events.

---

[6] Creston Davis, Marcus Pound, and Clayton Crockett, eds., *Theology after Lacan: The Passion for The Real* (Eugene: Cascade, 2014), 1.

[7] Jacques Monod, *Le hasard et la nécessité: Essai sur la philosophie naturelle de la biologie moderne* (Paris: Seuil, 1970) lays out this conflict.

[8] Wolfram Hogrebe, *Echo des Nichtwissens* (Berlin: Akademie Verlag, 2006).

The paradox of representing divine order by contingency is apt because any order that *can* be humanly apprehended and expressed would be inadequate to represent the divine Mind. This is why God's incomprehensible plan and dispensation of order in the universe must remain inscrutable. In *Convivio* IV. iv. 11, Dante refers and defers to "divine providence, which is above every human reason" ("divina providenza, che è sopra ogni ragione"). The divine nature in its infinite order transcends all finite human order and is incommensurable with it. "To whom then will ye liken God? or what likeness will ye compare unto him?" (Isaiah 40:18). As Isaiah prophesied, God's ways are infinitely beyond and incommensurable with our ways: "For my thoughts *are* not your thoughts, neither *are* your ways my ways, saith the Lord. For *as* the heavens are higher than the earth, so are my ways higher than your ways, and my thoughts than your thoughts" (55:8–9). As Pseudo-Dionysius the Areopagite, quoting his "teacher" Hierotheus, writes concerning the perfect order of divinity: "It sets the boundaries of all sources and orders and yet it is rooted above every source and order."[9]

The contingent – yet transcendent – writing displayed in Dante's heaven signals a short-circuiting and, in effect, a deconstruction of linguistic mediation. There is no calculable relation here between signified and signifiers – which have become thereby merely traces of the Unrepresentable.[10] Sparking emerges as, in many ways, the key image in which these ideas are imagined. The far-reaching consequences of the imagery of sparking as a deconstruction of conventional, or intentional, semantic signification perhaps become fully evident and reflective only in light of radical modern creations of poetic language such as those of Stéphane Mallarmé, whose language veritably "scintillates" with sensory perceptions that signify beyond all possible semantic reckonings of sense. Mallarmé throws poetic composition open to chance with a toss of the dice that no stroke of art can master ("Un coup de dés jamais n'abolira le hazard").[11] Yet poetry's shattering, splintering, or sparking of sense into

[9] Pseudo-Dionysius, "The Divine Names 648C" in *Pseudo-Dionysius: The Complete Works*, trans. Colm Luibheid (New York: Paulist Press, 1987), 66.

[10] For the notion of the trace as a reference to what cannot be represented, see Emmanuel Levinas, "La trace de l'autre," *Tijdschrift voor Filosofie* 25/3 (September 1963): 605–23, translated as "The Trace of the Other," in *Deconstruction in Context: Literature and Philosophy*, ed. Mark C. Taylor (Chicago: University of Chicago Press, 1986), 345–59.

[11] Mallarmé's identification of chance with divinity is made explicit by innumerable commentaries and is brought to a high pitch of philosophical sophistication, building on the seminal work of French philosophers Alain Badiou, Jacques Rancière, and Quentin Meillassoux. I connect this reflection with Dante in "De Dante à Mallarmé à travers l'*Hamlet* de Shakespeare: Négativité de la révélation

infinite constellations of sensations is arguably realized as powerfully as it ever would be already by Dante.

Speaking as Sparking, or a Randomness within the Order of Language

On the face of it, the imagery of sparking connotes chance action or random play, but Dante's spark imagery reverses this connotation and resolves into the revelation of a transcendent order. The sparking here intimates that, despite appearances, all that happens in heaven, and even in the whole universe, is guided by the hand of Providence and is governed, therefore, in the end, by divine Justice. Furthermore, since the sparks form *letters*, they reveal that the order in question, as pictured by the imagery of sparking, is closely connected to the order of language. Indeed, by the mutation of a single letter, the word for spark, "fav*i*lla," is deformed into the word for speech, "fav*e*lla." Similarly, the word for sparking, "sfavillare," is transmuted by slight alteration into a key word for speaking, "favellare." The ear is actually obliged to connect speaking ("*favellare*") with sparking ("*sfavillare*") by the occurrence of both words in the opening *terzina* of the heaven of Jove in consecutive verses ("I saw in that jovial torch / the sparking [*sfavillar*] of the love that was there / signal to my eyes our speech [*favella*]," XVIII. 70–72). This phonetic modulation, at the level of the signifier, between the word for sparking and the one for speaking reverberates with subliminal hints of a fusion also at the level of signified meaning between the concepts – and events – of speaking and sparking. Sparking infiltrates speech. By this subtle phonetic suggestion, speaking is grammatologically wedded to – or contaminated by – sparking. Dante's poetic diction surreptitiously insinuates that speaking is, in essence, a sort of sparking, which makes it, in a Derridean sense, "writing."

 Most conspicuously, sparking entails the random motion of a multitude of elements. Consequently, the phonetic connection between sparking and speaking suggests that the order of speech is itself the result of something like the chance motion of particles in the universe of Leucippus or of Democritus. The latter, as the *Inferno* recalls, "subjects the world to chance" ("che 'l mondo a caso pone," IV. 136).[12] These Atomist

poético-prophétique dans la modernité," in *Dante et Shakespeare: Cosmologie, politique, poétique*, eds. Pascale Drouet and Isabelle Battesti (Paris: Éditeurs Classiques Garnier, 2020), 65–83.

[12] The principal source here is Aristotle, *Metaphysics* 985 B 13–19. See Kurt von Fritz, *Philosophie und sprachlicher Ausdruck bei Demokrit, Plato und Aristoteles* (New York: Steichert, 1938), 24ff. But Dante seems likely to be informed most directly by Cicero, *De natura deorum* I. 66: "Ista enim flagitia

philosophers themselves had hinted that the same randomness as they found operating in the world applies, perhaps even in a primary sense, to the universe of language. The term *stoicheia*, meaning literally "elements," was used by the Stoics, following the Atomists, for the letters of the alphabet, as well as for the elements of the universe. The cosmic order was understood, thus, on the basis of the analogy with language, as a conjunction of material elements. This combination could be construed as given over to chance (as it was by the Atomists, including Lucretius) or as governed by fate (as in the view of Stoics like Seneca). But whether fate or chance was postulated as the ruling principle of the universe, in either case language, with its material "elements," was seen as a universe in itself and as a paradigm for the universe as a whole.

Dante is clearly sensitive to and even transmits the strongly negative connotation of this doctrine – at least in its first form, that given it by the Atomists – as denying Christian faith in divine providence. The Christian doctrine of providence postulates rather a free, intelligent planning of the universe and of everything that comes to pass within it. But the Atomist doctrine also challenges Dante to the bold gesture of actually basing his demonstration of providence and justice in the heaven of Jove on imagery precisely of the sort of random motion of particles envisioned by the pagan philosophers whom he otherwise condemns. He thereby incorporates and integrates the most antithetical vision imaginable into his own vision of divine Justice. Rather than denying and refusing it, Dante poetically admits this metaphysic of irrational motion into his own world-view, absorbing it at the level of his imagery. He thereby undertakes to show that even this erroneous pagan doctrine has a deeper basis and meaning, after all, in divine providence as disclosed by Christian revelation.

In fact, Dante derives his imagery in this heaven of the just souls from a biblical passage in the Book of Wisdom. The Scriptural source whose *incipit* serves as the theme-text and visionary object of this canto also furnishes the *Leitmotif* of its imagery, for the Book of Wisdom, too, in depicting the resplendence of the just, employs the figure of sparking specifically as an image for random motion. "Fulgebunt justi, et tamquam

---

Democriti sive etiam ante Leucippi, esse corpuscula quaedam levia, alia aspera, rutunda alia, partim autem angulata et hamata, curvata quaedam et quasi adunca, ex iis effectum esse caelum atque terram nulla cogente natura, sed consursu quodam fortuito . . ." ("For these wicked teachings of Democritus, or even earlier of Leucippus, that there are certain corpuscles, some smooth, some rough, some sharp, some hooked, curved and turned inwards, out of which heaven and earth are made without natural necessity but by chance encounters . . .").

scintillae in arundineto discurrent" ("The just shall shine, even like sparks running about among the stubble [or reeds]," Wisdom 3:7).

The force of the spark image as it occurs in the Book of Wisdom resides in the strong and, after all, astonishing contrast between the paltry material, the minuscule sparks in a field of humble growth, and the splendor of justice that shines out of their apparently random, disorganized shootings to and fro. This contrast precisely informs the spirit of Dante's recreation of the scene blazoning Justice in the heaven of Jove gloriously out of the midst of innumerable blessedly humble souls' apparently haphazard – yet actually divinely concerted – sparking.

It is also striking that in the Latin Vulgate, which Dante uses, this seemingly random motion is described by the word "discurrent." This term denotes literally a "running around" but lends itself to being heard, especially through Italian ears, as ambiguously meaning a "discoursing." This *double entendre* inherent in the word already forges the link between the order of material motion and that of speech, or more exactly writing, that is a key feature of Dante's vision. In the preceding cantos, Dante has already depicted shooting stars as "discoursing" with sudden spontaneity ("discorre ad ora ad ora sùbito fuoco," XV. 14) in the firmament of Mars.

In this way, the apparently random interaction of particles in sparking becomes a peculiarly privileged image for representing the intricate, albeit basically arbitrary and accidental, patterns of sound that produce meaning in speech. Speech is concretized by Dante's imagery as a form of sparking – of random motion of particles bursting with unpredictable energies. This sparking, for all the seeming arbitrariness and uncontrollability of its individual particles, is orchestrated, nevertheless, to form meaningful patterns, particularly a sentence from Scripture, with all its subtly significant harmonies and paradoxes. By such means, an ideality of sense is produced, as if miraculously, through the radically material, unstable, and irregular phenomenon of the spark. In this respect, "speech" is understood to be like writing – that is, to be an effect of meaning produced by material elements that in themselves are radically contingent and meaningless.

In this image of sparking, then, the poem offers an image of the universe, but also of itself. The poem itself is an explosion of sparks that miraculously form into the practically perfect order of the speech (or writing) that communicates Dante's Paradise. The divine order of Paradise can be embodied in the verbal order, or rather disorder, of the poem only on condition of the poem's being – when considered from a human point of view – a phenomenon of random sparking. For its order must be incalculable, that is, it must transcend any finite, human, conventional calculus and rather spring up, instead, as a mysterious, divine prodigy from the (humanly) uncontrolled release of energies in speech. That much is expressed by the imagery of sparking, which is, in fact, pervasive throughout the *Paradiso*.

The present discussion can accommodate only a summary and fugitive glance at a few examples of Dante's spark imagery and its employment in the larger context of the *Paradiso*. This imagery reverberates all through the third canticle, playing a key role, for example, in the point of light described as "the pure spark" ("la favilla pura") that images God in the *Primum mobile* (XXVIII. 38), the point from which heaven and all nature depend (XXVIII. 41–42). In the Empyrean, "live sparks" ("faville vive") spring from – in order then to be resubmerged in – the river of light. All these images taken together are qualified in Canto XXX (lines 64 and 78; cf. 95) as offering "shadowy prefaces" ("umbriferi prefazii") of the truth revealed in the Empyrean.

Like the ultimately ineffable reality of the Empyrean, virtually everything else in Paradise is touched in the end by the visual language of sparking. In the heaven of Mercury, the image is used in relation to God's giving of himself in Creation through the sparkling love generated from within him ("ardendo in sé, sfavilla," VII. 65) and then unfolding also outward in created beauty. Indeed, in every heaven Dante makes some use of this image or its cognates, and as a result he raises it to the level of a constitutive metaphor that becomes indispensable to his representation of Paradise. The spontaneous behavior of the sparks serves to characterize a free and unconstrained nature. As with the insistent animal images for paradisiacal phenomena, the conventionally lower elemental nature of the spark is taken to mirror a "nature" paradoxically more highly ordered in its incalculable complexity than all rational intentions whatsoever that can be *humanly* imposed on speech.

The imagery of sparks ("faville") and sparking ("sfavillar"), in counterpoint with that of speech ("favella"), indeed forms an intricately connected network that weaves in and out of Dante's text and knits it together. It does so even while playing up explosions in its sounds along with improprieties and splinterings of its sense. In Canto XIV, in the exclamation "O true sparking" ("O vero sfavillar," 76), the sparking in question is the flame of the Holy Spirit, the spontaneous sparking of the tongues of flame, which are brought into a series of equivalences: flaming = sparking = speaking. At the next ascent, the souls of the martyrs in Mars are seen brightly scintillating ("scintillando forte," XIV. 110) on the Cross of Christ. These pyrotechnics constitute further revelations of an occult, divine order and message emerging as if from chaos, for which the "spark" (Latin: *scintilla*) serves as pivotal symbol.

In light of the present discussion, it is not so surprising that this pervasive image of the spark should be associated so often with phenomena of language. In fact, the spark image, understood as suggested here, may be spotted as a hint, and indeed a constant reminder, of the specifically *written* status of the phenomena presented in every heaven. In *Purgatorio* XXI. 94–95, Dante had already brilliantly exploited the literary connotation of the spark of inspiration in the famous tribute paid by Dante's Statius to Virgil's poetry: "Al mio ardor fuor seme le faville / che mi scaldar, de la divina fiamma / ... / de l'Eneida dico" ("Seeds of my ardor were the sparks / of the divine flame that warmed me ... / of the *Aeneid*, I mean"). The spark, like the seed, multiplies and disseminates. It is used obsessively by Dante for intellectual engendering through literary tradition and for poetic fertility.

In the very first canto, with reference to his own effort to sing Paradise and his hope of inspiring future poets to follow him, Dante declares,

> Poca favilla gran fiamma seconda. (I. 34)

> (A great flame may follow a little spark.)

One could start by surveying poetry just in English – by Chaucer, Spencer, Milton, and Blake – as fulfilling this prophecy of his poem's sparking a blaze of visionary successors. Dante returns to a very similar wish and image at the end of his journey:

> e fa la mia lingua tanto possente
> ch'una favilla sol de la sua gloria
> possa lasciare a la futura gente.
>
> (XXXIII. 70–72)

> (and make my tongue so potent
> that it be capable of leaving even just one spark
> of its glory to future peoples.)

The figure of the spark only slightly disguised, furthermore, is present in the final "fulgore" or lightning bolt. In this figure, the impossible vision, which remains finally beyond image and figure, is nevertheless given to Dante's dumbstruck mind (XXXIII. 141). This is the spark that becomes the seed of the poem that Dante writes in the wake of his mind-shattering vision.

From Speech to Letter to Image: Metamorphoses of the Spark

This embarrassment of riches notwithstanding, it is in the heaven of Jove itself and in Canto XVIII in particular that the spark image for speech and its incalculable powers achieves its most impressive and intense realization – a celestial performance that culminates in a startling poetic apotheosis. The sparks that Dante witnesses here form speech: literally, the "countless sparks" ("innumerabili faville") become constituents of the letters of the alphabet – "our language" ("nostra favella"), as they are explicitly called from the opening verses of the heaven. Speaking as sparking here subsumes the evidently random emission of sparks within the order of language and speech, which, in turn, in Dante's linguistic humanism, is itself the basis of the whole political and social order. At the same time, conversely, speech in this heaven is brought into intrinsic contact with what appears to be a completely uncontrolled burst of sheer energy. As a simile for the metamorphosis of the letter M, innumerable sparks are pictured rising up pell-mell from firebrands that have been violently struck while burning:

> Poi, come nel percuoter d'i ciocchi arsi
> surgono innumerabili faville,
> onde li stolti sogliono agurarsi; . . .

(100–2)

> (Then, as when burning logs are struck
> innumerable sparks surge up,
> whence fools are accustomed to practice augury; . . .)

After its initial punning appearance in introducing the heaven of Jove, equivocating between spark (*favilla*) and speech (*favella*), the spark imagery, with its double aspect as representing paradoxically ordered contingency, is most unmistakably significant and literally striking in this concluding letter **M** at the grand finale of the vision of the verse from the Book of Wisdom. The image is wrought to an explosive climax at the moment when Dante sees the last of the thirty-five letters, which he describes as a gothic ꟿ.

This letter is transformed by a combustion of sparks to become the new symbol of total world order, namely, Monarchy, a scintillating blazon for Dante's political theory.[13] This graphic *image* then becomes *pictorial* as the

---

[13] A number of other possible meanings are inventoried by Federica Brumori Deigan and Elisa Liberatori Prati, "'L'emme del vocabol quinto': Allegory of Language, History, and Literature in

M suddenly metamorphoses into the image of an eagle's head and neck –
unmistakably the escutcheon of Empire.

> e quietata ciascuna in suo loco,
> la testa e 'l collo d'un aguglia vidi
> rappresentare a quel distinto foco.   (XVIII. 106–8)

> (and when each one was quiet in its place,
> I saw the head and neck of an eagle
> represented by that distinct fire.)

The emblem of universal imperial order emerges astonishingly out of an
image of chaotic and violent release of uncontrolled energies, an explosive
sparking. Dante exalts the chance play and blind violence of the striking of
the log, but also the preordained plan that is thereby realized, as the directly
following verses make explicit:

> resurger parver quindi più di mille
> luci e salir, qual assai e qual poco,
> *sì come 'l sol che l'accende sortille.*
>   (XVIII. 103–5)

> (thence more than a thousand lights
> seemed to surge and rise, some much and some little,
> *as the sun that ignites them alots.*)

The crowd of uncounted particles ("più di mille") is dispersed in a
differentiated and apparently ("parver") unaccountable way, yet divinity –
"the sun that ignites them" – nevertheless still operates here by assigning
lots ("sortille") behind the scenes and by determining the degrees of their
resurgence and ascent in a carefully discriminating manner ("qual assai e
qual poco").

The invisible hand is present again, just a little later, in the bird
metaphor, specifically in the reference to "the power which is the formal
principle of being in nests" ("quella virtù ch'è forma per li nidi"), a power
which "puts us in mind of him" ("e da lui si rammenta," XVIII. 110–11). It
is a power, in other words, that we recognize as "from God" ("da lui"). As
in the case of the birds in flight forming letters, so again with the sparks
composing speech, a phenomenon of mass and chance is given a unified,
determinate, legible form. These are reminders of how the Creator orders

---

Dante's *Paradiso* 18," *Quaderni d'italianistica* 19/1 (1998): 7–26. The M also links with the humanist
theme of *uoMo*, and thereby of the human social order, in the acrostic of Purgatory XII.

the instinctual behavior of animals and the mindless motion of matter alike to supremely intelligent ends. Here again, Dante unfailingly emphasizes that the phenomenal forms he sees written have a meaning determined by the control and intention of the divine Author. All this tends to turn writing back into speech ("nostra favella"), or to comprehend writing as a secondary materialization and externalization of speech taken as immediate self-expression.

Nevertheless, however much it may be possible to see this writing as essentially a form of speech, as an articulation of what the author means to express, Dante insists that the Word of God is revealed here in an unmistakably and irreducibly *written* form. He could hardly have made this point more *graphic* than in this scintillating display of letters across the heaven. The fact that in this "speech" the letters are formed out of what is at first an apparently random activity resulting from an uncontrolled release of elemental or instinctual energies suggests something radical about the very grounds and nature of speech. The most compact way of expressing the insight depicted here is to say that speech is based on, or is at its origin, a kind of writing.

The implication, indeed, is that speech, at least divine speech, is to be understood radically as a kind of writing, where writing inflects (and, in Derrida's terms, infects) sense with external elements subject to contingency. That speech itself depends on some system of differences, and thus in effect on "writing," in order to make sense, is the seminal insight theorized by Derrida with his notion of "archi-écriture" ("archi-writing").[14]

Completely relinquishing the deliberate, ideal intentions of speech as destroyed and overtaken by the random chances of matter in writing nevertheless enables order and intention – even in the form of divine providence – to reappear as transfigured and as expressing something beyond ordinary comprehension. Truly transcendent intentionality beyond every worldly order can only come out of what cannot but seem chaos to any finite intelligence. Dante's text thereby proclaims an order beyond its own invented order and beyond any human capacity to impose order.

Dante describes the order of the heaven as reposing upon the random sparking of letters that, at least to us, cannot but appear as chaos. Although the program of the poem brings all this playing with wild fire back into

---

[14] Derrida expounds this notion, for example, in *De la grammatologie*, 88.

harmony with the perfect order dictated from above, the revelation *in writing* is not thereby canceled out. The sense that writing is inherently contingent and precarious remains throughout the poem to its very end. Particularly the allusion in the concluding canto to the leaves of Sybil scattering to the winds (XXXIII. 64–66) functions as an image for the poem itself in its ultimate failure to synthesize and unify the contents of Dante's revelatory experience. The reflections prompted by the vision in Jupiter show this dispersion to be an ineluctable consequence simply of the poem's being written. There is, of course, a higher instance of unity symbolized in the final lightning bolt from above (XXXIII. 141), in which the divine vision is purportedly achieved, yet this unity exceeds representation and expression and even mortal, bodily life. Hence Dante's loss of consciousness and memory. Afterwards, however, Dante still has to live and write his experience in worldly terms and with finite means.

Precisely the worldly fragmentation and finitude of his vision, which is transfigured by some higher, incomprehensible power, enables the poem to simulate or recreate the experience of paradise or of divine presence. When all human, artificial forms imposing order break down, then the really miraculous and transcendent order underlying the apparent chaos of the world and history finally breaks through, even if it can become apparent and be represented only as unrepresentable. The breakdown of all manifest order, order that can be made legible through humanly comprehensible codes, becomes an apotheosis of a transcendent – albeit latent and invisible – order.

Paradoxically, the material or visible manifestation of divinity must be totally contingent in order to make manifest the absolute transcendence of God, his eternal and necessary Being. Only the contingency of everything – of every *thing* – clears the field for all things altogether to become a manifestation of the transcendent, absolute, and necessary God, who is *no* thing. Only this revelation of all things as contingent could make discernible – by its being absent from all possible objective appearances – a non-contingent Ground on which they all depend. Dante, along with Scholastic theology generally, accepts the notion that God, and God alone, is necessary Being. This postulate goes back at least to Avicenna and to the Arab graft of Aristotelian metaphysics on to a monotheistic doctrine of God.

Thus, if Dante exposes his grand vision of unity and divine presence astonishingly as writing at this juncture in Jove, it is not just because writing offers an attractive image with which to decorate the sky. Writing represents the breakdown into material parts and contingent events of the whole scheme and order of the cosmos – which, in Dante's poem, is nothing if not written. The insistence on the writtenness of the vision in this heaven marks the exposure of its radical vulnerability to dismemberment and dispersion, its apparent disorder in any finite perspective, its propensity to disintegration. But precisely therein – in its reduction to the sheer immanence of the medium in its material immediacy – lies writing's capacity to allude to a transcendence altogether higher than and beyond every definable, finite order of things.

In this negative way, in the heaven of Jove, Dante depicts intelligible order as being achieved immediately at the level of the signifier. The letters do not just signify a perfect, transcendent being and order: they embody and become it, and thereby identify themselves with an ambiguous presence of divinity *in* the signifying event itself. They incarnate God not iconically, not by pretending to imitate by semblance or likeness, but rather in their action of self-subversion and self-erasure, in being broken down to a mere matter of sparks. Relinquishing significance through their material reduction and disappearance, the letters are enabled to signify, or more profoundly to incarnationally and kenotically enact, the unsignifiable.

Perfect order is, of course, absolute simplicity, that of the Tri-Unity itself (as Dionysius indicates in *De divinis nominibus*, 649B–C), and of this simplicity the letters can be only a remote approximation, only a very inadequate image. The letter (and number) "I" most obviously embodies this ideal simplicity by virtue of being a simple unity, a single stroke without differentiation. Still, the imitation of the signified divine simplicity by any signifier whatsoever remains infinitely incomplete and inadequate. Only representing its own failure can establish a relation of immediacy that signals the collapse of signification and the realization of theophany in the (vanishing) immanence of the medium.

Dispersion of Sparks and the Wholeness of Sense

The images of contingency and chaos, in effect, are crucial to Dante's attempt to present the medium as unmediated revelation. In chaos, precisely, all mediation breaks down. Dante's stress on the sheer contingency of the medium – made visible in its conspicuous writtenness – disencumbers it, in the first instance, of any functions extraneous to and transcending it as medium. A mere medium is purely contingent, and in Dante's vision it shows up as present in and for itself as a material fact – even one that explodes into apparently senseless chaos.

Whatever is contingent is simply there, given, without cause or necessity, without reason or why. It is like Silesius Angelus's rose: "The rose is
without why" ("Die Ros' ist ohn warumb," *Cherubinischer Wandersmann*,
I, 289). A flower, the lily (*giglio*), briefly forms, also in Dante's vision of the
letter M ("ingigliarsi a l'emme," XVIII. 113) that emerges out of the chaos of
apparently random sparking, but it is soon to break apart and be reformed
into another image, being joined to that of the head and neck ("la testa e 'l
collo," 107) of the eagle. The lily image thus melts down to part of the
heraldic emblem of Empire, when "the design is completed" ("seguitò la
'mprenta") by adding a body (at least its wings) to the eagle's head (see
Figure 5). All these overdetermined significances emerge out of and are
revealed as grounded in the indeterminacy of the spark.

The objectification and materialization of "speech" – in this case,
actually a phrase from the Word of God, specifically the Book of
Wisdom, formed into a succession of written characters – thoroughly
determines its fragmentation into parts. The single, whole line taken
from Scripture is parceled out, not only into its five component words
(which Dante totals up in the phrase "vocabol quinto"), but even into *their*
constitutive "elements," the letters which appear in his vision *ad seriatim*.
Each letter, in turn, is itself an artificial composite formed out of innumerable sparks that are actually illuminated souls or "live lights" ("vive luci").

In all these ways, the "parts" of this "speech" are spread out in space,
separated from one another, divided up by intervals of temporal and spatial
difference. Not the ideal and seamless unity of the divine intention in the
Word, but the extendedness and externality of fragmented forms in space
and time, are what here become visible in the language that is written.
Dante's Scriptural visualization of the Word of God opens it up and strings
it out in such a way as to make its unity not an immediate given, but rather
a complicated pattern built up by synthesis of a multitude of differentiated
and exteriorized phenomenal elements. The immediacy of the letters'
presence thus turns out to be a complex and elusive way of signifying
something transcendent as immediately present. It is present not as such, in
a unified iconic image, but rather in the chaotic display and dissemination
of the sparks that do not linguistically signify Justice or God so much as
make this meaning immediately manifest – or at least felt. So Dante attests.

Dante indicates, particularly through the imagery of sparking, that in a
natural perspective only random chance, or total chaos, can actually be
discerned. The miraculous result that language made up out of what can be
perceived as no more than a conglomeration of contingent, randomly
shooting material particles should in the end make integral and ideal

sense shows that some transcendent ordering principle must, after all, be operative in it. In fact, the language displayed here, by virtue of its power to create meaning through synthetic unity, reveals the presence of a divine Mind. This presence makes a sense that is not guided by any objectifiable principle ("Quei che dipinge lì non ha chi 'l guidi"). Such an immediate presence is not within the dimension belonging to objective beings at all but is rather their ontological ground, their "forming power" ("quella virtù ch'è forma per li nidi," XVIII. 111), as Dante's rhetoric argues. Only so is it possible to justify all that happens in the world, revealing its apparent senselessness to be the effect of heavenly justice.

Dante's angle of approach to the crucial questions of ethics and politics contemplated in the Heaven of Jupiter is the order of language and specifically of writing, the sphere of the *grammè*. The mysterious synthetic power of language and its ability to make sense are not invested in any analyzable structure, nor in identifiable elements of language that are certifiably meaning-bearing. This deficit or default is what suggests the mysticism of the letter for which Dante opts. He has faith indeed in language, but it is faith in spite of the breakdown of all guarantors of sense external to the miraculous event of language in his poem. The letter as such is a bare geometric form, without intrinsic meaning, and decomposable into infinitesimal material particles.

The relinquishing of reference, and the unsparing anatomization of the structure of the sentence, dramatize the lack of wholeness in the objectively given phenomena of language per se. The elements of language appear in this text as purely external and as materially given. It is their meaning or sense that makes all elements of a linguistic statement hang together in the end, but such meaningful sense as emerges from chaos is not itself visible. It is necessarily a creation of the mind and partly even a matter of faith in something that vastly exceeds the concrete chaotic play of random material signifiers.

Some such faith determines what Dante perceives in the letters. Although he does not (and perhaps cannot) understand how, *some*how the combustion of sparks resolves into the display of letters and shows him that "our justice" in human history is indeed grounded in a divine Justice. He sees that the apparently senseless events on earth do make sense and will be justified in the end from a heavenly vantage point. God's very presence in these scintillating signs answers all his doubts and reassures Dante that justice reigns in the universe, after all, since it is all steered from above, from this heaven of justice, the "star" (in Dante's vocabulary) of Jupiter:

O dolce stella, quali e quante gemme
mi dimostraro che nostra giustizia
effetto sia del ciel che tu ingemme!

(XVIII. 115–17)

(O sweet star, what gems, and in what numbers,
demonstrated to me that our justice
is the effect of the heaven that you bejewel!)

The transcendent sense of the Word – which in this heaven is revealed to be Justice – is not attenuated or dispersed by its phenomenological realization and poetic objectification. On the contrary, it is thereby first made truly accessible to experience. It is precisely the contingency and fragmentation of human language that serves to throw into relief the unifying, gathering power of the transcendent Word. That language articulated in time should hold together and make sense cannot be explained by any merely temporal phenomena. That the language in Dante's vision should be writing, furthermore, and therewith be conditioned by spatial separateness, compounds the difficulty of explaining, let alone of producing, synthesis.

The letter *per se* is apt to spell disaggregation for Dante. A little later in this very heaven, in fact, the image of "mutilated letters" ("note mozze," *Paradiso* XIX. 174) concretizes this intrinsic propensity of the letter to fragmentation. In the *Convivio*, moreover, Dante chooses precisely the letter to serve as his example of an object that may be difficult to perceive as a unity: "things do not appear united but disjoined, almost the way a letter of ours appears on paper that is wet . . . on account of which . . . many hold the writing at a distance from their eyes . . . and this gives the letter a more distinct resolution" ("le cose non paiono unite ma disgregate, quasi a guisa che fa la nostra lettera in su la carta umida . . . per che molti . . . si dilungano le scritture da li occhi . . . e in ciò più rimane la lettera discreta," III. ix. 14; cf. IV. vi. 3). For Dante, the letter resolves into a perceptible image only at a distance. The letter may have been chosen here as example because it is not normally considered in itself, but only as part of a larger ensemble – for example, a whole word of which it is a part. A letter, according to Aristotle's classic definition in *De interpretatione* 2, is inherently a fragment, since the smallest meaningful unit of language is the word.

However, in some ways, Dante's description of his vision in the heaven of Jupiter contradicts this traditional value of the letter as inherently only a fragment. As Chapter 3 will demonstrate in detail, his grammatical analysis of language discovers below the level of intention realized in the sentence an eminently meaningful order in the letter itself – in what is supposed to be a non-meaningful element of language. This transcendent sense inherent in the very elements of language is elicited and brought out onto the stage of the heaven by the decomposition of a sentence into letters as its component parts. In this way, language is at first exposed not as a whole structure conveying a user's intention, but as a differential structure of arbitrary oppositions such as the system of marks that are coded into an alphabet (Excursus II). Yet the very structure of arbitrariness or randomness, along with the chaos on which it rests, is deployed to re-establish the meaningfulness of these bare atomic components at a more elementary level as expressing even more immediately the intentions – or, more simply and immediately, just the presence – of a transcendent Mind, the Creator and Governor of all nature and being.

Theological Revelation via Punning: Linguistic Contingency at Play

The theophany in *Paradiso* XVIII features an appearing of divinity in language, specifically in letters. Yet, like any representation, it cannot really show God in his transcendence. It can only mediate an experience of unrepresentable contact with God that generates confidence in divine providential order. Hence Dante's emotionally charged exclamation ("O dolce stella," etc.) thanking the heaven for showing him that *our* justice ("nostra giustizia") is *its* effect ("sia effetto del ciel"). Dante affirms that he can see divine Justice spelled out plainly in the heaven and understands, consequently, that even justice on earth is brought about by heaven. But what he "sees" is precisely that we cannot actually see God's Justice. Indeed, the letters "signify" what cannot be represented. There is an infinite disproportion between God and the Creation – or any thing within it. The divine Word is infinitely "in excess" ("in infinito eccesso," XIX. 45) of the universe it creates, and to that extent it remains "occulted" ("occulto") even in this self-manifestation:

> Colui che volse il sesto
> a lo stremo del mondo, e dentro ad esso
> distinse tanto occulto e manifesto,
>
> non poté suo valor sì fare impresso
> in tutto l'universo, che 'l suo verbo
> non rimanesse in infinito eccesso.
>
> E ciò fa certo che 'l primo superbo,
> che fu la somma d'ogne creatura,
> per non aspettar lume, cadde acerbo;

e quinci appar ch' ogne minor natura
  è corto recettacolo a quel bene
  che non ha fine e sé con sé misura.

(XIX. 40–51)

(He who turned the compass
  at the limit of the world, and within it
  distinguished so much that is hidden and manifest,

could not so impress his worth
  throughout the whole universe that his Word
  would not remain infinitely in excess of it.

And this makes certain that the first proud one,
  who was the highest of every creature,
  because he did not wait for light, fell unripe,

and thus it appears that every lesser nature
  is an inadequate receptacle for that good
  which has no end and measures itself by itself alone.)

As representation of the unrepresentable, therefore, Canto XVIII's theophany of letters must also somehow disqualify itself. For this purpose, Dante uses the motif of contingency. Not only is the arrangement and motion of the spectacle like random motion, but writing itself, and with it language in general, is exposed as founded on contingency – or at least on what to us appears to be contingency, since the order actually governing it transcends our comprehension. This turns out to be true of the providential order of the world and history as a whole, whose justice is inscrutable to us. Dante's imagery attempts the impossible – to represent the unrepresentable, transcendent order of the divine – by rendering all *manifest* order insufficient. In this case in particular, he does so by giving up on representing divine order, except through representation of apparent chaos.

In connection with the imagery of randomness in nature, Dante explores randomness in the constitution of language itself and, moreover, exploits randomness in the very language in which he represents all this. Indeed, before leaving the birds-as-letters simile too far behind, we should observe something actually quite striking about Dante's own language as used in this description. The birds are described literally as "congratulando," a word that contains a synthesis and that needs to be broken down into its component parts, "con" and "gratulando," in order to be readable as "being gratified together" in a shared satisfaction over their feeding ("a lor pastura"). This is the most natural sense for the word as it is used of the birds in the simile. Of course, the birds are metaphors for the blessed souls rejoicing in heaven, and these souls may also be seen as congratulating one another ("congratularsi") on the happiness that they have gained, as well as "congratulating" or giving glory to the divinity whose unending praise is their ceaseless occupation and fulfillment.

Thus, even the normal, proper meaning of the word "congratularsi" ("to congratulate") obliquely takes on pertinence, adding metaphorical resonances that, as if by a lucky coincidence, enrich the meaning of the scene. But this superposition, as if by mere serendipity, of the proper meaning upon an improper, unnatural combination of semantic elements points towards far-reaching aspects of the conception of language that Dante literally depicts in this heaven. Its radical openness to contingency is seen to be indissociable from its realization of a theophany. A purely contingent language, such as Dante's poetry pretends to emulate, is the only language suitable for representing a totally transcendent, divine, providential order. Such order cannot be represented except negatively. No matter how perfect any calculable order of justice may be, divine transcendence, the ultimate source of all true justice, can only assert itself in contingency and in the negation of every representable, worldly order, however right or just such order may appear to be in merely human terms.

This is one example of how Dante does not just offer images of apparent contingency resolving miraculously into providential, evidently transcendent order. He also, in his own writing, enacts this principle in some remarkably subtle and revealing ways. Perhaps the most obvious way in which this order in contingency registers is by playful punning right from the opening verses of the heaven of Jove. The very name of the heaven, which is also the name of the Olympian monarch, with its connotations of central rule and hierarchical order, reverberates punningly from the first line describing the heaven in Dante's text: "Io vidi in quella giovial facella" ("I saw in that jovial torch"). The same pun is virtually repeated at the other end of Dante's writing on this heaven, when it is explained how the soul of the Emperor Trajan has been able to come to this jubilant rejoicing, this jovial "play" or "game" ("venire a questo gioco," XX. 117). The name of the heaven of Jove ("Giove") now works anagrammatically in a noun ("gioco") rather than in an adjective ("giovial"), as at the outset.

A pun is a significant effect of apparently random coincidence in the sounds, the phonetic materialities, of language. It hints that there may be a sovereign, unexpected order in apparent chaos, in the mere, material substrate of speech, which is, at bottom, a sort of writing, an accidental effect of the exterior medium used to convey the ideal meaning or intention of speech. The surprising "accident" of the pun reflects a playful, not to say a gaming, aspect of God that runs very deep. The image of God as Gambler ("Giocatore") is another face of what shows up in the playful punning of this heaven. It communicates the inscrutability and *apparent* arbitrariness of a God not bound by human logic.

Giuseppe Mazzotta offers an interpretation of Dante's *theologia ludens* that brilliantly illuminates all that contingency can mean as revelation of God's freedom and playfulness in the universe and in history. Concerning the figure of the "divine Gambler," the *Dio Giocatore*, Mazzotta pertinently writes: "The image communicates inscrutability and apparent arbitrariness, on the level of salvation, of a God who, unbound by human logic, acts freely with regard to the work of his hands" ("L'immagine comunica l'imperscrutabilità e apparente arbitrarietà del piano della salvezza, di un Dio che, non legato alla logica umana, agisce liberamente verso l'opera delle sue mani").[15]

Palpably, the mood changes quite suddenly with Dante's entry into this heaven, leaving behind the martyrs in the Heaven of Mars, where the personal hardships in store for Dante, too, are harped upon with dramatic pathos. The lines in which Dante commences writing about the Heaven of Jupiter have, in contrast, something light and lively about them, something that is felt immediately in their rhythm and consonantal pattern depending especially on the interplay between rather sizzling fricatives (sf, f, s, v) and lilting liquids (l, ll). Let us hear them again:

> Io vidi in quella giovial facella
> lo sfavillar de l'amor che lì era
> segnare a li occhi miei nostra favella.
>
> (XVIII. 70–72)

Beyond the impression given, at least diffusely, by sound, the jocularity that is present here sharpens to a conceptual point. For the joviality of this beginning is inscribed literally into the name of the heaven of Jupiter or, as Dante writes, "Jove" ("Giove," XVIII. 95). "Jove" is originally just a genitive declension of "Jupiter." In such occurrences, the word weaves its associated concept of joviality together textually with the sounds used to express and articulate this "jovial" heaven. In the device of punning, the sonic material of words can displace their conventional meanings and constitute   semantically   accidental,   but   conceptually   compelling,

---

[15] Giuseppe Mazzotta, *Confine quasi orizzonte: Saggi su Dante* (Rome: Edizioni di Storia e Letteratura, 2014), 64.

significance. This type of contingency inevitably begins already where words take on an exterior, sensory, sonorous form of expression in being enunciated. As such, they are already a kind of "writing" by virtue of their using a material clang that is not transparent – but only diacritically related – to their meaning. Sound exploited in this way is "writing" already inherent in speech itself.[16]

Punning, as in Dante's "giovial" ("jovial"), plays, as punning quite generally does, upon contingencies of language. But what could appear to be relatively trivial or even pointless word-play becomes peculiarly apt in this thematic context. For, in this instance, what is apparently a linguistic accident produces what is just right, the "right" word. Here, in the heaven of justice, calling this the "just" word seems eminently justified. Precisely contingency (at least what appears as such from our point of view) is conceptualized, or rather imagined, here as a constitutive principle of this heaven and thereby of Justice itself. As the very name of the heaven hints, Dante affirms unified rule and authority in the world as dictated by the demand for conformity to the heavenly kingdom's own order. But this order, paradoxically, is discovered and presented through radical contingency.

Such virtuosities at the level of technique embody the overall significance and philosophical viewpoint of the poem. For Dante uses the order–chaos (or order–contingency) polarity in order to articulate an analogous juncture between the unrepresentable divinity and its objective representation. The two are made virtually to coincide in the miraculous event of revelation in the poem, even though in theory they are polar opposites and incompatible. The most random activity imaginable, the random motion or "sparking" of purely material elements, underlies the intellectual order of the transcendent Word of revelation.

The contingency in question, fundamentally, is not that of the material universe. The representation of divine presence as material contingency is but a figure for the contingency of whatever objective realities can be perceived in relation to the Unrepresentable Divinity – God, the necessary Being par excellence that they, nevertheless, are supposed, unaccountably, to signify. That the sheerly contingent should reveal the absolutely necessary is the miracle of revelation already in the Creation, as well as in the

---

[16] This idea of writing as constituted by an external, material signifier, whether graphic or sonic, one which is arbitrary with regard to inner intention or meaning, is crucial to Derrida's deconstructive analysis of speech in *De la grammatologie*, 15–41: "the exteriority of the signifier is the exteriority of writing in general" ("l'extériorité du signifiant est l'extériorité de l'écriture en général" (26).

Incarnation. That precisely *writing* should be employed to represent the Word of God, in keeping with the value of Scripture, is the wonder of wonders that this heaven ponders and celebrates. That *writing* should become not just a disposable means but itself be the form of revelation in which God speaks, and thereby makes himself present, is an incredible claim worthy of all the subtle and spectacular elaboration that Dante lavishes upon it.

We have seen how, at the climax of Canto XVIII, the wholeness and intentionality of speech are fused in Dante's imaginings with the blind explosiveness of sparking in all of its unpredictable dynamism. Much necessarily intervenes, given the essential nature of writing as mediation, before we can come to this moment of recuperation of wholeness and immediacy of the divine intention appearing in the visionary form of a writing that is theophany.

The opaqueness of writing as a contingent, material medium that intervenes and disperses the immediacy of speech must be pursued further. It emerges as a means of penetrating the mystery of revelation of the divine in Dante's thematizing of the grammatical "parts of speech." With this latter image, Dante emphasizes the breakdown of language as a stream of speech into fragments that is characteristic of writing. This susceptibility to decomposition is a liability intrinsic to writing as an externalized and materialized form of language. The next chapter brings to focus, in Dante's differential terms and images, this paradox that the purely contingent – writing – should serve to reveal necessary being – God.

CHAPTER 3

The Parts of Speech: Mediation and Contingency

Contingency as Key to Revelation

The spotlight on writing in Dante's vision of letters in the Heaven of Jove raises far-reaching philosophical and theological questions. The kernel of them is the status of writing as a medium or a means, but also as an immediate revelation, of God – or at least a symbol for such immediacy. Writing, in Dante's vision, is made to function as both. By its interposition of arbitrary and secondary signs, writing renders impossible any direct or immediate vision of the absolute – or even simply of the real. But thanks particularly to the exemplar of the Bible as Word of God and as book, writing can also stand symbolically for God's revealing "Godself" in an apparently stable, concrete, objective form of words and, consequently, even in a visible form of letters.[1] The conundrums caused by this ambiguous status of writing come out fully in later theoretical reflection, notably among thinkers of *écriture* or *Schrift* in contrast with the living word of speech. They are, however, already intensely realized and reflected on by Dante in the *Paradiso*.

This chapter focuses on how Dante's attempt to present the medium as unmediated revelation relies on images of contingency through breaking language down into parts, for in contingency all mediation breaks down. Literally, *con-tingere* is an immediate touching together without anything in the middle. Dante's stress on the contingency of the medium disencumbers it, in the first instance, of its function as medium of referring to something else that stands outside it and so sets limits on and conditions it. Representing its contingency presents the written medium simply on its own as an immediate presence. The medium, as contingent, becomes

---

[1] I borrow the vocabulary of "Godself" from Karl Barth. I use it in order to respect God's absolute exorbitance of any genre of selves other than Godself. God's way of being a self is incomparable and cannot be comprehended in the same way as that of any other individual's being "itself," "herself," or "himself."

present in and for itself. Whatever is contingent is presented as simply there, as given and as unaccounted for by any reason or necessity – as not dictated by any higher law or superior purpose.

It is crucial for Dante to represent the contingency of his medium, namely, writing, in order metaphorically to present something as absolute – the unmediated reality of God. In theory, the medium as such has a purely instrumental role. There is presumably nothing in it that is not subjected to the higher purposes of a controlling mind. Language is used as a medium to express a speaker's intention. However, as we saw in Chapter 2, the motion of sparks is invoked as a metaphor for Dante's medium of writing in order to suggest a random, uncontrolled, unmediated, explosive presence. The spark simply surges up, as if out of nowhere and in the most unpredictable fashion. That this medium (writing, the letter, the external and material mark) used for signifying the divine Mind and conveying divine Intentions should itself be manifest as an immediate presence and event, yet precisely with the emphasis on its contingency as a random sparking, constitutes a spectacular sort of reversal of the ordinary, earthly logic of mediation. Mediation is thereby turned into a kind of higher immediacy. Dante dramatizes this reversal of mediation into immediacy programmatically in this heaven and in more diffuse, capillary fashion throughout the *Paradiso*.

Through the dialectical interpenetration of writing and speech, indeed "The Presence of Speech in Writing," which we have just examined (Chapter 2), writing is exalted to the status of a superior, whole, unmediated – and therefore also authoritative – revelation. Such is writing's status, finally, in the religions of the Book, in which God is present in and through his Word in Scripture. This is what Derrida leaves out of his history of writing as always only the secondary, derivative, underprivileged, and contingent partner in a binary opposition with speech.

In *De la grammatologie*, Derrida acknowledges this flip-side to the story about writing, but he ripostes that it is only *metaphorically* that writing is attributed high worth as transcendent and eternal (27–28). As a literal, technical means, writing still remains subordinate and in subjection to speech, indeed devalued and depreciated. Yet Dante's vision deliberately and conspicuously exalts writing precisely in its most mechanical, technical, and "literal" aspects – as literally and perceptibly made of letters. He fundamentally deconstructs Derrida's dichotomy by valorizing writing's transcendence precisely in its externality and materiality – and in all its consequently contingent characteristics.

Derrida's view, in reality, holds only for a certain tradition of logos *philosophy*. Contrary to the tradition transmitted by Plato's *Phaedrus*, which portrays writing as an inferior stopgap for weak memory, in broad strands of the often hieratic and sacred culture of the West, writing has been viewed as *superior* in its authority and as endowed with an unfathomable plenitude of meaning and power. Writing is often made to stand for the transcendent and eternal, and it has also very often been credited with magical or supernatural powers.[2]

Some strands of this tradition are traceable especially to Egyptian origins. Writing was key to the arts of magic through which the Egyptian god Thoth maintained the universe. And writing conserved the records by which Thoth judged the dead. In spiritual and mystagogic traditions, more than in rational philosophical traditions, the written character has been thought to contain the innermost essence of the Creation. The letter expresses the principles of things that regulate and dictate their interactions.

Writing, by virtue of its visible markers, brings untold mysteries out of the depths of being to the surface to be perceived. Written marks condense an infinite content with unfathomable potency into finite, empirical forms. These forms are deemed to harbor an unmasterable force. That is why attempts are frequently made to manipulate them by various techniques that often verge on sorcery. This temptation seems inevitable once such written signs are seen as inhabited by a divine power that is humanly incalculable – even though inscriptions, nevertheless, remain accessible in their immediate empirical givenness as finite and contingent objects.

Dante does not efface or even attenuate, nay, he rather highlights the contingency of writing – at the same time as he exalts its almighty power and command over the Creation, as well as over History. Dante pays homage to the divine letters, above all, because of their revelation of universal Justice. But this revelation proves to be mediated by the sort of baser, uncontrolled, chaotic elements that are least expected where an incontrovertible vindication of divinity is to be made manifest. This revelation is complicated by many folds, and even by tearings, that let the other side of revelation as a (for us) unmasterable chaos show through. These aspects of Dante's vision will be evidenced and minutely scrutinized in this chapter, but we need first to look at the whole picture as Dante sees it.

---

[2] Extensive documentation for this superior status of writing in the Christian Middle Ages is provided by Jean-Claude Schmitt, *Le corps des images: Essais sur la culture visuelle au Moyen Âge* (Paris: Gallimard, 2002), especially "Écriture et image," 97–134.

The Central Vision and Its Differential Grammar

The representation of writing and its constitutive differences or "parts" actually makes up the thematic core of Dante's vision of Scripture as theophany in the Heaven of Jove. In relation to this core vision of writing, the motifs exfoliated up to this point reveal themselves as preliminary and propaedeutic. Among the elaborate preliminaries, the finely wrought epic similes that frame the vision (lines 58–60: "E come, per sentir più dilettanza . . ."; 73–75: "E come augelli . . .") contribute to a momentous build-up of dramatic intensity. A similar effect is achieved also by the invocation "O diva Pagasea" that decomposes a classical poetic divine name into an adjectival form ("diva" or divine) and a mythic figure (Pagasus) in alluding to the longevity of the glory of both poetic genius and political states ("che li 'ngegni / fai gloriosi e rendili longevi, / ed essi teco le cittadi e' regni," 82–84). This allusion to the traditional aspiration of poetry to eternalize the glory of kings and kingdoms sets up the problematic of mediating between time and eternity. Dante's visionary performance of Scripture is indirectly, yet intimately, concerned with making eternity happen in time and language – and thereby with enabling a transcendent divinity to be somehow experienced.

Riding the crest of these rhetorical embellishments, Dante's fantasy mounts to the main description of his vision of writing with a "dunque," meaning something like "now then," punctuating his transition to the central tableau of the vision itself. At this point, the actual vision of the complete sentence of Scripture in the eighteenth canto of the *Paradiso* is articulated in a surprisingly neutral tone and in plain, fact-stating terms. At this climactic moment, the subjective, affective point of view is muted, blended out, and transcended as the letters show *themselves* to a purely receptive instance of the "me" ("mi"):

> Mostrarsi dunque in cinque volte sette
>   vocali e consonanti; e io notai
>   le parti sì, come mi parver dette.
> "DILIGITE IUSTITIAM" primai
>   fur verbo e nome di tutto 'l dipinto;
>   "QUI IUDICATIS TERRAM" fur sezzai.
> Poscia ne l'emme del vocabol quinto
>   rimasero ordinate; sì che Giove
>   pareva argento lì d'oro distinto.

(XVIII. 88–96)

> (Now then five times seven vowels and consonants
>   showed themselves; and I noted

the parts, even as they appeared to me dictated.
"DILIGITE IUSTITIAM," were first,
the verb and noun of the whole painting;
"QUI IUDICATIS TERRAM" were the last.
Then in the M of the fifth word
the souls remained arranged; so that Jove
appeared there to be silver chased with gold.)

The primary emphasis in this spectacular display of Holy Writ in the heavens falls, first, on its being made up out of letters. This "literal" content of the vision, moreover, enfolds metaphorically a certain appearance as painting, or more specifically as manuscript illumination. The ambiguous significance of this painting metaphor goes all the way back in tradition to Plato's *Phaedrus*, already evoked in Chapter 1. Painting is ambiguously thing-like, yet also intentional – an external medium and yet, in this instance, a perfect rendition of the Mind of God. Furthermore, beyond simply conveying an idea, writing becomes here a visible spectacle, literally letters "painted" in the sky. Each letter takes on a certain substantial thickness, the opacity of a physical object absorbing vision.

The pictorial verve and audacity of this vision, which is literally made up out of letters that then become a painting ("dipinto") metaphorically, can be felt to be in tension with the prosaic articulation of the description in precise and perhaps even somewhat pedantic grammatical terms. We cannot but be struck by the analytical exactness and technical precision that Dante brings to this description of the inspired words of Wisdom even in the ecstatic throes of this literally flaming blaze of a celestial theophany. His attention to the mechanics of grammar, vowels and consonants, noun and verb, is conspicuous and meticulous in this otherwise overtly splashy, showy scene featuring giant letters broad-brushed over the canvas of the heaven.

The scene has been singled out by critics like Pertile, for instance, as "one of the most stupefying events in the whole poem."[3] It has been treated by John Freccero as "perhaps the most daring of all the sequences in the poem."[4] Anna Maria Chiavacci Leonardi designates its invocation as the most impassioned in the poem.[5] Yet even in the ecstasy of his visionary intensity, Dante notes down in a curious, perhaps even incongruous, way

---

[3] The phrase, "uno degli eventi più sbalorditivi di tutto il poema," is quoted from Lino Pertile, "*Paradiso* XVIII tra autobiografia e scrittura sacra," *Dante Studies* 109 (1991): 38.
[4] John Freccero, *Dante: The Poetics of Conversion*, ed. Rachel Jacoff (Cambridge: Harvard University Press, 1986), 213.
[5] Dante Alighieri, *Paradiso*, ed. Anna Maria Chiavacci Leonardi (Milan: Mondadori, 1997), 511.

what in the grammar class are called the "parts of speech" ("Partis orationis"). His own text, perhaps even somewhat awkwardly, describes the
language he observes as "le parti sì, come mi parver dette" ("the parts
such as they appeared to me spoken"). Scripture, the Word of God, is thus
disassembled into the separate letters of the vision, which are analyzed into
conventional grammatical categories.

The language of revelation would seem *prima facie* to lend itself to being
understood as simultaneous presence, a flash of lightning in which all is
immediately apparent and manifest. Indeed, just such imagery is also
employed intensively by Dante, signally for his "final" vision in "un
folgore" ("a lightning bolt") before he loses consciousness at the end of
his journey. But already this scene in Jove is as ostentatiously flashy as any
in the poem. Nevertheless, in this vision of Scripture in the Heaven of Jove,
which serves as dress rehearsal for the final vision, Dante perceives language
rather as an ensemble of parts in the manner – and using the terms –
specifically of grammatical analysis.

Why does Dante see this Scriptural phrase as a composite of noun and
verb, vowel and consonant, five times seven *letters*? To what exactly is he
drawing attention? And what does this imply about the language in which
revelation is communicated? What, for instance, does this visual dissection
into parts imply about the representation of God's absolute simplicity and
unity? Divine unity is manifest in this theophany as a *multiplicity* of
chaotically jostling sparks. It is crystallized through *different* parts of speech
divided into series of binary opposites. In addition to the grammatical
categories of noun and verb, vowel and consonant, the theme-sentence
itself is deliberately divided into two contrasting components, first ("primai") a main clause (DILIGITE IUSTITIAM) and then, finally, or "at
last" ("sezzai"), a relative clause beginning with "who" (QUI IUDICATIS
TERRAM). Intercalated, descriptive verbiage separates the two parts. This
serves to render more perceptible their different grammatical functions and
so to coordinate them. Moreover, the numerical binary of five times
seven – together with the contrastive color scheme of gold and silver –
reinforces the principle that only binary pairs constituted by significant
differences, not positive terms or attributes as such, can be perceived.

This sort of parceled perception in terms of binary oppositions is all the
more provocative because it is conjoined with a visionary immediacy and
wholeness ("tutto 'l dipinto" – "the whole painting") flaunted as something spectacular in the scene that Dante contemplates. Notwithstanding
the rapturous transport of this epiphany, Dante relentlessly insists on how
speech is broken up into "parts" in the line from Scripture that he views.

And these parts are described from a specifically grammatical point of view. Dante's description evidently brings out a systematic patterning by means of formal distinctions parsed in accordance with the grammatically codified "parts of speech." Language is taken no longer simply as an indivisible whole – at least not in its phenomenological appearance and mode of presentation.

In this visionary grammatical anatomy, Dante brings to the visual surface the deep structures of mediation by which language generates unified meaning. He grants us to look upon language's mediating mechanisms articulation of vowel by consonant, predication of subject by verb, qualification of statement by relative clause) as themselves immediate objects of vision. The means by which language mediates meaning are presented here as objects in their own right, as discernible and meaningful components of the vision. Scripture is presented – and is even put on display – in its articulation into the parts of speech by which its sense is generated. This anatomy of language, and specifically of writing, places under a magnifying glass its structures of mediation and offers them up as objects of vision, as immediate presences. Rather than remaining only subterranean, invisible meaning-producing operations, these grammatical functions are themselves exhibited as the contents of the vision – expressly through their technical grammatical names. What Dante's vision of God in the heaven of Jupiter purports to present directly and concretely, then, is a vision of the occult mediations by which language mysteriously produces meaning. At least, by naming them, it calls attention to the grammatical structures and operations through which language functions to create meaning and through which we experience meaning when we read or speak.

Speculative grammar in Dante's day (as we will see in Chapter 4) was engaged in probing how language works to bring unified sense out of its structurally diverse components and even out of its constitutive material elements. Dante brings its terms and concepts into the visible focus of the events in heaven related by his narrative. These terms are valid still, in certain basics, for modern structural linguistics. As Ferdinand de Saussure was to show with scientific exactitude in seminal formulations in his *Cours de linguistique générale* (1916), binary opposition is the underlying structure by which linguistic sense is produced. In fact, this is exactly how Dante presents language in his vision – as a series of binary oppositions.

The mediating structures are, in effect, examined by Dante in the light of linguistic and grammatical theory for what they reveal about the nature of divinity in its possibility of being manifest to us in and through language. To see divinity in action in and through linguistic mediation entails a strong statement in favor of a manner of seeing God that departs from traditional substance metaphysics narrowly conceived. God is perceived, instead, in and as mediation such as it is performed by language and particularly by the grammar of writing. This suggests that we might do best to try to see God, not so much in himself, or as a separate entity, but rather in and through the worldly mediations in which we and our understanding are inextricably immersed especially by virtue of our immersion in language. God is everywhere present in our always mediated perception of the universe, but this divine presence is discernible to us only, in some sense, as "writing."

Structuralist and post-structuralist understandings of language help to sharpen this type of insight into the differential nature of (linguistically produced) meaning (Excursus II). These theories stress that meaning arises from difference – from the differences of reciprocally defined terms – and has no positive existence as a discrete entity or pure presence. Meaning is found always only in mediations of meaning and never becomes directly present as such.

Grammar analyzes language into parts and disperses its sense into a system of differences. Only through the mutual mediation of such coordinated, differential terms as noun and verb, or consonant and vowel, is unified meaning engendered. Speculative grammar was the avant-garde linguistic theory of Dante's own time and is comparable, in certain respects, to the more recent (post-)structuralist linguistics. Like structuralist linguistics, speculative grammar abstracts from concrete elements as meaningful in themselves and derives meaning from formal differentials within a system. Yet Dante wishes at the same time to affirm a transcendent unity of sense in a manifest Presence. For this purpose, he uses the figure of the immediacy of "vision." He also seems at times to evoke something like a Kabbalistic view of language as possessing magical energies. There is an immediate, sensible music vibrating in the letters themselves, each of which is literally, and visibly, dancing or "moving to its note" ("a sua nota moviensi").

Writing is projected by Dante in this heaven as a higher immediacy, an even more immediate revelation than discursive speech, one that nevertheless turns out paradoxically to consist in, and to reveal, nothing but *mediation*. At the core of his vision of writing, Dante concretely envisages not just the reified form or image of the letter but the mediating activity of the basic grammatical structures of language – noun and verb, vowel and consonant, main statement and relative clause. What is explicitly envisioned is not even directly an actual activity of mediation so much as the differential structures that are at work in such mediation and in its generation of significance. Not the concrete visible presence, but the invisibility of a system of differences is revealed thereby as the generating source of the significances displayed in the heaven and as signifying the presence of "the love that was there."

The principles of this differential production of meaning that are operative in Dante's vision need to be placed into the frame of speculative grammar and, furthermore, of a negative theology in order to approach Dante's medieval understanding of them, as well as their broader cultural significance in later ages, including our own. Negative or apophatic theology reminds us that none of the poem's representations are adequate to represent God.[6] These representations signify, rather, what they *cannot* represent. The divine source of all meaning is itself a perfect unity; however, it cannot be grasped as such. It can be apprehended and expressed only through its *difference* from everything that *can* be comprehended and expressed.

The image of random sparks rising up helter-skelter from a burning firebrand when struck (XVIII. 100–2) serves Dante to encapsulate the radically contingent nature of the composition of the souls into the order of letters blazoning a providential significance. The incomprehensibility of this vision to human understanding emerges as the *sine qua non* of truly divine revelation and becomes a key for discerning divine providence. Reading Dante's *Paradiso* as a negative poetics that mirrors and is based on negative theology inscribes him into medieval traditions, but it also projects him forward to the negative literary-critical and philosophical analogues of negative theology in our own time.[7]

In this connection, it proves illuminating to remember that traditions of negative theology are a crucial matrix for the thought of Derrida, Blanchot, Foucault, Irigaray, Cixous, and others among the thinkers of difference whose reflections have enriched our contemporary consciousness of the philosophical and theological underpinnings of writing as *écriture*.[8] An often surreptitious sensibility for negative theology forms a vital link that binds us as postmoderns to Dante's premodern vision of the otherness in excess of human making, in which he recognizes the mysterious movement of divinity.

---

[6] Marco Ariani, *Lux inaccessibilis: Metafore e teologia della luce nel Paradiso di Dante* (Rome: Aracne, 2010), presents a formidable digest of this background in mystic or apophatic theology, most specifically in the tradition of the *Corpus Dionysiacum* or *Corpus Areopagiticum*.

[7] See my *On What Cannot Be Said: Apophatic Discourses in Philosophy, Religion, Literature, and the Arts* (Notre Dame: University of Notre Dame Press, 2007), vol. 2: "Modern and Contemporary Transformations."

[8] Graham Ward, *Theology and Contemporary Critical Theory* (New York: Macmillan, 2000) effectively brings out theological subtexts (what I call "theo-logics") of postmodern theological discourses.

However, Dante embraces the ideal of a truth that requires our attempting to envision things as a whole, an ideal that is often attacked and may seem scarcely tenable in the intellectual climate of postmodernism. Still, it is as language, and on the model of language as system, which was revived, in ways still compelling for us, especially by Saussure, that Dante envisions this ideal. Language is always inhabited by latencies. It speaks whatever it speaks only on the basis of the *unsaid*. This unsaid, which dwells in any saying, comprises the rest of language that conditions and contextualizes any given enunciation within the whole of language. Dante's idea of universal order, because it is essentially linguistic, is also essentially conditioned by the unsayable and remains *negative* in character. *Paradiso* constantly recalls this by incessantly recurring to the ineffability topos. Linguistic negativity, furthermore, demands to be understood in terms of the apophatic theology that our own time has radically renewed.[9]

Ineffability is certainly not peculiar to the *Paradiso*, although it takes on there a peculiarly penetrating theological urgency and radicality. The *Inferno* and *Purgatorio* have their moments of impasse to speech, and ineffability characterizes a fundamental aspect of the experience of Beatrice starting from the *Vita nuova* (III. 1, XLII. 1, etc.). Dante had already established a doctrine of "two ineffabilities" – of thought and of language, of concept and word – in the *Convivio* (III. iii. 14–15 and III. iv. 1–8). His poetry of love – for wisdom, Philosophy, the daughter of the Ruler of the universe – stands already under the sign of the ineffable. His theosophical poetry leads Dante to the limits of the expressible, where he is forced to resort to a diacritical approach to divinity through writing.

Signifying the Ineffable Other and Its Differential Logic

To the extent that language signifies by difference, it cannot be understood except by being broken down into parts. The possibility of language's having significance originates with and from the differences between consonant and vowel, noun and verb, and so on, as an abbreviated way of alluding to all manner of significant binary oppositions. This is why, in our effort to sound the significance of grammatical analysis in Dante's vision of writing, we are obliged to consider the paradigm of language as a differential structure and system. This model has been developed into

---

[9] I outline this renewal in a number of publications already cited, but I advocate it as urgently needed to address our current dilemmas in areas ranging from the canon crisis and identity politics to intercultural philosophy and cognitive science in *On the Universality of What Is Not: The Apophatic Turn in Critical Thinking* (Notre Dame: University of Notre Dame Press, 2020).

a comprehensive theory in modern times, but it already registers its paramount importance in Dante's descriptions, even if in what appears to be an inchoate form.

Indeed, the creation of a system of differences for purposes of signifying an ideality and absolute unity without difference, namely, God, is what happens in various ways in each of the heavens that make up the *Paradiso*. The entire work is based on a principle of hierarchical differentiation and gradation that binds differences into unifying structures. This feature of Dante's poem may seem to evince merely a passion for typological distinctions and classificatory schemas, but more deeply considered this absolute hierarchy, modeled on the Dionysian celestial hierarchy, expresses a metaphysical principle. If God is the only ultimate reality, and all else has being or reality only thanks to its relation to this one true Being, then only difference enables apprehension of this Being, which in its own proper nature is simple and, as such, inconceivable.

From its opening vision, the poem's leading theme is that of unity in diversity, of God's glory penetrating more or less in one part of the universe or another ("La gloria di colui che tutto move / per l'universo penetra e risplende / in una parte più e meno altrove," I. 1–3). The *cantica*'s overarching problem is that of how to represent or signify a reality that in and of itself is without difference, when signification works only on the basis of difference – as Dante and medieval semiology generally were well aware. What in reality is a seamless whole without difference – since the Being of God rigorously excludes difference – can only be represented as nothing but a play of differences. This is the general paradoxical predicament of representation of absolute reality, which absolutely repels representation, and it riddles this theological poet's work in every word.[10]

In effect, then, Dante takes writing in the sense of a divine *Logos*, the Word totally one with itself and self-present in the Trinity and still unified by one sense in Scripture, and he re-presents it as writing in the guise of a play of differences. The differences are not only between the letters punctuated each by a temporal interval, as remarked already in the preliminary generalized description: "*now* D, *now* I, *now* L ... ." The differences between vowel and consonant, noun and verb, five times seven (the number of the letters), are likewise presented as systems of binary oppositions. There is constant recourse to binary structures of differentiation in

---

[10] The all-important semiological principle of difference guides Jeremy Tambling's reading in *Dante and Difference: Writing in the Commedia* (Cambridge: Cambridge University Press, 1988). Tambling's reading is set up, however, I think unnecessarily, in opposition to "the kind of reading that justifies the movement towards unity" (3).

order to establish the whole significance of the scene in the heaven of Jove. Even the color scheme is envisaged as operating on a principle of binary opposition between silver and gold – the gold of the soul-sparks is distinguished against the argent background of Jove ("pareva argento lì d'oro distinto," XVIII. 96). This metaphorical reference to an illuminated manuscript again structures the pictorial/written phenomena that Dante records in terms of binary distinctions when he describes how he saw the head and neck of an eagle "represented by that *distinct* fire" ("rappresentare a quel *distinto* foco," XVIII. 108).

Fire, the element of Heraclitean flux, and the active element of this heaven imagined as a jovial "facella" ("torch"), becomes representable only by virtue of the difference introduced by the shining souls against the background of the firmament. The silver of the heaven's ground-tint in coordination with the gold of the souls' fire together articulate a perceptible field and figure, not to mention a significant sight replete with symbolic suggestions. The color scheme further suggests a richly ornate illuminated manuscript.

The constant operation of differentially engendered significance is presupposed by Dante's art as poet even at the purely phonetic level. Light and dark vowels make up a binary system that Dante can exploit to create meaningful sound patterns, as in a pair of lines such as

> Poi, come nel percuoter d'i ciocchi arsi
> surgono innumerabili faville,
>
> (XVIII. 100–2)

> (Then, as in the beating of burnt brands,
> numberless sparks spring up,)

The heavy, thudding "o"s and "u"s with "r"s of "percuoter" and "surgono" are contrastively brightened by sprightly, acute "i"s in quick succession in "i ciocchi arsi" and ". . .-abili faville." The blunt beating of the brands and the nimble darting and springing of the sparks signify oppositionally, and in this way the signifiers are made to parallel the contrasting quality of their respective signifieds: blazing fire versus bulky lumber.

This principle of differential signification is adumbrated and embraced near the beginning of the *cantica* in a passage that defines the general principles of the *Paradiso*'s poetics. This passage in *Paradiso* III is set up as parallel to those in *Inferno* III. 1–12 and *Purgatorio* III. 13–51 defining each cantica's respective poetics. In his description of the first appearances to him of the blessed in heaven, Dante limns the images of soul lights appearing in the "star" (the moon) as a nearly vanishing difference in color tone between pearl and white:

debili sì, che perla in bianca fronte
non vien men forte a le nostre pupille

(III. 14–15)

(so weak that pearl on a white forehead
does not strike our pupils more)

This difference, attenuated practically to the point of being extin-guished, embodies the principle of binary opposition in a limit-case of minimally perceptible difference. Beyond this threshold, where difference is erased completely, language disappears. Precisely that effacement is the prerequisite for an apophatic experience of the "beyond" of language. In the poem as a whole, and shifting from a visual to an auditory register, this is the experience of silence so often celebrated by poets and zeroed in on by Dante at moments through his mystical poetics of ineffability. A crucial figure for what lies beyond language as order and intelligibility, one that Dante uses to spectacular effect in this heaven, is that of contingency.

Contingency as Manifestation of the Non-manifest and as Revelation of Unrepresentable Transcendence

Dante witnesses to the letters as a transcendent presence, the embodiment and sign of a divine order: they reveal to him a providential justice reigning in the universe. But this cannot be seen in the letters except, paradoxically, by their contingency (their not *needing* to be) and even, finally, by their vanishing altogether (their not being at all). The order of language, in the case of divine speech, should presumably be flawless and all encompassing. It should be one systematic order governed by strict necessity, since the divine will is supposed to be without chance or arbitrariness. Dante is constantly at pains to empha-size just this about God's order in the other world, for example, in Statius's explanation that nothing happens without divine order on the mountain of Purgatory ("Cosa non è che sanza / ordine senta la religione della montagna," *Purgatorio* XXI. 40–45). Thus, the realm of the saved, even in Purgatory, is said by Statius to lie outside the range of contingency. But especially in heaven and in the Empyrean, there is literally no place for contingency:

Dentro a l'ampiezza de questo reame
   casüal punto non puote aver sito,
   se non come tristizia o sete o fame:
ché per etterna legge è stabilito
   quantunque vedi, sì che giustamente
   ci si risponde da l'anello al dito;

> e però questa festinata gente
>   a vera vita non è *sine causa*
> intra sé qui più e meno eccellente.
>
>   (*Paradiso* XXXII. 52–60)

(Within the largeness of this realm
   there is no place for an effect of chance,
   any more than for sadness or thirst or hunger:
since eternal law establishes
   whatever you see here, so exactly
   that it fits like the ring on the finger;
and thus this early-arriving folk
   in the true life are, not without cause [*sine causa*],
   more or less excellent among themselves.)

The souls in Paradise are ranged in ranks of differentiated degrees of merited blessedness. Similarly, as manifestations of divine presence, the letters represent perfect order. Yet the principle of this divine order and presence exceeds our comprehension. Consequently, it appears to us as randomness. Dante unveils the display to be, at least to our perception, pure contingency. It is not by realizing any formulas of order, but only by abandoning itself to indeterminacy and errancy in writing, that the divine can be made manifest in its transcendence.

Contingency functions thus as the negative or anti-image of a divine order that cannot be represented in its totality because it exceeds every finite structure. In other words, contingency indicates that the principle that orders the universe according to justice really transcends human comprehension. This will become explicitly the theme of the ensuing cantos XIX–XX of the Heaven of Jove, the heaven of justice. Only where no stated or discernible ordering principle seems to be operative, and therefore where there is no supreme law susceptible of being objectively represented, can the invisible divine principle or order that nevertheless miraculously governs and holds the universe together be inferred to exist.

Contingency here becomes the sign of an order that transcends every recognizable rational principle or objectifiable rule that could comprehend it. What happens apparently by chance (*casu*) is taken as a sign of providence already by Augustine in his *Confessions* and by Boethius in his *Consolation*, to cite two indispensable models for Dante. In Book VIII, Augustine's providential conversion is placed under the sign of a series of chance occurrences beginning with a visit from one Ponticianus and his sighting by chance (*forte*) a volume of Paul's epistles. What is implicit in Augustine's narrative is made explicit in Boethius's philosophical lesson.

Lady Philosophy teaches Boethius that there is no such thing as absolute chance ("nihil omnino casum esse confirmo"), since divine providence foresees everything. Things appear to happen by chance only because we ignore their causes (*De consolatione* V. 1).

A further important anthropological background for Dante's representations are practices of divination based on consulting apparently random phenomena. A prolonged historical purview shows the extent to which representing rationality of a higher nature as deriving from divinity has always resorted to modalities of chance as practiced in the mantic arts and methods of interpreting events and determining judgment. Decisions concerning war and peace, election of officials, verdicts in jurisprudence, etc., in myriad institutional forms, have since antiquity relied on chance – presumably guided from above – to discern the truth, act propitiously, and do justice.

In this perspective, Wolfram Hogrebe has extensively researched the mantic origin and foundations of philosophy and jusrisprudence alike.[11] This angle of vision helps us to realize how firmly ensconsed Dante's sense of divine revelation through contingency is in millenary institutions of Western cultures. Comparable practices register equally in Eastern cultures, for example, in the Vedas and in Daoist classics. Dante explicitly appeals to divinatory techniques in *Monarchia* II. ix, where he presents trial by duel (*duellum*) as a divinely sanctioned method for resolving disputes between conflicting earthly authorities, particularly princes and peoples vying for empire. Such chancy combats allow providence to determine the outcome.

In the passage under examination, Dante maintains that this revelation of the transcendent in the contingent transpires through God's writing in the heaven, and perhaps also through his own writing in the *Paradiso*, which is itself flagged as determined by random chance and fortuitous felicities of speech right from the pun on "jovial" in the opening line. This is quite a leap from Dante's earlier mortal terror of contingency in Purgatory, for example, when the mountain trembles and shakes his belief that the world is fully under the sway of divine order:

> quand' io senti', come cosa cada,
>   tremar lo monte; onde mi prese un gelo
>   qual prender suol colui ch'a morte vada.
>
> (*Purgatorio* XX. 127–29)

[11] Wolfram Hogrebe, *Metaphysik und Mantik: Die Deutungsnatur des Menschen*, 2nd rev. ed. (Berlin: Akademie Verlag, 2013).

(when I felt, like a thing that falls,
   the mountain shake; whence I was taken with a chill
   like what usually takes one who goes to his death.)

Momentarily, Dante is in the death throes of doubt that contingency might infiltrate even this world of the saved, or that God and the Good might *not*, after all, have everything under control and in perfect order. Our life would then be tragically abandoned to evil vicissitudes of history such as had perplexed, notably, Boethius before him – at least, before Boethius received the reassurances of rational instruction from Lady Philosophy. Dante is so terrified that Statius's exhaustive explanation of the non-natural cause of the earthquake (*Purgatorio* XXI. 40–45, cited above, p. 99) needs to be brought forth to tranquilize him and exorcise the spectre of contingency in this realm of the saved – saved, above all, from contingency. Nevertheless, contingency (to all appearances and, in any case, to us) turns up in heaven all the more stubbornly irrepressible – now as inseparable from the life and manifestation of the divine itself.

Dante uses writing to realize his theophany of the Word of God. This makes sense against the background of the fetishistic exaltation of the letter in Bible traditions such as the Kabbalah. Yet he is passionately interested in writing not only as an object, but also as his own medium in the poem. The realization of revelation actually occurs in its being broken down into the materiality and contingency of its medium. It is *as writing* that the divine is made manifest, but this impossible representation implicitly admits that divine transcendence remains beyond all manifest form and order. The manifestation in question is, at the same time, the demonstration of the impossibility of manifestation (of God as object). In an analogous form of the same paradox, time in its disappearing is the only manifestation of the ever-present eternity, which is itself beyond representation, as Augustine realized profoundly (Excursus III).

Dante's writing performs a total mediation of its transcendent sense by the immediately manifest medium of the poem. Yet this results not in circumscribing the divine as object of the poem. Instead, this mediation points towards what lies still outside it. The writing's own porousness and inadequacy is obsessively pointed out and dwelt on by Dante in countless forms of declared ineffability. Transcendent order and sheer contingency mediate each other reciprocally and totally, so that contingency is taken up entirely into order at the level of representation – becoming its manifestation and even incarnation. Still, at the same time, the poem acknowledges that no order, however perfect, can be any more than an arbitrary representation of something that remains in itself quite beyond representation. All representation is contingent in the face of the Unrepresentable. Dante's images of total mediation in the letter come to pass and pass away – and thereby gesture toward the Unmediated, the Unconditioned.

The Redemption of Contingency through the Artistic Medium

The concern with contingency is a major preoccupation of Dante throughout the *Comedy* and serves as a structural axis of the poem. This concern runs also all through Karlheinz Stierle's essays in *The Great Sea of Sense: Hermeneutic Explorations in Dante's Commedia.*[12] In chapter 4 on "The Horror of Contingency" ("Der Schrecken der Kontingenz"), Stierle traces Dante's "suspicion of contingency" ("Kontingenzverdacht") from the beginning to the end particularly of the *Paradiso*. Stierle begins from Aldo Vallone's observation that "the reign of doubt is proper to the *Paradiso*" ("Il regno del dubbio è proprio del *Paradiso*").[13] Dante's unallayable doubts become a force that actually propels him through the successive heavens. Dante questions whether the universe is perfectly under God's control or not and doubts whether it might not rather be subject, in the end, to contingency. What is more, he worries about this increasingly as he goes higher. Contrary to what one might expect, the closer he comes to God, the more doubtful Dante becomes. For Stierle, the poem builds up to the protagonist's finally losing himself in the absolute indeterminacy of the divine: humans are thereby left behind in utter incomprehension (102–19). This constitutes a sort of apotheosis of doubt, or at least of unknowing.

Stierle finds the signature of Dante's modernity in his persistent, or at least recurrent, impulse to skeptical doubting. Dante's doubting witnesses to his recognition of uncertainty and his lack of an assured rational grasp of the ultimate principle of reality. Stierle considers the presumed hierarchical ordering of the universe to be called into question continually by Dante's poem: "The 'more or less' of the divine order does not ground Dante's poetics; these poetics, instead, unfold in unforeseeable movements, in a language of the depth of Being, which withdraws from every dogmatic fixation" ("Das 'mehr oder weniger' der göttlichen Ordnung begründet

---

[12] Karlheinz Stierle, *Das große Meer des Sinns: Hermeneutische Erkundungen in Dantes "Commedia"* (Munich: Fink, 2007).

[13] Aldo Vallone, "Paradiso III," *Studi Danteschi* LXII (1990): 69–83 (citation 77), cited by Stierle (267).

nicht die Dantesche Poetik, die sich stattdessen in unvorhersehbaren
Bewegungen entfaltet, in einer Sprache der Tiefe des Seins, die sich jeder
dogmatischen Fixierung entzieht," 281).

As crucial as this is, I would underscore, nevertheless, that the dynamism
of doubting belongs also to Dante's access to the realm of perfect peace.
Such doubt is not a contradiction so much as an enabling condition of
imagining its own quelling.

Stierle reads Dante as having a modern sense of fear of ultimate ground-
lessness, as made manifest already in the opening scene, where the protagonist is lost in a forest and very near to committing suicide. He is in despair
because "the world in its entirety could have no sense at all" ("daß die Welt
in ihrer Ganzheit keinen Sinn haben könnte," 262–63). Stierle allows,
nevertheless, that, for Dante, contingency is overcome through poetry,
where nothing is purely contingent, where the severance of signifier and
signified is healed, for instance, by rhyme, in which sound and sense
coalesce. Dante would thus fulfill the impossible dream of which
Mallarmé had despaired, with his declaration that "A throw of the dice
will never abolish chance" ("Un coup de dés jamais n'abolira le hasard").
According to the reading that I propose in these pages, Dante would have
already answered Mallarmé. In effect, Dante shows that *only* – and precisely – through a throw of the dice (or of contingent sparks) can chance (or
disorder in human experience) be overcome.

Arthur Rimbaud, another poetic visionary sojourning in Hell, would
eventually write, "I ended up finding the disorder of my mind sacred" ("Je
finis par trouver sacré le désordre de mon esprit," "Délires II, Alchimie du
verb," *Une saison en enfer*).[14] Upping the ante, Dante finds even in Paradise
what to his mind appears as total disorder to be a sign of the sacred.

The scene of skywriting in Jove suggests that, at bottom, the entire order
of nature can be apprehended by us only as chance – as contemporary
science corroborates through its theories of chaos and complexity.
Historically also, science continually confirms this through the inevitable
collapse of all its paradigms, along with the semblance of the orders they
project, as is famously demonstrated by Thomas Kuhn in *The Structure of
Scientific Revolutions* (1962).

Dante generally designates matter as resistant to artistic purpose and as
recalcitrant to the ideal form or "seal of ideality" ("segno / idëale," XIII.
68–69) that divinity would ideally give to nature and that the poem would
confer upon language as its matter. This idea is molded basically on the

[14] Rimbaud, *Poésies* (Paris: Bookking International, 1993), 135.

prototype of the *Timaeus*. Plato represents creation as a struggle between intelligence or reason (*nous*) and necessity (*ananké*), crystalized in matter. He explains the world's malfunction as due to the influence of a further factor, which takes "the form of an errant or variable cause" (τὸ τῆς πλανωμένης εἶδος αἰτίας), or chance (48a).

However, escaping from such outside influences, the art of poetry can make its own matter – or can at least make its matter its own: it can *re*make its medium in its own image. Stierle argues that "poetry can absorb even the materiality of writing as its medium into the play of the poetic feigning of language" ("Aber auch die mediale Materialität der Schrift wird in das Spiel der poetischen Einbildung einbezogen," 211). Although the linguistic matter of the poem may never be completely pliant and subject to the poet's intention, Dante makes "the materiality of language fully present as poetic actuality" ("Materialität ganz in poetische Aktualität aufgeht," 219), which is a way of appropriating and, to this extent, neutralizing its contingency.

Stierle shows how, especially as hinted by the rhyme scheme *viso – riso – paradiso* (look – laugh – paradise), Dante's eroticized gazing upon Beatrice, with her eyes and smile, becomes itself identical with paradise. This suggests powerfully how Dante's experience of God, to whom Beatrice constantly directs and refers him, is in continuity with his erotic experience and ultimately not to be separated from it. When Dante experiences Beatrice's smile again, after ten years of privation, he celebrates the glorious and blessed beauty of a saint in heaven, with her "holy eyes" ("li occhi santi," *Purgatorio* XXXI. 133), whose light is eternal and divine splendor ("O isplendor di viva luce etterna," XXXI. 139). Still, however, Dante's own eyes again *happen* to be caught by Beatrice's smile in the *trap* of erotic passion: "thus the sacred smile" ("così lo santo riso") "drew him in with the ancient net!" ("a sé traéli con l'antica rete!," XXXII. 5–6).

Containing contingency, by which he is here again overtaken, is detected by Stierle as the driving preoccupation of the whole poem. Dante becomes increasingly captured by contingency as he mounts higher through Paradise. Contingency is the source of Dante's primordial fear and of the questions that give rise to the action and exposition alike from beginning to end. This is a sign of Dante's modernity.[15] Not unlike Mallarmé's "maître" ("master"), who hurls himself into, and is engulfed

---

[15] In the concluding remarks of his exhaustive study of the question, Albert Russell Ascoli, *Dante and the Making of a Modern Author* (Cambridge: Cambridge University Press, 2008), 402–5, emphasizes the "radical contingency" of Dante's construction of himself as author, or more exactly "poeta," and therewith its anticipation of modern, secular, and Petrarchan models.

by, the unmasterable sea (*Un coup de dés*, IV), Dante masters chance artistically not by excluding or depotentiating it, but rather by embracing it in its full force, without constraint or limit. Random chance is inscribed into the revelation of Scripture in Dante's vision as the signature of a providential purpose and power.

Dante's portrait, in *Inferno* VII, of *Fortuna* as a minister of divine providence already prefigures this original and paradoxical solution to dealing with contingency. Dante absorbs contingency by not resisting it but rather by throwing his poem and his language open to it. Paradoxically, contingency itself (for humans) becomes the revelation of God and of his providential mastery throughout the universe. The very opposition between contingency and divinely directed purpose is broken down. In *Paradiso* XVIII, the mediation (letters) becomes itself the im-mediate (the divine vision). The conceptual opposition between the two is overcome and flips over into a synergism in Dante's actual engagement with the specifics of the making of poetry. The same thing happens in our inextricable involvements in actual living, in which means and ends tend to become mixed up – to subvert and short-circuit each other – and fuse together.

Stierle pays attention especially to Dante's reflection on the way the medium conditions his art ("ihre medialen Bedingungen," 180) in *Purgatorio*.[16] Just as Purgatory is a temporal and transitional realm to be transcended, so the arts that this canticle concentrates on are likewise mere heuristic forms that serve for human development and purification especially in being transcended. Stierle characterizes Dante's art as a "transcending in act" and finds this to be the source of art's new dignity in Dante's work ("auch die Kunst ist in eigener und anderer Weise ein transcendere in actu. Gerade dies gibt ihr bei Dante ihr neue Dignität," 193). Different artistic means and media are all exploited for all that they are worth. Precisely their status as media, and thus as mediators, their "mediale Logik," enables the arts to afford an anticipation of completion and perfection ("Vollkomenheit") in another world or life.

Dante discovers in the *Paradiso* that to keep pursuing his journey in a poetic form he has no choice but to turn his attention back self-reflexively upon his own medium. Divinity offers him no other matter on which to work. Consequently, he has to negate the very medium of his art in order to make his way into the transcendent world. This other world cannot be presented as such, not even by the most ingenious of artistic inventions

---

[16] *Das große Meer des Sinns*, chapter 6: "Das System der schönen Künste im *Purgatorio*."

imaginable. The medium of Dante's art becomes crucial as the material of the negation that enables him to continue to signify, albeit negatively, his experience of Paradise. This means, furthermore, that his experience of Paradise is constantly at risk of being confounded with an experience of art, however much art, in theory, is transcended at this stage. Still, an ineliminable gap remains, for Dante, between art and religion, between "aesthetics" and "faith."[17] Dante achieves his vision of God in writing only by dissolving and transcending his artistic means. He dissolves and transcends these means through an absolute focus on them. Such is the symbolic and sacramental significance of "writing" as a concrete presence or signifier of an absent signified that, in this case, is specifically the unlimited signified "God."

The art of grammar was deemed by Dante to be the science par excellence through which chance in language could be mastered and brought under rational rule. Thus, grammar features centrally in Dante's vision of justice in this heaven and in its self-reflexive contemplation of poetic language as its medium. Just this highlighting of grammar, however, shows up the final inadequacy of all rational means and instruments of mediation: it turns them, instead, into elements of, and occasions for, immediate vision, which alone can convey an authentic sense of the divine. The next chapter follows grammar to speculative heights that finally transcend the grammatical point of view altogether.

---

[17] Giuseppe Mazzotta, "Literature and Religion: The Error of Narcissus," *Religion & Literature* 41/ 2 (2009): 29–35.

CHAPTER 4

From Speculative Grammar to Visual Spectacle and Beyond

The Grammatical Vision of Language Culminating in Speculative Grammar

The grammatical description of language betrays certain far-reaching and revealing biases that are built into Dante's vision of Scripture in the Heaven of Jupiter. For the discipline of grammar in the Middle Ages, although certainly diversified by Dante's time, nevertheless entailed a determinable intellectual outlook.[1] The development of grammatical study in the centuries leading up to and including Dante's lifetime had focused on progressively greater theoretical understanding of language in its global order. The twelfth-century Scholastic author William of Conches complained against Priscian, the fifth- to sixth-century grammarian who remained the principal source and authority on grammar throughout medieval tradition, that "he had neglected to deal with the causal basis of the various parts of speech and their accidents" ("causas vero inventionis diversarum partium et diversorum accidentorum . . . praemetterit").[2]

By Dante's day, a new kind of inquiry concentrating on the causes of the differentiation and invention of the parts of speech was coming into full swing on the intellectual horizon of university centers in Paris and Bologna. A new interest in the theoretical basis of grammar supplanted the older merely pragmatic approach of the school manuals. The so-called

---

[1] See Aldo Scaglione, "Dante and the Ars Grammatica," in *The Divine Comedy and the Encyclopedia of Arts and Sciences*, ed. G. Di Scipio and A. Scaglione (Amsterdam and Philadelphia: John Benjamins, 1988), 27–41; Paola Feltrin, "Il ruolo della grammatica nell'organizzazione medievale del sapere," *Rivista di storia della filosofia* 40/1 (1985): 159–66; Ermenegildo Bertola, "La Grammatica ed il problema degli universali nel medioevo cristiano," *Rivista di filosofia neo-scolastica* 3 (1994): 491–505; and Giuseppe Mazzotta, *Dante's Vision and the Circle of Knowledge* (Princeton: Princeton University Press, 1992), chapter 2: "Sacrifice and Grammar."

[2] William of Conche, *Glosae super Priscianum* as cited in R. H. Robins, *A Short History of Linguistics* (London: Longmans, 1967), 76.

"speculative grammar" is the most conspicuous, programmatic manifestation of this interest, and Dante's text clearly reflects his fascination with
grammar as a revelation of the structure of thought and of being itself. It is
within the horizon of this intellectual movement that Dante's specifically
grammatical outlook on language and reality develops.[3]

The later Middle Ages saw a flowering of this speculatively grammatical
thinking as elaborated and advocated by the so-called "modistae," who
were distinguished by their analysis of the logical modes of language and
expression.[4] This thinking was nurtured by expositions of a universal
grammar such as Roger Bacon's *Summa Grammatica* (1245). The ground
had been prepared by Peter Helias's commentaries on Priscian (*Summa
super Priscianum*) in the twelfth century that began to apply Aristotle's
rediscovered logic to the art and science of grammar. Aristotle, particularly
in his *De interpretatione*, I, 1, was understood as having postulated a purely
mental language characterized by certain modes of thought as common to
all languages and speakers. A generation or two more of such speculative
grammarians led to the *modistae*, who propounded a universal grammar
reflecting the structure of reality independently of the accidental differences of specific languages. This language of pure thought was supposed to
be the same in the minds of all – "una in tutti," as Dante phrases it in
Paradiso XIV. 88–89, where he describes such a language as being used in
an act of silent devotion or sacrifice consummated in his heart:

> Con tutto 'l core, e con quella favella
> ch'è una in tutti, a Dio feci olocausto
>
> (XIV. 88–89)

> (With whole heart, and with that speech
> that is one in all people, I made sacrifice to God).

Pursuing this insight, the *modistae* proposed a universalizing philosoph-
ical reformulation of the doctrine of the parts of speech inherited from
Priscian, and through him from the Alexandrian grammarians of
Hellenistic Greece in the third and second centuries BCE. Particularly
Boethius of Dacia among the *modistae* has been linked with Dante.[5] This
perspective on language, which integrates the Greek speculative and

---

[3] See Carlo Alessio, "La grammatica speculativa e Dante," *Letture classensi* 13 (1984): 69–88.
[4] G. L. Bursill-Hall, *Speculative Grammars of the Middle Ages: The Doctrine of Partes Orationis of the
Modistae* (The Hague: Mouton, 1971); Jan Pinborg, *Die Entwicklung der Sprachtheorie im Mittelalter*,
2nd ed. (Münster: Aschedorff, 1985); and Rita Copeland and Ineka Sluiter, *Medieval Grammar and
Rhetoric: Language Arts and Literary Theory AD 13–1475* (Oxford: Oxford University Press, 2013).
[5] Maria Corti, *Dante a un nuovo crocevia* (Florence: Sansoni, 1982).

metaphysical tradition, based on Aristotle's *Categories*, with Latin rhetorical theory of the parts of speech, is crystallized also in the works of Siger de Courtrai and Thomas of Erfurt, both of whom wrote speculative grammars in the first half of the fourteenth century. However, already two centuries of ferment had prepared the terrain that nourishes Dante's speculative thinking about grammar. Dante's reformulation turns especially on this thinking's already tense relation with theology.

Marie-Dominique Chenu reconstructs the emergence of the speculative grammar out of conflict between the proponents of classical grammar and theologians whose authority was not Cicero but the Bible.[6] Faced with solecisms in the language of Scripture pointed out by the masters of the arts (*maîtres ès ars*), theologians retorted that the divine Word of the Holy Spirit was not to be subjected to grammatical rules ("Pagina sacra non vult se subdere legi / Grammatices"). The trouvère Henry d'Andeli makes a version of this strife over the authority of grammar the subject of an allegorical epic: "La bataille des sept ars" ("The Battle of the Seven Liberal Arts") staging bitter confrontation between the humanist proponents of grammar at Orléans (William of Auvergne) and the champions of dialectic in Paris (Peter Abelard). Eventually, however, these diverging perspectives became integrated. In the Scholasticism of the universities, where the arts faculties and theological faculties existed side by side, grammatical theory came to be recognized as indispensable for theological speculation. This development laid the groundwork forging the complementarity of grammar and dialectic pursued in the course of the thirteenth century and issuing in the approach of the speculative grammarians. Before all, Roger Bacon is called as witness by Chenu (8).

Particularly the idea that there is a universal grammar, the same for all human beings, although its expressions are variable in historical languages, animates the outlook of the speculative grammarians called *modistae*. This guiding idea still survives today and even thrives, notably in the transformational grammar of Noam Chomsky. However, Chomsky reformulates this insight within the frame of modern subject-based philosophy with its roots in the Enlightenment.[7] As already suggested, in the Middle Ages this outlook was shaped by the development of logic pursuant to the rediscovery of Aristotle's logical works in the eleventh and twelfth centuries. The *modistae* combined this speculative perspective with that of school

---

[6] M. D. Chenu, "Grammaire et théologie aux XIIᵉ et XIIIᵉ siècles," *Archives d'histoire doctrinale et littéraire du Moyen Âge* 10 (1935): 5–28.

[7] This genealogy is laid out by Chomsky in his *Cartesian Linguistics: A Chapter in the History of Rationalist Thought*, 3rd ed. (New York: Cambridge University Press, 2009).

grammar in producing their philosophy of language. Predicated on the universality of human reason, and on the universality of the things in the created universe that all people share in common, a universal language could also be hypothesized, and in part be discerned, as mediating between the mind and the world, even while varying in its vernacular instantiations.

Neither strict realists nor integral nominalists, the *modistae* stressed language's necessary adherence to the reality of things, but at the same time they recognized an irreducible subjective factor at work in setting the world into words. The modes of signifying are not just *figmenta* of the mind: they must have correlatives in the properties of things ("correspondet aliqua proprietas rei seu modus essendi rei").[8] Transmitting the ideas derived through Priscian from the Hellenistic Alexandrian grammarians, and in particular from Dionysius Thrax (first century BCE), the *modistae* also focused on grammar as stabilizing language. This ideal evidently resonates with Dante's model in *Convivio* I. v. 7–8 of Latin as unchanging, thanks to its fixed grammatical rules.

The evolving manners of vernacular speech can serve to throw into relief the unchangingness of the *principles and ideals* embodied in such speech. In fact, in *De vulgari eloquentia*, Dante identifies the universal language not with Latin, but with the ideal vernacular, the *vulgare illustre* that he searches for in vain among the dialects of the Italian cities. It proves, in the end, to be not an empirical language at all but rather an ideal and perhaps in some ways a transcendent language. It belongs to "all Italy" ("totius Italie est," *De vulgari eloquentia* I. xix. 1), and is to be approached through the search for perfection in poetic language conducted by "illustrious" authors in all regions of Italy. Arguably, it exists nowhere as such and as a whole but rather shows through the cracks of human language thanks to Dante's *failures* to express his ineffable experience of God in the *Paradiso*.

Walter Benjamin's speculations in "The Task of the Translator" ("Die Aufgabe des Übersetzers") on "pure language" ("die reine Sprache") as present fragmentarily like a broken vase in the shards of existing languages ("Scherben eines Gefäßes") offers some fascinating opportunities for thinking through this ideal of an original transcendent language in contemporary theoretical terms (see Excursus VI). Benjamin's essay on the task of the translator introduces Baudelaire's *Fleurs du mal* as a modern poetic classic acceding to a more universal afterlife ("Nachleben") through

---

[8] Thomas of Erfurt, *Novi modi significandi* 6.2.2, §4, in *Große Denker Erfurts und der Erfurter Universität*, ed. Dietmar von der Pfordten (Göttingen: Wallstein, 2002), 59.

translation. The *modistae*, too, exalted the literary classic as a durable standard against the constant and inevitable shifts of colloquial speech. Such enduring, region- and epoch-transcending value is crucial, of course, also for Dante's notion of a *vulgare illustre* for use by authors of the most excellent type of literature. He begins to create a canon of literary models in Book II of his treatise on vernacular eloquence. His own effort to produce an exemplar of this ideal would eventually issue in the *Divine Comedy*.

Embodied in the grammatical imagery of Dante's vision in Jove are certain basic epistemological assumptions of speculative grammatical study and consciousness – particularly the idea of an essential deep structure that remains constant in spite of varying linguistic forms and manifestations. This is especially evident if we see the speculative grammar as an evolutionary outcome of increasingly rational reflection about grammar. Dante's age had become acutely conscious of grammar in its general philosophical import and speculative significance. Grammar analyzes the originally indivisible whole of language, the "stream of speech," into the distinct parts that were familiar to Dante, particularly from the tradition of Donatus (fourth century) and Priscian (flourished *circa* 500 CE), as the "parts of speech" ("partibus orationis").

R. H. Robins explains that "grammatical study begins whenever in the stream of speech or the expanse of writing there are observed, and in some way systematized, similarities of form or patterns of arrangement, and these are at least partly correlated with the meanings or functions of the utterances in which they occur."[9] Dante's description of the differential and even diacritical unity of language in the Heaven of Jupiter evidently brings out just this beginning of systematic patterning by means of formal distinctions such as those between noun and verb, consonant and vowel, word (or lexeme) and sentence.

Language is taken no longer simply as an indivisible whole, at least not in its phenomenal appearance and mode of presentation. Robins, from his historical-linguistic perspective, notes that "One of the earliest grammatical distinctions to be discussed in antiquity was the division of words into the categories of noun and verb ..." (14). He emphasizes that specifically this differentiation of noun and verb, which is explicitly named also in Dante's text, was key to the development of a characteristically grammatical understanding of language: "The really important grammatical

---

[9] R. H. Robins, *Ancient and Medieval Grammatical Theory in Europe* (London: Longmans, 1951), 14. Further insight on this is to be garnered from Frédérique Ildefonse, *La naissance de la grammaire dans l'antiquité grecque* (Paris: Vrin, 1997).

achievement of Plato was the definite segregation of the noun and what we must call 'the verb' ('onoma' and 'rhema')" (17).

This is the first big step to achieving a rationalization of language as an articulated system – an ensemble of classifiable elements governed by rules – that was developed further by Aristotle and thenceforward indelibly stamped upon the destiny of Western thought. Aristotle makes *predication* into the foundation for the distinction between verb and noun. In his *De interpretatione*, the predicative statement is based on distinction between the signs for *what* is predicated (attributes and accidents) and signs for that *of which* it is predicated (substances). Thus, from Aristotle on, language came to be understood largely on the basis of predicative logic.[10] No longer viewed as an originary phenomenon in its own right, language was reduced to grammar, which derived from logic. However, only with the reintroduction of Aristotle's greater logic, including his *Prior* and *Posterior Analytics*, into circulation from the middle of the twelfth century did this point of view achieve ascendency.

Dante shares in these rationalist biases, vigorously reinforced in his own Scholastic age of culture. Nonetheless, in his poetic work, language, with its intrinsic powers of synthesis, reaches far beyond all such analysis by grammatical criteria. He appropriates the logical-grammatical analysis of language and blends it into his own visionary, poetic experience of language. His poetry, in ways that call to be elucidated and contemplated, refuses to conform to logic – unless it be that of the transcendent Logos beyond every law of grammar. His enthusiastic reception of the new grammatical science and terminology catapults it high into the sky of metaphysical and mystical speculation, upending and ungrounding it, resituating it in vision and revelation beyond the reach of any finite rational analysis.

In principle, a language conforming to God should be without grammar and without distinctions of any kind so as to be able to emulate the perfect simplicity of the unitary Godhead. Grammar grounds the art of language and undergirds the recognition or reformulation of language as *artifice*. Dante, nevertheless, takes the whole Scholastic apparatus on board, even in his poetic navigation with his "little boat" ("piccioletta barca," as figured in *Paradiso* II. 1–18) steering toward that metaphysical oneness on mystic seas. Language belongs essentially to the art and artifice that Dante embraces as his vessel ferrying him over to such transcendent experience. This existential experience induces him to repudiate some of the assumptions of the

---

[10] Illuminating here is M. Frede, "Principles of Stoic Grammar," in *The Stoics*, ed. J. M. Rist (Berkeley: University of California Press, 1978), 27–76.

grammarians, with their artificial analysis of language. He ultimately transcends their anatomizing of language. He subsumes their analytic breakdown of language into binaries of vowels and consonants, nouns and verbs – even silver and gold he distinguishes in a coordinated system of differentiated signification ("argento lì d'oro distinto," XVIII. 96). Yet he recreates this breakdown and reverses its point of view in his vision of language as approaching a mystical wholeness.

Dante's poetic intuition of the original oneness of language ("one in all" – "una in tutti") is theologically inspired (the divine Word being the perfect image of the one God), but it can nonetheless also be anthropologically grounded. The differentiated parts of speech are introduced as abstractions from an originally undifferentiated wholeness of primordial human speech that poetic language, through its powers of synthesis, can endeavor to regain and emulate. All grammatical distinctions are but artifices vis-à-vis the originally whole phenomenon of speech.

Robins goes so far as to suggest that the word itself, as an isolable unit of meaning, may be considered to be "largely the creation of linguists and self-conscious speakers trying to analyze and classify sentence meanings in terms of smaller components."[11] Though the formulation is not undisputed, there is a basically valid and highly provocative observation lying at the roots of Bronisław Malinowski's dictum that "isolated words are in fact only linguistic figments, the products of an advanced linguistic analysis."[12] The same basic idea is formulated in a different vocabulary in the aesthetic philosophy of Benedetto Croce: "The primary thing is precisely speaking as a *continuum*, similar to an organism, and the words and syllables and roots are something secondary, the anatomical sample, the product of intellectual abstraction and not at all the original fact."[13] Such a conception is, after all, present throughout the tradition from Plato's *Cratylus* (402b), with its etymology of speech as a kind of flow (ροή) detected at the base of the name of *Rhea*, sister and wife of Chronus and "the mother of the gods," to all of whom she gave birth in a prodigious flow, like a stream. It is important to realize the intuitive appeal and wide diffusion of this vision of language in order to fathom how Dante's

---

[11] R. H. Robins, *A Short History of Linguistics* (London and Bloomington: Indiana University Press, 1967), 139.
[12] Bronisław Malinowski, *Coral Gardens and Their Magic* (London: Allen & Unwin, 1935), vol. 2, 11.
[13] Benedetto Croce, *Aesthetica in nuce* (Rome and Bari: Laterza, 1954), 45–46, in a discussion of "Retorica, grammatica e filosofia del linguaggio": "il *prius* è appunto il parlare come un *continuum*, simile a un organismo, e le parole e le sillabe e le radici sono il *posterius*, il preparato anatomico, il prodotto dell'intelletto astraente e non punto il fatto originario."

employment of precise grammatical terms can undermine and transform their status as binary and analytic in reaching towards a radically poetic and holistic understanding of the origins of language.

In fact, it seems that to speak of words at all as existing prior to the advent of grammar is anachronistic. Primordially, "speech" forms a whole with thought and action and is itself a continuum; it is not yet segmented into parts with distinct meanings, but is itself a functional whole. We learn from studies of language in a very long anthropological perspective that originally language is undifferentiated even from the phenomena and events of the world.[14] In pre-literate societies, words or speech are whole actions. But the development of language, and especially of linguistic self-consciousness, leads to its differentiation from a world of objects. Eventually language stands outside of and over against the world so as to be able to reference it in objectifying terms. This entails the differentiation within language itself of component parts, with their distinct functions within what previously had been apprehended simply as an indivisible unity.

Of course, Dante cannot be expected to have had our anthropological awareness of these sorts of perspectives on language in primordial cultures. Nevertheless, as poet, he considers and experiments with ideas of what it would be to recreate language in its primordial state as simulating the unfallen language created by God. He does so imaginatively, even while apprehending this possibility only by projection backward from within the most sophisticated scientific, grammatical understanding of language available in his time. Yet, by actually picturing grammar as a spectacle rather than only letting it operate invisibly in the making of sense, he raises awareness of the making of meaning in and through language to a new level. The parts of speech and the mechanics of grammar work together in their fragmentation and dispersion to produce the whole of sense. Dante's foregrounding of the means of mediation tends to make them disappear as means and become, instead, visible as whole objects of contemplation in their own right. As such, they are no longer just mediations: they become immediate vision.

This reification of language circumvents its function as mediating a sense or meaning in order to turn it into an immediate presence, the substance of the vision itself. Still, however, what is presented as immediacy is achieved through endless mediation of the whole by its parts. Each part is taken not

---

[14] This insight, which has been widely and diversely applied in literature and linguistics, was a master thesis of Edward Sapir, *Language: An Introduction to the Study of Speech* (New York: Harcourt, Brace and World, 1921). It was developed in influential ways by Benjamin Lee Whorf, *Language, Thought and Reality: Selected Writings of Benjamin Lee Whorf*, ed. John Carroll (Cambridge: MIT Press, 1956).

just as a part, but also as itself an instantiation of the whole and as being a worthy object of vision in itself. The result is that divinity may be declared to be present as a whole – as undifferentiated "love" – in each letter Dante sees. This fusion of the many with the one through language is rendered programmatic by the sign of the eagle, whose speech is articulated by "I" and "me" in order to mean "we" and "our" (XIX. 11–12). This phenomenon is presented by Dante as a wonder previously unheard of, never before written nor even imagined ("non portò voce mai, né scrisse incostro, / né fu per fantasia già mai compreso," XIX. 8–9). It seems to enact a miraculous transcending of the very dichotomy between the categories of individual and collective. This can happen by virtue of a logic of total mediation, realized linguistically, that reverses or collapses together mediation and immediacy. In language, as Dante envisions it, precisely endless mediation of the whole by its parts is immediately given to be perceived. However, this makes language lead naturally to images and cede to them, turning itself into vision and even into a picture.

Just this infinite mediation (of noun by verb, of vowel by consonant, of inner by outer, of ground by figure, etc.) is what Dante, in effect, takes as his object, for this is the Absolute – the divine, insofar as it can be made manifest and present in any kind of representation. In other words, the absolute of infinite mediation is manifest in the event of representing as such rather than in any determinate representation. This event is ongoing and infinite in Dante's text, a realization of the infinite in an undelimited act. Most fundamentally, it is neither the author's nor the reader's act: they only participate in an act attributed originally to God. This event is what medieval Scholastic theology called God as "pure actuality" ("actus purus") and what in mathematical terms can be called an "actual infinite."[15] In order to express this imaginatively, Dante pretends that this infinite creative activity of language can itself be represented as a Word or Letter or Image that directly "presences" the Creator and reveals divine Justice.

Intuitive Truth Expressed Allegorically as Imaginative Vision of Infinite Mediation

Propensities intrinsic to speculative grammar hypostatize grammatical structures as universal truths of language. The supposed speculative truths

---

[15] Mathematician Georg Cantor proposed his theory to the Vatican as proof of the existence of God. See "On the Theory of the Transfinite: Correspondence of Georg Cantor and J. B. Cardinal Frenzelin (1885–1886)," trans. Gabriele Chaitkin, with an afterword by Lyndon H. LaRouche, Jr., *Fidelio* 3/3 (1994): 97–110.

of grammar are fully apprehended somewhat similarly to Platonic ideas contemplated in an intelligible heaven. As a rationalism envisaging universal forms, speculative grammar is driven by a visionary *élan*. In general, contemplating whole truths and not just isolated facts encourages using visual metaphors and therewith underscoring also immediacy in the apprehension of truth. These proclivities lie behind Dante's impulse to turn into a visual spectacle writing that purports to reveal divine truth.

We can only intuitively "see" truth of this order, especially divine truth, not demonstrate it logically, nor grasp it discursively. Dante's linguistic acrobatics, in effect, throughout the *Paradiso*, with its paralogisms and oxymorons, its neologisms and equivocal rhymes, its deployments of contradiction and anacolouthon, of ellipses and litotes, use language against itself. Such forms of apophatic rhetoric outmaneuver language so as to approach negatively an im-mediate apprehension of truth. However, this is not the purely positive apprehension of divinity, without any discursive means, such as the angels and the blessed souls enjoy. Dante frequently invokes this latter doctrine, for example, in conversation with Cacciaguida in *Paradiso* XV. 55–63, and he expounds it in *Convivio* III. xv. 5–10. But his goal in the visionary poetry of *Paradiso* is rather to approximate this type of intuitive awareness poetically – *through language*.

We see in embryo here a momentous revolution in the relations between writing and the image. The possibility that the image could be a more true and complete revelation of divinity than the word represents a radical departure from Augustinian principles and the general suspicion of images, which were widely held to be inferior to writing in the Middle Ages. Adducing detailed historical documentation in his essays on medieval visual culture, Jean-Claude Schmitt demonstrates that, "Between the Book and images, there is a difference in dignity. The image (including man as 'image of God') counts as inferior to the prototype: the dream image is often fallacious . . ." ("Entre le Livre et les images, il y a une différence de dignité. L'image [y compris l'homme 'image de Dieu'] passe pour inférieure au prototype: l'image onirique est souvent fallacieuse . . .").[16]

This difference in dignity between writing and images applies specifically and especially to their value and "unequal roles in affording a knowledge of divinity" ("À l'écriture et aux images étaient également assignés des rôles inégaux dans la connaissance du divin," 99). Writing, under this Augustinian paradigm, was rational and permitted intimate

---

[16] Jean-Claude Schmitt, *Le corps des images: Essais sur la culture visuelle au Moyen Âge* (Paris: Gallimard, 2002), 98.

participation in the divine Logos. "The techniques of the image, in contrast, were tied to the function of *imaginatio*, intermediate in status between spirit and the corporeal senses; dreams and fantasms, held in suspicion, proceed from this function, among others, of the soul in its proximity with the body" ("Les pratiques de l'image relevaient au contraire de la function de l'*imaginatio*, dont le status était intermédiaire entre l'esprit et les sens corporels; les rêves et les fantasmes, tenus en suspicion, procèdent entre autres de cette fonction de l'âme plus proche du corps," 99).

Schmitt emphasizes the unequal status of writing and images in an art-historical vein and especially from a cultural-anthropological perspective. Initially in Christian tradition, the true revelation of God was deemed to be lodged in Scripture, whereas the image was cut to the measure of man. Hence, "The material image is invested with no sacred power" ("L'image matériel n'est investi d'aucune puissance sacrée," *Le corps des images*, 103). However, the great reformer Gregory the Great, from 590 onwards, began to rehabilitate the value of images and to legitimate their use in liturgy and festival, as well as in private devotion. The relationship between writing and images evolved in a tug-of-war, with successive reversals, through the course of the Middle Ages down to Dante's time. Schmitt summarizes this situation in "Écriture et image": "Certainly, in the thirteenth century, the Scriptures remained the essential depository of the Word of God, and the clergy principally retained the control of writing, which was still the foundation of their legitimacy. But, at the same time, a new Christian culture was affirming itself, one more open to lay participation: in the processions, in the confraternities, in private devotions, a Christian visual culture was affirming itself more and more" (*Le corps des images*, 133). Dante deserves to be placed in the vanguard of this movement. His *Convivio* is a manifesto for breaking up the clerical monopoly over writing and distributing its cultural, and even divine, riches more widely and equitably. All are invited to the convivial table to share in the knowledge even of divinity.

For Dante, ineluctably, as a mortal human, any intuition of the divine requires leaning heavily on the imagination. He discovers that human intuition of the purely intellectual Divinity is forced to turn self-reflexively upon its own faculty of imagining. This faculty specifies itself as the medium also of language itself, especially in its concrete, visible form as writing. This reflexive turn is necessary in order for imagination to have a concrete material substrate to work with. There is nothing concrete to start from in imagining the divine world, given its absolute difference from ordinary empirical reality, unless the intellectual life of imagination itself, in its *infinite* striving, be taken as its own subject. This characteristic feat of the modern subject identified with its own ceaseless, self-reflective striving is still being performed by Goethe's Faust, although it has at this point become more a tragedy than an itinerary to God.

Vision or intellection of the purely spiritual (God) is humanly possible only through the mediation of this self-reflexive capacity of the imagination taken as its own "material." Thinking self-reflection's own material conditions in the faculty of the imagination thus becomes eminently fecund. Dante sees materiality as enriching human expression and potentially as ennobling humans even above the angels ("ardisco a dire che nobilitate umana, quanto è dalla parte di molti suoi frutti, quella dell'angelo soperchia," *Convivio* IV. xix. 6). We have noticed repeatedly how the materiality of the image figures prominently in Dante's representation of writing as imaged in the Heaven of Jupiter.

In the dialectic of writing and the image that had swung between alternating ascendencies of iconophobia and iconolatry, Dante wills to exclude nothing from the truth but, instead, to totally mediate writing and image by one another. Indeed, Dante fully integrates the two. He realizes that, finally, the one can be conceived of and talked about only in terms of the other and that the divine encompasses both. The image takes on a new status, consequently, as contributing to a higher revelation. Dante's vision in the heaven of Jupiter turns Scripture itself into an image, a visual phenomenon, and thence into a visual "sign" or emblem.

The skywriting in Jupiter places a "graphic God" on stage.[17] The artificiality of the scene is captured in this metaphor, as well as in the fact that the scene Dante stages lets itself be construed specifically as the animated page of an illuminated manuscript featuring decorated letters as capitalized *incipits* (D, I, L), with text and glosses – Dante's narration and commentary – in the margins. Its being dependent on writing makes this a totally artificial kind of vision or "intuition." After all, writing can count as the original human artifice, the cradle of all human arts and industry. This graphic stunt has been flagged by Hollander as "[p]erhaps the single most self-conscious, 'artificial' passage in the poem."[18] Dante's far-reaching intuition is that the mystery of God can be glimpsed in contemplating the primordial fact of human artifice dramatized in the event of writing.

[17] I borrow here the wording ("mettere in scena un Dio 'grafico'") of Lucia Battaglia Ricci, "Con parole e con segni: Lettura del canto XVIII del Paradiso," *L'Alighieri* 6, n.s. (1995): 7–28. Citation, 28.
[18] Dante Alighieri, *Paradiso*, trans. Robert and Jean Hollander (New York: Anchor Books, 2007), 452.

Images were typically faulted, in a long tradition with Biblical roots, as merely copies and as the work of human hands and artisans. Dante, however, exalts certain images in their revelatory immediacy, even while simultaneously exposing them in their artificiality. He exposes writing as artifice, yet, even so, as penetrated by divine purposefulness. This constitutes Dante's move of total mediation of nature by artifice. Nature *is* God's artifice according to *Inferno* XI. 97–102 ("natura lo suo corso prende / da divino intelletto e da sua arte"), and human artifice is an imitation of nature that can bring humans closer to God as Maker. Human writing, at its most authentic, stands in the image of divine Scripture. Dante makes writing itself into an image by turning its letters into spectacles.

If images, on the one hand, are artificial, they can, on the other hand, be immediate manifestations of the supernatural. This conviction is deeply rooted in popular medieval traditions that Dante arguably leverages for his own purposes. Schmitt recalls that, for the Christian Middle Ages, the *imago* is often more an apparition or epiphany of a higher, spiritual world than a representation of empirical reality (*Le corps des images*, 24–26). While the artifactuality of images in artworks makes them merely human, images appearing in dreams and visions can have the opposite valence: they can count as revelations from a higher world beyond.

Dante uses visual symbols in his poem in this revelatory register. Looking just to the heavens immediately preceding and following Jupiter, the Imperial Eagle is ranged in series with the Greek Cross of martyrdom in Mars and the Golden Ladder of the contemplatives in Saturn. The verbal and grammatical dynamics of the scene in Jupiter, with their insistence on the written status of everything that Dante's poem presents, enable us to see these pictorial emblems as themselves springing out of the contingent dynamics of writing and so as signifying something quite other than what they represent in the form of visible likenesses. These images use their iconic content somewhat like the Orthodox icon as a means of evoking an absolutely *dissimilar* and invisible divinity. Such is the anagogic and apophatic way of Dionysius the Areopagite.

Analogy (which, referred to God, is really dis/analogy) serves Dante as a visionary vehicle rather than as a constructive principle for making a simulacrum: it takes him to the point of his having to kick it away like a ladder that has served its purpose and would afterwards become an impediment to immediate vision. All that Dante himself can give to the reader are the images that mediate his unmediated vision – *plus* an enactment of the generating source of these images in poetic imagination understood as deeply inextricable from the process of writing. Dante allegorizes the infinite imaginative process of creation fantastically in his representations of the mediating function of writing.

Immediate Vision of the Invisible in the Visible

The medium of Dante's allegorical journey is not just a static and finite object. It opens up into a dynamic process of mediation. This process is open-ended and infinite. It is an Incarnation of the Infinite. We could even speak here of an "actual Infinite" in a vocabulary that will reach from medieval metaphysics (particularly as reconstructed by Duns Scotus) to modern mathematics, with Georg Cantor's set theory (*Mengenlehre*, 1895–97).[19]

The Infinite becomes the principal definition of God in the new rational-scientific metaphysics that is being articulated in Dante's time by his exact contemporary Duns Scotus (1265–1308). Scotus redefined God as an infinite degree or *intensity* of being (*esse*).[20] Of course, divinity is never completely present to finite intelligence. Yet the exhaustive presence of the medium gestures towards a completeness in meaning as the condition of possibility of any of its manifestations. Similarly, the material process of language in a sentence, proceeding word by word, alludes to the completeness of its sense. This linguistic principle was the basis of Augustine's apprehension of the relation between time and eternity (Excursus IV).

The medium disappears as such and breaks down into an infinite process of mediation. This process of mediation is realized with unprecedented intensity in Dante's vision and is all that can be seen of God. However, we can also see its ultimate nullity, its disappearance. It thus becomes also an invitation to look beyond the visible altogether and to acknowledge the *invisible* presence of God – even as Christ is "the image of the invisible God," according to Colossians 1:15. As Paul writes, broadening this relation to the invisible, in his letter to the Romans: "the invisible things of him since the creation of the world are clearly seen, being understood by the things that are made, even his eternal power and Godhead" (Romans 1:20).

God is "seen" negatively, or is understood (by Dante in heaven) through the invisible divinity's being manifest analogically in an infinite process of mediation that then dissolves and so points back to its invisible source. This is allowed to occur by Dante's making the linguistic, and specifically written, medium itself his object of contemplation – in effect, the *visio Dei*.

---

[19] See, further, my *Dante's* Paradiso *and the Origins of Modern Thought: Toward a Speculative Philosophy of Self-Reflection*, part II.

[20] *Ord.* I, d. 3, pt. 1, qq. 1–2, n. 58. Scotus's *Ordinatio* (accessed April 2, 2021) is available at www.logicmuseum.com/wiki/Authors/Duns_Scotus/Ordinatio/Ordinatio_I/D3/Q2.

God can be given to experience only through mediations, specifically through their infinity, and Dante's vision of divinity in the mediations of language says as much. It admits and works with this predicament. Yet his vision presents this truth immediately in picture language broad-brushed across the heaven. In some sense, Dante suggests, his vision of the medium (writing) gives rise to an immediate vision of the divine. Understanding such a sense calls for intensive theoretical reflection.

In *The Visible and the Invisible*, Maurice Merleau-Ponty applies himself to showing how the invisible is always perceived along with anything visible and as its condition and ground. He maintains that "The invisible is there without being an object; it is pure transcendence, without an ontic mask. And the 'visibles' in the last analysis themselves exist only as centered on a core of absence as well." ("L'invisible est là sans être objet, c'est la transcendance pure, sans masque ontique. Et les 'visibles' eux-mêmes, en fin de compte, ne sont que centrés sur un noyau d'absence eux aussi."[21]) Seeing is selective and makes invisible what it excludes from its focus.

This suggests, in phenomenological terms, how Dante's visioning of his material, scriptural medium might include im-mediate vision of the invisible divine transcendence as embedded in an unfocused and non-objective way in his perception of his medium as an object. The seeing of the visible is immediately – because un-thematically – a seeing of the invisible. Visibility presupposes and brings *in*visibility along in its train as an unfocused background condition.

The "immediate" vision of the invisible envisaged by Merleau-Ponty is to be understood as interior, as engendered by imagination, but not only that: it is best understood as situated somewhere between exterior and interior vision – or perhaps "above" them, in the dimension that Merleau-Ponty designates as "pure transcendence." It is, in effect, prior to reflection and to divisions into inner and outer.

Merleau-Ponty, in the highly secularized context of mid-twentieth-century French philosophy, is anxious not to let this invisibility be hypostatized into an independent realm. He is careful to explain:

> When I say, therefore, that every visible is invisible, that perception is non-perception, that consciousness has a "*punctum caecum*," that seeing is always seeing more than one sees, – this must not be understood in the sense of a contradiction – one must not think that I add to the perfectly definite visible something like a non-visible Itself, (which would only be an objective absence) (which is to say an objective presence *elsewhere*, in an *elsewhere* in

---

[21] Maurice Merleau-Ponty, *Le visible et l'invisible*, ed. Claude Lefort (Paris: Gallimard, 1964), 278.

itself) – It is necessary to understand that visibility itself brings invisibility along with it.

> Quand je dis donc que tout visible est invisible, que la perception est imperception, que la conscience a un *"punctum caecum"*, que voir c'est toujours voir plus qu'on ne voit, – il ne faut pas le comprendre dans le sens d'une *contradiction* – Il ne faut pas se figurer que j'ajoute au visible parfaitement défini comme en Soi un non-visible (qui ne serait qu'absence objective) (c'est-à-dire présence objective *ailleurs*, dans un *ailleurs* en soi) – Il faut comprendre que c'est la visibilité même que comporte une non-visibilité. (295).

Merleau-Ponty thus guards against turning the invisible into an object-ive other world, such as Dante, in effect, poetically imagines. The perceived absence is not itself, for Merleau-Ponty, a presence elsewhere in another world. It is inherent *in* the visible object. However, to fully and concretely imagine the invisible is the part of poetry, and this is where Dante's imagination excels. Indeed, Merleau-Ponty, too, understands how this perception of a lack or blind spot (*punctum caecum*) gives rise to compensating *discourses* imagining what cannot be seen. And a host of philosophically minded art theorists in Merleau-Ponty's wake likewise emphasizes this displacement of blind vision to discourse.

Eminently, Georges Didi-Huberman documents the myriad ways in which the proliferation of figuration is the direct consequence of the invisibility of what is figured as divine. In his reversal of the commonplace declaring the unfigurability of the mystery of the Incarnation or divine truth, Didi-Huberman quips, "The mystery, because it is ungraspable, *cannot but be figured*" ("le mystère, parce qu'il est insaisissable, *n'est que figurable*").[22] Didi-Huberman argues that the loss of the thing itself, of the face to face with divinity and with the "end" of truth ("la perte de la 'chose même' . . . du face à face et du 'terme' de la vérité"), obliged early Christian thinkers or theologians to take the "detour of figuration" in order to "regain the thing itself" ("un detour obligé par la figure hors de la chose . . . pour retrouver la chose," 211).

Didi-Huberman stresses that images in outer, public space always work on us in conjunction with inner images. Any strict division between the mental and the real in vision collapses. The image itself is located no more really in outer, public space than in inner, mental space. The forms that images take in either dimension derive from their common unlimited

---

[22] Georges Didi-Huberman, *L'image ouverte: Motifs de l'incarnation dans les arts visuels* (Paris: Gallimard, 2007), 31.

potentiality, which Didi-Huberman conceives of as a formless, or more exactly an unformed, center from which all forms emanate. It resembles, in effect, the blind spot or *punctum caecum* that, according to Merleau-Ponty, is *in* everything visible. There is always an "unformed center" ("centre informe") in every form.[23] This, indeed, serves as a good general, theoretical formula for capturing an unrepresentable or "apophatic" dimension of images.

In a kindred perspective, Schmitt, in *Le corps des images*, specifically with reference to the Christian Middle Ages, underscores "the mediation between the visible and the invisible that the image operates" ("la mediation qu'opère l'image entre le visible et l'invisible," 24–25). He stresses the "epiphanic function" of images as rendering present or "presentifying" invisible reality that is not, except inessentially, imitated from models in the empirical world. Instead, the image functions as a "transitus," either transporting the mind from earth to heaven or rendering invisible heavenly realities "incarnate" in sensuous forms for human perception.

Writing about "the body of images" in the Middle Ages, Schmitt focuses especially on the insufficiency of images, which gives the impetus to imagining the invisible, as powered by the dialectic between the shown and the hidden ("dialectique du montré et du caché," 324). This supplementing of images takes place especially in, and by means of, discourse. As running up to a threshold of impossibility, the translation between verbal and visual communication in artworks has been a subject of intense reflection throughout the history of art theory on the topic of "ekphrasis" (Excursus V). Jean-Louis Schefer, in *Scénographie d'un tableau*, underlines the ineluctable discrepancy between images and the words about them in ekphrasis.[24] Schefer details how the writer becomes, in effect, a movie director recreating a scene in another medium. A more stunning illustration for this than Dante's scene in the heaven of Jupiter can hardly be imagined.

Writing as the Concrete Presence of an Infinite Absence

Theoretical reflection about the pictorial dimension and function of writing in our own day has reached a high pitch of intensity and regained certain speculative heights that serve for reflecting back on Dante's archetypal scene

[23] Georges Didi-Huberman, *La peinture incarnée, suivi de Le Chef-d'œuvre inconnu par Honoré de Balzac* (Paris: Minuit, 1985), 35. Didi-Huberman develops this theme further in *La resemblance informe ou le Gai Savoir visuel selon Georges Bataille* (Paris: Macula, 1995).
[24] Jean-Louis Schefer, *Scénographie d'un tableau* (Paris: Seuil, 1968).

of Scriptural writing. Contemporary art historians and theorists have meditated deeply on the role of images in making absence present. Some of them
glimpse, moreover, the unlimitedness of this absence, sometimes even in its
theological implications and connotations.[25] A theologization of the presencing of absence through the image can surely be discerned in Dante's
"scenography" in the Heaven of Jove. Through emphasizing the writtenness
of his vision of God in Paradise, Dante is already bringing out into the open
what particularly Didi-Huberman and Schmitt, as well as Hans Belting,
emphasize about images as *making absence present*. This realization of
absence can become a kind of enactment of divinity, an incarnation in
mental experience – and, even more to the point, in an aesthetic medium –
of God.

Belting has analyzed the paradox that images are or mean the presence of
an absence by focusing specfically on their identification with their
medium. Images make an absent object really present by virtue of the
substantial material presence of the *medium* in which they are presented.
"We are willing to credit images with the representation of absence,
because they are present by virtue of their chosen medium. They need
a presence as medium in order to symbolize the absence of what they
represent."[26] As a result, "In the riddle of the image, presence and absence
are inextricably entangled" ("Im Rätsel des Bildes sind Anwesenheit und
Abwesenheit unauflösbar verschränkt," 23). In Chapter 1, I dwelt in detail
on this particular phenomenon with regard to the scenography of Dante's
vision of Scripture. Writing, turned into vision, was expounded as ambiguously signifying, and even as imagistically embodying, the presence of an
incorrigibly uncontainable, unrepresentable divinity.

The imaging of the necessarily and incorrigibly absent has been thought
through intensively by Belting, and not without regard for this theological
problematic. Their uncanny sort of presence makes images apt to serve as
intermediaries between the living and the dead and even as means of
reintegrating the dead into the community of the living. For archaic
societies, with their rites and cults and religions, images were experienced
as real presences of the dead and of the gods (*Bild-Anthropologie*, 143ff.).

---

[25] The theological implications of such absent presence are directly addressed by the sacramental,
Eucharistic theology of Louis-Marie Chauvet, *Symbole et sacrement: Une relecture sacramentelle de
l'existence chrétienne* (Paris: Cerf, 1987), trans. Patrick Madigan, S.J. and Madeleine Beaumont as
Symbol and Sacrament (Collegeville: The Liturgical Press, 1995), 178.

[26] Hans Belting, *Bild-Anthropologie: Entwürfe für eine Bildwissenschaft* (Munich: Fink, 2001), trans.
T. Dunlap as *An Anthropology of Images: Picture, Medium, Body* (Princeton: Princeton University
Press, 2011), 6. This citation from the "Introduction for English Readers" is not in the original
German edition, which I otherwise cite and translate.

Dante's representation of souls restores something of this archaic power to
the image, but in a more artificial vein: real presence is conjured through
the artifice of poetry. As in the anthropological theory formulated by
Belting, exogenous and endogenous images (ones originating from outside
and from within the human subject, respectively) coalesce in producing
a virtual reality that is neither merely external and physical, nor merely
interior and psychic, but rather conjugates and transcends both (*Bild-
Anthropologie*, 19–22).

The interpolation of aesthetic artifice into relations with dead souls
tends to undermine the dichotomy between real bodies and mere images.
Dante's mimesis of dead souls as living bodies still intends to respect the
difference: his representation of his own shadow in the other world,
specifically in Purgatory, where his body is exposed to sunshine, differentiates it from the souls, who are bodiless (*Purgatorio* III. 16–45). Dante's
perception of the dead *as if* they had bodies is an artistic invention without
a grounding in theological dogma.[27] It is rather the brainchild of Dante's
theological imagination.

The artistically created body was destined to replace the resurrected body
as the primary reality in Renaissance artistic representations of the afterlife.
At the height of this movement, Michelangelo (1475–1564) represents souls
in the afterlife on the ceiling of the Sistine Chapel as fully realized physical,
even hyper-physical, bodies.[28] For Giotto (1266–1337), in Dante's own age,
painted bodies are not as such real and do not cast shadows. Massaccio
(1401–28) first gives painted images the realistic quality of casting shadows at
the beginning of the Florentine Renaissance in the visual arts.

The new Renaissance realism in painting represents the triumph of art as
illusion, collapsing the difference between the body and the image, the
living and the dead, and making what is in principle absent seem fully and
immediately present. Dante's daring to represent his own living body and
its shadow in the world of the dead lies at the origin of this movement of
illusionary mimesis.

Nevertheless, Dante's art in the end aims not at life-like representation
but rather at a realization in another world through transformation beyond
any this-worldly actualizations. Hierarchies between spiritual and physical,
between bodily and merely imaged reality, are still clear for Dante. Yet he
invents the fiction of an imagined body inserted into the real world and

[27] Étienne Gilson, "Trois études dantesques: Qu'est-ce qu'un ombre?," *Archives d'histoire doctrinale et littéraire du Moyen Âge* 4 (1965): 71–93.
[28] Hans Belting, "Bild und Schatten: Dantes Bildtheorie im Wandel zur Kunsttheorie," in *Bild-Anthropologie*, 189–212.

interacting with eternal realities that it will eventually, in progressively secularized culture, void. In our headily virtual culture more than ever, the image usurps and empties the body of its reality.

Artistic representation discovers itself as not merely reproducing or copying external, empirical reality but rather as opening another dimension of the real. For Dante, this is the higher reality known through theological revelation and not properly representable by human means. Therefore, he foregrounds the artificiality of artistic representation as a means of blindly relating to a transcendent order of existence. Dante's theological reference, however, will be largely elided by modern art, with its generally secularized outlook. The presence of the image will be taken in and for itself rather than as a reference to another metaphysical reality that is absent from the visual field. This modern image, bereft of its relation to an absence, becomes mournfully impoverished.

The dialectic between presence and absence in the image can be traced in its anthropological ramifications from rites and cults of the dead (Belting, "Bild und Tod," *Bild-Anthropologie*, 143–88) – of which the *Divine Comedy* reads as a consummate epic projection. Through the death of persons, images representing them became entangled in the mystery of their absence. The dead truly exist in another world, and "Their presence as images [Bilder] in our world is secondary and in the mode of a medium" ("von der Art eines Mediums," Belting, "Bild und Schatten," *Bild-Anthropologie*, 189).

Images are used cross-culturally to negotiate relations between the living and the dead and in order to face the anguish of human finitude. The image often – and, in any case, potentially – has a longer past and future than those of the one who views it. Art critics and cultural historians are concerned to recuperate the power of images that has been eclipsed in our technological age, with its erasure of the mode of ritual through which images were animated in former ages.[29] Above all, the tying and binding function of language is essential to understanding the spellbinding power of the image in Dante (Excursus V).

Didi-Huberman likewise speaks of the image as the "visual detour" ("le détour visuel") of something else which is not presently there ("n'est pas là présentement").[30] Images dwell in "the cave of the octopus" of our

---

[29] Régis Debray, *Vie et mort de l'image: Une histoire du regard en Occident* (Paris: Gallimard, 1992) meditates provocatively on this problematic. Also instructive here are Ernesto Grassi, *Macht des Bildes: Ohnmacht der rationalen Sprache. Zur Rettung des Rhetorischen* (Cologne: DuMont Schauberg, 1970); and Louis Marin, *Études sémiologiques: Écritures, peintures* (Paris: Klincksieck, 1975).

[30] Didi-Huberman, *L'image ouverte*, 195.

unconscious psyche, which remains "outside of our purview because located at the center of ourselves" ("hors de notre vue puisque au centre de nous-mêmes").[31] Since there is always a core of invisibility ("nucleus d'invisibilité") at the intersection between memory and desire, imagination and body, consciousness and the unconscious, an absence interpretable as God's is always present in the dimension of the imagination. Poets like Dante are specialists in bringing this theoretical predicament to full expression in verbal imaginings.

For Didi-Huberman, furthermore, constitutive of making the absent present is the interchange between the tenses. The image is anachronistic and, while it does not abstract itself from history, it upsets the usual chronological ordering of history. An image is capable of juxtaposing the Garden of Eden with the chamber of a first-century Hebrew girl at the moment of the Annunciation from the angel Gabriel.[32] Even more than just anachronistic, the image is "achronic" or even "polychronique" (22). It opens up linear history into a complex interactive relation among the time dimensions of past, present, and future. This casts some light on Dante's eagle image, and on the doctrine of providence in Jupiter, as well as on the tableaux of Roman history as a triumph of divine justice in *Paradiso* VI. We will consider language in its binding function in Excursus V and examine how such binding can depict the transcendental origins of time.

Grammatical Shattering of Wholeness and Presence Restored through the Image

Dante is exploring an irreducibly *linguistic* logic of incarnation – of an incarnate *Logos*. Nevertheless, the divine Presence is linguistically manifest in *Paradiso* XVIII in the fragmentary *vision* of letters. Vision is the privileged mode of immediate presence, and the fragment can stand for, and actually *be*, the whole (at least in our experience) because there is no other mode in which the whole can be present. This operation is not a dogmatic and idolatrous coercing of the representation into identity with God. It works, instead, on a logic of (non-)identity – of the fragment presented as a splinter or spark. It is because there is no adequate representation of the presence of the whole that Dante can absolutize the partial elements of his subjective visionary experience as mediating a "vision" of whole truth. He

[31] Georges Didi-Huberman, *Ninfa fluida: Essai sur le drapé-désir* (Paris: Gallimard, 2015), 143.
[32] Georges Didi-Huberman, *Devant le temps: Histoire de l'art et anachronisme des images* (Paris: Minuit, 2000).

can, moreover, accommodate the external, spatial dimension of writing into his vision through a total mediation of inwardness by outwardness.

Dante includes in his exalted vision even the technical terms of writing and of grammatical science that appear, at first, unamenable to total internal mediation in any synthesis and transcendent unity. This amounts to a paragon instantiation of the interdependence and interpenetration of endogenous by exogenous images that Didi-Huberman and Belting alike frequently rehearse. The inwardness of mind is made miraculously visible in the externality of the written. In fact, the new *speculative* outlook on grammar in Dante's age would make grammar, too, a revelation of the mind's synthetic capacity, and this capacity is celebrated by Dante as an image and an echo of the unifying, creative power of God.

Dante's image of the eagle is considered to be "one of the most memorable figures of Western literature" ("una de las figuras más memorables de la literatura occidental") by Jorge Luis Borges in his essay "El Simurgh y el águila."[33] The simurgh, in Persian mythology, is a bird that is somehow all birds and thus a symbol of divinity – even as God is all things in one, however self-contradictorily. Dante's eagle is similarly superindividual, condensing all the blessed jovial souls into one.[34] The notion of a being that is composed of other beings ("un ser compuesto de otros seres," Borges, *Nueve ensayos dantescos*, 139) and, at the limit, of all beings, is an abstraction, but it is made concrete and present in such images. Artists from Giovanni di Paolo to Gustave Doré have pictorially rendered this image of uniplurality (Figures 2–4), which Dante creates poetically from letters.[35]

Dante poetically represents the wholeness of the divine Mind mainly through representing the miraculously appearing linguistic fragments – letters – forming themselves into the completeness of a whole sentence. The evolution towards an analytic of language as a differentiated system, which is fundamental to grammar, entails essentially the spatialization of "speech" transformed into "the expanse of writing" – exactly like the canvas in the heaven of Jove depicting Dante's vision of God's speech in the form of writing. It was characteristic of grammarians in antiquity to treat language as a substantial medium that could be surveyed and measured and molded at

---

[33] Jorge Luis Borges, *Nueve ensayos dantescos* (Madrid: Espsa-Calpe, 1982), 139–44. Citation, 140.

[34] Michelangelo Picone, "Canto XVIII," in *Lectura Dantis Turicensis: "Paradiso,"* eds. Georges Güntert and M. Picone (Florence: Franco Cesati, 2002), 265–79. Reference, 275.

[35] Suggestive images can be viewed online at https://eclecticlight.co/2019/09/02/the-divine-comedy-paradise-4-the-just-and-the-contemplative/ (accessed April 2, 2021). These include Francesco Scaramuzza (1803–86), Spirits of the Sky of Jupiter, *Paradiso* 18, British Library (Figure 2), and an anonymous engraving of the composite Eagle, Biblioteca Medicea Laurenziana (Figure 6).

will. In order to do so, they hypostatized and reified its elements, abstracting them from the temporality of speaking.

Dante, in his vision of Scripture, envisions a spatialized representation of language as writing such as is found in the ancient grammarians, but at the same time he also emphatically reinscribes this vision back into the temporal phenomenon of speaking and its generation of meaning that is "nostra favella" ("our speech"). He uses the exterior, material, evidently recalcitrant aspects of writing as further means of subjective expression of his visionary experience (Excursus IV expands on this). Dante thus sees the disintegrative aspects of grammatical analysis in a reintegrative perspective centered on the perceiving subject.

Gerald Bruns has observed that the older grammarians "tended to regard human speech as a wholly spatial and visual affair, the utilization of a phenomenon of quantity and extension."[36] Bruns examines Donatus's treatise, the *Ars Minor*, which details various categories of words and the eight parts of speech, but in detached abstraction from use and meaning, with attention only to their grammatical inflections of gender, number, person, and so on. Bruns maintains that this approach "describes not an act of speech but the behavior of language, not the articulation of thought but a spatial and visual field in which discrete particles 'fall away' from one another according to a fixed design. Language, as it is systematized by the grammarians, becomes a phenomenon of quantity and extension: like all systems, it is perfectly self-contained . . ." (33).

This last remark, nevertheless, suggests how the analytical breaking-down characteristic of grammar is not necessarily equivalent to the destruction and dispersion of all unified order. As Bruns also remarks, "the breaking-down of the stream of speech into 'isolatable fragments' is at the same time a breaking-down into *patterns* – into a subject–verb pattern, for example, if we are thinking of Greek, or into any number of formal patterns, which determine how the 'fragments' are to enter into combination" (28). This is how (speculative) grammar is presented by Dante – as breaking down the sentence in order to reveal not only its structure as a whole ensemble, but also, at its most elementary level, an ordered pattern. Dante stresses, furthermore, that the pattern reveals an order beyond any humanly apprehended and established order. The

---

[36] Gerald Bruns, "Rhetoric, Grammar, and the Conception of Language as a Substantial Medium," in *Modern Poetry and the Idea of Language: A Critical and Historical Study* (New Haven: Yale University Press, 1974), 14.

latter, after all, may be only apparent and is, in any case, always fragile and vulnerable to destruction.

Reaching beyond the mechanics of grammar, Dante embraces a mystical sense of language as ordered to an intention transcending that of any of its human users. The finite orderings of speech by speakers are comprehended within an infinite, but not so readily perceptible order, something of which, nevertheless, is revealed exceptionally to Dante in this heaven. In this way, the system of language shows itself to possess a certain infinity in its capacity of infinite self-mediation. In later, speculative, Hegelian terms, this is a kind of higher life of the concept and a transcendence of sense or meaning with respect to its natural, verbal vehicle.

While grammar analyzes language into its component parts, thus inviting the disintegration of a presumed primordial wholeness of speech, it also furnishes the rules for fitting these parts together into a meaningful whole. Grammar, in its initial manifestations, analyzes language into its component parts and shatters the wholeness of the event of speech. Nevertheless, its rules and structures are, at the same time, what bind the elements of language together into meaningful whole statements. Dante does not actually dwell on or abide by grammatical rules. Instead, he apprehends the wholeness of language immediately as image and even as divine Word. Dante's descent into the disintegrating abyss of writing, his "grammatology," so to speak, does not prevent him from reintegrating his experience of language once again into the living Word of God. In the end, language for him is also a participation in the outspoken life of divinity (see, further, Excursus III).

For Dante, in his treatises, grammar has the connotation of stable, universal, rule-governed language. These are its chief characteristics in Dante's discussions of the ideal of a perfectly grammatical language and of Latin in particular as a grammatical language in *Convivio* I. v–vii and in *De vulgari eloquentia* I. ix. 11. The latter defines grammar as "a certain unalterable identity of language across diverse times and places" ("gramatica nichil aliud est quam quedam inalterabilis locutionis idemptitas diversis temporibus atque locis"). Grammatical language is, in this sense, timeless or eternal and, on that account, the more perfectly reflects divinity. However, in the *Paradiso*, language opens to eternity not by instantiating or mirroring unchanging laws, but rather by violating and twisting them in its discovery of absolutely singular and inimitable modes of expression. Not by resisting change and dynamism, but rather by committing itself wholly and without reserve to the vernacular, by dissolving itself into time through its performative character as a unique event, paradisiacal language indirectly elicits the eternal, which shows up in its shadow as its Other.

Dante's thematizing of the anatomization of language by writing does not, in the end, work to the detriment of unitary metaphysical structures, which in philosophical tradition have been associated rather with speech (and by Dante ultimately with divine speech). Such unitary structures are constantly affirmed and even *imaged* – by the poem, especially in Jupiter. For Dante, the unity of language and the transcendency of its sense can actually be realized in and through analysis and anatomization. For unity and transcendent order are not just a construct: they are inherent in the underlying medium of language. They are already present in writing and in its material substrates as belonging to a divinely ordered Creation. By breaking down all conventional orderings and intentions, the miraculous order beyond all finite, human intentions is allowed to emerge into view directly from these elements themselves – as the visionary images of letters in Jupiter.

The starting point of the description in this heaven is the presence of "the love that was there." This is also its endpoint, inasmuch as the carnivalesque play of letters and sparking is all ordered to the divine Good that moves the soul-lights to itself ("il ben ch'a sé li move," XVIII. 99). This recalls the Aristotelian God that moves all things in the universe through final causation by being loved. Of course, Dante adds a Christian conception of God's intentional and loving calling of all things to himself, but this source as such remains invisible. Dante's theological inference, in any case, is based on interpretation of the phenomenal elements that are manifest to his sight in their very disintegration.

The fragmentation of the wholeness of language into parts by writing is constantly in play with representations of speech as controlled by the mind, with its guiding intention, giving the wholeness of sense to the whole painting ("tutto 'l dipinto"). This wholeness is subtended, furthermore, by the Mind that initiates the motion of the heaven. Even the metaphor of painting, which hews very closely to writing in the crucial respects of externality and spatiality, is used to affirm God's intentional control of all that Dante has seen written by sparks in the sky. Dante expressly prays to the Mind in which all that happens in the heaven has its ground and origin: "For which I pray to the mind in which your motion and virtue originate" ("Per ch'io prego la mente in che s'inizia / tuo moto e tua virtute ...," XVIII. 118–19; cf. also 105). Dante keeps this imagery of the transcendent source of signifying in play together with that of randomness and of the evidently spontaneous origination of the spark; he even integrates it with the imagery of the breakdown of speech into writing.

Transcendent Sense: From Linguistic Epistemology to Love of Justice

The breakdown of language into its grammatical components featured in their own right opens the sentence up from inside to a meaning contained within its elements that is not the meaning imposed from without by the intentions of its users: it is a higher sort of meaning than ordinary linguistic sense. The very elements themselves are already intrinsically meaningful. This is not (or, at least, is not limited to) the human speaker's meaning – the intention for which language is made to serve as an instrument of communication. Instead, this "sense" is made manifest immediately to the senses, as if inscribed into sensations themselves.

This sort of immediacy is pictured metaphorically as intuitive intellectual apprehension that transcends the analytical comprehension of logic and grasps true, intellectual being in its wholeness. This whole meaning belongs ultimately to the intellectual ideal of Justice, as the theme sentence of the heaven of Jupiter arrestingly proclaims. The five physical senses, moreover, are all subsumed into Dante's intellectual vision. They also furnish the most apt metaphors for it. The senses are all intellectual or "spiritual" at the point where they serve to reveal true being, not just material qualities but "things themselves" ("les choses mêmes"), as they do again later in the phenomenology of Merleau-Ponty.[37]

In Dante's vision, the senses become synaesthetic. As such, they become instruments for disclosing transcategorically a metaphysical reality. As employed in poetry of this order, at this metaphysical height, the senses reveal the synthesis of being rather than just its isolated, objectifiable features or qualities. This synthesis, however, is pre-thetic rather than a summation of separate impressions in differentiated sensory modalities. For painters, as Merleau-Ponty understands them, sensation becomes a self-reflexive circuit of "magical" revelation rendering vision "total or absolute, outside of which nothing remains, and which closes on [the painters] themselves" ("une vision total ou absolue, hors de laquelle rien ne demeure, et qui se referme sur eux-mêmes," *L'œil et l'esprit*, 34). The painters are themselves regarded, and are even enveloped, by the visions they create through their painting.

The sentient body of Dante as poet, like that of the painter for Merleau-Ponty, recreates the world on the basis of its own emanations "echoing" what it senses. Dante's senses similarly engender a "subjective correlative"

---

[37] Maurice Merleau-Ponty, *L'œil et l'esprit* (Paris: Gallimard, 1964), 13.

(this notion will be developed in the next chapter) for experience that escapes them – definitively in XXXIII. 58–63, distilling a "sweetness" in his "heart" in place of the obliterated vision. Painting, for Merleau-Ponty, aims to expose "the secret, feverish genesis of things in our body" ("cette genèse secrete et fiévreuse des choses dans notre corps," *L'œil et l'esprit*, 30). This perception pierces to "the depth of the existing world and that of the unsoundable God" ("la profondeur du monde existant et celle du Dieu insondable," 57), the "abyss of being" ("Être abyssal," 58) that the "technicized" thought of science and its constructed beings ("ces êtres comme de *constructa*") cannot fathom. This attention to the bodily genesis of images is being pursued interdisciplinarily in conjunction with neuroscience today by many researchers including Belting ("Medium – Bild – Körper," in *Bild-Anthropologie*, 11–56).

Yet even this autonomous structure generated by the body is itself a sign of an otherwise. In Cézanne's art, "vision regains its fundamental power of manifesting or showing more than itself" ("La vision reprend son pouvoir fondamental de manifester, de montrer plus qu'elle-même," Merleau-Ponty, *L'œil et l'esprit*, 59). For Merleau-Ponty, the things of the world give themselves in and as the tearing or rupture of Being ("le déhiscence de l'Être," *L'œil et l'esprit*, 85) and its opening to invisible reality. "This means finally that the proper of the visual is to have a lining that is invisible in the strict sense, one which it renders present as a certain absence" ("Ceci veut dire finalement que le propre du visible est d'avoir une doublure d'invisible au sens strict, qu'il rend présent comme une certaine absence," 85). Objects such as "the apple and prairie 'form themselves' and descend into the visible, as if coming from a pre-spatial hinterworld" ("la pomme et la prairie 'se forment' d'elles-mêmes et descendent dans le visible comme venues d'un arrière-monde préspatial," 73).

The divine Word that Dante sees, and is addressed by, is expressed in letters that break it up into separate pieces. The letters themselves disintegrate into what appears as a chaos of the elements that is imaged by Dante as random sparking. Yet this is how whole sense is grasped as the vision descends into visibility from the invisible. Precisely in this literal breakdown and fragmentation of language, the guiding hand of divine Providence, its sense and intention, is discerned and confidently affirmed in its infinite autonomy and transcendence: "He who paints there has no guide" ("Quei che dipinge lì non ha chi 'l guidi," XVIII. 109). Precisely the autonomy of this expressive act, its freedom from conditioning by anything outside itself – such as normally inheres in anything that is materially caused – is unequivocally affirmed. Paradoxically, what Dante seeks to realize in and through the temporalization and spatialization of language as a concrete and incarnate medium is precisely the transcendence of linguistically created sense.

Language essentially transcends time and space through a meaning that is self-reflexive in structure. Language is self-generating and autonomous in its capability of originating sense – thanks to its enactment of a transcendent Word that becomes incarnate, sensual, fleshly, in a sense that Merleau-Ponty's epistemology of painting renders perspicuous. Merleau-Ponty reverses the distanced viewing of an object typical of centuries of idealizing oculocentrism by making perception proceed, rather, from within the dark depths of the flesh. Such a view was intuited, in effect, by the medieval extramissive theory of vision in which sight was engendered by emissions from a bodily organ, the eyes. Dante's Christian incarnational understanding of perception similarly grounds it in the material body and its senses. Dante's visionary experience is idealized, but also de-idealizing, given its emphasis on materiality and contingency (Chapters 2 and 3).

This chapter (4) has moved from the rational philosophy of language called speculative grammar to art-historical and phenomenological theories of invisibility in the image. In both cases, rigorous rational analysis winds up in a kind of radical self-critique leading to a self-deconstructive move that breaks down our usual finite logic and opens to a kind of mystical horizon of the "beyond" of language and of the image. The power of language and of the image is ultimately a power of surpassing all finite representation toward an infinite and unknowable power that is not grasped by rational science but rather shows through at its limits.[38]

Dante realizes in the space-time of the Heaven of Jove a perfect ordering of elements – of the souls that inhabit and animate it in the form of sparks. Just as, at the Creation, all things were made by the Word, here again we are given to see the Word of Scripture in action. This enactment of order in space reenacts the original ordering of the Creation, together with the restorative reordering of history according to the time of Redemption. This ordering of letters into a sentence manifests the divine ordinance for history and its ideal of justice. In the Heaven of Jove, Dante presents a controlled, symbolic ordering of the space-time of the heaven as a revelation of the way in which God's will and justice are in control of the whole of universal history. His vision is an epitome of the providential

---

[38] Ernesto Grassi, *Die Macht der Phantasie: Zur Geschichte abendländischen Denkens* (Frankfurt am Main: Syndikat, 1984) combines the resources of Italian humanism with those of German idealism in developing a persuasive speculative cultural history along these lines.

ordering that made the founding of Rome by Aeneas simultaneous ("a una ora") with the founding of the Davidic dynasty, out of whose root Christ the King was to be born (*Convivio* IV. v. 3–9).

From our standpoint within it, this history looks like a chaos of random sparks in a general conflagration. However, seen in its totality, from a point of view beyond history, this world of events will reveal its design to be fully worthy of the transcendent justice of an omnipotent and perfect God. Dante breaks language down into letters and reduces it to the sheer materiality of its elements (*stoicheia*). Yet this turns out to be a revelation of justice from beyond the horizon of what humans can rationally see in their analysis of language as a phenomenon.

Still, not even justice, taken alone as a self-sufficient concept, can give us the whole picture: what Dante sees in the heaven of justice is "the *love* that was there." The experience of love undoes and undermines all our preconceived ideas about justice. For Dante, finally, in the vision of the *Paradiso*, there can be no justice without love, and this radically transforms the notion of justice as equality. Particularly Dante's Heaven of Jupiter demonstrates that "divine justice is at every point moved by love" and "at every point cedes to love."[39]

Justice itself becomes a source of paradox, doing violence by love, as suggested in an enigmatic passage of the Gospel of Matthew 11:12: "The kingdom of heaven suffereth violence, and the violent take it by force" ("Regnum caelorum vim patitur, et violenti rapiunt illud"). Dante echoes this statement in his Heaven of Jupiter: "*Regnum celorum* violenza pate / da caldo amore" ("The Kingdom of heaven suffers violence / from ardent love," XX. 94–95), interpreting the violence in question as a violence of love willingly, but passionately, "suffered" on the part of heaven. Love exceeds every possible rational calculus of retributive justice, so that the only true justice, finally, is that of love. This constitutes an ethical correlate of the ultra-grammatical epistemology that Dante envisions in the heaven of Jupiter.

Dante's *Paradiso*, all throughout, is concerned with transcendence of normal epistemological limitations, particularly of time and space, through absorption in the vision of the infinite Being of God. And Dante's indispensable resource and medium as the vehicle of this transcendence is language. How does language mediate this transcendence? Not by abstracting from the temporal and spatial but, contrariwise, by sinking

[39] John Took, "'Diligite iustitiam qui iudicatis terram': Justice and the Just Ruler in Dante," in *Dante and Governance*, ed. John Woodhouse (Oxford: Clarendon, 1997), 137–51; citation, 150.

itself into them and, at the same time, also transfiguring them. Whereas space and time would ordinarily count empirically as language's necessary conditions, Dante's poetic making reverses this dependency and makes space and time over again as imaginative forms emanating from and falling within the range and animation of language.

"Living language" has perhaps become a lame phrase and highly suspect in our contemporary critical climate, but it is not so wrong for intimating the self-engendering and creative capacities that are intrinsic to language as Dante discovers it at the visionary heights of his poem in its "visible speech" ("visibile parlare") in heaven. The latter phrase is borrowed from *Purgatorio* X. 95, but it applies also, and conspicuously, to Dante's vision of the skywriting in *Paradiso* XVIII. Rendering the concatenation of words simultaneous through visualization liberates language from unilateral syntactical relations and makes its elements polysemous and multidirectional vectors.[40]

As a differential play of significances, of values and vectors that are always mediations and relations to something other, writing, letters, literature inevitably *virtualize* the real, making it omnipresent, yet only as a negation of absolute reality. The *absolutely* real can only be revealed as an *other* world – for which Dante's poetic universe is emblematic.[41]

Dante's poetry makes language fill space and time with phenomenal energy and presence. The vision of the letters from the Book of Wisdom in Canto XVIII symbolizes the peculiar virtue and working of Dante's language by its exploitation of spatial and temporal dimensions in order to present Scriptural language in a totally spectacular way. This intensive phenomenalization of language also illustrates, and even shows off, some of the special powers of poetry. Yet the phenomenal incarnation of language is held firmly together with the transcendence of sense, which Dante's text represents as equally fundamental to language, especially to its poetic and specifically revelatory nature. This paradoxical interpenetration and co-inherence of the transcendent (sense) and the immanent (sensation) in the phenomenon of language is the fascinating mystery contemplated by Dante in his vision in the Heaven of Jove. It takes the form momentously of the presence of speech in writing (Chapter 2), and this becomes an emphatically *sensuous* presence – an incarnation of the word – that Chapter 5 undertakes to explore more concretely.

---

[40] Compare Giovanni Pozzi, *Sull'orlo del visibile parlare* (Milan: Adelphi, 1993), 13–14.
[41] Theories of virtual reality are pioneered in their application to Dante by Jacob Abell, "Medieval and Postmodern Virtual Realities: Embodiment, Disembodiment, and the Ends of Experience from Marie de France to Dante to Char Davis" (Vanderbilt dissertation, 2021).

CHAPTER 5

Sense Made Sensuous and Synaesthesia in the Sight and Sound of Writing

The apotheosis of sense or meaning as the final moment of language, whether in the stream of speech or in the sequence of writing, is dramatized spectacularly in the explosive transformations of the last letter – M – of the theme-sentence that Dante selects from the Book of Wisdom and lights up with the soul-sparks in the Heaven of Jupiter. Once the conceptual sense of the sentence has been realized with the appearance of the final letter, this Gothic insignia M (Figure 1(a)) metamorphoses into two successive pictorial emblems – first, the lily (Figures 1(b) and 2) and then the eagle's head and neck ("la testa e 'l collo," XVIII. 108) and wings or body, as depicted in Figure 1(c). The latter pictogram (variously imagined in Figures 3–6) sensuously and holistically displays, in visual phantasmagoria, the meaning and majesty of Empire. It means, and superessentially *is*, Justice: it emblematizes Dante's utopian vision of the ideal state.

In Dante's ideal vision, World Empire is itself made in the image of the perfect order of the created universe. Dante's ideal of a universal World Government is modeled on God's own intrinsic order and unity in the spiritual heaven. Monarchy alone, Dante believes, can guarantee justice in history and society. He demonstrates this at length in the logical syllogisms of Book I of his political treatise *Monarchia*, as well as in his construction of universal history in *Convivio* IV. iii–v, and he recurs to this theme obsessively as a *Leitmotif* throughout the *Commedia*.

The sense of the Scriptural sentence on justice and love addressed to the rulers of the earth is thereby rendered concrete in a symbolic language of imperial heraldry. The message of Scripture is converted into – and is transmitted by – the emblem of the eagle and its historical realization by Rome. Emerging as a metamorphosis of the M, this textual eagle is a transformation of *writing* in the final character that, literally, "takes off" once the letters of the sentence are complete. The sense of the sentence – its meaning – is put into play and on display through sensations both visual and audible. Dante's description insists on this, with its persistent pairing in a sustained parallelism of impressions in each of these sensory modalities. Dante pursues this transformation of sense – or meaning – into a supersensory type of sensation and presence by the alchemy of poetic language further in the subsequent cantos, XIX and XX, of the heaven of Jove that flesh out the intellectual meaning of the vision presented in XVIII. 70–117 by elaborating on its phenomenal form.

For Dante, the signs in the heaven of Jove are important as presences that can be *sensed* – that can be perceived by his physical senses. Marguerite Chiarenza calls the sign of the eagle a "real presence."[1] This is true primarily in a metaphysical sense. Still, we must also recognize that, considered poetically, this presence is sensuously real in the modality not only of sight but also of hearing. The letters are presented throughout this heaven as sights in constant and explicit conjunction with sound and, furthermore, with movement. The holy creatures *sang*, but they also formed their collective shapes into choreographed flights of letters, "now D, now I, now L":

> sì dentro ai lumi sante creature
> volitando cantavano, e faciensi
> or D, or I, or L in sue figure.
>
> (XVIII. 76–78)

> (so within the holy lights creatures
> flying sang, and made themselves
> now D, now I, now L in its figures.)

This suggests that sight and sound and kinetics belong originarily together and are only artificially, or analytically, distinguished. Nothing more specific is said as to *what* the holy creatures sang. Presumably it was, in one way or another, the ineffable God. In any case, we can assume that it would have been integral to what they then make visibly manifest, especially considering the symmetrical coordination of sight and sound that governs the *cantica* all thoughout, from the first canto – with its flood of light taken in together with the music of the spheres (I. 82). Dante's senses of both sight and hearing are overwhelmed by such novel sensations

---

[1] Marguerite Chiarenza, "Canto XX," *Lectura Dantis* 16–17 (1995), *Special Issue: Lectura Dantis Virginiana, III Dante's* Paradiso: *Introductory Readings*, 301. These terms are made even more resonant by George Steiner's *Real Presences* (London: Faber & Faber, 1989), an eloquent rebuttal to Derrida's attack on the metaphysics of presence. Steiner is inspired by the power of presence as demonstrated in literature just such as this scene insisting on language as present through its literary means.

beyond what is normally possible for human perception. A desire unprecedented in its acuteness to know their cause awakens in him:

> La novità del suono e 'l grande lume
>   di lor cagion m'accesero un disio
>   mai non sentito di cotanto acume.

(I. 82–84)

> (The newness of the sound and the great light
>   ignited in me a desire to know their cause
>   never before felt with such acuteness.)

Taken as experience of the superessential reality of Paradise, what Dante records here as sensation is ambiguously intellection that can be expressed in diverse sensory modalities.

The principles of such poetic composition, as well as of such a metaphysics and theophany, favor the song and its uncomprehended meaning's being as closely bound in unity as possible with what is then shown visually: meaning almost seems to dissolve into sensation. The grammar here, moreover, suggests that the letters are first sung and that subsequently each is made into "its" figure and becomes a written form and shape. The immediately following lines clearly distinguish two such moments or phases – the resolution into song and then into a figure that is sustained momentarily in silence:

> Prima, cantando, a sua nota moviensi;
>   poi, diventando l'un di questi segni,
>   un poco s'arrestavano e taciensi.

(XVIII. 79–81)

> (First, singing, they moved to its note,
>   then, becoming one of these signs,
>   they paused for a little and kept silent.)

The souls, singing, move first in time to its ("sua") – that is, the letter's (or possibly the song's) – note. Whatever it may mean for a letter to have "its" own note, such individual attunement of letters is familiar from the Kabbalah's letters, with their numerical valences, and is not unlike certain Pythagorian conceptions of universal harmonics. This lyrical, melodic, and rhythmic manifestation of the letter then metamorphoses into a spatial image recognizable as one of the chosen letters of the alphabet. At this stage, stasis and silence are reached, which consistently mark the moment in which meaning can finally be construed, even in the representations of heaven.

Music and motion culminate in silence and stasis: the phenomenon is consummated by its own negation. This must be the case in order to signify supersensory perception, since such perception can only be constituted dialectically by a negation of ordinary sense perception. Dante's text does not offer unequivocal resolutions but rather vibrates between voice and written character or inscription, between sound and sight. The two are perceived as inextricable from one another, each somehow necessarily referring to and calling forth the other. The coextension, coordination, cohesion, and apparent coincidence of the sensory modes here hint that they are metaphors for supersensory experience such as Dante's intellection of Paradise can only be.

When Dante actually presents in his text the letters that are given to his vision in Paradise, the vision by which he beholds them is not simply vision in a literal sense. Ordinary empirical vision needs to be transcended or deconstructed in order that Dante's "visionary" experience, his *written* vision, can take place. Vision and audition here become finally metaphors for a supersensory experience of intellection. As merely physical, both sight and sound are equally inadequate and become self-destructing sensations.

Sight and sound in heaven, as intellectual sight and sound, are indeed interchangeable. In *De trinitate* XV, Augustine remarks that, "When, then, these things are done outwardly through the body, speech and sight are different things; inwardly, however, when we think, both are one. Similarly, hearing and seeing are two mutually diverse things in the bodily senses; however, in the mind, seeing and hearing are not different."[2] This inner relation of sight and sound in the mind becomes focused particularly in relation to the use of synaesthesia in Canto XX.

A theological grounding for Dante's undertaking can be found in the miracle of the Incarnation, whereby the ineffable divine Word becomes accessible to being seen and heard and touched. In many instances in the Gospels, Jesus's sensuous contact with others is treated with marvel and produces miracles. However, the Scriptural divine Word, too, in certain traditions, is held to produce sensory miracles. Dante's synaesthetic treatment of the supersensible becomes most intelligible within the tradition of the spiritual senses discerned in religious experience and particularly in

---

[2] Sancti Aurelii Augustini, *De trinitate Libri XV*, 2 vols., ed. W. J. Mountain, in *Aurelii Augustini Opera*, Pt. XVI, 2, Corpus Christianorum, Series Latina (Turnhout: Brepols, 1968), XV. x. 18. "Foris enim cum per corpus haec fiunt aliud est locutio, aliud uisio; intus autem cum cogitamus utrumque unum est. Sicut auditio et uisio duo quaedam sunt inter se distantia in sensibus corporis, in animo autem non est aliud atque aliud uidere et audire."

reading Scripture.[3] There is, in this tradition, some speculation on the ineffable divine Word's being neither properly visible nor audible, though both sensory channels can be valid as ways of translating metaphorically what cannot be properly expressed. Talk of "vision" of the divine Word has the advantage of connoting an immediate apprehension of a totality. This is one essential aspect of how the illumination of the Word is understood to occur theologically. Of course, precisely the check to realizing total vision is what makes the finite created intellect transcend itself and jump to a higher sort of apprehension of what it cannot adequately know. The first reason or ground of things ("prima cagion") is exactly what created intellects do not see totally ("non veggion *tota*," XX. 132).

Indeed, the *Paradiso*, in a peculiarly strict and conspicuous sense, is precisely about the invisible. The visual image is an index of something that is not properly visible. As with all imagery of Paradise, we must ask: Is the object then a kind of writing? It is, in the sense that it is significant, in the end, not for its perceptual qualities, but only for that which they index by virtue of the differences that signification engenders. This interpretation might seem to be dispelled by the lavishness and elegance and energy of this "writing" in images. Dante's writing in the sky, moreover, neutralizes what we ordinarily expect as the property of all writing, namely, the interrupting of the transparency of speech. Dante's skywriting conjures divine meaning (or presence) immediately and transparently out of the self-referentiality of signifiers and their highly performative signifying. Instead of relying on the conception of writing as a conventional, purely arbitrary, effaceable sign for bearing intellectual meaning, the concept of writing in play or at work in this heaven conspicuously mobilizes a sensory orgy of the written character shown off with "calligraphic" flourish.

Dante, of course, in ways recalling and at least indirectly influenced by Augustine, is generally anxious that the signifier not block or delay access to the signified. God, the ultimate *significatum*, must not be deflected or obscured by any opacities of language. And yet, here the opaque signifiers themselves become identical with the divine vision. The heaven of Jupiter in particular, and Dante's poetry in general, give great emphasis to the sensible form of signifiers: they enact an apotheosis of the written letter. In this respect, Dante agrees with much contemporary theory of poetic language since Mallarmé, for which the materiality of the signifier is

---

[3] Traditional texts and backgrounds are presented in Paul L. Gavrilyuk and Sarah Coakley, eds., *The Spiritual Senses: Perceiving God in Western Christianity* (Cambridge: Cambridge University Press, 2012).

recognized as essential to the poeticality of language and to its visionary truth.

Philippe Sollers views Dante from a perspective informed by Mallarmé, Blanchot, Jakobson, and Saussure. He stresses how "the *attachment to the letter* was at the enigmatic origin of poetry, especially vedic poetry" ("l'*attachement à la lettre* était à l'origine énigmatique de la poésie et surtout de la poésie védique"). Mallarmé's phrase "this reciprocal contamination of the work and the means" ("cette réciproque contamination de l'œuvre et des moyens"), from "L'Action restreint,"[4] suggests rather a mutual determination of literary means, such as writing, and the poetic work: Sollers envisages eventually even the "paradise" created by their working together.[5] Dante's visionary poetry pivoting on the letter in the cantos that concern us here is itself an effort to lay bare something of the enigmatic origin of poetry. Pictographic and hieroglyphic languages are typically considered to be closer than phonetic languages to things themselves, and in this sense to be more "original."[6]

The importance of this iconic aspect of Dante's language has not been overlooked by Dante scholarship. It has been explored particularly by Roger Dragonetti through reading Dante in the quasi-Cratylist tradition of Isidore of Seville.[7] It was made macroscopic, furthermore, by Egidio Guidobaldi, who, in describing the sensory intensity of Dante's representations, emphasized their harmonic expansiveness ("espansione armonica") and their fullness as spectacle ("pienezza spettacolare"). Starting from Horace's motto *ut pictura poesis* and following Jacques Maritain's Neo-Thomist theory of aesthetic synthesis, Guidobaldi treats Dante's poem as a *Gesamtkunstwerk* englobing music, theater, song, scenery, and dance in its compression of the literary genres of novel, drama, and lyric, with varying emphases as it progresses through the three canticles.[8]

Within the more circumscribed compass of the prophetic word of the Bible taken as Dante's model, Giuseppe Mazzotta highlights the concrete quality of Dante's poetry in terms that likewise bring out its multi-medial dimensionality appealing simultaneously to several senses. "Characterized

---

[4] Stéphane Mallarmé, *Œuvres complètes* (Paris: Pleiades, 1945), 371.

[5] Philippe Sollers, "Dante et la traversée de l'écriture," in *Logiques* (Paris: Seuil, 1968), 107. See, further, Philippe Sollers, *Vers le Paradis* (Paris: Desclée de Brouwer, 2010).

[6] See Franz Dornseiff, *Das Alphabet in Mystik und Magie* (Leipzig: Teubner, 1922); and Ernest Fenollosa, *The Chinese Written Character as a Medium for Poetry*, critical ed., eds. Haun Saussy, Jonathan Stalling, and Lucas Klein (New York: Fordham University Press, 2008).

[7] Roger Dragonetti, *Dante pèlerin de la Sainte Face* (Gent: Romanica Gandensia, 1968).

[8] Egidio Guidobaldi, *Dante Europeo III: Poema sacro come esperienza mistica* (Florence: Olschki, 1968). See especially "Primato lirico e compresenza di forme," 611–20; cf. 633–87.

by material consistency, as palpable and edible substance ('taste,' 'nutri-ment,' 'digested,' are the terms employed to define it), the poetic word of Dante situates itself in the tradition of the *nabim* for whom the word is never merely a simulacrum or receptacle of things, nor the formal, funereal image of the real. The prophetic word exists as a tangible icon and is rather a reality capable of itself transforming the deceptive appearances of the world."[9]

And yet, at the same time, sensuous form in the *Paradiso* is to be understood ultimately as an aesthetic expression of a totally invisible and imperceptible reality. Dante's most spiritually attuned critics have for generations written fervently of a process of spiritualization, whereby earthly reality is transfigured and even distilled into theological significa-tion. For Augusto Guzzo, earth, *terra*, is volatalized into celestial nature ("volatilizzata in natura celeste"), while according to Giovanni Getto, images are dissolved and transformed into theological content ("non solo spiritualizazzione artistica, ma un vero e proprio processo di trasforma-zione in cui 'l'imagine si dissolve quasi in contenuto teologico'").[10]

For Chiarenza, the eagle belongs to Dante's techniques for representing immateriality. The eagle represents a stage in the progress towards a supposedly "imageless vision."[11] However, concretely, Dante gives us only images and their disappearance. The vision consists in the apprehen-sion of a meaning, but only after the image has already disappeared. The letters in the series, moreover, are never present all together but only in serial form, one letter at a time. Chiarenza stresses how "symbolic meaning overshadows concrete form" (86). This intuition elucidates the fact that what Dante sees in this vision of language as the divine Word in Jupiter is specifically writing. For writing is, by its nature, a fragmentary form, or at least a diacritical function in which meaning is not immanently present but is rather dynamically produced and then dispersed (like the leaves of Sybil) or disseminated (as "seeds" and "sparks"). In a sense, this suggests how the whole vision of Paradise is to be understood as writing – as coinciding,

---

[9] Giuseppe Mazzotta, "Teologia ed esegesi biblica," in *Dante e la Bibbia* (Florence: Olschki, 1988), 100. "Caratterizzata da materiale consistenza, come sostanza palpabile ed edibile ('gusto', 'nutri-mento', 'digesta' sono i termini adoperati per definirla), la parola poetica di Dante si colloca nella tradizione dei *nabim* per i quali la parola non è mai mero simulacro o ricettacolo delle cose, né è l'immagine forma funerea del reale. La parola profetica esiste, tangibile icona e anzi, realtà essa stessa capace di trasformare le ingannevoli apparenze del mondo."

[10] Citations of commentaries in Dante Alighieri, *La Divina Commedia*, vol. VI (Milan: Fratelli Fabbri Editori, 1965), 299.

[11] Marguerite Mills Chiarenza, "The Imageless Vision and Dante's *Paradiso*," *Dante Studies* 90 (1972): 79–91.

therefore, with the *Paradiso* as a written work. Writing entails rupture and distance between sensible form and intellectual or spiritual meaning. Dante invests so intensively in the visual form of the letter in order ultimately to discard and surpass it. He works his vision of writing up to its own dissolution, literally and thematically, in the skywriting of Jupiter that explodes into incalculable trajectories of sparks, which then metamorphose into a visual emblem.

Divinity in the *Paradiso*, in conformity with the *Phaedrus* tradition, is conceived essentially as intellectual light, and the appeal "illustrami di te" ("make me illustrious with yourself") suggests some sort of union with God in this transcendent dimension of being, as well as alluding once more to the painterly dimension of writing that is so persistently present throughout the passage. Painting is akin to writing, thus understood, precisely in its rendering an invisible significance visible. As Paul Klee's aphorism famously states: "Art does not render the visible, but rather renders visible" ("Kunst gibt nicht das sichtbare wider, sondern macht sichtbar").[12]

Painting works as a substitute for writing also in Derrida's theory in *The Truth in Painting* (*La vérité en peinture*, 1978). Considered as modes of representation, painting and writing alike are apt to stand initially in the way of the transparency of sense, but in the end this barrier turns inside out and both media convey a deconstructed sense that is transparent and immediate. The *purely* sensual sign has an indeterminate, perhaps even infinite, significance. Empty of determinate conceptual content, it can be grasped only by its negation of all conceptual significances. Such signifying might be taken as a *pharmakon* – the poison that heals, serving also as medicine. Dante enthusiastically embraces the painterly potentialities of writing, even as he affirms and explores the disruptive characteristics of writing – not unlike Derrida – but all for the purpose of indirectly delivering a higher, invisible truth, a kind of healing in and through the breach.

Dante seeks to realize consciousness of time and eternity simultaneously in the ecstatic temporality of open, infinite semiosis betokened by the sparking of signs. The concrete presence of sensory features in language is an elusive, vanishing presence, one that alludes, in Dante's perception, to presence of another kind – an eternal presence, which, however, can have no distinct form or feature. For all their sensory flashiness and choreographed spectacularity, the scenes in these heavens are not enduring, but momentary. The impressions they make are not indelible in themselves, so much as

---

[12] From *Creative Credo*, 1920. Paul Klee, *Kunst-Lehre* (Leipzig: Reclam, 1991), 60.

suggestive of "something else." They are intriguing moments that, by vanishing, clear the way and point further along the paradisiacal path converging on a divine Other. The reader is not given anything stable or solid to hang on to, no sense of grasping reality *tel quel* – as revealed in its nakedness. The figures traced in the heaven are transparently artifices, even enigmatic codes. They are only *indicative* of an otherworldly reality known theologically to be beyond representation, and thus beyond any manifest feature or figure. This reality is *experienced* in the sparking or signifying, but it cannot be contained or circumscribed objectively in any realized shape or form, since these are constantly metamorphosing into something other.

The eagle, that "beautiful image" ("bella image," XIX. 2), has an artificial but transcendentally infused life as a "sign" ("quel segno") that is fabricated and literally woven or made into a text by divine grace ("de la grazia divina era contesto," XIX. 37–38). Part of the strategy, then, is for the signs of Paradise to expose themselves as signs, for them to declare themselves pure signs, and thereby to vanish before that of which they are not even precise indicators, with determinate content, so much as incalculable traces and miraculous manifestations. Their concrete forms become sacramental manifestations. The ineffable experience of poetry itself stands in for and trumps every more externally perceptible object of experience.

The Pure Sign Incarnate (Canto XIX)

Readers of *Paradiso* XIX have underlined the peculiar, unprecedented visionary space opened from its first word "Parea" ("appeared"). Edoardo Sanguineti describes this as "An absolutely thematic word, ... the visionary 'to appear' sets the tone of the new page of the *Paradiso*" ("Un verbo assolutamente tematico, ... il visionario 'parere', intona la nuova pagina del *Paradiso*").[13] Along similar lines, and citing Sanguineti, Vittorio Russo maintained that the objective narrative is suspended and replaced by a temporal unfolding interior to consciousness: "The temporality of diegesis seems to be suspended or transferred into the continuum of the interior dimension of consciousness" ("Il tempo della diegesi sembra sospendersi o trasferirsi nel *continuum* della dimensione interiore della coscienza").[14] In this inner dimension of what appears to consciousness, signs can incarnate absolute meaning in their own right.

[13] Edoardo Sanguineti, "*Paradiso* XIX," in *Il realismo di Dante* (Florence: Sansoni, 1966), 103–4.
[14] Vittorio Russo, "Pd. XIX: Similis fictio nunquam facta fuit per aliquem poetam," in *Il romanzo teologico: Sondaggi sulla "Commedia" di Dante* (Naples: Liguori, 1984), 149.

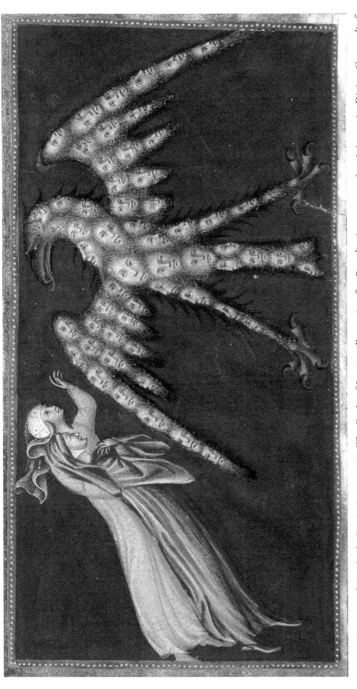

Figure 4 Giovanni di Paolo di Grazia (1403–1482), The Eagle of Justice, illustration for *Paradiso* (*c.* 1444–1450), miniature in *Divina Commedia* for Alfonso V, king of Aragon, Naples, and Sicily, British Library, London. Photo ©The British Library Board (shelfmark: C13232–27)

A clue to the peculiar ontological consistency of this canto (together with the one that follows) can be found in the insistent references to the emblem of the eagle. This "sign" (XIX. 37, 101; XX. 8, 86; cf. VI. 32, 82, 100, 104) or "image" (XIX. 2, 95; XX. 79, 139), with its dominant speaking part, imposes itself indelibly as the protagonist of the whole heaven.[15] The sign here takes on a life of its own. It is not just a formal marker for a reality external to itself but rather makes manifest the intrinsic life of form. This is achieved especially by rendering its sense (or meaning), which is the unity and essence of the sign, sensuous. Dante is obsessed in this canto with synaesthetic hearing and seeing of the words of his text. To show how textual experience develops senses of its own, senses that perceive not the properties of external objects but rather sensuous qualities inherent in the sign, qualities that are instrisically (and infinitely) meaningful, constitutes the extraordinary experimental undertaking of these cantos.

Nevertheless, the theme of canto XIX is a theological argument, even a theodicy, and to this extent it is abstract. In XIX. 70–78, Dante expresses doubt concerning the justice of condemning people who had no opportunity to hear the Gospel or receive baptism, and the balance of heaven elaborates an answer. Dante's task is to make even this doctrinal material poetically concrete. This becomes most evident in the lyrical flourishes, particularly the bird similes, with which the complex argumentation is punctuated.

Precisely where the most difficult questions of justice corner reason into impasses, Dante's bird images take wing and celebrate in lyrical raptures the mysterious ways of God that exceed our comprehension. This tactic serves even as a framing device, since before the Eagle's first discourse in answer to Dante's doubts, the simile of the falcon that is unhooded and looks around rejoicing ("Quasi falcone ch'esce del cappello, / move la testa," XIX. 34–39) intervenes and sets the tone.

The aporias of the discussion of "divine justice" ("la divina giustizia," XIX. 29) are placed from the start into a visionary register, since no discursive way out is in sight. The Eagle explains that divine justice exceeds human comprehension, and its speech is book-ended by another lyrical flourish with the stork image (XIX. 90–93). Fundamental philosophico-theological

---

[15] John Leavey, "Derrida and Dante: Différance and the Eagle in the Sphere of Jupiter," *MLN* 91/1 (1976): 60–68, quotes indefatigably all the numerous occurrences of "segno," "imagine," "imago," "'mprenta" to designate the eagle as a kind of heraldic figure rather than a bird that could be real and present. He comments that "These references register the formality of the eagle in this sphere" (p. 66). This is true, yet, *pace* Derrida, I wish to stress that for Dante purely formal being attains to a higher degree of reality than that of the ordinary, empirical reality of things.

problems are dissolved more than they are resolved – as also by Wittgenstein in his *Tractatus Logico-Philosphicus* (1921).

The sensuous images of the *Paradiso* are presented as vanishing subjective impressions. Not concreteness, in the end, but evanescence is their essential characteristic. This has long been observed in the criticism, for example, with regard to the river simile in XX. 19ff.: "Precisely because the visual image resolves into the musical image of murmuring, these verses differ from the celebratory verses of the *Inferno* dedicated to the green streams of the Casentino (XXX. 64–67), in which the image maintained its concrete actuality, its determination as a thing seen and almost tasted. The eagle itself is still only a stylized image, without profundity; accordingly, the sound can issue through its *hollow* (*buggio*) neck."[16]

This ephemerality of the image is enacted in an especially emblematic way from the opening of *Paradiso* XX, with the disappearing daylight soon substituted for by starlight used to allude to raising consciousness to an altogether higher level of reality. Dante's technique entails rendering sense or meaning sensory, especially in the auditory or visual modes of poetry, but also relativizing all sensations (mutually) through their reference to the supersensory. Already *Inferno* III. 28–30: "l'aura sanza tempo tinta" ("the timelessly tinged air"), and V. 28: "io venni a luogo d'ogni luce muto" ("I came to a place where every light is silent"), begin to take recourse to the synaesthesia necessary to speak of the eternal realms.

The conversion of sense (intellectual) into sensation (physical) is a major aesthetic goal of Dante and of aesthetic artists generally. It becomes self-conscious especially among modern artists. It can be found again at its intensest, for example, in Marcel Proust's transubstantiation of his experience into art through the remembrance of things past, for which the taste of a madeleine proves instrumental. Everything that the book's protagonist, Marcel, has experienced in time, and that has therefore been lost ("le temps perdu"), can be recovered through the agency of the imagination in its creation of art.[17] Art presents concretely, sensuously, the time that is lost to mere experience and its successiveness. Linked together in an

---

[16] "Proprio perché l'immagine visiva si risolve in quella musicale del mormorio, questi versi si differenziano da quelli celebrativi dell'*Inferno*, dedicati ai verdi *ruscelletti* del Casentino (canto XXX, versi 64–67), nei quali l'immagine manteneva la sua concreta attualità, la sua determinatezza di cosa vista e quasi assaporata. Or a invece tutto perde capacità e peso. La stessa aquila è pur sempre un'immagine stilizzata, senza profondità, cosicché il suono può sortire attraverso il suo collo *bugio*." This commentary in Dante Alighieri, *La Divina Commedia*, vol. VI (Milan: Fratelli Fabbri Editori, 1965), 315, cites and synthesizes readings of this canto by Vittorio Rossi and Attilio Momigliano.

[17] Gianfranco Contini develops this comparison in "Dante come personaggio-poeta," in *Varianti e altra linguistica: Una raccolta di saggi (1938–68)* (Turin: Einaudi, 1970), 335–61.

order that is not just that of "intelligence," but rather of a fully sensuous resurrection, the images of art and of literature in particular constitute what Proust calls "time regained" ("le temps retrouvé").

Karlheinz Stierle underscores how "language is the medium that dialogues with the multiplicity of other artistic media" for both Proust and Dante ("bei beiden steht das Medium Sprache im Dialog mit der Vielfalt der künstlerischen Medien") in the works to which each dedicated their lives.[18] And in both works, constructed in language that can endure, time is made an object of poetic contemplation. However, whereas for Proust the work withdraws from time in order to represent time as an object of consciousness, Dante dissolves representation and its work *into* time in order to brush with eternity in its withdrawal from consciousness. Not aesthetic stasis, but a dynamic event of eternity: this is Dante's goal, and it points him beyond the bounds of art and representation. Nonetheless, he does *provisionally* represent time as it unfolds in all manner of concrete images.

Julia Kristeva might call this "sensible time" ("le temps sensible"): it is time that is made accessible to experience of the senses from the point of view of the eternal rather than of what vanishes. She relates such a temporality expressly to Dante's work of recovering and redeeming lost time by imagining that the modern "I" who speaks in Proust's fiction, in effect, says: "*I offer you the Divine Comedy of life: not of mine but of yours, of ours, of Being – it is the Absolute*" ("*Je vous offre la Divine Comédie de la vie: pas de la mienne, mais de la vôtre, de la nôtre, de l'Être – elle est l'Absolu*").[19] The reader thus becomes the protagonist of the poem in ways provoked by Dante's addresses to the reader. As Kristeva's Dantesque reference suggests, Dante is emblematic of this enormous sea change in the entire purport of literature in the modern era. Dante manifests his awareness that the readers' reenactment of the poem in their own imagination and sensory experience lends it its concrete meaning and existential truth.[20] This subjective dimension of the event of truth in the poem underlies and subverts the strictly objective logic of representation in specific, separate sensory modalities.

---

[18] Karlheinz Stierle, *Zeit und Werk: Prousts "À la recherche du temps perdu" und Dantes "Commedia"* (Munich: Hanser, 2008), 7.
[19] Julia Kristeva, *Le temps sensible: Proust et l'expérience littéraire* (Paris: Gallimard, 1994), 211.
[20] Just this structural relay to the reinvention of meaning in the experience of the reader is the premise for my approach to the poem in *Dante's Interpretive Journey*, beginning from chapter 1: "The Address to the Reader."

Canto XX. Visionary Writing: The Sight and Sound of the Word

Canto XX presents a fusion of sense (meaning) and sensuousness through images of speech made into music, and vice versa. Dante describes auditory sensations in visual terms. Strikingly, he *visualizes* the rising of notes on a cithar to the neck of the instrument, or to the hole in a wind instrument, where the sound is emitted. He is imaginatively seeing sound. Such synaesthetic effects belong essentially to Dante's creation of the experience of Paradise and to the sensory experience that can be elicited from letters, as the vision in XVIII. 71–113 so powerfully demonstrates.

Conception translated into sensation can be recorded – in the heart. The musicality of language is mnemonic and makes it apt to be learned by heart. The intensive musicality of the canto's exordium can be placed into evidence by an alignment of its rhymes:

> discende – s'accende – risplende
> parvente – mente – tacente
> canti – t'ammanti – santi
> flailli – lapilli – squilli
> lume – fiume – cacume

The canto's musical themes are re-echoed in the music of these rhymes.

The *Paradiso*'s images are most characteristically also images bearing a transcendent sense that has been made sensuous. Sense is, then, the sensuous form of music rising in the strains of sound taking shape along the neck of a cithar that breaks unexpectedly into speech – into words exactly such as are awaited by Dante's "heart," where he writes them (XX. 30).

Canto XX, the so-called "canto of the just spirits," begins with Dante remembering what the heaven does ("e questo atto del ciel me venne a mente," 7) when the sun sets (1–3) and the sky, which before had been illuminated by the sun alone, shows up again. However, now the sky is lit by many lights, even though according to Ptolomaic astronomy all the stars reflect one light alone, that of the sun:

> Lo ciel, che sol di lui prima s'accende,
>   subitamente si rifà parvente
>   per molte luci, in che una risplende.

> (XX. 4–6)

> (the heaven, which before from him alone was lit,
>   suddenly turns again to appearing
>   due to many lights, in which one is reflected.)

In effect, the canto begins with a visual image to describe an acoustic phenomenon. The appearance of the whole host of stars after sunset comes to mind as the one voice of the eagle finishes and, after a silence, gives way to the many-voiced singing of the individual souls. The analogy with the appearance of the stars adumbrates, at the same time, the theme of the one and the many that lies at the heart of Dante's imperialist doctrine (*De monarchia* I. viii), as well as of his poetic metaphysics of the realm of Paradise (*Convivio* II. iii–v). From its opening lines, the *Paradiso* describes a unity of all in God, but also the multiplicity and diversity of participation in divine glory throughout the universe ("in una parte più e meno altrove," I. 1–3). This earthly memory is an analogy for what Dante does *not* remember: the phenomena (or rather noumena) of paradise proper that he experiences are not themselves within time, which is a condition of all memory. Dante does not state this threshold of memory as absolute: instead, he describes how the notes he heard are effaced gradually from memory ("canti / da mia memoria labili e caduci," 12). There is a virtuality of eternity in Dante's representation that enables it to be faintly captured in such residual images.

Dante repeatedly describes his unrememberable experience through images of sight that is sound and sound that is, in effect, sight. Neither modality taken in and for itself, as we know it through our empirical senses, proves adequate to represent the experience. It is somehow in the transposition from one to the other that poetic expression is found for an experience that itself escapes description and even memory, in whatever sensory modality. The canto presupposes at its beginning a silence ("tacente," 9) after the eagle's words of denunciation of corrupt Christian princes at the close of Canto XIX. And when, at the beginning of XX, perception starts up again, as conveyed by the analogy to stars coming out after sunset, Dante states that this comparison is suggested by the living lights, which become more bright and sing:

> però che tutte quelle vive luci,
>   vie più lucendo, cominciaron canti
>   da mia memoria labili e caduci.
>
> (XX. 10–12)

> (because all those living lights,
>   shining much more brightly, began songs
>   that for my memory are labile and extinguished.)

The blending of light into song here will be pursued throughout the canto. It is patent, not to say blatant, in the expostulation in the next tercet –

> O dolce amor che di riso t'ammanti,
>   quanto parevi ardente in que' flailli,
>   ch'avieno spirto sol di pensier santi!
>
> (XX. 13–15)

> (O sweet love who mantle yourself with smiling,
>   how ardent you appeared in those pipes
>   that were blown by only holy thoughts!)

Dante apostrophizes the sweet love that is mantled with a smile and exults over the ardor that makes the one love appear in the many "flailli," variously translated as "torches" (Latin *flacellum* through Old French *flael*) and as "flutes" or wind instruments (*flauto* from Latin *flare*, to blow), in what perhaps is, after all, not a merely accidental uncertainty.[21] This ambiguity encapsulates the undecidability between the registers of seeing and hearing that traverses the whole heaven. In the following *terzina*, the resplendent gems ("lucidi lapilli") silence the angelic notes ("puoser silenzio a li angelici squilli"). And Dante seems to hear the murmuring of a river ("udir mi parve un mormorar di fiume"), which, however, is described with a splendidly visual image of water "that descends crystalline from rock to rock, / showing the abundance of its peak" ("che scende chiaro giù di pietra in pietra, / mostrando l'ubertà del suo cacume," 20–21). And at this point begins the intensely heard – or is it rather seen? – description of how sound arising at the neck of a cithar "takes its form."

> E come suono al collo de la cetra
>   prende sua forma, e sí com' al pertugio
>   de la sampogna vento che penetra . . .
>
> (XX. 22–24)

> (And as sound at the neck of a cithar
>   takes its form, and as at the hole
>   of the zampogna wind which penetrates . . .)

---

[21] Manuscript variations include *frailli, flavilli, fravilli,* and *favilli*. See Giovanni Carsaniga, "Flailli," in *Miscellanea di studi in onore di Vittore Branca*, vol. I: *Dal medioevo al Petrarca* (Florence: Olshki, 1983), 305–9. Interesting pages on light operating sonorously as language in the *Paradiso* can be found in Didier Ottaviani, *Dante: L'esprit pèlerin* (Paris: Seuil, 2016), 84–89.

Similar also to wind moving through the hole in a bagpipe, without any time lapse, the murmur of the eagle rose through its neck, as if it were hollow:

> così, rimosso d'aspettare indugio,
>   quel mormorar de l'aguglia salissi
>   su per lo collo, come fosse bugio.

(XX. 25–27)

> (so, without any interval of waiting,
>   the murmur of the eagle rose
>   up through the neck as if it were hollow.)

This emptiness is the medium of the sound in question. The sound, however, is rather "seen" by being localized spatially. This strict inter-dependence of sound and sight suggests an experience that was perhaps in some sense independent of both, in such a way that the sounds cannot properly be described except by resorting to what they are *not*, namely sights, and vice versa.

This hybrid phenomenon issues in words, but words that are perhaps neither seen nor heard in any external sense because they are rather words written interiorly in the heart:

> Fecesi voce quivi, e quindi uscissi
>   per lo suo becco in forma di parole,
>   quali aspettava il core ov'io le scrissi.

(XX. 28–30)

> (Here it made itself voice and went out
>   from its beak in the form of words
>   such as the heart awaited, where I wrote them.)

Here, too, the sounds are localized as issuing "from the beak," but their shape or form seems to be determined by the expectation of the heart. So even before they are heard or seen, they are pre-delineated: they take shape in response to the expectation of the heart, where they are already *written*. These words produced first in the heart correspond to the words "dictated within" of Dante's poetics as formulated in *Purgatorio* XXIV ("a quel modo / ch'e' ditta dentro vo' significando," 52–54): they first suggest a possible dimension of interiority of the written word. They are an interior word like Augustine's *verbus interiorus*, but written. This word, it seems, Dante *can* remember in his mind's eye. Or perhaps he does not need to remember it at all because it belongs to the creative moment which first shapes and grants time. A stable form is apparently attained by writing, but the act of creation itself stands outside of time as its condition, and poetic making enables Dante to participate in that dimension of time transcendence. (Excursus V pursues the phenomenology of transcending time through poetic making, as well as the reversible ekphrastic transposition between verbal and visual registers.)

The eagle's speech draws attention immediately to its eye, specifically to the part that in mortal eagles sees and suffers the sun ("vede e pate il sole," 31). The eye of this eagle, following a well-established convention concerning the ability of the eagle to stare directly into the sun (cf. I. 46–48), is focused not upon the wide demesne below, taken in from its lofty height. The eagle's gaze is trained, instead, on the sun: symbolically, it is absorbed in the contemplation of God. This seeing is also a suffering, active and passive, and the individuality of the eagle and of the ego here is transcended. The picture is not one where all objects are unified by rays ending in the eagle's eye, but rather one where the eagle's eye itself is being trained upon a center outside itself. Self-transcendence of each sense into other senses and of each consciousness into another is the persistent theme of these representations.

The inadequacy of human sight or insight is compensated for only by a poetic transfer that slides from one modality to another – suggesting something of an untransmittable experience of an incomprehensible reality. The mechanism of this modal shift is employed one last time to bring the canto to its conclusion. The winking of the soul-lights, which confirms what has been communicated, is compared to a riff on cithar strings that gives expression to and enhances what has been sung.

> E come a buon cantor buon citarista
> fa seguitar lo guizzo de la corda
> in che più di piacer lo canto acquista,
> sì, mentre ch'e' parlò, sì mi ricorda
> ch'io vidi le due luci benedette,
> pur come batter d'occhi si concorda
> con le parole mover le fiammette.

> (XX. 142–48)

> (And as a good guitarist follows up
> a good singer with a riff of the chord,
> in which the song acquires extra pleasure,
> so, while the eagle spoke, I remember
> that I saw the two blessed lights,
> as if in one blinking of eyes concordant,
> moving with the words their flames.)

The speech of the eagle had emerged from pre-articulate sounds figured as a murmuring river, a babbling brook, or as the notes emitted from the neck of a string instrument (a lute or *cetra*) or the hollow pipes of a wind instrument (*zampogna*) in *Paradiso* XX. 16–30. And here, finally, at the canto's end, its "speech" comes with the winking of an eye of celestial soul-lights. By these synaesthetic images, Dante exposes the ground and spring of articulate speech in the feeling or sensation that precedes and renders it fertile.

Gary Cestaro points out that the "fertility" ("ubertà") remarked by Dante in XX. 20 for the exuberant abundance of a flowing spring is based etymologically on the breast (*uber* in Latin) and thus ties in with the fertility motives of the nursing body.[22] As again decisively in the closing images of the whole poem (XXXIII. 106–8), in order to figure the ultra-linguistic experience of Paradise, Dante traces language essentially to its beginnings as baby talk.[23] This molten state of language contains all in potential, even without differentiation of the senses from one another, or of the sensory and the intellectual. Dante pursues language, the medium of differentiation, upstream to its source at a point where all is one.

Specifically here, in the Heaven of Jupiter, Dante deploys and thematically focuses this synaesthetic language that overcomes all contradictions by groping back to a common source for all meanings and sensations. This occurs, not by accident, precisely where Dante confronts most directly the intractable question of God's justice in salvation, following up on the question raised in Canto XIX regarding the pagan born on the bank of the Indus out of earshot of the Gospel. In XX, the ecstatic celebration of the incomprehensible salvation of the pagans Trajan and Riphaeus leaves, nevertheless, the gnawing question, which is even closer to home for Dante, of why not Virgil? Already Dante has brought the lark simile onto the scene (XX. 73–78) in order to cover over the gap in rational explanation with sheer lyrical rapture. Dante has already been told bluntly that he cannot understand what he hears. He believes, but cannot "see" ("non vedi"), what the eagle is telling him (XX. 88–93). He knows the things he is told by their names, but not by their essences (*quiditate*).

---

[22] Gary P. Cestaro, *Dante and the Grammar of the Nursing Body* (Notre Dame: University of Notre Dame Press, 2003).

[23] Robert Hollander, "Babytalk in Dante's 'Commedia,'" in *Studies in Dante* (Ravenna: Longo, 1980), 115–29.

Dante has to resort to the admission that divine grace is simply beyond human comprehension. The eagle evokes this amazing grace with regard to the soul of Riphaeus:

> L'altra, per grazia che da sì profonda
> fontana stilla, che mai creatura
> non pinse l'occhio infino alla prima onda . . .
>
> (XX. 118–20)

> (The other soul, through grace that flows
> from so profound a fountain that no creature
> has ever pierced with its gaze to the first welling . . .)

However, this also implies that the final verdict concerning who will be blessed is not yet known to us. The final words of the eagle emphasize the inscrutability of divine predestination and thus leave the door open to what to us may seem impossible:

> O predestinazion, quanto remota
> è la radice tua da quelli aspetti
> che la prima cagion non veggion *tota*!
> E voi, mortali, tenetevi stretti
> a giudicar: ché noi, che Dio vedemo,
> non conosciamo ancor tutti li eletti; . . .
>
> (XX. 130–32)

> (O predestination, how remote
> is your root from those regards
> which do not see the first cause whole!
> And you, mortals, restrain yourselves
> from judging: since even we, who see God,
> do not yet know all the elect; . . .)

The synaesthetic images are integral to how Dante answers the enigmas of justice that riddle the heaven. He is made lyrically to feel the harmony of the universe, even where its justice remains unfathomable to his sight or understanding. Dante shifts into an aesthetic register a theological problem, the classical conundrum of theodicy: Why do the wicked prosper? or, How can an omnipotent, loving God allow evil? This move has a biblical precedent in Job, with the incomparably sublime poetry spoken by the Voice out of the Whirlwind in chapters 38–41 in answer to Job's exasperated questionings.

Dante, in effect, offers an aesthetic solution to a moral problem; or rather, he does not offer a solution at all. He leaves open the mystery of divine providence as beyond our human capacity for understanding. His way of entering into and participating in this mystery is through the experience of language as also opening to a unity of all that it is not able to say but nevertheless expresses by exceeding the limits of sense and of the differentiated categories of the senses. Where the ability of argumentative theodicy to explain God's justice breaks off, Dante displays the incapacity of language in general to explain, but also its uncanny power to suggest and evoke and allude to the fathomless – to its meaning in excess of all finite form and content.

As key to this move, Dante turns reflection from merely objective consideration in a direction of *self*-reflection. He reflects on the sensory modalities of his vision and thereby dissolves their distinctness as separate senses. Each sense tends to overflow its own boundaries because each is a channel opening to something beyond sensation and beyond objective form and definition. This self-reflexive turn is integral to the focus of the poem – and of this passage in particular – on its own mediality. Taking the medium as metaphor for immediacy has to be understood, finally, as a form of the poem's self-reflexivity.

What remains for us, then, in order to complete this reading of Dante's vision of Scripture in the Heaven of Jupiter, is to see his focus on his written medium as an instance of a self-reflective focus characterizing revelation in general, beginning from the Trinitarian God. Writing attracts special attention in this heaven, but the focus on the means and medium as a way of breaking open a horizon of the in-finite is the pattern of Dante's aesthetic revelation of divinity throughout the *Paradiso*. It works by dramatizing the encounter with the limits of our own understanding. The self-reflective focus on the self dwells on the *limits* of the self and breaks consciousness open to its Other, through a human sense of inadequacy or "disaggualianza" (*Paradiso* XV. 82).

The artistically self-conscious preliminaries in Canto XVIII building up to Dante's vision of Scripture in the Heaven of Jove introduce the self-reflective structure that is actually key to interpreting why the medium becomes the enabling means of a transcendent vision: the linguistic means does so through exceeding its function as medium and becoming the substance of the vision itself. The synaesthetic images in Canto XX serve further to suggest and illustrate this compression. They cannot be taken straightforwardly but rather signify something else in another modality. They call attention to and, at the same time, negate themselves in their own literal content. They have, therefore, come to be called "anti-images" by modern critics such as Chiarenza and Hawkins (*Dante's Testaments*, 223), in the wake of Freccero ("Introduction to the *Paradiso*," *Poetics of Conversion*, chapter 14). Such images constitute an instance of self-reflection opening the way to reflecting what utterly exceeds and transcends the self. As with the senses, so with reflection, Dante inscribes a movement into otherness into their own intrinsic mode of operation, at least as it is revealed from the height of heaven.

Self-Reflection and the Limits of Understanding

In his encounter with Cacciaguida, Dante stresses that the blessed have total knowledge even of contingent facts by contemplating all as reflected in the mind of God figured as a book decreeing final destiny, or, more exactly, a "great volume, where neither black nor white mutates" ("magno volume / du' non si muta mai bianco né bruno," XV. 51). Consequently,

> Così vedi le cose contingenti
>   anzi che sieno in sé, mirando il punto
>   a cui tutti li tempi son presenti . . .
>
> (XVII. 16–18)

> (Thus you see contingent things
>   before they in themselves are, looking at the point
>   at which all times are present . . .)

Such necessary knowledge of contingent events is possible here because everything is known as united in the One, who is God. Every heaven includes some statement to the effect that this One is the Truth or Good that alone is ontologically self-sufficient: "that good / that has no end and measures itself with itself" ("quel bene / che non ha fine e sé con sé misura," XIX. 52–53), as is said in this heaven. This idea is expressed consistently in terms of structures of self-reflexivity. God is totally self-referential – he "measures himself with himself" ("sé con sé misura"). Analogously, our only access to apprehending divinity is through our own self-reflexivity.

The metaphysics of self-reflection that dominate the entire canticle need also to be factored into our reflections on the way that the Scriptural medium of revelation is taken as the object of divine vision in the Heaven of Jupiter. This vision is an instance, and is even paradigmatic, of turning knowledge reflexively upon its own means and medium in order to dissolve or deconstruct the finite self and open it towards the infinite at its core and source. The images that the self gives itself prove to be "self-consuming artifacts."[24]

God's totality and self-sufficiency is understood as his ability to self-reflect and thus to "give" everything to and from himself. Metaphysically dependent, finite creatures, including Dante, imitate this self-reflexiveness and become more God-like in doing so. Dante's ascent entails his reflecting on himself more and more perfectly. In the opening lines of Canto XVIII, the canto in which Dante enters into the Heaven of Jove, Cacciaguida provides a model of self-reflexivity of the inner word that is reflected and imitated by Dante:

> Già si godea solo del suo verbo
>   quello specchio beato, e io gustava
>   lo mio, temprando col dolce l'acerbo.
>
> (XVIII. 1–3)

> (Already that blessed mirror was enjoying
>   his word alone, and I was tasting
>   my own, tempering the bitter with the sweet.)

As is captured here *in nuce*, Dante's reflections on his own emotions in experiencing Paradise are intrinsic to the "imparadising" of his "mind" ("'mparadisa la mia mente," XXVIII. 3). When he sights Beatrice in Canto XVIII, he finds that he cannot describe her and so abandons the attempt. What he *can* tell is the *effect* upon him – what could be called the "subjective correlative."

> . . . e qual io allor vidi
>   ne li occhi santi amor, qui l'abbandono;
> non perch'io pur del mio parlar diffidi,
>   ma per la mente che non può redire
>   sovra sé tanto, s'altri non la guidi.
>
> (XVIII. 7–12)

> (. . . and what love I then saw
>   in the holy eyes I abandon (describing);
> not only because I distrust my speech,
>   but for the mind itself that is not able to retell
>   what is so far above it unless an Other guides it.)

---

[24] Peter S. Hawkins invokes this paradigm in "Dante's *Paradiso* and the Dialectic of Ineffability," in *Ineffability: Naming the Unnamable from Dante to Beckett*, ed. Peter S. Hawkins (New York: AMS Press, 1983), 5–21.

Dante insists that he can relate not what he actually saw, but only how he felt in experiencing it:

> Tanto poss'io di quel punto ridire:
> che rimirando lei lo mio affetto
> libero fu da ogne altro disire.
>
> (XVIII. 13–15)

> (So much of that point I can retell:
> that gazing on her my affections
> were free from every other desire.)

This pattern is repeated again a few lines later in the canto. A state of feeling is invoked in lieu of any objective description of what Dante experienced upon his entry into the higher potency of the sphere of Jupiter:

> E come, per sentir più dilettanza
> bene operando, l'uom di giorno in giorno
> s'accorge che la sua virtute avanza,
> sí m'accors'io che 'l mio girare intorno
> col cielo insieme avea cresciuto l'arco,
> veggendo quel miracol più addorno.
>
> (XVIII. 58–63)

> (And as through feeling more delight
> by functioning well, a man from day to day
> is conscious that his virtue is advancing,
> so I became aware that my rotating with
> the heaven had increased its arc,
> seeing this miracle yet more adorned.)

Dante can tell us only of the changes that he felt in himself as he experienced this higher heaven. Objective reality is captured and recorded in terms of its *subjective correlative* in Dante's own experience. This structure actually repeats God's own self-reflective manner of being and acting by substituting self-reference in Dante for reference to an exterior other. Dante thus experiences God in himself by imitation and assimilation.

God is the One from whom all good and truth and beauty come. He is self-engendering, whereas everything else that has any being or truth or goodness or beauty is derivative from him – a reflection of his absolute plenitude. In this sense, all that is or is valuable is one in God. The "eternal pleasure" radiates directly in Beatrice, from her beautiful face (XVIII. 16–18). All that positively is, and all that is positive, at its source and in truth, is simply God, or from God.

In every place short of the Empyrean, light is but a kind of shadow. Thus, the eagle explains that only the light that comes directly from God is not darkness:

> Lume non è, se non vien dal sereno
> che non si turba mai; anzi è tenebra,
> od ombra de la carne, o suo veleno.
>
> (XIX. 64–66)

> (There is no light, unless it comes from the serenity
> that never is disturbed; otherwise, it is darkness,
> or a shadow of the flesh, or its poison.)

This implies that all finite light is at risk of exposure as mere vanity or, even worse, as "poison": it can be secured and sustained only by reflecting divine light. The radiating of this divine light causes all that is and all that has any good whatsoever to be:

> nullo creato bene a sé la tira
> ma essa, radïando, lui cagiona.
>
> (XIX. 88–89)

> (no created good draws it to itself
> but rather is caused by its radiating.)

In Dante's metaphysics, there is one source of all that is true and real, and anything that does not devolve from this one fount is spurious. The nature of the One, accordingly, is to be related ultimately only to itself. Canto XIX's explanations regarding theodicy are one more occasion to emphasize how the divine being or goodness is sufficient unto itself and cannot be measured by any other.

> La prima volontà ch'è da sé buona,
> da sé, ch'è sommo ben, mai non si mosse.
>
> (XIX. 86–87)

> (The first will that is in itself good,
> from itself, as highest good, has never been removed.)

Dante emphasizes the disproportion between any created being and the infinite divine being of the Creator, who is imaged as the Ancient of Days tracing the limits of the Creation with a compass. Dante again makes

Figure 5 *Paradiso* XIX, from *La divina commedia*, 1793. Engraving by Tommaso Piroli after a drawing by John Flaxman. Fiske Dante Collection, Division of Rare and Manuscript Collections, Cornell University Library

the point that God can be understood only on Godself's own terms – hence the necessity of God's self-reflection. The divine Word is in "infinite excess" ("infinito ecesso," 45) of any possible instantiation within the created universe.

No receptacle is adequate to the infinite divine goodness, which can be measured only by or against itself – a lesson that bears constant repeating:

> e quinci appar ch'ogne minor natura
> e corto recettacolo a quel bene
> che non ha fine e sé con sé misura.

(XIX. 49–51)

> (and thus it is evident that every lesser nature
> is a cramped receptacle for that good
> that has no end and measures itself with itself.)

The closest humans can come to apprehending some inkling of this is to experience infinite self-reflection within themselves. The self reflects itself into its own object and thus becomes an immediacy for itself. It thereby negates its own infinity and the infinity of the act of mediation by positing itself as a finite object. Yet, as thus negated, the self is opened infinitely to what is other than itself. It cannot comprehend this infinite otherness but can only be torn open in relation to it. We have already alluded to the importance of bird images in Jupiter for traversing gaps in its discursive logic and argument. They rely especially on self-reflexivity in performing this feat. An infinite negation of self enables a transcending of given, objective limits of representation, and the bird images in particular are called on to illustrate this. Dante's bird images poetically take flight, but precisely through reflecting back on themselves.

Bird Images of Lyric Self-Reflexivity

A number of the most beautiful and compelling lyric images of the poem occur in the Heaven of Jove. A series of ornithological figures in particular encapsulates its poetics of self-reflexivity. The bird serves Dante as a symbol for singing and love, an affective plenitude that becomes articulate in poetry. Poetry is an outpouring that turns back reflectively on itself and on its own linguistic medium in the turning of the "verse," which derives from Latin *vertere* (to turn).

The eagle is the main pictorial figure in this heaven, emerging from the sky-launched letters in Canto XVIII. This image opens Canto XIX:

> Parea dinanzi a me con l'ali aperte
> la bella image che nel dolce *frui*
> liete facevan l'anime conserte.

(XIX. 1–3)

(Before me appeared with open wings
the beautiful image of the sweet *frui*
making the concerted souls glad.)

The beauty and openness, as well as the happiness in sweet fruition (*frui*),
expressed in this "image" are developed in a series of bird portraits constituting variations on a theme. The Latin *frui* recalls Augustine's term for
disinterested heavenly enjoyment as distinct from earthly use or *uti*. The
latter tends to instrumentalize its object.

In poetic realization in concrete media, both graphic and sonic, as well as
fantastic, an apotheosis takes place. It involves a realization of unity and
transcendent sense in material media of voice and ink. These media
produce a lyric ecstasy that is linked with the creation of unity, even
miraculous unity that is not merely aesthetic. It is a spiritual unity such
as actually establishes – or discloses – justice as real throughout the
universe. In a statement reflecting intensively on his technique in this
passage, Dante presents this poetic production as an unprecedented
miracle:

> E quel che mi convien ritrar testeso,
>   non portò voce mai, né scrisse incostro,
>   né fu per fantasia già mai compreso;
> ch'io vidi e anche udi' parlar lo rostro,
>   e sonar ne la voce e "io" e "mio,"
>   quand'era nel concetto e "noi" e "nostro."

(XIX. 7–12)

> (and that which it falls to me now to retell
>   was never borne by voice nor written in ink
>   nor was it ever comprehended by fantasy;
> I saw and also heard that the beak was speaking
>   and sounded in its voice both "I" and "me,"
>   while in its conception it was "we" and "our.")

The same elements of a self-reflexive lyric construction of surpassing
gaudium, in which creaturely will and divine grace coincide, are met in
a second bird image a little later in the canto, that of the falcon
rejoicing in freedom. Here, too, the bird is designated as "sign"
("segno"): it is presented as a formal, semiotic, textual construction
("contesto") largely out of self-reflexive verbs ("si plaude," "faccendosi," "farsi," "si sa"):

> Quasi falcone ch'esce del cappello,
>   move la testa e con l'ali *si plaude*,

voglia mostrando e *faccendosi* bello,
vid'io *farsi* quel segno, che di laude
de la divina grazia era contesto,
con canti quai *si sa* chi là sú gaude.

(XIX. 34–39)

(Like a falcon that emerges from its hood,
  moves its head and with its wings *applauds itself*,
  demonstrating desire and *making itself* glorious,
so I saw that sign *form itself*, which with praise
  of the divine grace is woven together,
  with songs *self-explanatory* to those who rejoice above.)

Dante's experience of grace does not occur purely by self-emptying and self-annihilation of will. That style of mysticism flourishes contemporaneously with Dante in Meister Eckhart and in his immediate predecessor, Marguerite Porete.[25] But Dante forges a somewhat differently inflected mysticism based on the self-reflexive constructedness of lyrical language. It is by *poiesis* – making, and specifically self-making, especially the self-referential making informed and performed by lyrical language – that Dante seeks mystical union with God. His making, furthermore, spills over into *un*making: he is aware that his self-reflexivity must transcend itself.

In this regard, the result ultimately coincides with the Rhineland mysticism of Eckhart, after all. And in the end, a self-reflective, courtly poetics is crucial for Marguerite, too. Yet Dante develops a distinctive lyric technique that turns especially upon an exercise of self-reflection that he drives to peculiar speculative heights especially through his bird similes.[26] The series of self-reflexive lyrical bird images that encapsulate this technique of lyric mysticism starts at the beginning of Canto XIX with the "bella image" of the open-winged eagle who gives gladness to concerted souls in sweet fruition. The artifice of self-reflection here is eminently productive, itself a supreme fruition in which all become one in will.

The third bird simile in XIX returns to this "conviviality" motif. The joy produced by self-reflexive lyric feeds and nourishes. It suggests how the

---

[25] Marguerite Porete, *Le Mirouer des Simples Ames*, ed. Romana Guarnieri (Turnhout: Brepols, 1986), trans. Ellen Babinsky as *The Mirror of Simple Souls* (New York: Paulist Press, 1993). On Eckhart, see Rubina Giorgi, *Dante e Meister Eckhart: Letture per tempo della fine* (Salerno: Ripostes, 1987); and my *On What Cannot Be Said*, vol. 1, 285–90.

[26] Neo-Platonic and Christian traditions of speculative self-reflection are pertinently discussed in Pierre Hadot, "Le mythe de Narcisse et son interprétation par Plotin," *Nouvelle Revue de Pyschanalyse* 13 (1976): 81–108 and by Julia Kristeva, *Histoires d'amour* (Paris: Denöel[Folio], 1983), "Narcisse: La nouvelle démence" and "Les troubadours," who relates them expressly to Dante.

eagle, this "benedetta imagine," is a formal construction and yet is productive of concrete nourishment. This occurrence of the image, a few more
verses into the canto, is also constructed on reflexive verbs ("si rigira," "si
fece"). Its reflexive verbal structure emphasizes particularly the self-
reflexive character of this joy associated with singing and with flight that
circles upon itself:

> Quale sovresso il nido *si rigira*
>   poi c'ha pasciuti la cicogna i figli,
>   e come quel ch'è pasto la rimira;
> cotal *si fece*, e sì levä i cigli,
>   la benedetta imagine, che l'ali
>   movea sospinte da tanti consigli.
>
>   (XIX. 91–96)

> (As above the nest the stork *turns (itself) about*
>   after it has fed its young,
>   and as the one just fed looks back upward;
> so the blessed image *made itself*, and so
>   I raised my brows, as the wings
>   moved, borne aloft by so many counsels.)

The nourishment motif, present here in the feeding of baby
storks by their mother, persists as at least a trace in the fourth bird
simile for the blessed sign of the eagle. Modeled on a poem by Bernart
de Ventadorn, this is the crowning instance of the aviary similes in
Canto XX:

> Quale alodetta che 'n aere si spazia
>   prima cantando, e poi tace contenta
>   de l'ultima dolcezza che la sazia,
> tal mi sembiò l'imago de la 'mprenta
>   de l'etterno piacere, al cui disio
>   ciascuna cosa qual ell'è diventa.
>
>   (XX. 73–78)

> (Like the lark, which flings itself into the air,
>   first singing, and then goes silent, content
>   with the ultimate sweetness that satiates it,
> so seemed to me the image of the imprint
>   of the eternal pleasure, at whose desire
>   each thing becomes what it is.)

This simile, with its reflexive verb ("si spazia"), summarizes the
series and encapsulates the metaphysical significance that lyric

experience takes on as Dante invents it in this heaven. Satisfied with its own singing, the lark bears the imprint of God's own pleasure in Godself. The sheer lyrical ecstasy that characterizes blessedness in this heaven is capped by still another simile, that of the guitar riff heightening the delight of song at the end of the canto (XX. 142–44).

Nevertheless, in the next heaven, yet another bird simile marks, in crucial respects, another culmination of the series. This turns out to be the most metaphysically provocative of all the bird similes. It emphasizes how poetic construction "anticipates time" ("previene il tempo") and opens into the experience of eternity:

> Come l'augello, intra l'amate fronde,
>   posato al nido de' suoi dolci nati
>   la notte che le cose ci nasconde,
> che, per veder li aspetti disiati
>   e per trovar lo cibo onde li pasca,
>   in che gravi labor li sono aggrati,
> previene il tempo in su l'aperta frasca,
>   e con ardente affetto il sole aspetta,
>   fiso guardando pur che l'alba nasca . . .
>
> (XXIII. 1–9)

> (Like the bird, amidst the beloved foliage,
>   posted on the nest of its own sweet brood,
>   during the night that hides things from us,
> who in order to see the longed-for visages
>   and to find the food with which to feed them,
>   which makes its heavy labor welcome,
> anticipates the time on the open branch
>   and with ardent affection awaits the sun,
>   fixedly looking, that the dawn be born . . .)

In this case, it helps to compare what the simile is standing for as well, since the simile consists no longer simply in the image of a real bird used to characterize some aspect of the emblematic eagle:

> così la donna mia stava eretta
>   e attenta, rivolta inver la plaga
>   sotto la quale il sol mostra men fretta:
> sì che, veggendola io sospesa e vaga,
>   fecimi qual è quei che disiando
>   altro vorria, e sperando s'appaga.
>
> (XXIII. 10–15)

(Thus my lady remained erect
  and attentive, turned toward the zone
  under which the sun hurries least:
so that, seeing her, suspended in longing,
  I made myself like one who desiring
  would like something else, and is fulfilled with hope.)

Dante is fed and satisfied self-reflexively ("s'appaga") by his desire itself. Again, as with the mother stork simile in XIX, motifs of feeding bring taste and smell and touch into the synaesthetic mix by which wisdom is dished out to Dante. They are an important supplement to the typically fore-grounded senses of sight and hearing. Dante's "vision" of Scripture is also a lyrical audition that enchants him and demands an outlet in *all* of his sense modalities because every one of them is infinitely exceeded. As media, moreover, their nature and function is to be exceeded by what they mediate.

The limits of knowledge are constantly exceeded by Dante's ques-tions (this continues in Canto XXI when Dante asks why Pier Damiani is especially chosen to speak with him), and Dante resorts to lyric plenitude to make up for his lack of positive explanatory content. The self-reflections of lyric substitute for what transcends human reflection. The Eagle does not mince words with polite man-ners in directly declaring to Dante this gaping hole in his understanding:

> "Quali
> son le mie note a te, che non le 'ntendi,
> tal è il giudicio etterno a voi mortali"
>
> (XIX. 97–99)

> ("As are
> my notes for you, who do not understand them,
> so is the eternal judgment for you mortals.")

Dante's and humanity's recourse, in the face of the unbridgeable distance to transcendent truth, is to employ structures of self-reflection. We can know ourselves and our own inadequacies, and this self-reflexivity gives us some intimation of divinity in its own intimate (Trinitarian) self-reflexiveness. Dante's concentration on the medium of Scriptural revela-tion in the Heaven of Jupiter is, in the end, an instance of turning knowledge self-reflexively on itself, on its own means and bases, in order to "know" experientially the infinite self-circulation of what cannot be known as a static object. The vision of writing featured in Dante's writing of the *Paradiso* is a form of self-contemplation of one's own activity as a means of intuiting the transcendent God – the template of Trinitarian self-contemplation – through one's own imitative self-reflexive enactment.

The poem is full of figures of spinning upon oneself and of circles turning within turning circles: "sperule" (XXII. 23); "it sang rotatingly" ("roteando cantava," XIX. 97); "Thus, the circulated melody / sealed itself" ("Cosí la circolata melodia / si sigilava," XXIII. 109–10). These engines of internally generated energy all figure the self-generating reflexivity characteristic of divine being, and therewith of all beings, insofar as all *qua* being imitate God. This figure is most clearly articulated in lyric language. The language of lyric can claim, as song, to be near to originary human language. This point of view was recovered in the eighteenth century by Vico, Herder, and Rousseau, all of whom maintained that language was originally sung.[27] The idea is certainly not foreign to Dante, for whom original utterance (like Adam's) had to express spontaneous joy in being and attunement to his Creator (*De vulgari eloquentia* I. iv. 4). Dante similarly anticipates the "discovery" of the eighteenth-century theorists that poetry is prior to prose ("prosaycantes ab avientibus magis accipiunt," *De vulgari eloquentia* II. i. 1) in the history of humanity's literary awakening and self-expression.

Metaphor and the Poetic Making of the Linguistic Substance of Paradise

The extraordinary status of the *Paradiso*'s signs as hypersensational is realized in the metaphors of Canto XIX. What they refer to is not always easily determinable, but their force lies in their sense rather than in their reference.[28] Dante's imagery in this heaven, as in the *Paradiso* generally, is attenuated in its representational or referential application. By hypothesis, its ultimate object is unrepresentable. This does not mean that Dante is not speaking in perfectly definite terms about clearly conceptualizable objects but rather that these objects are themselves mentioned always only in order to evoke further ineffable and unrepresentable "things." Leveraging

---

[27] I treat this topic in "Metaphor and the Making of Sense: The Contemporary Metaphor Renaissance," *Philosophy and Rhetoric* 33/2 (2000): 137–54.

[28] A distinction between sense or meaning ("Sinn") and reference ("Bedeutung") is made by Gottlob Frege, "Über Sinn und Bedeutung," *Zeitschrift für Philosophie und philosophische Kritik* 100 (1892), 25–50. Up to a certain point, this is the difference between connotation and denotation in terms of the Anglo-Saxon linguistic theory inaugurated by John Stuart Mill. The first is a meaning intrinsic to the word, what it conjures up and suggests to the mind when presented as word alone. The second is the extralinguistic object that the word denotes.

Neo-Platonic negative theology, Marco Ariani has explained this most cogently with regard to Dante's use of metaphor or, more exactly, "transumptio" as a *dissimilar* similitude. Concerning the Heaven of Justice, specifically cantos XIX and XX, Ariani writes:

> We are facing a true and proper imaginative system, a long, complex *transumptio* that crosses and connects the two cantos centering on a nuclear image from which the verbal texture radiates, that of an unimaginable liquid light occulted in the inscrutable splendor of divine Justice. Synaesthetic technique thus dominates the weave of these tentacular metaphorical systems with which Dante attempts the impossible: to "syllable" the emanation of being through domestic comparisons in the form of *dissimilar similitudes* taken from the metaphorical legacy of Neo-Platonism (plenitude, the sea, the fountain, the wave, the root). This technique is without recognizable precedents in the poetic tradition. One can find something analogous only in philosophical and theological sources, even if we must clearly realize that Dante surpasses their tendency to antimetaphorical diffidence by his intrepid exercise of fantasmatic images, convinced as he is that they are always impressed with the seal of informing divine light.[29]

Dante actually goes well beyond simple negation and enriches this first-order Neo-Platonic, or more exactly Plotinian, negative theology in creating a positive sensorium of his experience of Paradise. Indeed, there always has to be a positive theology working in tandem with every negative theology. This has remained a key postulate of Christian negative theology ever since Dionysius the Areopagite, who is often recognized as its founder. However, Dante creates a metaphorical universe based on the negative experience of finding himself face to face with the ineffable God. His positive theology thus lies on the far side of this negative experience, which he expresses and elaborates in the exquisite and intoxicating fantasies of the *Paradiso*. Dante uses the resources of poetry to elaborate a metaphorical paradise, or a paradise of poetic metaphor, that is positively

---

[29] "Siamo di fronte ad un vero e proprio sistema immaginale, una lunga, complessa *transumptio* che travalica e connette i due canti accentrandosi su un'immagine nucleare da cui irradia la testura verbale, quella di un'inimmaginabile luce liquida occultata nell'imperscrutabile splendore della Giustizia divina. La tecnica sinestetica domina dunque la filatura di questi tentacolari sistemi metaforici con i quali Dante tenta l'impossibile, sillabare il mistero dell'emanazione dell'essere con domestiche comparazioni in forma di *dissimiles similitudines* tratte dal lascito metaforico del Neo-Platonismo (il ripieno, il mare, la fontana, l'onda, la radice). Tecnica senza riconoscibili precedenti nella tradizione poetica, per la quale si può trovare qualcosa di analogo solo nelle fonti filosofiche e teologiche, anche se si deve avere ben chiaro che Dante ne supera la tendenziale diffidenza antimetaforica per un impavido esercizio delle immagini fantasmatiche, convinto come è che vi siano sempre impressi i sigilli dell'informante luce divina." (*Lux inaccessibilis*, 260–61).

sensual, following up on his passage through the negative-theological moment of the ineffable. Comparable in this regard is John of the Cross, who arrives at sensuous poetic expression in and through his dark night of the soul in "La noche oscura."

The Letter to Can Grande uses the word "metaphorismorum" to describe a mythic style of representation characteristic of Plato. A closely related aspect of Dante's understanding of figurative language is captured in another term current in the Middle Ages: "transumptio." The Letter to Can Grande elencates also "transumptivus" (XIII. 9.27) among the rhetorical modes employed in the *Paradiso*. Considered rhetorically, the *transumptio* is a fine flower of ornate style, both *ornatus facilis* and particularly *ornatus difficilis*.[30] The *transumptio* was often taken as master trope in the Middle Ages, following indications in the *Rhetorica nova*, attributed to Cicero. It is discussed at length by Geoffrey de Vinsauf in his *Poetria nova* (vv. 765–1093).[31] As a consequence, *transumptio* is studied intensively also in the thirteenth-century Bolognese school of *ars dictaminis* rhetoricians, particularly by Bene da Firenze and Boncompagno da Signa. *Transumptio* connotes especially a capacity to absorb all the figurative powers of language into one. Its basic metaphorical operation consists in "sumere ex alio" – summing up under another head (Forti, "La magnanimità verbale," 110). This suggests that it is by the transfer to the improper that it becomes possible to unify a multiplicity. Pushing this to the extreme case, Buoncompagno's *Rhetorica novissima* derives the *transumptio* originally from the Word of God.[32]

Fiorenzo Forti's researches bring out the extent to which Dante's use of the *transumptio* is far more vital than that of the rhetorical tradition. Forti compares it particularly with Boncompagno's rhetorical use of *transumptio* for decorative purposes ("De transumptionibus que fiunt per imagines"): "With all the panache of Boncompagno, the rhetorical devices he disassembles and reassembles appear always mechanical in comparison with the most pallid instances in the *Comedy*" ("Con tutto l'estro di Boncompagno, i congegni retorici che egli va smontando e rimontando appaiono sempre meccanici a confronto del più pallido luogo della *Commedia*," 122). Rather than codified images that belong to

[30] Fiorenzo Forti, "La magnanimità verbale: La transumptio," in *Magnanimitade: Studi su un tema Dantesco* (Bologna: Pàtron Editore, 1977), 106.
[31] Geoffrey de Vinsauf, *Poetria nova*, in *Les arts poétiques du XIIᵉ et du XIIIᵉ siècle*, ed. Edmond Faral (Paris: Champion, 1924), 221–31.
[32] https://web.archive.org/web/20070207233146/http://dobc.unipv.it/scrineum/wight/rnprol.htm (accessed April 2, 2021).

the immense medieval repertoire of symbolic systems, for example, those linking animals to moral qualities, Dante furnishes new metaphorical inventions, genuinely live metaphors.[33] Dante's place of unparalleled originality in the history of literature needs to be accounted for also by his rediscovery and activation of the lively invention of metaphor. Dante makes this codified rhetorical schema for the first time fully poetic, indeed the essence of poetry as the invention of a world in desire. As such, metaphor becomes tantamount to the "reinvention" of Paradise – literally, coming (*venire*) back (*re*) into (*in*) it. Dante's Paradise is, in effect, a paradise of poetic metaphor.

A model of Dante's use of *transumptio* singled out for citation by Forti is the description of the river of light said by Dante to deliver "shadowy prefaces" ("umbriferi prefazii") of the divine vision:

> E vidi lume in forma di rivera
> fulvido di fulgore, intra due rive
> dipinte di mirabil primavera.
> Di tal fiumana uscian faville vive
> e d'ogni parte si mettean ne' fiori
> quasi rubin che oro circunscrive.
> Poi, come inebriate da li odori
> riprofondavan sé nel miro gurge
> e s'una intrava, un'altra n'uscia fori.
>
> (XXX. 61–69)

> (And I saw light in the form of a river
> refulgent with lightning, between two banks
> painted with miraculous springtide.
> And from this torrent stormed living sparks
> and in every part they produced flowers
> like rubies that gold circumscribes.
> And then, as if inebriated by the fragrances,
> they plunged back into the miraculous gorge,
> and if one entered in another came back out.)

This elaborately ornate passage certainly displays Dante's gothic sensibilities. But it also intimates the kind of knowledge of substantial, spiritual meaning that Dante's metaphors embody.

---

[33] Giuseppe Ledda, *Il bestiario dell'aldilà: Gli animali nella* Commedia *di Dante* (Ravenna: Longo, 2019) studies the immense richness and complexity of animal images in the *Commedia*. For ample background particularly on the series of bird similes brought to focus in the preceding section, see chapter 9: "Parole, visioni, scacchi: Immagini aviarie nel cielo di Giove," 233–45.

It had been observed already by early commentators such as Benvenuto da Imola that Dante's metaphors are all *figural*, that is, they are not just pleasing to aesthetic taste but have a substantive, didactic meaning as well. It was typical medieval exegetical practice to interpret all the elements of a complex imagined scene according to their discrete meanings. Dante's images seem susceptible of this sort of interpretation, though they also tend to remake all previously established meanings in light of the new whole that they themselves forge.

Dante's complexes of metaphor are also effectively mixed together, branching out into organic – even if uncontainable and only equivo-cally identifiable – wholes. The experience of God in Paradise is described as a feast, according to the recurrent *convivio* motif, and also, most intensively, as a metaphorical seeing. The two semantic fields are fused together when Dante's eyes are said to drink from the river of light so as to be annealed for the vision of God: "as soon as from the water the eaves of my eyelids drunk" ("e sì come di lei bevve la gronda / de le palpebre mie," *Paradiso* XXX. 88–89). "Eaves" adds in a further architectural motif to this fusion of metaphorical constructions.

Metaphor is traditionally understood as "picture language" – "bildliche Sprache" – as German says. Meaning is mediated by image and becomes sensuously concrete in untold and untellable ways. The transfers and transfusions typical of metaphors are forms of mediation, even mediation of an unattainable Immediacy. And mediation, as we have been arguing all along, becomes a master metaphor for the unconditional im-mediacy of divinity. Metaphor, to this extent, *performs* divinity in Dante's poem. The letter, taken as icon, as visible speech, becomes such a metaphorical per-formance in Dante's vision of writing.

Geometrical Imagery and Perspective Opening to Infinity in the Heaven of Jupiter

We have seen that Dante's metaphorical imagination is also specifically geometrical in this sixth heaven, which features God as a Geometer turning his compass in the act of creating the world:

> "Colui che volse il sesto
>   a lo stremo del mondo, e dentro ad esso
>   distinse tanto occulto e manifesto . . ."

>   (XIX. 40–42)

("He who turned the compass
  at the limit of the world, and within it
  distinguished so much that is hidden and manifest . . .")

Dante associates the sixth heaven with geometry programmatically in the *Convivio*'s system of correspondences between the seven planetary heavens and the seven liberal arts. We must realize that these arts are not merely circumscribed areas of technical knowledge. They open upon the contemplation of the infinite. The geometrical point provides an image of the infinitely small and indivisible – and therefore not measurable. The impossibility of squaring the circle offers another (anti-)image of the impossible and, in principle, imageless, and therewith also another figure for divinity.

> Sì che tra 'l punto e lo cerchio sì come tra principio e fine si muove la Geometria, e questi due alla sua certezza repugnano: ché lo punto per la sua indivisibilitade è immensurabile, e lo cerchio per lo suo arco è impossibile a quadrare perfettamente, e però è impossibile a misurare a punto. E ancora: la Geometria è bianchissima, in quanto è sanza macula d'errore e certissima per sé e per la sua ancella, che si chiama Perspettiva. (*Convivio* II. xiii. 27)

> (Thus, Geometry moves between the point and the circle as between beginning and end, and these two are antithetical to its certainty, since the point on account of its indivisibility is immeasurable, and the circle because of its curvature is impossible to perfectly square and is thus impossible to measure exactly. Furthermore, Geometry is superlatively white inasmuch as without stain or error and superlatively certain in itself and through its handmaiden, which is called [the science of] Perspective.)

Space is the dimension and the medium of representation that geometry in its perfection employs in order to represent that which is, in principle, unrepresentable or "impossible." It creates for the eye a perspective on what remains otherwise ungraspable for the mind. Geometrical imagery is concretely visual and spatial, and yet geometrical concepts open this spatial reality to an infinite dimension that cannot be concretely represented. This is what makes geometry apt for figuring divine Justice as incomprehensible.

Justice is imagined by Dante as a matter of symmetries and balance, and geometrical figures furnish some of its most precise and intuitive expressions. Linear or central perspective, as it begins to enter medieval art with Giotto and his follower Pietro Cavallino, raises this issue acutely as the issue of divine versus human vision of justice.[34] Giuseppe Mazzotta

---

[34] For a reading of this important transition in art history, see Alessandro Parronchi, *Cavallini: "Discepolo" di Giotto* (Florence: Polistampa, 1994).

intriguingly suggests that Dante reconciles the new modern aesthetic of painting based on the perspective of the subject, which begins to emerge in Giotto, with the medieval, Byzantine, theocentric aesthetic realized in the mosaics of Ravenna.[35] The perspective of the subject as first-person protagonist is affirmed with unprecedented force in Dante's poem. Yet true perspective remains God's rather than the human protagonist's. In the still medieval perspective of the mosaics, which has validity also for Dante, the direction of the regard is reversed and the viewer is scrutinized by the divine view of the saints and Christ as *Pantocrator* looming above on the ceiling of the Ravennese Basilica Sant'Apollinare in Classe.

Perspective for Dante is instrumental to the realization of infinite, divine vision rather than simply replacing the latter by humanly calculable and controllable artifices. And yet, even if justice is divine, nevertheless its representation remains human. In response to this predicament, Dante represents God himself as drawing, designing, and painting. Can God be apprehended as the source of our own representations? Can the limits of their human mediation, in some way, be neutralized and overcome? Can justice on earth, as done by humans, succeed in executing the divine will? How can the particularity of their perspectives be transcended? These questions are pressed by Dante's text.

Virgil's and Ovid's Roman epics remain national epics of a certain race or people. But Dante, as Mazzotta pertinently comments, takes up "a position beyond the idolatrous fascination with any particular place" and beyond the purview prescribed by the "myths of a specific culture" ("una posizione di estraneità da ogni fascinazione idolatrica con un particolare luogo o con i miti di una particolare cultura," *Confine quasi orizzonte*, 94). The Heaven of Jupiter's economy of salvation, with its references to pagans (Riphaeus and Trajan) and Hindus (XIX. 70–72), relativizes Christian and Roman cultural chauvinism and turns Dante's work into a self-critical, open, dynamically global vision. The virtuous Ethiopian and the Persian are able to put to shame the righteous hypocrisy of those who "call out Christ, Christ!" ("gridan Cristo, Cristo," XIX. 103–14). These "outsiders," finally, are not overlooked; instead, they will themselves look down with the blessed in judgment on damned Christians. The opening of particular perspectives of peoples and civilizations, including the Roman and Christian, to reconciliation with universal humanity and cosmic destiny

[35] Giuseppe Mazzotta, *Confine quasi orizzonte: Saggi su Dante* (Rome: Edizioni di Storia e Letteratura, 2014), 84, chapter VI: "Spettacolo e geometria della giustizia (*Paradiso* XVIII–XX): L'Europa e l'universalità di Roma," 81–96.

extends infinitely the scope of Dante's calling. Ensconsed within his own well-defined Catholic Imperial culture, Dante nevertheless projects a self-critical, self-subverting universality open to other peoples and cultures and trained upon absolute otherness.[36]

Dante is certainly seeing and writing from a European perspective, yet he sees Europe as in relation to its others and as intrinsically penetrated by alterity. Christian European society is put to scorn by the Jew within, laughing at its typical hypocrisies (*Paradiso* V. 81), and it is defined from without, emblematically by Justinian's legal code, the *Corpus iuris civilis*, which Dante reminds us was forged in Byzantium at the extreme confine with Asia ("ne lo stremo dell'Europa," *Paradiso* VI. 5). This legal constitution is framed by an Emperor under the sway of the Eastern heresy of monophysitism. Europe is constituted by heterogeneity not only outside its porous borders but also from within and at its own core. It is characterized not by static, seamless, self-identity but by the intrinsic contradictions and limits of its ownmost characteristics.

In Dante's vision, as Mazzotta understands it, Europe is defined spiritually by its characteristic philosophy, theology, and jurisprudence but also by the flaws and limits of a civilization for which knowledge is transgressive (Ulysses's passage) and love violent (Europa's rape). It is especially the self-critical knowledge of these limits that Dante underscores and that distinguishes him and the European *Geist*. Dante is acutely conscious of the bias built into any *perspective*, not least the European. Mazzotta elicits such insight from Dante: "since every perspective brings with it a self-limitation, he reflects on his own no less inevitable limits and on his own possible errors" ("perché ogni prospettiva comporta un'autolimitazione, egli riflette sui suoi non meno inevitabili limiti e sui suoi possibli errori," *Confine quasi orizzonte*, 84).

The concluding sentence of Mazzotta's chapter on Jupiter and geometry, linking with the previous heaven of Mars and Dante's encounter with his great great grandfather Cacciaguida reviewing the Florentine past, expresses this deliberate delimitation of perspective within an open horizon in lapidary terms: "On the basis of Roman and Christian universality, the gaze of Dante rises up, and his poetry, which is the very voice of Western spirituality, exposes nakedly the belonging of every familiar, subjective perspective to the vast latitude of the Earth" ("Sulla scorta dell'universalità

---

[36] Dante's peering beyond Europe, anticipating our own contemporary critiques of Eurocentrism, is documented and analyzed by Brenda Schildgen in *Dante and the Orient* (Urbana: University of Illinois Press, 2002) and in "Dante and the Crusades," *Dante Studies* CXVI (1998): 95–125.

romana e cristiana, lo sguardo di Dante si solleva, e la sua poesia, che è la voce stessa della spiritualità dell'Occidente, mette a nudo l'appartenenza di ogni prospettiva familiare e soggettiva alla vasta latitudine della Terra," *Confine quasi orizzonte*, 96).

This naked self-exposure brings Dante's vast visionary outlook home to its rootedness in his own personal experience and encapsulates Dante's universalism without abstraction from his particular historical situatedness. Dante owns up to his own human and historical particularity in some disarming ways that are virtually unprecedented in the thoroughly Greek-influenced culture and language of his medieval civilization still based, to a large extent, on Platonic idealism and Aristotelian essences. These acknowledgments become, paradoxically, means of fulfilling his universal vision.

Geometry is about perspective and, just like theology, enables us to distinguish between our own perspective, based on our own measures, and the incommensurable that lies beyond our coordinates. The limits of human measures and reason are self-critically met with and acknowledged in confronting that which is in "infinite excess" ("infinito eccesso") of them. We cannot measure the divine judgment with our short vision ("con la veduta corta d'una spanna," XIX. 81), just a handbreath ("spanna") in geometrical terms. Our lines and circles and spheres never comprehend the Whole. We cannot, with our short receptacle, fathom the Good without end that measures itself with itself alone:

> E quince appar ch'ogne minor natura
> è corto recettacolo a quel bene
> che non ha fine e sé con sé misura.

(XIX. 49–51)

> (and thus it appears that every lesser nature
> is an inadequate receptacle for that good
> which has no end and measures itself by itself alone.)

Yet the divine abyss, nevertheless, adheres to and informs the surface that we *can* map and draw – analogously to the way that theology, with its incalculable "ultimate concern" (Paul Tillich), subtends the measured reasoning of philosophical discourse ("l'abisso inerisce alla superficie, così come la teologia sottende il discorso filosofico," Mazzotta, *Confine quasi orizzonte*, 91). Human arts pushed to their limit collapse and open to unfathomable divine knowledge. An ungraspable depth undergirds any finite subject's inevitably perspectival knowing.

Mazzotta emphasizes that the divine Geometer is an Artist and that an aesthetic outlook forges some kind of contact of this divine geometry with the human world. The design of the cosmos infinitely surpasses us, and yet we have our perspective for receiving it as an aesthetic experience. Our perspective does not, like God's, command unlimited vision, nor does it enable us to create the universe. We are rather within it – under the mobile gaze of the divinities figured in the mosaics in Ravenna. Their infinite gaze follows us as viewers wherever we go and from whatever strictly limited angle we might choose to look.

This awareness of limitations makes the universal perspective of salvation history, which historically emanates from Europe, unable to totalize and close itself off as European but, instead, opens gateways upon other regions and cultures. The idea of salvation history itself, so dear to Western Christianity, derives from the Holy Land in Asia Minor. Thus the purported universality of its civilization breaks down in Europe's own internal contradictions stemming inevitably from divergent human perspectives. Still, the projection of a truly universal divine perspective has been a persistent and irrepressible aspiration of European culture. Perspective, as *perspectiva artificialis*, is already announced in Giotto and Cavallini, but it is not yet confined by the limits of the subject. It remains open to a mobile and all-enveloping divine perspective that is envisaged and imagined, even though it is unattainable for a finite human subject – as Dante reminds us in admonitions delivered from the height of the Heaven of Jupiter.

Geometries of self-enclosure break apart in Dante's heavens: they are burst open to a Justice that is superhuman. It is not that Dante does not express the desire for completeness and perfection, but these values are imagined as attainable only in a comprehensiveness that includes everything that geometrical, geographical, and ideological or cultural limits would exclude. Dante's "uni-verse" is a "turning into one" of the All that follows a curvature that only God can master. Thus, human perspective needs to be kept always open to infinite vision, to the vision of the Infinite that is always other than our own.

CHAPTER 6

Infinite Script: Endless Mediation as Metaphor for Divinity

Revelation of the Divine in and through Infinite Linguistic Mediation

The grammatically analyzed mode in which language is presented in Dante's vision of writing illustrates the proclivity of writing to shiver and splinter meaning. Writing tends to partition and fissure the presumed wholeness of sense as it occurs originally in oral communication and in the indivisible event of intuitive understanding. What Dante especially emphasizes in his description of the vision of Scripture in the heaven of Jupiter is the way that writing breaks language down into its component parts. By doing so, Dante places into evidence the grammatical anatomy of language as intrinsic to its transfigured appearance even in this purportedly authoritative revelation of universal Justice. It is precisely the mechanical and material, the artificial and mediated aspects of language – particularly its grammatical composition out of differentiated and coordinated parts of speech – that become conspicuous in Dante's inspired vision of the transcendent "speech" of Scripture. The wholly, holy, "hole-ly" divine Word, accordingly, is incarnated by the partial, profane, fragmentary, and material elements that make up its written characters or letters.

We have dwelt on how the reification of language in the spectacle of the letter circumvents its function as mediating a sense or meaning in order to turn the medium into an immediate presence, the substance of the vision itself. This foregrounding of the means of mediation at first tends to make them disappear as means and become visible as objects of contemplation in their own right. They present a "painting" that makes up a kind of whole ("*tutto* 'l dipinto"). As such, the letters are no longer mediations but become, instead, themselves the principal objects of the vision in their immediate visual presence. Yet, when Dante elaborates the scene in more detail, this unmediated vision opens up into a display of grammatical parts working in coordination with one another. In effect, the image seen in the heaven puts on display the endless mediation of the whole by its parts and of the parts by the Whole.

We have interpreted the immediacy of Dante's vision of writing in the Heaven of Jove as a metaphor for the unmediated vision of God, but the vision's articulated content turns out to be nothing other than mediation. Dramatically displaying the mediations in which language consists becomes itself a metaphorical realization of divine revelation. Something comparable to this happens again at the end of the poem. The vision of God is presented metaphorically as a single volume ("un volume") in which the universe is compacted with all its substances and accidents and their mutual relations conflated together ("sustanze e accidenti e lor costume / quasi conflati insieme," XXXIII. 85–90) in one bond of love ("legato con amore"). The divine essence is revealed here in and as the mediation of everything in the universe – both in the Creation, treated as the "book" of nature, and in the universe of language.

The analogy of the poem, as the book that Dante creates, to the created universe as God's book is here set out as a corollary alongside the analogy of Dante's book to Holy Scripture. Already, in Dante's culture, the universe was most apt to be understood as itself a form of writing, as a communication of God's glory. This becomes patent, for instance, in the Psalms: "The heavens declare the glory of God / And the firmament sheweth his handywork," 19:1. Yet the universe, too, no less than any kind of writing, including Holy Scripture, offers direct experience only of mediations rather than of God's presence as such. God is experienced in our intuiting the unity of these mediations, the substances and accidents of the universe – or, analogously, in the binding of the pages of the book into one volume. By such analogical means, Dante's poem delivers in these lines (XXXIII. 85–90) a self-reflexive image of itself. These verses build an analogy between the temporally experienced universe and Dante's book bound into one volume from the separately circulating fascicles in which he may initially have released it.[1]

It is, then, precisely mediation – and, above all, writing as mediation – that makes up the divine vision as this text presents it. To see God, or "the Love that was there," is practically equivalent to seeing the mutual determination of all things together through the mediating structures of language. God is present, or at least appears, *as* this mediation that makes

---

[1] John Ahern, "Binding the Book: Hermeneutics and Manuscript Production in Paradiso 33," *PMLA* 97/5 (1982): 800–9.

everything connect with everything else. Thus writing, as the visible medium of this mediation, miraculously makes the nature or essence of the divine manifest. God's writing (Scripture) appears in the Heaven of Jupiter, but Dante envisions and analyzes it for us as the essence of language as such by opening to view its anatomy as writing. This anatomy reveals writing as a system of differences in the act of mutual mediation – as best this action can be understood according to the most advanced linguistic science of Dante's time and of our own (Excursus II).

Whereas we emphasized at the outset of our examination of this heaven that Dante presents his medium, which is writing, and specifically the letter, as an immediate object of vision, by the end we see that what he sees in writing is precisely the structure by which it mediates its diverse elements in producing a unified sense. In a first step, we saw how mediation and the medium – writing, by virtue of being made into the object of the vision – became a metaphor for the immediacy of seeing God, the divine vision. In a further step, we see that this mediation, having itself become an object of vision, is no longer just the fact of the unmediated presence of the written letter. We see, instead, a display of the concrete workings of language as mediation, its structures and mechanisms, as they mediate between its various complex component parts in generating their unity of meaning. Dante renders visible these linguistic dynamics – replete with the material mechanics of tracing letters that operate in the making of sense. This anatomy of sense-making is surely one of the earliest feats of the secular, scientific spirit and its anatomizing gaze, decomposing unfathomable divine vision into observable sensible parts that can be grasped by human cognition.

Dante has a prescient grasp of how language can disclose and display no ultimate ground of meaning that is not identical with its own mediations. In his vision in the Heaven of Jupiter, and actually throughout the poem, just these mediations are what we see in their immediacy. Of course, Dante understands the terms of grammar and linguistics as metaphors for theological realities – for the divine Word and its self-expression or revelation. A certain dogmatic theology would posit hypostases and imagine divine Persons who underwrite sense or meaning, as well as being. Dante's poem reveals, however, behind these symbolic idealizations, the mediating activity of language itself. Language, as mediation, therewith becomes a poetic revelation of divine presence in and as the linguistically mediated interdependence and connectedness of all things. It is as if divinity simply were – or, more exactly, were to appear as – the significant interconnectedness of things that is disclosed by language as well as in the universe itself understood as divine speech. God's transcendence, in this perspective, would be the transcendence of the process of mediation itself with respect to all of the elements that are mediated within and by it. Still, none of this excludes or undermines expressing and figuring divinity via all manner of theistic representations as supremely a person.

To say that God is in, or appears as, these mediations is not to reduce divinity to something merely worldly. The process of mediation is endless; it is open and infinite. We never exhaustively perceive what is present and at work in it, since it leads always to unforeseen further mediations. This entails, furthermore, that we can never definitively comprehend God. We cannot, therefore, abide with any abstraction telling us what God is, not even with concepts such as the Unrepresentable or the Incomprehensible, the Nameless or the Transcendent. We must rather find this unmediated, unrepresentable God always present again in new and different ways that are made manifest in and through the mediations in which our lives are totally enveloped. "Mediation," too, can serve as another metaphorical figure for the Unrepresentable. Since we live as persons, mediation and what is mediated are bound to have a personal aspect for us.

When we become aware of these mediations *as* mediations and allow for them as belonging to something else that might be imagined as an infinite, incomprehensible Whole, then we live in and through them as relating us to something (or someone) else that cannot as such be exhaustively mediated. This something or other is manifest to us only negatively in the contingency of our lives in the world – a something (or nothing) that cannot be grasped, not even as "the Unmediated" or "the Whole." It leaves Dante speechless before what he insistently declares to be ineffable. This ineffable he-cannot-say-what is what Dante envisions as immediate vision – but only in and through the mediations of his vision of writing.

From Representation of Mediation to the Unrepresentable and Im-mediate

Through the intricacies of the imagery of Dante's vision, God's appearing as letters in the theophany of the heaven of Jupiter thus transforms itself into God's appearing in the *mediations* of language. Usually mediation operates unobserved, as attention is focused on *what* is mediated, but Dante's linguistic, poetic, and theological vision features the *means* of mediation as its direct object. Nonetheless, it is not exactly the medium, or writing as such and as an object, that most fascinates him – and us – in the end. It is rather something that is not objectifiable – mediation itself in its infinity – that is the *source* of unlimited power and fascination in both the poetic *mise-en-scène* and the universe that it models and enacts.

Grammar, as an analysis of language into its component parts, is ultimately aimed at letting the wholeness of sense spring forth from an articulation of the seamless stream of speech into the complexity of differentiated parts. Grammar is presented, in Dante's vision, not as a law governing its expressions, but as *figuring* in a playful display – the random play of sparks in speech, or of material elements in the inscription of letters. Miraculously, from these irrational sparkings and shootings, apparently just random scribblings, the rational order of language in grammar rises up in all its ordered configuration of components comprising a spectacular unity and universal wholeness. The uncontrollable dynamism of the letter reveals itself to be the generating source of order in language. And this order presents an analogy for divine order in the universe as a whole, despite its apparent chaos from our inevitably limited perspective. By reflecting on itself in this way, language reflects a total order that ensures, however encrypted, an inscrutable justice in the universe. Writing, as the paradigm par excellence of such endless self-mediation, which is alone what can be a revelation of the whole and total, becomes the revelation of God, his self-manifestation here and now in the Heaven of Jupiter.

To my mind, what this text is saying is that the mediation taking place in language and specifically in writing, as projecting a unity of sense, is itself the presence of God such as it can be experienced and expressed in letters. In the vision of Dante's poem, God is directly experienced not as a distinctly representable individual but rather in and through the mutual connections of things that the poem brings home to us, the relations in and through which all things are created and become what they are ("ciascuna cosa qual ell'è diventa," XX. 78). This kind of unity through interconnectedness is experienced paradigmatically in the case of writing as a differential system. The structural linguistics of Saussure and the deconstructive critical reflection of Derrida are both discernible here in embryo and still as squarely ensconsed in their originally theological matrices.

What Dante envisages in his vision of writing in the Heaven of Jupiter is indeed the presence or the appearing of God. God is present as the mediation that operates at every point in our language, as well as in the differential grammar of the Creation and of History as culminating in the providential Justice established by the Roman Empire as the image of a World Government that remains, however differently, imaginable still for us today. Divinity is made visible by Dante, above all, in writing, but that is because, *qua* mediation, writing is also essentially the substance of what we live in our lives as finite, signifying, sense-making creatures. We deal with one another and our world always only through mediations that are traversed by what to us is unmasterable contingency, and yet these mediations and contingencies, Dante maintains, belong to a higher unity or synthesis that is beyond what we can comprehend.

God is envisaged in the mediation of all things by one another, and the vision of God is attained through our experience of mediation. By presencing mediation in language as an object directly of vision – indeed of a prophetic, visionary experience – Dante expresses the recognition, which is made explicit in his declarations of ineffability, that the true nature of the divine in itself cannot but be imagined as im-mediacy. His vision of mediation negates itself and awakens him to the not-to-be-mediated absolute simplicity of the divine nature. When he exclaims to the sweet star (Jupiter) that it demonstrated to him how our (human) justice is actually the effect of heavenly justice, of "the heaven that you bejewel" –

> O dolce stella, quali e quante gemme
>   mi dimostraro che nostra giustizia
>   effetto sia del ciel che tu ingemme!
>
> (XVIII. 115–17)

> (O sweet star, what gems, and in what numbers,
>   demonstrated to me that our justice
>   is the effect of the heaven that you bejewel!)

– what Dante presents is not *simply* mediation (the visible interplay of parts of speech, etc.), but also its negation in a (non-)vision, a declaration, of im-mediacy. What he actually sees is only an "effect." Dante does not simply identify the divine with the mediations he sees – which would lead to a sort of idolatrous pantheism, or else to a secular atheism in the manner of Spinoza or Hegel, or perhaps, in our own age, to a totalizing informatics. Instead, he represents mediation in its own inherent negativity (like everything belonging to the created universe, the world of beings) as pointing to an unrepresentable immediacy (Being, God), Whom he directly apostrophizes.

The letters in their immediacy as presences show Dante God's just ordering of the universe. This he cannot actually see, but the immediate presence of God's Word assures him of it. His direct address of the heaven mirrors its demonstrating to him immediately by its speaking presence that human justice is an effect of divine Justice – despite the manifest breaking-up of the sentence and the composition of its letters out of apparently incoherent sparking. The presence of divinity in direct address, in the immediacy of language – more than any objectively formulated mediations of meaning – is the "demonstration." (Excursus VI will elucidate this link between language and im-mediacy by leveraging the ultra-phenomenological thinking of Levinas.)

In Dante's vision, most forcefully through this linguistic address, the mediations of language are negated as mediations and are made rather to appear as immediate presences. Mediation and immediacy are thus made practically to coincide. In the terms of a tradition running exemplarily from John Scott Eriugena to Nicolas Cusanus, Dante's vision here presents a *coincidentia oppositorum*. This is the tradition that also informed Hegel's dialectical thinking in its theistic version as based on the "negation of negation" (*negatio negationis*).[2]

By presenting mediations of language in the place that has been pre-pared supposedly for the unmediated vision of God, Dante suggests that God, the Unmediated, is to be seen in the mediations of language. At least this is so when the latter are seen in a perspective of infinity – *sub specie aeternitatis*. Still, the Unmediated does not finally appear per se in these mediations, which are only finite phenomena, but rather in their *effacing* themselves as mediations in order to gesture towards what they are not and cannot represent or mediate. God is, indeed, "seen" in mediation, but only in the moment in which it fails as mediation and opens up, breaking open from within, to the Unmediated.

What is seen of God are mediations – language, letters, writing, sparks. But these mediations are not content simply to be mediations. Taken as a whole, they call for and refer to the *un*mediated. God is what you do *not* see in the phenomena of the universe and of language. Nevertheless, these phenomena allow you to see that there is something more *in relation to which* they, as a whole, are negations. Mediations are revealed as transitory and negative in their own being, as dependent upon and referred to something other than themselves – the Unmediated and Whole. This Unmediated, paradoxically, becomes manifest as a material presence of the medium. In other words: Incarnation. The Roman Imperial Eagle incarnates, with the immediacy of an image, the whole history of the world as culminating in a universal order of divine Justice. In the eagle, Justice

---

[2] Stephan Grotz, *Negationen des Absoluten: Meister Eckhart, Cusanus, Hegel* (Hamburg: Meiner, 2009).

itself, which is normally but an abstract attribute, speaks presently as a kind of concrete presence or persona. Although just an abstract and emblematic sign in itself, the Eagle becomes a metaphor for the heightened reality of universal Justice incarnated historically, according to Dante's ideal, by the Roman Empire. Such trans-substantiation becomes possible, and is made actual, by the Eagle's real presence in Dante's vision.

Nevertheless, the mediation achieved in, and performed by, writing is inextricable from contingency and materiality. The order that writing displays is not just an ideal form of the mind but rather penetrates an intractably external and material reality. This order cannot simply be imposed by a subjective act of consciousness. Its creation requires and witnesses to the unlimited power of the divine Creator over all being, starting from its material roots.

The poem di-sports and dis-plays its Scriptural medium in order to stage-manage an experience through metaphor of the Unmediated, which is the Divine Vision. Dante witnesses the articulation of his medium into incomprehensible complexity. He nevertheless sees it as inscribing a higher order and as the best, or perhaps the only, means of conveying the transcendent wholeness – the vision of God – that he has been given to envision and has thereby been incited to believe. His flaunting of his medium is designed, ultimately, to make it disappear as medium so that we are left face to face with at least the *place* prepared for the Unmediated.

Only mediation that subverts itself as mediation in order to become the metaphor of unmediated presence can produce (or rather prepare for) the appearing of God – theophany. The unmediated presence of God is the non/showing of the Unrepresentable that Dante never tires of acknowledging through obsessively repeated rehearsals of the ineffability topos. However, in this case, the Unrepresentable coincides with, or at least appears as, the totality of representations mediating the divine message and meaning of the whole poem. The technical virtuosity of Dante's descriptions runs through and plays out all the possibilities of representation to the limit where representation exhausts its possibilities and points beyond itself to what it cannot represent or even fathom – the ineffable. Yet, neither does the ineffability topos simply remain in place: it, too, has been made to turn vertiginously around the center that moves the sun and the other stars.

PART II

Philosophical Reflections

EXCURSUS I

Writing and Visionary Immediacy: Mechanics and Mysticism of the Letter

Diligite iustitiam – "Love justice." Befitting its peremptory immediacy as the divine Word and as an imperative command from God, Scriptural revelation in the Heaven of Jove is presented emphatically as a spectacular visual display of writing. Nonetheless, Dante shows and deliberately exposes how his "vision" is synthesized out of the differentiated elements of grammar. In crucial ways, this anatomical dissection can be applied to the vision of the poem as a whole. A distinctive poetics of linguistic form, taken as whole and revelatory, is operative at the level of Dante's unprecedented language from the beginning to the end of the *Paradiso*. However, its grammatical presuppositions and infrastructure are also constantly probed, nowhere more deeply than here in the Heaven of Jupiter, where the "parts" of the vision are cast in specifically grammatical terms.

Tendencies inherent in language to amalgamation and to anatomization are thus placed in tension. The Name and the Letter can become objects of vision and veneration in their own right in a quasi-cultic worship of writing. But Dante, at the same time, embraces a rational view of language in which meaning is produced mechanically by systematic differentiation. He lets these perspectives play suggestively with and against one another. They can even collapse into each other.

The apparition from the outset of the vision of the letter or character (γράμμα, *gramma*), which is itself composed of written lines or traces (γραμμή, *grammé*),[1] obliges us to begin by speculating on the sense inherent in the letter as such – and even in its constitutive marks – taken as visual phenomena. The focus on writing throws into relief the startling fact that Dante finds the sublime order of poetry not only in the overarching

---

[1] This terminology is purveyed by Martianus Capella, *De nuptiis Philologiae et Mercurii*, 229: "quod γραμμή linea et γράμματα litterae nuncupantur." https://archive.org/details/martianvscapellaoomar tuoft/page/56 (accessed April 5, 2021).

191

metanarrative of divine Providence but already in the subsemantic particles of the alphabet in which poetry consists.

The poem relies openly on the mechanics of writing and difference to produce its effects of unified vision and presence. Still, this disclosure need not be demystifying. Nothing in the rapt tone and fascination of the scene in Jove appears to warrant such a conclusion. The breakdown into the grammar of writing, with its differential systems of vowel and consonant, noun and verb, statement and subordinate clause, seems in this case to suggest rather the opposite. It evokes a mysticism of the letter. This scene's grammatical anatomy projects an ocular revelation of theological truth more inward and unitary than any merely discursive exposition could possibly convey.

Of course, at one level, Dante is certainly following the rationalization of language by grammatical science. This is undeniably an element of his vision, since he explicitly employs its vocabulary of technical terms. The traditional parts of speech parsed in the grammatical manuals of Priscian and Donatus serve as the basic "elements" (στοιχεῖα, *stoicheia*), sounds or letters, out of which the vision is made. Yet grammar seems here in the heaven of Jupiter to be linked with a kind of mysticism of language that makes the letter, like the Pythagorian number, into an object of contemplation and of revelation of a superior truth. Even the single letter, as contemplated by Dante in this scene, is revealed as a veiled Name of God.

Such an understanding of Scripture was undoubtedly known to Dante in the form of the Kabbalah, which happened to attain to a particularly notable flowering in Dante's time in the so-called "prophetic" or ecstatic Kabbalah of Abraham Abulafia. Yet Dante is not taking sides between the scientific and the mystical outlooks on language in order to champion one over against the other. Instead, he is treating the two outlooks as compatible and as each expressing important aspects of his comprehensive and perfectly unified vision of a total reality everywhere penetrated by divinity. Nevertheless, the tension between the science and the mysticism of language entirely stuctures his text and vision.

A language that aspires to homogenize all elements in the name, ultimately the Name of God, would undo the fundamental statute of language as meaningful by virtue of differentiated elements. The Name of God is, in principle, absolute: it is in and of itself the plenitude of all conceivable meaning, which it gathers into totality and into the absolute simplicity of the divine. Ultimately, as infinite and unutterable, God and his Name are one (Zechariah 14:9). Something of this way of thinking is represented in contemporary theory by Theodor Adorno's reflections on music as like the

Name of God in indistinctly suggesting endless meanings, while actually articulating none.[2]

Dante, in effect, practices a kind of Cratylism of proper names, attributing to them intrinsic significance as revelations of the hidden nature of what they name. The first and most crucial and conspicuous case is the name of "Beatrice," his "beatifier." Beginning from the *Vita nuova*, with its doctrine that *Nomina sunt consequentia rerum* (XIII. 4), Dante meditates explicitly on the meaning and beatifying action of this name. He states at the outset of his *libello* that his lady was spontaneously called "Beatrice" even by those who did not know her name ("fu chiamata da molti Beatrice li quali non sapeano che si chiamare," II. 1). Evidently, the effect of her beatifying presence instilled in them an inspired knowledge of her name.

Dante undescores the power of this name over him still in Paradise, for example, in declaring himself motivated by the mere syllables "Be" and "ice": "But that reverence that makes itself mistress / over me wholly, just for *Be* and for *ice* ..." ("Ma quella reverenza che s'indonna / di tutto me, pur per Be e per ice ...," *Paradiso* VII. 13–14). The power invested in names – and even in their component particles – depends typically on their natural significance buried in their etymologies.

The etymological connotations of names such as Saint "Dominic" ("of the Lord"), together with those of his father "Felice" ("felicitous") and his mother "Giovanna" ("dispensing of benefits"), are called to attention expressly by the text of *Paradiso* XII. 67–81. The father, Felice, was "truly happy" ("veramente felice"), and the mother, "truly Giovanna," was made a prophet ("ne la madre, lei fece profeta," 60), like John the Baptist, her namesake ("Govanni," with a gender switch), by the baby in her womb. Most explicitly, Dante underlines the fact that Saint Dominic's name comes from the genitive form or "possessive," literally "*of* the Lord" (*Domini* from *Dominus*). His name is a declension of the name of the one to whom Dominic entirely belonged and was consecrated ("nomarlo / del possessivo del cui era tutto," 69). Dante constantly plays with such root meanings of proper names.

In the *Paradiso*, almost any name, from Francis (frank, free) to Benedictus (blessed), read with a little ingenuity, yields a true index to the character named and an implicit prophecy concerning their exalted

---

[2] Theodor Adorno, "Fragment über Musik und Sprache," in *Quasi una fantasia* in *Musikalische Schriften I–III, Gesammelte Schriften*, vol. 16 (Frankfurt am Main: Suhrkamp, 1978), 252–56, trans. Rodney Livingstone, *Quasi una fantasia: Essays on Modern Music* (London and New York: Verso, 1992), 1–6. Adorno refracts Benjamin's thought on language as originally and essentially a naming of God.

destiny. These instances are fairly plain, but other such etymological suggestions of proper names constantly play anagrammatically throughout Dante's poetry also in barely visible nuances. Microscopic reading of the subtexts of Dante's poem enables us to flush out innumerable other subliminal suggestions of intrinsic meaning in the proper names that Dante employs.[3]

However, this is only one side of Dante's understanding of language. His representations presuppose a mystical conception of language, and specifically of writing, even while, at the same time, synthesizing such conceptions with a rational, grammatical sense of language. Whereas, according to Scholem's Kabbalistic sources, "God's language, the inner Word, has no grammar" ("die Sprache Gottes, das 'innere Wort', . . . hat keine Grammatik"),[4] we have seen that Dante's vision of "our speech" – and, in fact, of written language – focuses it as grammatical and consequently exposes it as differentially structured. Dante's breaking of Scripture down into its structural components is potentially and implicitly a desacralizing maneuver. Yet grammar is itself marvelously transformed into a metaphor for divine vision by Dante's envisioning of letters as a display of sound and light (*son et lumière*) in the heavens.

In contrast with a structuralist outlook and indeed with all scientific linguistics based on the postulate of the arbitrariness of the sign, individual letters as such, for Dante, are not necessarily devoid of significance. Poetry – and not least Dante's poetry – is most apt to demonstrate this. Although, scientifically speaking, in order to be understood linguistically, they must be apprehended as operating in a system, still the letters taken as atomic particles of language may themselves be viewed by Dante as names for God and thus as manifestations of divine presence. In the case of the vision of Scripture in *Paradiso* XVIII, immanent within each letter is the Name of God from which the whole of language and even the whole of Creation is understood to be derived by a process of emanation – as in the Kabbalah. The divine essence was understood to be present in the Name of God, as well as in each originary letter from which the Creation was held to have proceeded by the Kabbalist thought of Dante's own time.[5] Whatever

---

[3] I discuss further examples in "The Place of the Proper Name in the Topographies of the *Paradiso*," *Speculum* 87/4 (2012): 1089–1124.

[4] Gershom Scholem, *Die jüdische Mystik in ihren Hauptströmungen* (Frankfurt am Main: Suhrkamp, 1957), 279.

[5] Gershom Scholem, "Der Name Gottes und die Sprachtheorie der Kabbala," *Eranos Jahrbuch* 39 (1970), 243–99 can be consulted for in-depth understanding. This essay gives the most concentrated exposition of what is treated in more detail, but more diffusely, in Scholem's *Zur Kabbala und ihrer Symbolik* (Zürich: Rhein-Verlag, 1960). Sandra De Benedetti Stow, *Dante e la mistica ebraica*

Dante's familiarity with this tradition may have been, he patently employs an (in some respects) analogous sort of letter mysticism in presenting his vision of Scripture.

In this way, Dante articulates a complex, Janus-faced understanding of language. He deploys a conception of language as a differential system, in which every element taken for itself, in isolation, is empty of meaning. However, at the same time, he hints at a conception of language based on the Divine Name as a unitary cipher infinitely saturated with significance.

For Dante, both visions are valid. The gist of the idea of divine presence in the letter as a Name of God is that the experience of meaning in language confers upon the letter whole – and even divine – sense. Nevertheless, Dante can clearly see that this making of sense is poetic. It is dependent on a subject's creative act and is even built out of the differential elements of signification. The mysticism of the Name ultimately effaces all differences, whereas Dante ultimately – or at least also – understands language as radically differential, and even as material and mechanical, in its ability to produce articulate meaning.

Dante definitely wishes to attain through language to a visionary transcendence. Just as for the Kabbalists, so for Dante, the letter, particularly the visionary letter such as it is sensuously displayed in his poem, becomes a vehicle of divine revelation and is even in itself a revelation of the divine. A key to this remarkable fact is language's capacity to transcend time, to encode something that is at least projected as timeless (Excursus III). Yet language achieves this in and through its consisting in, and operating with, temporalizing structures of difference (Excursus IV). Dante's immediate vision of the letter opens a penetrating x-ray view into the differential, mediating operation of language as the Logos that binds everything in the world together (Excursus V).

Poetics of Revelation in Transition from Oral Culture to Written

When language is written, it is susceptible of grammatical analysis and can be subjected to certain attendant demystifications. At the same time, the written word can also be the source of new myths exalting language and its mysterious powers. The polarity of the oral and the written can work in both directions, moving between rationalism and mysticism and, in fact,

(Florence: Giuntina, 2004) applies the Kabbalah background specifically to Dante, as does also María Rosa Menocal, *Writing in Dante's Cult of Truth: From Borges to Boccaccio* (Durham: Duke University Press, 1991).

Dante has it both ways: his mysticism is not an alternative to rationalism but rather its intensification and apotheosis. In the way that Dante places writing on the scene, it supersedes speech and orality as the matrix of the revelatory, prophetic poetics that he proposes.

Dante reproduces ekphrastically the effect of a page of an illuminated manuscript by his description of the letters in his self-reflective *mise-en-abyme* of his own literary medium. He begins, as is customary in an illuminated manuscript, by highlighting the initial letters of his Scriptural text: D, I, L. His description evokes a manuscript page, with its decorative initial letters, which are made to stand out in his own text through capitalization and fanciful elaboration of the letters of the biblical text. This illuminated "page" is, furthermore, replete with glosses in the form of Dante's own narration and commentary on the scene. He then continues to imitate specifically the artwork of illuminated manuscripts with his pictorial representation of the emblematic eagle.[6] Dante's remarkable representation, in effect, constitutes an enactment of an epochal transition from oral to written culture that proved prophetic, especially when seen with hindsight from a post-Gutenberg vantage point.

Certain of the critical stakes of Dante's exaltation of writing as theological revelation in the scene in Jove are helpfully contextualized as expressing this epochal transition from oral to written culture characteristic of the Middle Ages. Dante effectively mimes a new and acute consciousness of textuality.[7] His awareness of the new possibilities of this medium registers obliquely, but explicitly, in *De vulgari eloquentia* II. viii. 5–6, where he envisages the *canzone* in its self-containedness as consisting in "the words on the page – without their enunciator" ("verba in cartulis absque prolatore"). He thus renders the words independent of their being enunciated by a speaker. In this way of considering them, the words become practically a stand-alone visual phenomenon.

Dante's poetry revives the prophetic word of the *vates*, the seer, but the text of his poem embodies it emphatically as a vision in *writing*. This written form of prophetic vision incarnates the miracle of the divine word of revelation in poetry in some scarcely precedented ways. This novelty helps account for the exceptional energy that Dante puts into the visual spectacle of this scene signaling an epochal transition.

---

[6] Gian Roberto Sarolli, *Prolegomena alla "Divina Commedia"* (Florence: Olschki, 1971), 291–98: "La 'M' che diventa aquila."

[7] John Ahern, "Singing the Book: Orality in the Reception of Dante's Comedy," in *Dante: Contemporary Perspectives*, ed. Amilcare Iannucci (Toronto: University of Toronto Press, 1997), 214–39.

Certain critics underline the "incantatory effect" that Dante achieves by writing the "Biblical Sapiential imperative" from the Book of Wisdom (DILIGITE, etc.) into his poem. For Federica Deigan and Elisa Prati, "In his metalinguistic allegory Dante is re-enacting and sacralizing the civilization's crucial passage from the auditory medium to the written one (it is, after all, the epochal metamorphosis of language)." Dante is sensitive to what is lost in this transition, but he is also receptive to the new powers acquired thereby: "as he tries to cope with the loss of evocative power that the word suffers in that passage Dante exploits in full the advantages of the written medium."[8]

In just this vein, Walter Benjamin, with his eye on baroque emblems, identifies the tendency of writing towards visualization of language as sacralizing, but he notes the tension between atomization and amalgamation. He identifies the wholeness of the visual figure with the holy, sacred character, literally the hieroglyph:

> For sacred script always takes the form of certain complexes of words which ultimately constitute, or aspire to become, one single and inalterable complex. So it is that alphabetical script, as a combination of atoms of writing, is the farthest removed from the script of sacred complexes. These latter take the form of hieroglyphics. The desire to guarantee the sacred character of any script – there will always be a conflict between the sacred and profane comprehensibility – leads to complexes, to hieroglyphics.[9]

Dante's writing becomes a hieroglyph in the Heaven of Jove, yet without refusing the atomization, and even the propensity to decomposition, that come with committing language to the material medium of writing. Dante holds together, in highest tension, this anatomized schema of alphabetical elements with the view of the letter as a visual whole figure aspiring to embody and express the perfect unity and wholeness of the divine.

This amphibolous approach bringing together the sacralisation and the pulverization of the image, its unity and disintegration in the same stroke, presents us with the letter as a site for the production of miracles. It prefigures the astonishing feats of the digital age, in which the numerical reduction of images makes possible their mechanical reproduction and thus enables them to proliferate infinitely. Benjamin's analysis in "The

---

[8] Federica Brunori Deigan and Elisa Liberatori Prati, "'L'emme del vocabol quinto': Allegory of Language, History, and Literature in *Paradiso* 18," *Quaderni d'italianistica* 19/1 (1998): 5–6.

[9] Walter Benjamin, *The Origin of German Tragic Drama*, trans. John Osborne (London: NLB, 1977), 175–76. Cited also by Deigan and Prati in "'L'emme del vocabol quinto.'" Benjamin's theory of language as revelation is pursued further in Excursus VI.

Work of Art in the Age of Its Technological Reproducibility" ("Das Kunstwerk im Zeitalter seiner technischen Reproduzierbarkeit," 1935) echoes this material reduction having as its theological flipside the production of an "aura" and thereby anticipates surprising features of religious revival in the media revolution of postmodern times.[10]

Conspectus of the Excursuses and Their Contents

Dante's unitary vision, for all its immediacy, is a vision of mediation through language and its constitutive binaries. This will be demonstrated in terms of Saussurian linguistics in Excursus II. Excursus III then proceeds to analyze how language in Dante's vision unfolds in a series of clearly differentiated temporalities – worldly, or objective, and inner, or subjective – which are subsequently synthesized into unity and projected to eternity. Excursus IV explores the transcendental subject that begins to emerge with Dante's "I" as the locus of this synthesis. Excursus V deepens this phenomenological analysis of the synthesis as essentially linguistic and as effected by the Logos and its action of binding things together into a universe. Excursus VI, finally, brings this vision of language to focus through comparison with contemporary phenomenology, particularly in Levinas, as ultimately aimed at an ethical imperative of justice.

Taken together, the Excursuses offer an abbreviated compendium of selected ideas from the philosophy of language comprised between the Middle Ages and Modernity. The first two Excursuses gather together divergent angles of approach to language as unified form and as differentiated structure. The middle two Excursuses contemplate language as the generator of time, but equally of intellectual essences and therewith of images of Eternity. The final two Excursuses concentrate on language's capacity to create a visionary wholeness, but only through rupturing representation by means of an ethical transcendence.

---

[10] Walter Benjamin, "Das Kunstwerk im Zeitalter seiner technischen Reproduzierbarkeit," in *Schriften*, vol. I, ed. Theodor W. Adorno (Frankfurt am Main: Suhrkamp, 1955), 366–405, trans Michael W. Jennings as "The Work of Art in the Age of Its Technological Reproducibility: Third Version," in *Selected Writings, Volume 4, 1938–1940*, ed. Howard Eiland and Michael W. Jennings (Cambridge: Belknap Press, 2003), 251–83. For substantial development of this point, I am obliged to defer to my essay "Amphibolies of the Postmodern: Hyper-secularity or the Return of the Religious?," in *Sacred and the Everyday: Comparative Approaches to Literature, Religious and Secular*, ed. Stephen Morgan (Macau: University of Saint Joseph Academic Press, 2021), 9–34.

Saussure and the Structuralist Idea of Language as a System of Differences

A unifying and synthesizing function of mind, in its making or shaping of meaning, has been recognized throughout humanities tradition as characteristic of language, paradigmatically of speech. In language, all elements are mutually dependent and mutually defining. Each part presupposes the others, and understanding how all fit together is understanding the utterance as a whole. Accordingly, in order to rationally account for its intelligibility, language is customarily analyzed into the "parts of speech." This "grammatical" type of analysis opens insight into how an utterance can be meaningful. Moreover, such an analysis into parts is how language makes anything else understandable – nothing, perhaps, more importantly than justice, the central theme of the Heaven of Jupiter.

Any state of affairs becomes scientifically intelligible in and through language by virtue of its parsing or articulation into functionally connected, but differentiated parts. This parsing begins in language itself, with differentiations of vowel from consonant, noun from verb, main statement (consisting of a predication, noun plus verb) from relative clause, and of language itself from the concrete things and situations it represents. Linguistic understanding is thus achieved through breaking down the continuous phenomenal flux of speech and, through it, of what comes to be known as the world.

Ferdinand de Saussure theorizes how this segmenting of the world can be achieved only in parallel with the breaking up of the stream of sound in speech into the mutually differentiated parts known as "phonemes."[1] Neither articulated sounds (phonemes) nor concepts (or "thoughts") can be sorted out and differentiated except by means of their reciprocal correlation into corresponding segments. This procedure produces articulation where before there was none – or it reproduces within us, and within our

[1] Ferdinand de Saussure, *Cours de linguistique générale*, eds. Charles Bally and Albert Sechehaye (Paris: Payot, 1955 [1916]), 155–58.

communication systems, the articulation necessary for making things intelligible to us. Before being articulated into "things" or discrete entities, the world is not as such comprehensible to us. Language is a differential system for articulating what, in itself, is absolutely simple or, in any case, undifferentated and therefore ineffable – "reality" per se before it is articulated.[2]

The differential operation of language, such as it is expressed by the binary oppositions ostentatiously displayed in Dante's vision, has been theorized in modern times most originally and comprehensively by Saussure in terms that correspond uncannily well to Dante's. Specifically the chapter in the *Cours* on "Linguistic Value" ("La Valeur Linguistique") elucidates the differential nature of language expressed by the binary oppositions detailed in picturesque display by Dante's representation of language in the Heaven of Jove. Saussure begins with a section describing "Language as thought organized in phonetic material" ("La langue comme pensée organisée dans la matière phonique"), where he explains that ideas and vocalized sounds in themselves, before being brought together into the differential relations constituting language, are nothing but "two amorphous masses." These "deux masses amorphes" (156) Saussure describes as consisting, on the one hand, of all possible thought and, on the other, of the sound of all orally producible noises. Only by being brought into correlation with each other in language are these two indistinct continuums segmented into intelligible thoughts and distinguishable sounds. As regards "thought" or meaning taken in itself, everything is "nebulous and nothing is necessarily delimited" ("Prise en elle-même, la pensée est comme une nébuleuse où rien n'est nécessairement délimité," 155). Phonetic substance or "sonority" in itself is equally mobile and indefinite, but it "furnishes a malleable material that divides itself up into distinct parts so as to supply the signifiers that thought requires" ("une matière plastique qui se divise à son tour en parties distinctes pour fournir les signifiants dont la pensée a besoin," 155).

Distilling the consequences of this analysis into an image, Saussure represents language as a synthesis of the continuums of indefinite thought and indeterminate sound segmented in correspondence with one another – like the recto and verso of a single sheet of paper ("Nous pouvons donc

---

[2] Wilhelm von Humboldt's Romantic linguistics and Sapir and Whorf's hypothesis concerning language and reality agree on this point. All in common give priority to language in structuring the world, which cannot even be apprehended *as* a world except through the structurations of language. Still, most illuminating and penetrating here is the light cast on Dante's text from the structural linguistics of Saussure, with its "diacritical" (see below) analysis of signification.

représenter le fait linguistique dans son ensemble, c'est-à-dire la langue, comme une série de subdivisions contigues dessinées à la fois sur le plan indéfini des idées confuses [A] et sur celui non moins indeterminé des sons [B] ...," 155–56). In these terms, Saussure analyzes, systematically rather than historically, how the stream of speech is broken by mutual differentiation between signifiers and by their difference from what they signify. The things signified (or concepts) are differentiated from each other thanks only to the differentiation between linguistic signifiers and vice versa.

Saussure's insight into the intrinsically relational or "diacritical" character of language constitutes a great idea in the tradition of the humanities. He himself calls attention repeatedly to its paradoxical (159) and mysterious (156) nature. It exposes a prior negation as constitutive of any positive phenomenon of language. As Maurice Merleau-Ponty explains concerning its impact on a later, post-World War II generation: "What we learned from Saussure is that, taken one by one, signs do not signify anything, that each one does less to express a sense than to mark a gap in sense between itself and the others" ("Ce que nous avons appris dans Saussure, c'est que les signes un à un ne signifient rien, que chacun d'eux exprime moins uns sens qu'il ne marque un écart de sens entre lui-même et les autres").[3]

The structuralist model of language as a system of differences without positive terms ("dans la langue il n'y a que des différences *sans termes positifs*," *Cours*, 166) was pervasively influential beginning in the 1950s in revolutionizing not only linguistics but also the whole spectrum of the humanities. As a result, the model of language asserted itself as the dominant paradigm in virtually every discipline. Saussure's idea of language was a crucial catalyst (alongside the language-based philosophies of Heidegger and Wittgenstein) to the so-called "linguistic turn" that swept across the humanities and social sciences. Like virtually all such historically pivotal, epoch-making ideas, this one was far from having been simply ignored until its "discovery" by the thinker who finally turned it into an acknowledged landmark of intellectual history. It shows itself all along in a variety of guises, but generally first in the intuitive insight of poets and as expressed in fanciful terms before being worked out systematically and in scientific fashion.

The special problem that Dante took on with the writing of his *Paradiso* forced him to confront directly the nature of language as signifying fundamentally by difference "without positive terms" because his divine

---

[3] Maurice Merleau-Ponty, "Le langage indirect et les voix du silence" (1952), in *Signes* (Paris: Gallimard, 2003 [1960]), 63.

subject was preeminently what could not be positively uttered or conceptualized. Dante's main subject – God – was what a millenary tradition of
negative theology averred could be signified only negatively or contrastively. For Dante, this tradition culminated especially in Thomas Aquinas,
relaying the authority of Dionysius the Areopagite.[4] In *Paradiso* IV. 28–63,
Dante lays out this problematic and the accommodation to which he
resorts. He models his approach on Scripture's "condescending" to represent God physically, as having "hands" and "feet" ("Per questo la Scrittura
condescende / a vostra facultate, e piedi e mano / attribuisce a Dio a altro
intende," 43–45).

To Saussure we owe the modern linguistic understanding of what Dante
adumbrates in the linguistic epiphany in Jove, namely, the differential
nature of language – in other words, the generation of meaning from
differences within language itself rather than by a direct relation of one-
to-one correspondence to the world of things outside language. The latter
is what Saussure calls "nomenclature." He exposes it as based on an
erroneous idea of how language works and of what language fundamentally
is ("Nature du signe linguistique," *Cours*, 97–100). In its place, Saussure
opened up insight into the generation of meaning by relations internal to
language understood as a system of differences – a total structure ("Le signe
considéré dans sa totalité," *Cours*, 166). This insight – based on the
scientific, empirical study of language – led to formulations and applications across fields, for example, by literary critics such as Roland Barthes
concerning the "intransitivity" of literary language. Likewise, Claude Lévi-
Strauss built his "structural anthropology" on this Saussurian foundation.

For Saussure, and for modern structuralist linguistics following him, the
crucial insight is bound up with the thesis ("premier principe") of the
arbitrary nature of the sign in chapter 1 on "The Nature of the Linguistic
Sign" ("Nature du Signe Linguistique," *Cours*, 100–3).[5] Dante, like
St. Augustine in *De doctrina christiana* (II. ii), would have taken the
conventionality or arbitrariness of linguistic signs pretty much for granted.
However, this does not prevent Dante from finding the substantial significance of things poetically coded into their names after the motto "Nomina
sunt consequentia rerum" (*Vita nuova*, XIII. 4), as discussed in Excursus I.
The poetic potential of names is made conspicuous by Dante's deployment

---

[4] Thomas Aquinas, *Summa theologica*, Ia, Quaestio 13: *De divinis nominibus* and S. Thomae Aquinatis,
In librum Beati Dionysii De Divinis Nominibus expositio, ed. Ceslai Pera, O.P. (Turin: Marietti, 1950).
See, further, my *On What Cannot Be Said*, vol. 1, 249–54.
[5] See particularly Louis Hjemslev, "Structural Analysis of Language" (1948), in *Essais Linguistiques*
(Copenhagen: Nordisk Sprog- og Kulturforlag, 1970 [1965]).

throughout his *œuvre* of etymological figures. This procedure is especially striking, as already observed, in *Paradiso* XII, with its self-exegesis of etymologically significant names.

The structural analysis of language, however, contended that meaning is not mysteriously immanent in the word as a presence or event and expression of the being that is named. Meaning is rather the effect of interaction between differential terms in a system in which no element has any meaning in isolation – by itself alone. The presupposition of the ultimate semantic emptiness of language's individual terms implies the need for difference in order to make something out of nothing. Only language's own internal differentiations can produce the effect of meaning. The whole of sense originates from the differentiation of linguistic elements – noun and verb, signifier and signified, etc., such as we see envisioned in Dante's breakdown of language into its functional "parts."

The individual signifiers of difference are nothing in themselves: they have no positive, definable quality of their own. They can be distinctly discerned at all only by their relation to something else. This need of difference in order to produce meaning applies not only within a series of signifiers, but also to any such series as a whole. They, too, are meaningful only in relation to other series. Thought itself becomes something distinct and discernible only in relation to meaningful units of language, and vice versa.

Thus, pushed to its limits, the structuralist conception of language implodes and shows the self-generating system in turn to be necessarily related to, and even contaminated by, an outside. It presupposes always further, more all-encompassing systems. The postmodern turn of the structuralist insight in so-called *post*-structuralist discourse thus brings to focus the crucial insight that it is not only *within* a given system that difference is the principle of intelligibility. A system, too, requires relation to something *other than itself* in order to convey any meaning at all and to bear upon the real.

The post-structuralist model is no longer that of the generation of meaning from within a single self-enclosed system. Meaning involves, instead, a regress of systems with relation always to other systems and ultimately to an Other by virtue of the irreparable breach or inherent openness of any system to what lies outside and beyond it.[6] Even in strictly

---

[6] Umberto Eco's semiological thinking of the "open structure" points unmistakably in this direction. This becomes his thesis notably with *L'opera aperta* (Milan: Bompiani, 1997 [1962]). The language-based philosophies of Derrida, Foucault, Lacan, etc., transform the structuralist paradigm analogously by turning it toward the Other.

scientific terms, without conjuring up numinous Others, any system such as language is intelligible only in relation to other systems in the society and world surrounding it. Language is embedded in myriad cultural and physical frameworks of reference. This predicament produces a series of systems in which each in turn requires reference to further systems in order to become fully intelligible. This series of relays produces a postmodern understanding of system as an open-ended series of systems always piggy-backing on other systems in an infinite regress.

The strict structuralist model, in contrast, preserves still a sense of meaning as immanent within language, albeit only in the system of language as a whole – and indeed as generated from within this system rather than as deriving to it from its relation to an external reality. The thrust of the structural paradigm is to think of language as a self-enclosed system of internal relations of difference without direct dependence on anything outside of and transcending language. It relates to any referential reality not directly, but always only indirectly and on its own terms. Language is not, as such, an imitation or representation of extralinguistic reality. And yet, only relation to external reality lends language its power and pertinence. Only the ineffable valences of material things lying beyond language (even though they are scientific-ally graspable only in and through language) are capable of making language useful and meaningful. This is made evident through structur-alist anthropology (Lévi-Strauss); through the semiotics of culture (Barthes); and through the morphology of folktales (Vladimir Propp), as specific applications of structuralist linguistics.

To this extent, structuralism, in its furthest consequences, is not strictly scientific, but remains akin to theology, given the latter's inherent reference to a transcendental signified – as has often been pointed out, sometimes in an accusatory tone, by post-structuralist writers. Derrida, in particular, critiques the theology inherent in the concept of the sign as such. The "epoch of the sign," for him, remains "essentially theological" ("L'époque du signe, essentiellement théologique, ne finira peut-être jamais").[7] Structuralism leaves a space for transcendent reference and meaning accrued through relation to an absolute Other – other to all signs and signification. Still, however, in its basic import and original intent, and in conformity with modern, scientific presuppositions, structuralism disre-gards, or at least demotes, any sources of meaning transcending the system itself and concentrates, instead, on the immanent generation of meaning

---

[7] Jacques Derrida, *De la grammatologie* (Paris: Minuit, 1967), 25.

sheerly by means of linguistic difference. The latter alone can be explained in scientifically precise terms.

Dante, too, concentrates on this immanent phenomenon of binary differences forming a system of self-generating meaning. Unmistakably, a foreshadowing of this idea of language that will lead to structuralism haunts Dante's totalizing artifact. Yet he still sees this autonomous system rather as a symbol of something else entirely, of a higher and more potent reality from which all meaning derives. Dante's tendency towards systematicity and his ambition aimed at discerning whole and total structure is evident in the architecture of his otherworlds and even in the stylistic fabric of his poem. As Ossip Mandelstam observed, "Dante's book is, above all, the entry upon the scene of the world of Italian of his time as a totality and system."[8] Yet, for Dante, the self-enclosed, self-referential structure of language is not the whole of reality. It is, in fact, nothing at all in and for itself. Language as such exists only as an expression of God's perfection – as a mirror of the divine, the only true reality.

Language encompasses these divergent possibilities rooted in its signifying by difference, as Dante so graphically illustrates in the Heaven of Jove. A magical, religious conception of language as revelation, and a rational, analytical conception of language as structure, jostle together in his works. As inextricably intertwined, both conceptions seem simultaneously to inform Dante's writing.[9] For Dante, language can be coextensive with both reason and revelation. This insight would return again later in the Romantic thinker Johann Georg Hamann: "Sprache – die Mutter der Vernunft und Offenbarung, ihr A und O" ("Language – the mother of reason and revelation, their alpha and omega").[10] This avatar suggests how Dante's poetry embodies some of the most provocative insights into language that would be worked out in the ensuing centuries both by scientific study and by speculative reflection.

---

[8] Ossip E. Mandelstam, *Entretien sur Dante*, trans. from the Russian by Louiz Martinez (Lausanne: L'Age d'Homme, 1977), 13: "Le livre de Dante, c'est, avant tout, l'entrée sur la scène du monde de l'italien d'alors comme totalité et système."

[9] The general problematic of rationalism versus unifying, symbolic vision is compactly surveyed in its great amplitude in Dante's work by Zygmunt G. Barański, "Dante commentatore e commentato: Riflessioni sullo studio dell'*iter* ideologico di Dante," *Letture classensi* 23 (1994): 135–58. Barański underlines the superiority of synthetic, symbolic vision to analytic, scientific knowledge for Dante.

[10] Hamann's phrase, from his famous letter of 1785 to Jacobi, is quoted by Scholem, "Der Name Gottes," 245, as well as by Heidegger at the beginning of "Das Wort," in *Unterwegs zur Sprache*. It is cited also by Walter Benjamin in "Über Sprache überhaupt und über die Sprache des Menschen."

Temporalization and Transcendence of Time through Language

Ephemerality as the Cipher of Eternity

Grammatical analysis presents the stream of speech as a written sequence arranged in a spatial field that is occupied by words as objects composed of spatial forms or letters. Dante enhances this tendency to objectification pictorially by imagining the letters as paintings and the particles that compose them as scintillating sparks. This spatialization departs from the conception of language as either a transparency to mental activity or a purely ideal structure of logic remaining rigorously separate from the world. Dante's vision reifies language, lending it something of the autonomous existence of the thing. He treats language as an object existing in space, translating its succession of moments into simultaneously present parts of a whole picture. At the same time, however, Dante's description illustrates the reverse tendency of absorbing this whole world of objective, spatial representation back into the phenomenal dimension of inner time-consciousness. For his description of the letters presupposes their disintegration and even vanishing, as each letter is erased by the formation and appearing of the next letter in the sequence. The last letter, M, finally, is erased by its transformation into the pictorial emblem of the eagle.

Language is thus spatialized in the depiction of its letters, but these in turn are temporalized, for the text that Dante as protagonist reads exists nowhere as a whole in objective space. It is produced only by the mental synthesis of his distinct perceptions of each successive, momentarily appearing letter. Only after the whole series strung out in time has appeared can the individual letters be bound together so as to yield the meaning of the sentence as a whole: Dante never sees the full phrase written out permanently in heaven. He sees the letters only one at a time. Such a serial mode of perception emphasizes rather the event-character of Scripture as he sees it. The visual objectivity of the letters is stressed with a certain exhibitionistic flair, but only as a phenomenon of the moment:

this "objectivity" is not, after all, of the kind that belongs to substantive and enduring entities. The "whole painting" ("tutto 'l dipinto") is to be seen nowhere except in the imagination, since it is not an object in space but rather exists exclusively in the synthesis of Dante's own mind and as represented in his text.

What, then, does it mean that, when Dante sees the verse of Scripture ("Diligite iustitiam, qui iudicatis terram," Wisdom 1:1) written in the skies, the phrase does not appear all at once, but only piece-by-piece? Dante presents writing visually, heightening its normally visual mode of reception into the conspicuous visuality of a spectacle. Yet, even in this mode of spatial synthesis and simultaneity of the souls forming each letter, the fragmentariness endemic to writing is displayed in the successive appearance and disappearance of the constitutive elements of the phrase.

It is from the end of the sentence that the meaning of the whole finally becomes intelligible. St. Augustine observes this property of the operation of syntax in general as based on the way that time elapses in the reciting of a psalm. The psalm as a whole can be grasped only by virtue of the synthetic activity of the mind in memory and in expectation (*Confessions* XI. xxviii). Even a single verse is never present all at once, but only word by word, syllable after syllable. Under any normal circumstances, meaning in language is revealed not immediately in instantaneous vision, but in time – the time of syntax, in which the sentence grows to completion and achieves the fullness of its meaning.

The "thing-like" quality of the letters that are seen comes out powerfully in the metaphors of sparking and painting. But, beyond this apparent connotation of the metaphors, what Dante actually sees are signifiers vanishing even as he sees them: they yield up their objective appearance as they *dis*appear into the whole of sense, in which alone they perdure and by which they are superseded. Thus, Dante does not, in the end, reify language into a thing, as critics, including Pertile, have been inclined to suggest. The substantiality and perduring quality of objective entities does not characterize the writing Dante sees. Instead, writing here vanishes into a presence that is realized only momentarily in Dante's (and his reader's) mind. Only so can the eternal, which Dante's vision intimates, be humanly apprehended.

This disappearance of the medium, sublated into a purely mental element, is what made Hegel exalt the hymn in his *Lectures on Aesthetics* (*Ästhetik*) and in the *Phenomenology* (*Phänomenologie des Geistes* VII. B. c: "Das geistige Kunstwerk") as the most perfectly spiritual form of art. This sublimation is, at least, one aspect of Dante's poetics in the *Paradiso*, and it may illuminate the motives for which Dante's poem, too, modulates repeatedly into hymn-like strains when reaching lyrical heights of poetry in the *Paradiso* (for example, at XIV. 28–33 and XXIV. 1–9) culminating in the hymnic prayer to the Virgin in the last canto (XXXIII. 1–39).

The presence in question in the event of speech is a coming to pass – and pass away.[1] It is present in that it vanishes. Such is the nature of speech, as Augustine famously analyzed it. And such, according to Augustine, is the very condition of the totality of sense. Paradoxically, language must pass away in order that the event of sense might come to take place and perdure. As Augustine remarked in his "confessions" to God: "certainly you do not wish the same syllable to go on sounding but to pass away [so] that other syllables may come and you may hear the whole speech" (*Confessions* IV. xi).[2] "For there never could be a whole sentence unless one word ceased to be when its syllables had sounded and another took its place" ("non enim erit totus sermo, si unum verbum non decedat, cum sonuerit partes suas, ut succedat aliud," IV. x). This way of reasoning comes to Augustine in the wake of the loss of the deceased friend of his youth. As in language, so in life, considered from the standpoint of eternity, the mortality of the parts is necessary to the life of the whole. God alone is the whole, and "He does not pass away and there is none to take his place" (IV. xi). By this showing, precisely the death of mortal creatures opens up the whole significance of eternal life.[3]

Augustine, furthermore, conceived all history analogically as a kind of sentence whose end-point is reached in Christ. Christ finally makes intelligible the providential order – the meaning – of all the ages and their seeming chaos (*Confessions* XI. vi, vii, xxviii). History reaches its conclusion with the Christ event in the same way as the last word in a sentence makes everything coming before it finally fit into a definitive order of sense. (This is especially true in a Latin sentence.) Without Christ, history seems to be nothing but random chaos, just as language, considered as a temporal, physical phenomenon of sound or sight, appears to be totally contingent until the miracle of sense suddenly emerges from the sentence and transcends the time in which each separate element transpires. In this respect, language is analogous to the divine Word in Christ. This presence of the

---

[1] Heidegger's thinking of the event (*das Ereignis*), notably in *Beiträge zur Philosophie (Vom Ereignis)*, insists on such language as deriving from the Greek φθορά (phthora) or "perishing."

[2] Augustine, *Confessions*, trans. F. J. Sheed (Indianapolis: Hackett, 1942). Latin texts in *Confessions*, ed. James J. O'Donnell (Oxford: Clarendon Press, 1992), vol. I.

[3] Marjorie O'Rourke Boyle, "Augustine's Heartbeat: From Time to Eternity," *Viator: Medieval and Renaissance Studies* 38 (2007): 19–43.

eternal Word as incarnate in history proves crucial for Dante's presentation of writing in this scene. The paradoxical conjunction of the temporal and the eternal is symbolized in this scene through a numerical cryptogram for Christ. The Christological sense of the writing Dante sees is ciphered into the number 35 (7 × 5) of the letters in the sentence.

The Christological – Mortal and Material – Sense of History and Language

There is thus another, and an even more fundamental, kind of order – one that is theological and world-historical, rather than only linguistic – underlying the explosive events in the sky of Jupiter. It is the rationality of the Incarnate Logos, Christ, written into the scene in its 5 × 7 = 35 letters. Dante's text expressly calls attention to how the letters in the phrase exhibited from Scripture are thirty-five in number, five times seven vowels and consonants ("cinque volte sette / vocali e consonanti"). This is the number of years, according to the *Convivio*, attained to by Christ on earth up to his death and resurrection – the decisive event that gives its true sense to his life and indeed to all human life since Adam. Dante reasons that Christ lived human life to perfection and so necessarily to the peak of thirty-five years of age, the apex of the arc of life spanning the proverbial three-score-and-ten (seventy) years of the Bible (Psalm 90:10). Dante reckons that Christ, being thirty-three years old when he died (as tradition holds), died just as he was about to turn thirty-four – that is, just before his thirty-fourth birthday. At age thirty-three, he was in his thirty-fourth year and was on the threshold of completing thirty-four years of life on earth. This means that he was just at the point where, by turning thirty-four, he would have *begun* his thirty-fifth year and therewith the descending curve of the arc of human life. Dante reasons symbolically: "The highest point of this arc [of human life] ... I believe, in the most perfect natures, is in the thirty-fifth year. And this is my reason: that our savior, Christ, who was perfect in nature, chose to die in the thirty-fourth year of his life; since it was not fitting for the divinity to remain in a life that was degenerating, nor is it credible that he did not want to be in this life of ours at its summit, seeing that he had been in the lower state of boyhood."[4]

---

[4] "Là dove sia lo punto sommo di questo arco [of the human life-span] ... io credo che ne li perfettamente naturati esso sia nel trentacinquesimo anno. E muovemi questa ragione: che ottimamente naturato fue lo nostro salvatore Cristo, lo quale volle morire nel trentaquattresimo anno de la sua etade; ché non era convenevole la divinitade stare [in] cos[a] in discresce[er]e, né da credere è

Since thirty-five is the mid-point of the three-score-and-ten years traditionally accorded to mortals and the high-point of the perfectly symmetrical arc of human life, it is only reasonable that Christ should have
consummated his earthly mission just as he was reaching this "perfect"
age: ". . . at his thirty-fifth year Christ was at the apex of his life" (". . . al
trentacinquesimo anno di Cristo era lo colmo de la sua etade"). Dante finds
corroboration in Luke's statement (23:39) that Christ died at "about"
("quasi") the sixth hour, or noon, which means at almost the height of
the day ("lo colmo del die"). By "quasi" Luke implies (says Dante) that
Christ's thirty-fourth birthday (the first day of his thirty-fifth year) would
similarly be the high-point of his life ("Onde si può comprendere per
quello 'quasi' che al trentacinquesimo anno di Cristo era lo colmo de la sua
etade," IV. xxiii. 11).

The 5 × 7 = 35 letters of the verse from Wisdom, then, could well count
for Dante as a Christological cipher. As the decisive event inaugurating the
eschaton, the Christ event makes manifest the final meaning of all history.
The phrase DILIGITE IUSTITIAM / QUI IUDICATIS TERRAM, with
its syntactical closure reached in the thirty-fifth letter, M, functions as an
analogue for history, with its syntax completed in Christ. Christ – the just
man in whom God's eternal justice throughout all history is fully and
finally revealed – is made present here by a code in writing and as dispersed
into differential signs rather than as a discrete, unitary individual.

Once syntactical completion is reached, all the elements of the phrase
are simultaneous: Dante has mentally retained and amalgamated the letters
appearing one at a time. To this extent, time is transcended – through
language. In the whole structure of the sentence, each individual element
or letter is up-rooted from its time-boundedness: each is tied to the others,
those arriving before and those occurring after, all bound together into one
sense and in one sentence, irrespective of the specific coordinates of their
own time of occurrence. Dante's Paradise, which in the strict sense is
ultimately just the Empyrean (XXXI. 52), lies outside of time. But it is
reached – to the extent that it can be reached at all, at least by the poem – in
and through language. This Paradise is timeless like the ideal unity of sense
achieved through language. And yet, any actualization of language can take
place only in time and indeed in history. Language, in this way, by enacting
time, images eternity. It is through the dissolution of its every element in

ch'elli non volesse dimorare in questa nostra vita al sommo, poi che stato c'era nel basso stato de la
puerizia." *Convivio* IV. xxiii. 10.

the flux of time that language gestures towards what is beyond time as the condition of unity of its temporal performances.

Dante proposes a theophany of the eternal Word by presenting it in temporalized images. He temporalizes and ephemeralizes the letters of Scripture in his vision, but he reveals this dynamic of disappearing to be the indispensable means of figuring the Word of God in its eternity. The letters making God manifest, in fact, signify by their number, thirty-five, the measure in years of the eternal Word incarnate on earth. Dante's epiphany, as an incarnate manifestation of the Godhead, is modeled on Jesus of Nazareth, the Incarnation of the Word. The number of the letters gives the ultimate Christian incarnational sanction to Dante's representation of theophany in the form of the letters phenomenalized in time and space.

Thus, it is paradoxically by being materialized poetically in time and space – and under the sign of the death of God in Christ – that the transcendent sense of language can be realized. This sense is realized as an ideality that transcends time and space. The conventional, semantic sense of language is destroyed by anatomization. Letters do not as such bear sense, according to the principle that the word is the smallest semantic unit, which goes back to Aristotle. The letter, on its own, is meaningless. It is but a part of a word, which needs in turn to be bound in a sentence with noun and verb in order to say something significant.[5] Precisely the decomposition of language into letters – as seen acted out in the Heaven of Jove – first allows its transcendent sense to be made manifest.

The last letter (M) turns into a visual emblem, the Eagle of Empire, which reveals to Dante, to the degree possible, given his human limits, the mystery of divine Justice. Out of language – in fact out of its isolated parts, that is, letters – the sense of the whole of the universe emerges. Although letters, in grammatical theory, were held to be below the level of sense, here they bear and immediately manifest the sense of the whole cosmos and of history. This sense is immanent in every part of language and even of language's own material substrate. Dante's poetic materialization and mincing of language brings this out into the open and into view, as especially the analysis of the image of sparking in Chapter 2 showed.

Dante presents this Christian-Kabbalistic theophany poetically in his visual display of letters metamorphosing into the emblem of the eagle. The

---

[5] Aristotle, *De interpretatione*, chapter 2. "The noun therefore is a voice signfying by convention, without time, no separate part of which voice is significant" ("Nomen igitur est vox significans ex consensu, sine tempore, cuius vocis nulla pars est significans separata").

implication is that a whole sense, the sense of the Whole, inheres in the very elements of language, namely, the letters, below the minimum semantic units of conventionally meaningful language (words). Particularly the letters of Scripture – and then even their component sparks – become here autonomous elements of a revelation. A supernatural meaning is thus attributed to the medium itself that language materially *is*, irrespective of its use to bear intentional meanings of speakers extraneous to itself.

The complete sense of language transcends whatever can be realized in time and in the consciousness of individuals. While Dante displays the fragmentation of language in time into separate constituents or letters, the whole sense of language remains precisely what cannot be limited to any one finite form. The phenomenal form is presented and is even shown off flagrantly in Dante's vision. By this means, the transcendent sense is made present without ever being limited to a specifiable intention. It is revealed, instead, by the phenomenal playing out before Dante's eyes of language in all its sensuousness as a lively presence. The last letter, M, occasions Dante's synthesis of the whole phrase. It connotes the whole world (*Mondo*) and the ideal, all-embracing government for this whole (*Monarchia*), as well as perhaps the *M*illenium to be established by the *M*essiah figure that Dante repeatedly prophesies from *Inferno* I. 101–5 to *Purgatorio* XXXIII. 40–48: DIL recalls *cinquecento diece e cinque* = 515.

Some even speculate that the M could intimate *M*ary at the origin of this salvific event, given her association with the lily that garlands the letter's gothic stem ("ingigliarsi a l'emme," XVIII. 113).[6] Indeed, in Apocalypse 12, the woman clothed in the sun and moon, prefiguring Mary giving birth to the Savior, is given two great eagle's wings ("datae sunt mulieri alae duae aquilae magnae," 12:14) in order to fly away from the dragon to a place prepared for her by God (12:6). Dante's M, too, eventually sprouts eagle's wings (XVIII. 104; XIX. 1). M is, in any case, the thirty-fifth letter – the last, a cipher for Christ's Passion, which gives it the superlative symbolic potential of signifying the revelation of the sense of all time in the final stroke of history in the incarnate divine Word.

Christ, as the revelation of divine truth in the flesh, is a paradox. Revelation of God is complete in him, but it also remains possible to see there only a man. Similarly, it is possible to see in writing only a material thing, and to miss the spirit that gives it meaning by animating its marks

---

[6] In his comprehensive review of the history of interpretation of the scene from Jupiter in the commentaries, Joseph Chierici, *L'aquila d'oro nel cielo di Giove: Canti 18–20 del Paradiso* (Rome: Istituto Grafico Tiberino, 1962) takes the M to stand for Mary and the eagle for Christ.

and endowing them with intention, making them a revelation of thought. Just as the meaning of Christ is revealed through history, and in full only at its end, so the meaning inherent in the written mark or character is revealed only by the syntax of the sentence: and it is revealed completely only at the sentence's end.

Elena Lombardi, in *The Syntax of Desire*, amplifies John Freccero's laconic remarks on syntax and desire through detailed examination of the intellectual matrices in medieval culture for the notions of synthetic unity that are articulated in terms of grammatical science by the *modistae*.[7] Similar notions are developed philosophically and theologically by Augustine and in poetry and poetics by Dante. As seen through these perspectives in the Middle Ages, syntax is highly ambivalent. The parts of speech break up the unity of the sentence. As such, syntax is complicit in the logic of the Fall from original unity into multiplicity, mortality, and corruption. Yet syntax also provides the means of recomposing the fragments of mortal and material existence into unity. As such, it is driven by desire for union and unity, which is to say for God, when understood theologically, as it was by Dante and quite generally in the Middle Ages. This makes language the key to unlocking the experience of eternity, as will be pursued further by resuming the discussion of Augustine begun in the first section of this Excursus.

The Transcendence of Time through Language: Augustine and His Legacy

Saint Augustine's speculation on time and its relation to eternity was fundamental for thought throughout the Middle Ages and has remained so down to modern-day philosophies, signally phenomenology. Edmund Husserl begins his *Lectures on the Phenomenology of Inner Time-Consciousness* (*Vorlesungen zur Phänomenologie des inneren Zeitbewußtseins*, 1928) with an acknowledgment that no further substantial advance in understanding the consciousness of time has been made since Augustine. An Augustinian understanding of time as subjective subverts the underlying cast of the modern subject. The subject is discovered as infinitely malleable in its continual conversion to the Infinite – and therefore as without any fixed essence of human selfhood such as is posited by the rigidly ordered essential hierarchies of the Dionysian

---

[7] Elena Lombardi, *The Syntax of Desire: Language and Love in Augustine, the Modistae, Dante* (Toronto: University of Toronto Press, 2007).

universe.[8] An immediate relation to the Absolute enables the human person *not* to be subject to time and to reject mediation by intermediaries in the hierarchy of beings.

This Augustinian self is articulated by language suspended on love. Augustine expounds the phenomenon of time not primarily on the basis of the movement of physical and eminently of heavenly bodies, as had been standard among philosophers following Aristotle's *Physics*, but rather on the model of language as analogous to the synthesis of syllables in speech. He construes time as the *syntax* of history.[9] Sometimes this model of the "syllables of time" turns out to be even more than an analogy: time itself is represented as given by the possibility of synthesis residing in language. Perhaps past and future cannot be apprehended at all except by synthesis in the present: hence as past present or future present. For Augustine, this synthesis has occurred always already, eminently in the Word (the second person of the Trinity) as Creator. Just as God exists in the fullness of Trinitarian Being anteriorly to Creation, so God's eternal Word (the Son) remains always intact and whole, even when sounded out in the syllables of time. This structural parallel between language and time is based on a structural difference between the Origin and all else – all that is originated. In *De genesi ad litteram* I. 2–6, Augustine elaborates on the contrast between God's original creation by his Word outside of time (since time is among the things created) and all words sounding within time. As Eugene Vance points out, "the meaning of the language of Scripture is strictly autonomous from the temporal, verbal signs by which it is expressed."[10]

This is again the paradox of the incarnation of a transcendent divinity taken to the level of language and informing even the poetic artifact as wrought by Dante. A temporal, material language, as the "support" for a sense or meaning that transcends it, makes materially manifest in time an order that is itself neither material nor temporal. With human language transpiring in time, it is necessary that the parts of a discourse all pass away, giving place to other parts that succeed them, in order that the whole may be realized. Dante registers this temporal necessity in his vision by noting how each part, each form of a letter, passes away before the next one comes. But he also "notes" the "parts" so that he can envision them as a whole, with each part simultaneously present in his mind. This is what he displays

[8] Alain De Libera, *L'invention du sujet moderne* (Paris: Vrin, 2015), 24–39.
[9] In addition to the *Confessions* as already cited, *City of God* II. xxiii takes up this theme.
[10] Eugene Vance, "Saint Augustine. Language as Temporality," in *Mimesis: From Mirror to Method, Augustine to Descartes*, ed. J. Lyons and S. Nichols Jr. (Hanover: Dartmouth University Press, 1982), 26.

in his text by placing the successively appearing letters alongside each other in a continuous and connected sentence.

It is in the achievement of a totality of sense – the meaning of the whole phrase – that the temporality of the phenomenal appearance of its separate parts, the letters, is transcended. Thus an experience of the eternal – God – as an experience essentially of language in its production of meaning is achieved. This experience of the eternal through ephemeral elements in time is the essence of the Incarnation, which Dante has, in fact, ciphered into the heart of his vision. Christ, as the eternal Word, is the indispensable key to the transcendence of time through language.

Augustine's analysis of language as temporal – and therefore as transpiring and vanishing – is inseparable from his theory of the transiency of all earthly things. Vance, among others, has called attention to this pervasive aspect of Augustine's thought and to the pathos with which it is invested. We remarked that its autobiographical origins lie in Augustine's first experience of death through the loss of a friend to whom he felt himself attached viscerally and without reserve (*Confesssions*, Book IV. iv–ix). The successive occurrence of human words, their statute as dis*curs*ive – literally running or "coursing" – differentiates them from the eternal Word of God, which is perfectly one with itself and without difference. Although we are constantly confronted with the impossibility of expressing the eternal Word in human language, paradoxically it is precisely language that provides the analogical, and even the real, experiential basis for apprehending this ineffable divine Word.

This paradox, namely, that focusing on an impediment to expression makes it into the means of surpassing language into another register beyond language, subtends the *Paradiso* as a whole. The linear nature of the signifier is a limit which, nevertheless, leaves it always open to further addition and orients it to an unrealizable totality. Saussure underlines "the linear character of the signifier" ("Le caractère linéaire du signifiant") as the second general principle of the linguistic sign (after the arbitrariness of the sign). As Saussure pertinently remarks, although simple and obvious, this principle is of "incaluculable consequences" (*Cours*, 103–4). Precisely this principle furnishes the crucial pivot for Saint Augustine's transition from time to eternity. Language, as an open-ended linear progression of particles (signifiers), can signify something of a wholly different nature – a whole intellectual sense (signified).

In Book XV of his treatise *De trinitate*, Augustine theorizes the interior word that remains intact and is neither divided, by being spoken, nor dispersed in time. It is a word that, rather than sounding exteriorly, lights up interiorly and is more truly word than the word that is heard through physical ears. Augustine draws this analogy explicitly: "Therefore the word that outwardly sounds is a sign of the word that inwardly shines and that better deserves the name of 'word'" ("Proinde verbum quod foris sonat signum est verbi quod intus lucet cui magis verbi competit nomen").[11] This word is a whole and is one with itself even in being proffered – the way that the divine Word remains eternally one with itself even in becoming flesh. It is not turned into flesh, even though it assumes flesh.

The word as "verbum" comprehends not only single words but also larger units of discourse such as sentences or statements. In Augustine's thought, the analogy of the human word or *verbum*, which already exists whole in the mind before any part of it is uttered, becomes fundamental to the Christian doctrine of the Incarnation. It provides a model for understanding the Incarnation not as a metamorphosis, like that of a pagan god into a material form, but as the utterance of a word. The mystery of language thus becomes the key to the mystery of the Incarnation.[12] Or, at least, language provides the best way of understanding how something that is an indivisible whole, an immaterial ideality, such as meaning, should become material and temporal as it transpires in speech or is materialized as text. "And just as our word becomes voice without being changed into voice, so the Word of God is made flesh but escapes being changed into flesh. Assuming flesh, not being consumed therein, even this (human word) becomes our voice and that (divine word) is made flesh" ("Et sicut verbum nostrum fit vox nec mutatur in vocem, ita *verbum* dei *caro* quidem *factum est*, sed absit ut mutaretur in carnem. Assumendo quippe illam, non in eam se consumendo, et hoc nostrum vox fit et illud caro factum est," *De trinitate*, XV. xi. 20). In both cases, the spiritual or intellectual assumes a material form without being consumed by it.[13]

The way Dante incorporates Augustine's thinking on language as disclosing the juncture between time and eternity is reflected in his use of the motif of the act of prolusion in speech that nevertheless leaves the agent unchanged. The whole thought that is expressed incarnate in material signs exists identically before and after articulation. The motif of "remaining one

---

[11] Sancti Aurelii Augustini, *De trinitate Libri XV*, 2 vols., ed. W. J. Mountain, in *Aurelii Augustini Opera* Pt. XVI, 2, Corpus Christianorum, Series Latina (Turnhout: Brepols, 1968), XV. xi. 20 (page 486).

[12] For the importance of the idea of the incarnation of the Word in the context of the history of Western thought, see Hans-Georg Gadamer, *Wahrheit und Methode* (Tübingen: Mohr, 1960), trans. Joel Weinsheimer and Donald G. Marshall as *Truth and Method*, 2nd rev. ed. (New York: Continuum, 2004), Part III, "Language and Verbum," 418–29.

[13] See discussion by Lombardi, *The Syntax of Desire*, 60–61.

in itself" ("uno manendo in sé come davanti," *Paradiso* XXIX. 145–47; cf. II. 36; XIII. 60), which informs the whole of the *Paradiso*, beginning from its opening verses, with their evocation of the one and the many, derives, by multiple routes, from such Augustinian, Neo-Platonic metaphysics.[14]

However, this metaphysical Word that remains beneath all actual words is not itself available as a given phenomenon. It is, in Giorgio Agamben's terms, purely "Voice" as the absolute taking-place of language prescinded from any articulated content.[15] A void in terms of determinate significance, such a divine Word is a *pure* presence. But that does not make it a simple, positive given. It can be affirmed only on the basis of self-reflection. The passage in *Paradiso* XXIX telling of God's "I" creating in order to be able to say "I subsist" in other "I"s ("potesse, risplendendo, dir 'Subsisto,'" XXIX. 15) expresses this predicament of linguistic self-reflection at the origin of Creation and thus of any possibility of presence.

This miraculous synthesis called "sense" (i.e. meaning), which takes place in language, manages to transcend time and to bring all that is dispersed through the universe – "substances and accidents and their modes" ("sustanze e accidenti e lor costume," XXXIII. 88) – into the self-reflexive unity of the word. The ground projected by this miraculous event, suspended in what is otherwise nonsense, is the presence of the Word. The Word's own presence is self-reflexive: it is the life of the Trinity (the Father being perfectly reflected in the Son, etc.). Thus, the poet of the ineffable, of God in the form of the Trinity, does not just say nothing: he evokes an infinite presence. Dante's language in the *Paradiso*, even while calling attention to itself and its immediate physicality, would also like to be transparent to the presence it evokes, disappearing before this invisibility, which, however, enables "vision" of all that is and of all that could never before be seen as a whole.

This idea of language as an eternal Word made perceptible in time had very wide currency in medieval Catholic theology. Accordingly, there are any number of medieval mediations of Augustine's thought on time and language that could have been part of Dante's cultural baggage. The idea is employed intensively, for example, by Saint Bernard. In his Fourth Homily "In Praise of the Virgin Mother," which is read in the lectionary

---

[14] Cf. Roland J. Teske, "St. Augustine's Use of 'Manens in Se,'" *Revue des Études Augustiniennes* 39 (1993): 291–307. This motif is investigated also by Jaroslav Pelikan, *The Mystery of Continuity: Time and History, Memory and Eternity in the Thought of Saint Augustine* (Charlottesville: University Press of Virginia, 1986).

[15] Giorgio Agamben, *Il linguaggio e la morte: Un seminario sul luogo della negatività* (Turin: Einaudi, 1982), 128.

every year on December 20, the Virgin is coaxed: "Answer with a word, receive the Word of God. Speak your own word, conceive the divine Word. Breathe a passing word, embrace the eternal Word."[16]

This idea is also the subject of fundamental metaphysical speculations such as those of St. Anselm in *Monologion*, cc. 29–36. In discussing the "unum verbum per quod facta sunt omnia" ("one word by which all things were made") of the Gospel According to John 1:3, Anselm emphasizes the absolute unity and transcendence of the divine Word with respect to all created things. Unlike human words, which resemble the things that they name (Anselm is a Cratylist), the divine Word is without similitude to the things created by it: it is of a different ontological order. Yet this heterogeneity cannot be the whole story either, and notably Aquinas will develop elaborate principles of analogy between creatures and their first cause, the Creator, the Word.

The Bible unequivocally affirms the Word as the principle of divine creation: "All things were made by him [the Logos, the Word]; and without him was not any thing made that was made" (John 1:3). Compare Colossians 1:16: "For by him were all things created, that are in heaven, and that are in earth, visible and invisible, whether they be thrones, or dominions, or principalities, or powers: all things were created by him, and for him." Creation through the Logos (the principle of language) is the linchpin between the world and God, time and eternity.

Poetry, like human language generally, is a corporeal phenomenon, and yet somehow it is able to reflect and express a non-material, a "transcendent" order of sense. Its successive parts make a whole that is itself not temporal in nature. Augustine explains this again in *De vera religione*, but here he places the accent on the *aesthetic* sense of order and wholeness more than he does in the similar passages in the *Confessions* that we have already noted:

> So it is that a metrical line is beautiful in its own kind although two syllables of that line cannot be pronounced simultaneously. The second is pronounced only after the first has passed, and such is the order of procedure to the end of the line, so that when the last syllable sounds, alone, unaccompanied by the sound of the previous syllables, it yet, as being part of the whole metrical fabric, perfects the form and material beauty of the whole. But the versifier's art itself is not dependent on time in the same way; its beauty is not portioned out in temporally measurable units. It is

[16] Ferrucio Gasteldelli (ed.), *Opere di San Bernardo II: Sentenze e altri testi*, trans. Claudio Leonardi (Milan: Fondazione di Studi Cistercensi, 1991). English version online at http://te-deum.blogspot.com/2012/12/st-bernard-on-blessed-virgin-mary-and.html (accessed April 6, 2021).

simultaneously possessed of all those virtues which enable it to produce a line – a line which is not simultaneously possessed of all its virtues but which produces them in order. For the beauty of things shows the last footprints of that beauty which art itself constantly and immutably watches over.[17]

Sic enim et versus in suo genere pulcher est, quamvis duae syllabae simul dici nullo modo possint. Nec enim secunda enuntiatur, nisi prima transierit; atque ita per ordinem pervenitur ad finem, ut cum sola ultima sonat, non secum sonantibus superioribus, formam tamen et decus metricum cum praeteritis contexta perficiat. Nec ideo tamen ars ipsa qua versus fabricatur, sic tempori obnoxia est, ut pulchritudo eius per mensuras morarum digeratur: sed simul habet omnia, quibus efficit versum non simul habentem omnia, sed posterioribus priora tollentem; propterea tamen pulchrum, quia extrema vestigia illius pulchritudinis ostentat, quam constanter atque incommutabiliter ars ipsa custodit.[18]

In poetry, as in music, material, sequential signs, "signa sonantia," can manifest a transcendent, intellectual order. But they cannot say what occurs to the soul in a moment of illumination in which truth shines, a moment which is outside time and cannot properly be remembered. Prescinding from its material medium, the art of poetry consists in imitating a purely rational harmony. In this regard, the truth of poetry resides not in its sensuous form, but in its intellectual content. Hence, Augustine writes in *De ordine* 2. xi. 34 that "Our praise of the meter is one thing, our praise of the meaning is something else" ("aliter metra laudamus, aliterque sententiam"). Augustine insists on the perversity of attachment to gratifications derived from the sensuous material of art as opposed to its intellectual sense (*De vera religione* xxii. 43).

Precisely with respect to this abstraction from the medium of language, Dante parts company with Augustine. In his vision of the transcendent sense of Scripture, Dante exalts the sensible, phenomenal medium rather than just the purely intellectual meaning. This can be seen immediately and strikingly in his presentation of the medium of writing in *Paradiso* XVIII. The modes of rendering sense sensuous are then explored and exploited with reference particularly to a transcendent ideal of Justice by the richly imaged and sensuous poetry of the remaining cantos of the

[17] This passage is quoted by A. D. Nuttal, *Two Concepts of Allegory: A Study in Shakespeare's The Tempest and the Logic of Allegorical Expression* (New Haven: Yale University Press, 2007), 44–45, whose translation I follow.
[18] Augustine, *De vera religione* xxii. 42. *Bibliotheca Patrum Latina*, ed. J. P. Migne (Paris: 1861), vol. XXXIV.

Heaven of Jove, Cantos XIX and XX. Whereas for Augustine it is necessary to transcend all mediations in order to apprehend the eternal, for Dante, with his poetic approach to the eternal, mediation is exactly where and how the absolute can be encountered. In this respect, Dante stands closer to the immanentist thinking characteristic of modernity, which declares itself in Spinoza, peaks in Hegel, and is continued by Deleuze, than to the Platonist dualism of sense and intellect handed down to the Christian Middle Ages by St. Augustine, among others. In this, as in so many other ways, Dante makes the decisive turn towards modernity.

Dante attempts in his poetry to create metaphors for the sound and sight of a transcendent, a soundless and invisible, Word. The goal is to learn to discern the wholeness of eternity articulated in time, and this act of synthesis is analogous to – and is even realized in – understanding the sense of language. The miracle of sense, as something whole and abiding, as it emerges in language, paradoxically by its nature as discursive or literally "cursive" – as flowing away into nothingness – is the miracle of eternity realized in time (albeit always fleetingly, and at the same time as this realization is undone). This intersection and integration of time and eternity, in fact, has been widely recognized as Dante's goal in the *Paradiso* and even in "the entire journey."[19]

Eternity cannot itself as such be experienced, but it can be sensed or suspected precisely where experience breaks down and runs up against its own limits. The utter contingency of experience points to something of the absolutely opposite order, something permanent. The latter is, to us, rather an ungraspable Nothing, yet it is more permanent than time itself and is thus, under any circumstances, necessary and, in a word, "eternal." The sensuous, given its ephemeral nature, has been interpreted, at least since Plato, as pointing to something other than the order of sense, something of the order of meaning, of Being. Being itself does not exist, any more than eternity, as an object that can be measured and verified. Yet the whole order of beings, taken for itself, collapses and disintegrates as not self-sustained, not founded on itself. It need not *be* at all. Yet it is. And although it is not rationally demonstrable, this miracle is what we experience, marvelously, when we experience anything. Only the deconstruction of our order of time lends credence to the intuition of eternity, just as the self-deconstruction or implosion of the order of beings, their showing themselves always to be at least as much non-beings as they are beings, induces

---

[19] John Freccero, "Dante's Prologue Scene," *Dante Studies* 85 (1966): 1–25, "The synthesis of eternity and time is the goal of the entire journey . . ." (22).

Plato to conceive the necessity of a superior ontological order, that of Being, on which they all depend.

Such is the experience that we as moderns call "contingency" and that paradoxically opens upon the eternal. Goethe intuited and reiterated this vision – which was originally medieval more than eighteenth-century in character – at the end of his *Faust* in declaring that all that is passing is but a sign of eternity as the final word. The drama's final "Chorus Mysticus" reads virtually as a recapitulation of Dante in Paradise, specifically of Dante's being drawn all the way to God through the erotic force of his attraction to a woman:

> Alles Vergängliches
> Ist nur ein Gleichnis;
> Das Unzulängliche,
> Hier wird's Ereignis;
> Das Unbeschreibliche,
> Hier ist's getan;
> Das Ewigweibliche
> Zieht uns hinan.
>
> (Part II, Act V)

> (All that is passing
> Is but a likeness;
> The unattainable
> Here becomes real;
> The indescribable
> Here is realized;
> The eternal feminine
> Draws us on.)

The "here" of immanence is experienced as a realization of an unattainably other reality. Exemplarily, the erotic, its inherent instability notwithstanding, becomes a manifestation of eternal Love. This points to a surprising transhistorical kinship between Goethe and Dante as arguably the two greatest philosophical epic poets in modern Western languages.[20] For both poets, nature, as rediscovered by new types and intensity of scientific scrutiny, was a direct revelation of eternity (Hösle, *Dantes Commedia und Goethes Faust*, 31–40).

---

[20] Vittorio Hösle, *Dantes Commedia und Goethes Faust: Ein Vergleich der beiden wichtigsten philosophischen Dichtungen Europas* (Basel: Schwabe, 2014). For a partial English version, see "Dante's Commedia and Goethe's Faust: Similarities and Differences," in *The European Image of God and Man*, eds. H. Günther and A. A. Robiglio (Leiden: Brill, 2010), chapter XV, 314–44.

Poetry makes the ideality of sense or meaning sensuous. It conjoins and commingles the rational and the sensuous components that Dante recognized as constituting the linguistic sign ("rationale signum et sensuale," *De vulgari eloquentia* I. iii. 2–3). This has been described, as we already observed, by Roman Jakobson as making sense sensuous, but it is also, certainly for Dante, the reverse. The sensuous is fleeting, but in poetry it is subsumed into the relative timelessness of intellectual sense as a determinate content of meaning. On the basis, then, of a kind of existential projection, this open space created by the ungraspable as a gap in our analytic understanding of the real is worked over by the imagination into a symbol of the absolute transcendence of time by God.

Negative Dialectic of Time and Eternity: From the *Commedia* to Modern Literature

The miracle of Dante's language consists in its realizing the only apparently static eternity of sense in the dynamic event of language. This is how human comprehension can open itself to the transcendence of sense – only negatively, by denying itself all self-made transcendence or stability, by surrendering itself to the temporal flux which claims it. Consciousness does this, for example, by commending itself into the mysterious, ungraspable "hands" that can reach around and hold this falling together. Just such a giving up of self to an Other (echoing Christ's final, dying words "Into thy hands I commend my spirit," Luke 23:46) is imagined in the verses of Rilke's "Herbstgedicht" ("Fall Poem") from *Das Buch der Bilder*:

> Die Blätter fallen, fallen wie vom weit
> Als welkten in den Himmeln ferne Gärten;
> sie fallen mit verneinende Gebärde . . .
>
> Wir alle fallen. Diese Hand da fällt.
> Und sieh dir andre an: es ist in allen.
>
> Und doch ist Einer, welcher dieses Fallen
> unendlich sanft in seinen Händen hält.
>
> (The leaves fall, fall as if from far off,
> as if distant gardens in the heavens were withering;
> they fall with gestures of negation . . .
>
> We all fall. This hand there falls.
> And just look at the other: it is in all.

And yet there is One, who this falling
infinitely, gently holds in his hands.)

The negative gestures ("verneinende Gebärde") of these "leaves" falling
out of the deep distance make them images of apophasis – of self-denying
discourse opening a peep-hole to transcendence. Dante's image of the
scattering of Sibyl's leaves (XXXIII. 64–66) makes the same gesture of
language's self-cancellation in the final approach to the vision of eternity.
Rilke is situated in a tradition running from Goethe and Hölderlin in the
eighteenth century through German Romanticism to Novalis: it is
a tradition of reaching out toward an ineffable eternity through negation
of the forms of time. Paul Celan, in *The No-One's-Rose* (*Die Niemandsrose*,
1963), succeeds Novalis and the Hölderlin of "Patmos" in this poetry
performing its own self-deconstruction through a negative dialectics of
language.[21]

This lineage links with what has long been recognized as the distinctive
innovation of Dante's poem in the history of thought, namely, that it
represents the eternal in the forms of time. This was lucidly proclaimed by
Hegel in his *Aesthetics* (III. 3. iii) and was made a commonplace among
Dantists by Auerbach, who was seconded by renowned critic and medi-
evalist Hans Robert Jauss.[22] It is commonly taken as a cardinal principle,
and is underlined as such for understanding Dante, by a wide variety of
criticism.[23] The American context, for instance, affords precedents such as
Jeffrey Schnapp's *The Transfiguration of History at the Center of Dante's
Paradiso* (1986). This insight was a starting point for my reading of the
Commedia in dialogue with contemporary hermeneutic theory in *Dante's
Interpretive Journey*. Broached in the Introduction, the argument for
historicity as the condition of transcendence is carried out in detail in
chapter 5 in a concluding section on "Hermeneutics, Historicity, and
Suprahistorical Truth." Dante's great breakthrough to genuinely historical

---

[21] I pursue this line of interpretation in "Poetics of Silence in the Post-Holocaust Poetry of Paul
Celan," *Journal of Literature and Trauma Studies* 2/1–2 (2014): 137–58. See, further, chapter 3 of my
A Philosophy of the Unsayable (Notre Dame: University of Notre Dame Press, 2014) and *On What
Cannot Be Said*, vol. 2, 387–93.

[22] Hans Robert Jauss, "Erleuchtete und Entzogene Zeit: Eine Lectura Dantis," in *Poetik und
Hermeneutik XIV, Das Fest*, ed. W. Haug and R. Warning (Munich: Wilhelm Fink, 1989), 64–96.

[23] Particularly interesting in this regard is the contribution of Anna-Maria Chiavacci-Leonardi, "La
Novità della *Commedia*," in *La fine dei tempi: Escatologia e storia* (Fiesole: Nardini, 1994), 154–58, as
well as that of Franco Masciandro, *La problematica del tempo nella Commedia* (Ravenna: Longo,
1976). Masciandro defines the *Commedia* as a whole as a "ricerca della totalità del tempo" ("search
for the totality of time") and an effort to "cogliere il tempo nella sua totalità" ("seize time in its
totality," 7–8).

interpretation began from his momentous discovery in *De vulgari eloquen-tia* of the vernacular as a changing language ("variari opportet," I. ix. 6) that nevertheless, paradoxically, proved most apt for the representation of eternity in his "poema sacro" (XXV. 1).

Karlheinz Stierle analyzes the ways that literature in general, yet emi-nently the poetry of the *Paradiso*, thinks time in images to its limits in order to envisage eternity.[24] Proust and Dante both respond to the crisis of secularization in which Time breaks up into fragments of subjectively experienced time. Already in Dante's time of crisis for the conception of time, on the threshold of the modern age, no longer does one overarching shape of time embrace and reconcile all actually lived temporalities of individual subjects. Time falls apart into subjective perspectives.[25] Dante's troubled poetic present, for Stierle, breaks through and unsettles any possible tranquility about time all the way through the *Paradiso*. Only the poetic work can shape time into a whole – and thereby mediate the wholeness of eternity to time-bound humans. Both authors, Dante and Proust, employ aesthetic means to reassemble time as a whole for the subject through memory. Temporalization through memorialization becomes an immanent eternity in which a kind of "second degree" tran-scendence is invented and made concretely real in the poetic work – Proust's and Dante's, respectively (*Zeit und Werk*, 135–36). Dante poetic-ally anticipates the modern philosophical problematic of a gap between lived time (*Lebenszeit*) and objective, worldly time (*Weltzeit*), in Hans Blumenberg's vocabulary. Stierle underlines the "incommensurablity" (*Zeit und Werk*, 137) of these temporalities.

We are thus directed to focus more sharply on the negativity that is inherent in this continuity and even renders it possible. Such an emphasis has characterized much recent criticism of modern authors facing the alterity introduced by time. Many leading authors from Romantics to modernists, in subtle ways, are Dante's heirs in this regard.[26] We can broaden Stierle's connecting of Dante with Proust in showing the repre-sention of time as a negation of eternity to be practically an overarching and enabling structure of Western literature.

---

[24] Karlheinz Stierle, *Zeit und Werk: Prousts "À la recherche du temps perdu" und Dantes "Commedia"* (Munich: Hanser, 2008), 167–94.
[25] For the medieval backround, see Analies Maier, "Die Subjektivierung der Zeit in der scholastischen Philosophie," *Philosophia naturalis* 1(1950): 361–68; and "Scholastische Diskussion über die Wesensbestimmung der Zeit," *Scholastik* 26 (1951): 520–26.
[26] William D. Melaney, *Alterity and Criticism: Tracing Time in Modern Literature* (New York: Rowman and Littlefield, 2017), especially chapter 7: "Eliot and the Uses of Dante: Thresholds of the Unsayable," 83–96.

Dante's apprehension of language as event, and as passing away, besides being displayed broad brushed in large letters on the scene of the Heaven of Jove, percolates into his constant manipulations and innovations with language. Specifically, the verbalization of all parts of speech – in unprecedented self-reflexive constructions like *s'inluia*, *m'intuassi*, *s'insempra* – characterizes the *Paradiso*'s unique language. Each of these neologisms vectorizes personal pronouns or a temporal adverb by fitting them with prepositions and turning the composite into a self-reflexive verb. This realization of language as event is what the whole scene in Jove consciously and conspicuously achieves. This heaven *performs* Scripture. By becoming event, language vanishes as static form and opens a space beyond itself. By defining the contours of time, language opens a "space" around itself that is sensed as harboring the opposite of time, namely, eternity.

Dante attempts to realize divine actuality in and as language. For this purpose, he requires a language of total verbalization – where namings are decomposed into verbal actions. Traditionally, language is thought to function by preserving and fixing identity against the flux of time. The epic poet confers longevity ("rendili longevi") and even perpetuity on the fame of the heroes and heroines who are sung. This function of language is duly rehearsed by Dante in his invocation to his inspiring Muse ("diva Pegasea") in the scene in *Paradiso* XVIII. 82–84. Yet what Dante, after all, shows in his vision is that true eternity is achieved only through the *passing away* of language. Language must realize pure actuality in order to attain to the eternal, and this it can do only in silence and in disappearing as a temporal phenomenon. By emphasizing these intrinsically self-negating aspects of language, Dante has language render itself up in sacrifice to the pure enactment and actualization of Being.

Dante's verbalization of nominal forms – the most characteristic pattern of his neologisms throughout the *Paradiso*[27] – has a metaphysical significance that speculative grammar illuminates. In the terminology of the *modistae* who developed this type of grammar-based philosophy, the noun stands for a static mode of being (*modus entis*), while the verb connotes becoming (*modus esse*).[28] Dante's transposition to verbal modes effects a heightening of perspective from the level of the entity to the act of Being, which in Thomas Aquinas's theology belongs properly only to

[27] See Brenda Deen Schildgen, "Dante's Neologisms in the *Paradiso* and the Latin Rhetorical Tradition," *Dante Studies* 107 (1989): 101–19. This aspect of verbalization is emphasized likewise by Joseph Luzzi, "'As a leaf on a branch . . .': Dante's Neologisms," *PMLA* 125/2 (2010): 322–36.

[28] G. L. Bursill-Hall, *Speculative Grammars of the Middle Ages: The Doctrine of Partes Orationis of the Modistae* (The Hague: Mouton, 1971), 118–19.

God.[29] In fact, for Thomas, just this pure actuality (*actus essendi*) of Being *is* God.

The totality of vision conferred by the poem flows from the simplicity of divine Being (which it realizes in rendering itself pure actuality) rather than from any all-encompassing system. It could only be an *inarticulable* wholeness – whole and entire, without difference. This totality is thus *ineffable* – unlike Hegelian totality, which is completely articulated in the System. The latter makes up a realized whole of all that can be said. Dante's is a totality *before* all saying, one in which Hegel does not believe and which he dismisses as merely empty and abstract, for he focuses rather on the *result* of mediation through history and discourse as alone the revelation of truth.[30]

We have seen that Dante perceives an underlying order at the level of structure. Ultimately, this is the divine Logos that structures all Creation. Yet his presentation of this structure is totally dynamic. The letters form a sense transcending time and change, but still their realization consumes itself in the dramatic choreography of the scene featuring their display and disappearance. In fact, Dante's constant technique in the *Paradiso*, with its irrepressible invention of neologisms for what was previously without words in his language, is to *verbalize* all language.[31] This is consonant with his daring choice of the vernacular for his ambitious bid to create an immortal work of literary art. Not static, grammatical Latin, but the evolving, disappearing, dynamic tongue of the vernacular can best evoke the eternity that perdures in the ineffable dimension beyond language. Language's self-consumption as an artifact makes it the *indicator* of an eternal presence. In order to grasp these possibilities theoretically as they could be conceptualized in the Middle Ages, we must extend yet further, in Excursus IV, Saint Augustine's thought about time and eternity, which pivots on his theory of language.

---

[29] An outstanding exposition of this aspect of Thomistic metaphysics is Cornelio Fabro, *Introduzione a san Tommaso: La metafisica tommista e il pensiero moderno* (Milan: Ares, 1983).

[30] However, the early Hegel's apophatic sensibility, before the exigencies of the System, and in some ways still silently underlying it, is elicited by Andrew W. Hass, "Hegel and the Negation of the Apophatic," in *Contemporary Debates in Philosophy and Negative Theology: Sounding the Unsayable*, eds. Nahum Brown and J. Aaron Simmons (London: Palgrave Macmillan, 2018), 131–62.

[31] In a comparative cultures perspective, this priority of verbalization was discovered as the vocation of poetic language by modernist poets under the influence of Ezra Pound and his work with Chinese characters as guided by Ernest Fenollosa (1853–1908). In 1919, Pound momentously published Fenollosa's posthumous *The Chinese Written Character as a Medium for Poetry*.

Transcendental Reflection: Time Synthesis and the Role of the "I"

Dante's vision of the Scriptural sentence "Diligite iustitiam, qui iudicatis terram" from the Book of Wisdom allows him, as already stressed, to glimpse only one letter at a time. He sees each of the thirty-five ("cinque volte sette") letters of the sentence in temporal succession. Thus, Dante's grammatical scansion of the phrase is also a temporal scansion. He "notes" it as an ensemble of "parts" and accurately distinguishes those that come first ("primai") from those that complete the picture ("sezzai"). His careful chronicling of the exact order of the action punctiliously demarcates what comes "next" ("Poscia") and then what follows in a distinct moment "afterwards" ("poi," 100). The schema of "Prima" and "poi" (used already in lines 79–80), which is ostensibly just a facilitator of the presentation, expresses what has emerged as one of the most essential things about Dante's vision in this reading, namely, its parsing of a meaningful whole into its distinct component parts separated by temporal intervals.

Why such insistence on the temporal scansion of Dante's vision of this line from Scripture? The complete written phrase, taken abstractly as a purely verbal form, is atemporal. Textually, the phrase appears written as a whole in the simultaneity of the characters that compose it. Still, in Dante's experience, it is vanishing and fragmentary and features but one character at a time. Why, above all here in heaven, where the ideal condition of *totum simul* is in principle realized, is Dante's experience – and then again his transmission of this experience – marked so conspicuously by temporal divisions and even by the temporal perishing of each separate element? This revelation of writing in its wholeness as biblical Word, and indeed as symbol of an eternal Justice, turns out by such accents to reveal the necessarily fragmentary and unstable nature of its apprehension by humans. The wholeness belongs exclusively to the *signatum* (signified), ultimately God, and not to the *signans* (signifier), human language. Still, there is a claim to revelation of some extraordinary experience and insight. Something of the divine reality is realized, albeit negatively and dialectically, in the writing in which the poem consists. Dante can glimpse the whole of being only partially via synthesis in the mirror of language.

Of course, any pretension to wholeness of vision is likely to raise suspicions in many critical spirits today. But should we not be equally suspicious of stopping short with fragmented pictures and only partial truths? Dante, in any case, treats the effort straining toward wholeness of experience that this language expresses as meaningful, even if not without obsessively registering also its aporias. Is the poem, then, a process that issues in a synthesis of sense in which time is finally transcended?

Time is indeed the element of division, but also of synthesis. It breaks the primordial wholeness of the unanalyzed, unprocessed world up so that it can be appropriated by the subject and be synthesized into the whole of an ordered experience. Dante's remarking the role of his own "I" in producing the synthesis of the sentence ("e *io* notai / le parti sí ...") builds the structure of what philosophers call "transcendental reflection" into his perception. The theoretical analysis in modern phenomenology of this structure as basic to human consciousness can help us to see much more clearly all that is implied in Dante's gesture by placing it in a perspective of intellectual history reaching down to our own time.

Phenomenology of time-consciousness underwrites Dante's entire experience of the letters appearing successively to him in the heaven of Jupiter and forming a whole only in his mental synthesis of their event. The spatial objectification and dispersal of intention that are implicit in writing meet their limit here. Dante's "io" ("I") remains at the center of his experience even of a transcendent center into which he is inscribed – all the way to the last giration of the poem's final tercet, pivoting on "my desire" ("mio disio," XXXIII. 143). To this extent, Dante does not, in the end, consign language to the status of an impersonal, atemporal system: it is not, finally, for him *langue* (Saussure). In his understanding, language is proferred and comprehended by a subject, an I, which is not only a category generated by the system (Benveniste), but itself an originating principle of sense by which – or whom – the synthesis of language is performed.

It is in the spirit and in the synthesis of transcendental subjectivity that Dante's truth takes root and grows. It is no accident that semioticians – such as Kristeva and Eco – thinking their theoretical premises through to the end, postulate the speaking subject at the center of the system. Semiotics emerges, in crucial respects, from ancient rhetoric: both disciplines very clearly accord foundational status to the speaking subject. Aristotle's *Rhetoric* establishes this principle for all subsequent rhetorical tradition in Book I – devoted to the orator as the transmitter of messages – before proceeding in Book II to the public, or the recipients of messages that work on the passions, and finally, in Book III, to the message itself, particularly in its figural elaboration. Roland Barthes, from the other end of this tradition, likewise stresses how the technical approach to signs that rhetoric and semiotics share in common at their roots, before becoming differentiated from each other, postulates an individual as artificer using language as a means of expression:

> What is perhaps more important than these definitions is the fact that rhetoric is a *techné* (this is not empirical), which means: *the means of producing something that can either be or not be*, something the origin of which is in the creating agent and not in the created object. There is no *techné* of natural or necessary things: thus discourse is part of neither one nor the other.[1]

Signs are not simply natural or necessary. They are contingent productions of a subject, and Dante, with his idiosyncratic, especially metaphorical creation of language in the *Paradiso*, pioneers this perspective, which becomes programmatic in the modern poets and in the revolution of modern thought that follow in his wake.[2]

However, this emergent dimension of self-reflective subjectivity in language need not isolate individual subjects. On the contrary, the subjective dimension of value in contingency has also a communitarian aspect, one to which Dante and Latin rhetoric and even Scholastic philosophy are all highly attuned. In a sort of parallel in contemporary thinking, and building on the later Wittgenstein, Richard Rorty recognizes the necessity for consensus forged by language in a community for any sense of value as transcending naked contingency.[3] Philosophical analysis in this vein leads to a view of value as arising always only within the parameters of communities of interpretation. Even in their arbitrariness and contingency, a certain kind of transcendental grounding for norms and standards

---

[1] Roland Barthes, "L'ancienne rhétorique: Aide-mémoire," in *L'aventure sémiologique* (Paris: Seuil, 1985), 95. "Ce qui est peut-être plus important que ces définitions, c'est le fait que la rhétorique est une *technè* (ce n'est pas une empirie), c'est-à-dire: *le moyen de produire une des choses qui peuvent indifféremment être ou n'être pas*, dont l'origine est dans l'agent créature, non dans l'objet créé: il n'y a pas de *technè* des choses naturelles ou nécessaires: le discours ne fait donc partie ni des unes ni des autres." Originally in *Communications* 16 (1970): 172–223.

[2] I develop some selective probes demonstrating this Dantean descendence in *Secular Scriptures: Modern Theological Poetics in the Wake of Dante* (Columbus: Ohio State University Press, 2016). I outline the revolution of modern thought by subjective self-reflexion in *Dante's* Paradiso *and the Origins of Modern Thought: Toward a Speculative Philosophy of Self-Reflection*.

[3] Richard Rorty, *Contingency, Irony, and Solidarity* (New York: Cambridge University Press, 1989).

remains possible – as Dante's transcendental "we" ("noi") presupposes and attests.

Transcendental Reflection and the Horizon of Modern Thought

What we have found Dante experimenting with in his metaliterary attention to the powers of writing is, in effect, what can be called, in the
vocabulary of modern philosophy, "transcendental reflection." He takes
the technique of writing as a "condition of possibility" of the world of his
poem and of its showing of something that, in principle, cannot appear.
Writing thus becomes tantamount to magic: it performs the trick of
inducing the ineffable to speak. Theophany, in this case, is made possible
by the art of writing. Writing has inexhaustible implications for the nature
of that theophany, and they are registered in Dante's representations of it.
What Dante discovers in his transcendental reflection on writing in the
theophany of Paradise (and most concentratedly in *Paradiso* XVIII. 71–117)
has been worked out in other forms by Western phenomenological tradition from Descartes through Kant to Husserl. The transcendental perspective that opens in this epic poem, in fact, coincides in essential ways
with the philosophical horizon of modern thought.

   The decisive importance for Western thought ever since Augustine of
the reflection carried out here on time as grounded in self-consciousness is
foregrounded especially by Thomas J. J. Altizer in his own prophetic
idiom. Viewing Western cultural history through theological lenses,
Altizer writes, "Not until Augustine's *Confessions* does self-consciousness
first fully realize itself in any form, for not only is the *Confessions* the first
extant autobiography, and therefore may justly be said to be the creator of
that genre, it is also the first full work of any kind in which self-
consciousness is present and realized as a grounding center, a center
which was destined to become a primal ground of Western culture and
society as a whole."[4]

   Not only is Augustine in some sense first, but his analysis of the
temporality of self-consciousness remains unsurpassed down to the contemporary period, as witnessed by Husserl, the founder of the modern
phenomenological movement:

> The analysis of time-consciousness is an age-old crux of descriptive psych-
> ology and of the theory of knowledge. The first one who deeply felt the

---

[4] Thomas J. J. Altizer, *History as Apocalypse* (Albany: State University of New York Press, 1985), 81.

powerful difficulties that reside here and exerted himself over them almost to the point of despair was Augustine. Chapters 13–28 of Book XI of the *Confessions* must be thoroughly studied still today by anyone who is occupied by the problem of time. For modernity, for all its proud knowledge, has not made any substantial advance over this great thinker who seriously stuggled with these matters. Still today we can say with Augustine: *if no one asks me, I know, if I wish to explain to an inquirer, I do not know.*[5]

Following Augustine's lead, Dante helps us to understand that transcendental reflection is (or can be) not all closed in upon itself. It can, instead, be an echo of and an answer to a higher instance of being and consciousness. It does not consume its significance within itself but rather points beyond itself. This capability inheres in the very meaning of "intentionality" in Husserl's jargon. In Dante, the capacity of transcendental reflection opens toward a higher ground than itself. The significance of transcendental reflection already embodied in Dante's poem is not to be taken just literally as the supposedly emancipatory act of self-reflective self-grounding that it is in Descartes, Hegel, and Husserl. More fundamentally, self-reflection is an allegory for transcendence that it cannot comprehend – a theological transcendence in whose image and shadow self-reflection stands. Dante is thinking out certain consequences of an insight in Plato's *Timaeus* into the necessary priority of eternity over time – for which eternity serves as model and archetype. This priority had already been thought further by Plotinus (*Enneads* V) and Augustine (*Confessions* XI).[6] Jorge Luis Borges, in "Historia de la eternidad" (1936), traces these traditions forward to Schopenhauer and to Nietzsche's Eternal Return.[7]

Transcendence of the "io" as Reflection of the Transcendent

"Io" ("I") is, in fact, the first word of the description of Dante's vision in the heaven of Jove: "*I* saw in that jovial torch" ("*Io* vidi 'n quella giovial

[5] Edmund Husserl, *Vorlesungen zur Phänomenologie des inneren Zeitbewußtseins*, ed. Martin Heidegger (Tübingen: Max Niemeyer, 1980), 2. "Die Analyse des Zeitbewußtseins ist ein uraltes Kreuz der deskriptiven Psychologie und der Erkenntnistheorie. Der Erste, der die gewaltigen Schwierigkeiten, die hier liegen, tief empfunden und sich daran fast bis zur Verzweiflung abgemüht hat, war Augustinus. Die Kapitel 13–28 des XI. Buches der Confessions muß auch heute noch jedermann gründlich studieren, der sich mit dem Zeitproblem beschäftigt. Denn herrlich weit gebracht und erheblich weiter gebracht als dieser große und ernst ringende Denker hat es die wissenstolze Neuzeit in diesen Dingen nicht. Noch heute mag man mit Augustinus sagen: *si nemo a me quaerat, scio, si quaerenti explicare velim, nescio.*" (First published in *Jahrbuch für Philosophie und phänomenologische Forschung* IX (1928), 368.)
[6] Jean Guitton, *Le temps et l'éternité chez Plotin et Saint Augustin*, 3rd ed. rev. (Paris: Vrin, 1959 [1933]).
[7] Jorge Luis Borges, *Historia de la eternidad* (Buenos Aires: Emecé, 1968).

facella . . .," 71). It occurs also at the center of the main vision, in "I noted"
("io notai," 89), in the *terzina* immediately preceding and introducing the
Scriptural citation. This essential word and ontological structure implicitly
enframes the entire scene of the vision and, beyond that, of Dante's whole
poem, starting from the *Inferno*'s initial "I found myself" ("mi ritrovai") in
a dark wood.[8] In addition to representing what Dante considered the
original name of God (*Paradiso* XXVI. 134), "I" signifies the unity from
which, according to *De vulgari eloquentia* I. xvi. 2, all numbers flow (cf.
Monarchia III. xi. 1). Not only does "I," here elongated and differentiated
into "io," constitute the general unifying framework of Dante's whole
autobiographical poem: it also forms, in general, a central framework of
modern Western culture.

These intellectual stakes make it highly worthwhile to seriously reflect
on that "io," the "I," who serves as organizing principle throughout
Dante's poem. Albeit inaugurated, in ways we have examined, by
Augustine, this is an historically new and revolutionary phenomenon in
which the individual comes to self-consciousness as constitutive source of
value. All that the poem directly presents is represented as enframed within
Dante's consciousness. The addresses to the reader relay this enframing
function to the poem's readers and make them participate in it.

Nevertheless, the *io* of the poem remains, indelibly, a *written* I, and its
transcendence is not pure or simple. This is registered, among other ways,
by the split of the instance that says *io* into the "I" of the protagonist
and that of the poet. This distinction has been a cardinal principle and
a powerful tool furnishing Dante critics, notably Contini, Freccero, and
Stierle, with interpretive leverage for reading the poem. The *io* of the poem
is created through the poem itself, through its writing, as Dante could
hardly have made more macroscopic. *Io* is the *archi-écriture*, the originary
writing, at work in the origin of the poem's sense. This "I" is temporal and
differential in nature and, as such, is never simply present but is rather of
the order of what Derrida calls a "trace": "[Such an I] is always already
engaged in the 'movement' of the trace, or in other words in the order of
'signification.' It is always already gone out of itself in the 'expressive layer'
of lived experience" ("Il est toujours déjà engagé dans le 'mouvement' de la
trace, c'est-à-dire dans l'ordre de la 'signification.' Il est toujours déjà sorti
de soi dans le 'couche expressive' du vécu").[9]

---

[8] This first-person orientation to the world is traced throughout Dante's complete *œuvre* by
Marco Santagata, *L'io e il mondo: Un'interpretazione di Dante* (Milan: Il Mulino, 2011).
[9] Jacques Derrida, *La voix et le phénomène* (Paris: Presses Universitaires de France, 1967), 96.

The being-outside-itself of Dante's *io* is also highlighted by this *io*'s being a *noi* (we), signaled from the first verse of the *Inferno*: "In the middle of the way of *our* life" ("Nel mezzo del cammin di *nostra* vita"). This duplicity of the first person is brought explicitly to thematic relief in the Heaven of Jupiter's celebration of the eagle's voice, which speaks simultaneously as "I" and "we":

> ch'io vidi e anche udi' parlar lo rostro,
>   e sonar ne la voce e "io" e "mio",
>   quand'era nel concetto e "noi" e "nostro".

(XIX. 10–12)

> (I saw and also heard the beak speak
>   and sound in its voice both "I" and "we"
>   although its concept was "we" and "ours.")

The "io" becomes identical with a "we," in fact, with a universal first person, to the extent that precisely through the category of the "I" all particularity can be subsumed into the universal. By such means, a transcendence towards pure being at the heart of language can be initiated. On these verses, Jacqueline Risset comments: "The I which speaks is in some sort the pure I of total language" ("le je qui parle ici est en quelque sorte le je pur du langage total").[10] Hegel famously defined "spirit" (*Geist*) as "The I that is we and the we that is I."[11] Dante similarly expresses spirit as language in a way that lines up with postmodern understandings of Hegel, especially among French thinkers in the wake of Heidegger.[12]

Yet in Dante's vision, the self-showing of being is grounded not just in individual human consciousness, but also in the contingent medium of history and in language as the ultimate horizon of sense. This is a crucial aspect of Dante's modernity. Likewise, in Hegel's dialectic, every immanence is already intrinsically related to an outside. Hegel's differing (or distinguishing) of Being from itself – its being equivocally Nothing – is subsequently disclosed by Derrida as *différance*, where the (external) sign is always presupposed for any sense, since sense can be determinately realized only by deferring to this external detour in its relation to itself.

---

[10] Jacqueline Risset, *Dante écrivain: Ou l'intelletto d'amore* (Paris: Seuil, 1982), 191.

[11] G. W. F. Hegel, *Phänomenologie des Geistes*, eds. Hans-Friedrich Wessels and Heinrich Clairmont (Hamburg: Meiner, 1988), 127: "Ich, das Wir, und Wir, das Ich ist."

[12] This connection is central to my *Dante and the Sense of Transgression;* I extend it in *Dante's* Paradiso *and the Origins of Modern Thought: Toward a Speculative Philosophy of Self-Reflection*, 107–12.

Figure 6 Anonymous, "Jove, Heaven VI," engraving, Biblioteca Medicea
Laurenziana, Florence Ms. Med. Palat. 75, f. 89r.
Courtesy of MiBACT.

In this manner, the content of Dante's *I* is opened into the scene of the heaven rather than being occulted into the pure subjectivity of an internal time sense. Dante's self-staging is a phenomenological reduction that has already gone through Derrida's deconstructive transformation: "The hearing-oneself-speak is not the interiority of an inside closed in on itself; it is the irreducible opening within the inside, the work and the world in the word. *The phenomenological reduction is a scene*" ("Le s'entendre-parler n'est pas l'intériorité d'un dedans clos sur soi, il est l'ouverture irréductible dans le dedans, l'œuvre et le monde dans la parole. *La réduction phénomènologique est une scène*," *La voix et le phénomène*, 96).

Dante's representation of his consciousness in the Heaven of Jove is nothing if not a theatrical scene. And Dante's *io* is the image of a (*D*)*io* which is both immanent and transcendent, an interior light that is none-theless above the me that it created – to invoke St. Augustine's version of the immanence-transcendence of God (*Confessions* VII. x. 16) so funda-mental to the incarnational theology with which Dante, too, is centrally concerned. God is interior and superior, present to and remote from, the I ("Tu enim, altissime et proxime, secretissime et praesentissime," *Confessions* VI. iii. 3; cf. I. iv. 4), more inward than my own most intimate me and higher than what is highest in me ("Tu autem eras interior intimo meo et superior summo meo," III. vi. 11). God is both "internis" and "externis": "more interior than every thing because all things are in him, and more exterior than every thing because he is superior to all" ("interior omni re, quia in ipso sunt omnia, et exterior omni re, quia ipse est superior omnia").[13]

Understood thus, subjectivity is the structure that deconstructs the opposition between immanence and transcendence. Mediation of a higher instance of Being here becomes an uncontainable presence. It is not encompassed by the "I" but rather explodes the "I" into ecstasy in interpersonal and interstellar space beyond itself. This is a way for the "I" to be in God and to be inhabited by God. As *Confessions* I. ii. 2 makes clear, the being of any creature is contingent upon God's being present in it. But this presence is also an absence, for God transcends every creature, infin-itely. God is present in all creatures "with the presence of divinity [*divini-tatis praesentia*] but not in all with the grace of indwelling [*habitationis gratia*]." This distinction, as made by Augustine in his letter to Dardanaus, designated by him as his *Liber de praesentia Dei* (*Epistulae* 187. 5. 16,

---

[13] *De genesi ad litteram* VIII. 26. 48 in *Œuvres de Saint Augustine* 49, 7th series (Paris: Desclée de Brouwer, 1970), VIII–XII.

Patrologia Latina 33), preserves the uniqueness of the Incarnation. But it also opens the space of a divine poetic creativity that will be exploited by Dante and by the modern poets in his wake.[14]

Centering especially on Hegel's discussion of the emergence of subjective self-consciousness through the struggle to the death in the figures of lordship and bondage, Alexandre Kojève emphasized the external realization of spirit historically in institutions as mediated by laws and language. Jacques Lacan developed this insight as a dialectic of desire, in which the self is first constituted through struggle for recognition from the other in a symbolic order.[15] Along with Maurice Merleau-Ponty, Jean-Paul Sartre and Simone de Beauvoir elaborate on the dialectic of recognition in an existential key that Dante's visionary scene uncannily anticipates in its linguistic and materialist emphases. Yet Dante avoids the anthropological reduction that vitiates interpretations following Kojève's. Dante's approach would, in effect, hold Hegel's phenomenology together with his logic, recognizing the Being beyond human subjectivity as the ultimate giver of sense. Jean Hyppolite, in *Logique et existence* (1952), brought these mutually supporting aspects of Hegel's philosophy – articulated between the *Phenomenology* and the *Science of Logic*, respectively – together (Russon, *Infinite Phenomenology*, 285–87) in a way that restores the balance that we see established by Dante's incarnate vision.

The vital role of subjectivity in the discovery and presentation of the transcendent world and experience of Dante has been appreciated over many centuries as perhaps the most significant breakthrough of the poem in the direction of inaugurating the modern age. In particular, Dante's personality stands forth in its uncompromised individuality and historicity in the poem, and this has earned the work fairly universal recognition as a dawning of modernity in literary history.[16] What interests us specifically is how Dante's *io* becomes the supporting structure for revealing a dimension of transcendence that leads to a revelation of God. The transcendence of the "I" is thus itself constituted through relation to something other – something absolutely Other and imaginably divine. This does not place the ego in the position of being the absolute source of its world. This later development in modern philosophy from Descartes to

---

[14] I flesh out this genealogy in *Secular Scriptures: Modern Theological Poetics in the Wake of Dante*.

[15] For more detail, see John Russon, *Infinite Phenomenology: The Lessons of Hegel's Science of Experience* (Evanston: Northwestern University Press, 2016), 271–92.

[16] Octavio Paz, *La otra voz: Poesía y fin de siglo* (Barcelona: Seix Barral, 1990) reads the Western tradition of poetry from this angle of vision that is pioneered by Erich Auerbach and is based on a deeper tradition in Hegel's wake in Germany (Burckhardt) and in Italy (De Sanctis).

Fichte has been taken by critical Enlightenment thinkers as determined fundamentally by the negation of faith in a religious transcendence of which subjectivity can be no more than a derivative image. But it is far from clear that the sense of subjectivity is such a denial even for these revolutionary thinkers.[17]

Dante takes the *I* as organizing framework and originary principle of the poem. But this *I* and the poem itself are put forward as mediations of a higher being, that of God. The discovery of subjectivity as in some sense superior to the world it acts within and is strongly conditioned by comes through very powerfully in Dante's poem. Modern thought shows its indebtedness to a breakthrough like Dante's precisely on this all-important point. Yet what needs to be stressed is not just Dante's discovery of the free individual subject, but rather his grasp of this principle as united with an orientation towards *another* transcendence, that of God. The transcendence of the "I" is to be understood fundamentally as the image of God's prior and grounding transcendence.

Dante's "I" is the discovery of a principle that will dominate the modern age and be reflected upon with unflagging intensity throughout modern philosophy. Husserl in particular attempted to bring a great tradition of philosophical reflection on the transcendence of the subject to culmination in his transcendental phenomenology. The far-reaching consequences of Dante's discovery of subjectivity in its transcendence can be gauged and placed in a revealing perspective by a glance forward at the systematic working out of such insight finally in Husserl's phenomenology. Ultimately, however, for Dante the transcendence of subjectivity fails to carry conviction and looks illusory *unless* it is taken as itself an image of another and higher transcendence. In fact, subjectivity consists precisely in this recursive capacity to reflect back on and transcend *even itself*. No determinate, finite entity could ever be definitely identified with this dynamic structure. It is the nature of such transcendence to be incapable of being definitively given in anything finite – save in the absolute paradox of God Incarnate in Christ.

In his *Phenomenology of Internal Time-Consciousness* (*Vorlesungen zur Phänomenologie des inneren Zeitbewußtseins*, 1893–1917), Husserl attempted

---

[17] Jean-Luc Marion's rereadings of Descartes, particularly *Sur la théologie blanche de Descartes* (Paris: Presses Universitaires de France, 1981) and *Sur le prisme métaphysique de Descartes* (Paris: Presses Universitaires de France, 1986), and Fichte scholarship, especially as catalyzed by Dieter Henrich, "Fichtes ursprüngliche Einsicht," in *Subjektivität und Metaphysik: Festschrift für Wolfgang Cramer*, ed. Dieter Henrich and Hans Wagner (Frankfurt am Main: Klostermann, 1966), 188–232, deeply question the secularist assumptions that have long reigned in reading these key philosophers.

to establish the priority of *perception* ("Wahrnehmung") as absolutely distinct from all *representation*. Perception was to be strictly the immediate presence of the perceived and therefore "not representative but presentative" ("nicht repräsentativ, sondern präsentativ"). The key to this pure presence in perception is the flow of time phenomenologically as absolute subjectivity (see section 36: "Der zeitkonstituierende Fluß als absolute Subjektivität"). But this simply furthers Descartes's – and following him modern philosophy's – presumable attempts to make the conscious self into the self-sufficient foundation of all knowledge. Husserl grounds all knowledge and life itself on transcendental consciousness as the source of all experience: "This source has the title *I myself*, with my whole actual and possible conscious life, finally my concrete life as such" ("Diese Quelle hat den Titel *Ich-selbst*, mit meinem gesamten wirklichen und vermöglichen Erkenntnisleben, schließlich meinem konkreten Leben überhaupt").[18]

In *The Crisis of European Science and Transcendental Phenomenology* (*Die Krisis der europäischen Wissenschaft und die transzendentale Phänomenologie*, 1936), Husserl defines the notion of "transzendental," in the largest sense, as that "original motive that through Descartes in all modern philosophies is the giver of sense and in all, so to speak, seeks to come to itself and attain the genuine and pure form of its task and systematic development. It is the motive of the questioning after the last source of all knowledge formation, the self-reflection of the knower on itself and on its knowing life" ("originale Motiv, das durch Descartes in allen neuzeitlichen Philosophien das Sinngebende ist und in ihnen allen sozusagen zu sich selbst kommen, die echte und reine Aufgabengestalt und systematische Auswirkung gewinnen will. Es ist das Motiv des Rückfragens nach der letzten Quelle aller Erkentnisbildungen, des Sichbesinnens des Erkennenden auf sich selbst und sein erkennendes Leben," 108). In effect, Husserl absolutizes the self-knowing of self-consciousness as the source of all knowing.

Dante's subjectivity, and the temporality in which it consists, in contrast, are not absolutized: instead, they are key to opening the dimension of transcendence towards what is absolute, beyond the limits of expression, in God. Dante does not isolate any inner stratum of self-consciousness as foundational, but rather opens subjectivity out into a textuality that nevertheless stands allegorically as a *sign* of absolute transcendence. The transcendence of the human subject and the inner unity of all things in God – by being represented in Dante's constructions and by making these

---

[18] Edmund Husserl, *Die Krisis der europäischen Wissenschaft und die transzendentale Phänomenologie* (Hamburg: Meiner, 1973), 108.

representations possible as their transcendental condition – points to the absolute transcendence of divinity. This is the crucial difference between the "egocentric" transcendental phenomenology of Husserl and the theo-centric analysis of the soul's transcendence by Thomas Aquinas.[19]

Likewise determined to escape this egocentric reduction, Emmanuel Levinas's revisionings of phenomenological philosophy have urged the need for an ethical transcendence of subjectivity reaching beyond the cognitive dimension: "Man would be the place where transcendence occurs, even if one can call this being-there or *Dasein*. Perhaps the whole status of subjectivity and of reason should be revised starting from this situation" ("L'homme serait le lieu où passe la transcendance, même si on peut le dire être-là ou *Dasein*. Peut-être tout le statut de la subjectivité et de la raison doit-il être révisé à partir de cette situation").[20] Levinas's approach will be taken up in the final movements of the final Excursus (VI) as foreshadowed by Dante's ethical reconceptualization of human knowing.

Recentering the Transcendence of the Subject in Modern Philosophy via Dante

There are many transcendences: for example, Plato's and the Bible's, to name just two relevant ones that have, in turn, themselves splintered into manifold different varieties. They give rise to as many different possibilities for seeking and cultivating an experience of, and a relation to, world-transcending reality. It is important to distinguish between, at least, cosmological, epistemic, ethical, and theological forms of transcendence.[21] Husserl's is typically modern, perhaps *the* modern transcendence par excellence – that of the conscious subject that engenders its world by being the active, living principle underlying all that can be represented to consciousness. Dante is certainly a poet of transcendence, yet his transcendence is not founded on and fulfilled or finalized by the "I" but rather points beyond it.

The *I*, in Dante's Christian view, is but a reflected image. It is the mediation of a higher Being. Dante concentrates on the mediated forms to

---

[19] This difference is worked out in detail by Edith Stein, "Husserls Phänomenologie und die Philosophie des hl. Thomas v. Aquino" (1929), in *Husserl*, ed. H. Noack (Darmstadt: Wissenschaftliche Buchgesellschaft, 1973), 73. However, for the intriguing view that Husserl's own reflection on divine transcendence, apparently marginal, is in reality quite central to his thinking, see Angela Ales Bello, *Husserl: Sul problema di Dio* (Rome: Edizioni Studium, 1985).

[20] Emmanuel Levinas, *L'Au-delà du verset* (Paris: Minuit, 1982), 10.

[21] Merold Westphal, *Transcendence and Self-Transcendence: On God and the Soul* (Bloomington: Indiana University Press, 2004).

the point where they disappear as mediated and show through to an immediacy presupposed by their function as mediators. A later dialectical terminology – that of Gadamer, deriving from Hegel – would call this "total mediation" (*Truth and Method* III. 3. b: "Language as Medium and its Speculative Structure"). (Excursus VI, in its opening sections, pursues this dialectic.) Self-reflexivity, as mediation of transcendence, is tantamount to concentration on mediation that leads to the unmediated because what is fully objectified is reduced to nothing but inert content and is not self-sustaining. Its totalization, therefore, summons forth its other and ultimately the absolute Other. Whatever is fully objectified (self-reflected) turns out to be only an image of something else, some Other, that transcends – and produces and sustains – it.

Dante discovers the transcendentality of the "io," what becomes fundamental for modern philosophers from Descartes to Husserl, without, however, like the philosophers, making this transcendentality the foundation for all knowledge and being. All human knowledge filters through the "I" as the point of synthesis – and, to this extent, all objective representations are intrinsically related to the "io" and to one another in and through it. Nevertheless, this *io* is understood by Dante not as its own foundation posited in a self-grounding act of transcendental reflection. The being of the *io* is radically inflected with nothingness, for it is created *ex nihilo*. Nonetheless, it mirrors the being of God, which *is* self-grounding in its transcendence and is constituted by an act of self-reflection. This is to say that the being of God is Trinitarian: God gives Godself in its Word, constituting itself by this self-relation as Spirit. In imitating God, the conscious ego creates a sphere of *relative* autonomy.

Dante presents an encyclopedic vision of the universe – but as reflected in the experience of a personal *io*, that is, himself. This structure of selfhood and even of self-reflexivity is the constant postulate for his poem and its world. In terms of the history of world poetry, the reorganization of the epic along the axis of the self can be seen as Dante's seminal innovation: "In Christian poetry, a new element appears: the poet himself as hero . . . . The ancient poem was impersonal: with Dante the I appears" ("En la poesía cristiana aparece un elemento nuevo: el poeta mismo como héroe . . . . El poema antiguo era impersonal; con Dante aparece el yo").[22]

But the self-reflexiveness that is constitutive of modern subjectivity is first and foremost a self-reflexivity of language, which alone permits the I or

---

[22] Octavio Paz , "Poesía y modernidad," in *La otra voz: Poesía y fin de siglo*, 14.

the "je" – for example, of Descartes or Rousseau or Proust – to be conscious of itself. The transcendence of the linguistic category of the "io" is to be understood in the first instance as a transcendence of language – and is so understood in medieval tradition, following the principle of Creation by the Word. There has been a return to this perspective in postmodern hermeneutic thinking since Heidegger.[23] The fundamental linguisticality of subjectivity has been researched with particular rigor by structural linguists, eminently Benveniste.[24] This insight has led to the hypothesis of the liquidation of the subject, at least as a substance, by post-structuralist thinkers such as Foucault and Derrida.

The situation for Dante is different from that in modern phenomeno-logical tradition, where the "I" as mediation of otherness is centered in itself rather than in this otherness. The self in the perspective of Dante's poem is a structure serving to relate to God as the absolute Other rather than simply encompassing all possible reality within its own parameters. Whereas in modern philosophy, popularly epitomized by the thought of Hegel, otherness has typically been comprehended as no more than a detour back to self and thus as an indirect mode of self-relation, we need to stand this insight on its head (or turn it inside out) in order to see things from Dante's perspective. Not the I, but God, is the ground and principle in Dante's theocentric world-view. The reality of the "I" is derivative: it consists of being "made in God's image."

Mark Taylor observes that in modern philosophy since Descartes "the subject's relation to otherness is mediated by and reducible to its relation-ship to itself."[25] This has made of modern subjectivity a vicious circle, and postmodern efforts have been bent on breaking out of it. Dante's subject-ivity moves in the reverse direction. The circle sets out from God and turns back to God. In theory, this is the case with Hegel's Logic as well, which is what makes his thought still so compelling today, even though the sense of transcendence is totally absorbed into the immanence of mediations of the

---

[23] See especially Karl Otto Apel on the transcendentality of language as a hermeneutic horizon: "Der transzendentalhermeneutische Begriff der Sprache" and "Sprache als Thema und Medium der transzendentalen Reflexion" in *Transformation der Philosophie II* (Frankfurt am Main: Suhrkamp, 1973), 311–57. Also Karl Otto Apel, "Die beiden Phasen der Phänomenologie in ihrer Auswirkung auf das philosophische Vorverständnis von Sprache und Dichtung in der Gegenwart," *Jahrbuch für Ästhetik und allgemeine Kunstwissenschaft* 3 (1955–1957): 54–76. These reflections are grounded in thinking about Dante and the tradition of linguistic humanism in Apel's *Die Idee der Sprache in der Tradition des Humanismus von Dante bis Vico* (Bonn: Bouvier, 1980).

[24] Émile Benveniste, "De la subjectivité dans le langage," in *Problèmes de linguistique générale* (Paris: Gallimard, 1966), 258–66.

[25] Mark Taylor, *Altarity* (Chicago: University of Chicago Press 1987), xxii.

Absolute Idea.[26] The difference lies in Dante's poetry and in how it concretely realizes the sense of otherness. There is here, in consequence, an important distinction that needs to be made between being mediated by, and being reduced to, something else. For Dante, the subject's relation to itself is mediated by relation to the wholly other – God. The self-enclosed structure of relatedness is, in the subject, only an image of God and perdures as a reality in God beyond the grasp of human understanding. Self-relatedness, as it is experienceable by humans in time, therefore, is always virtual, never final.

My purpose in rereading some key moments in modern philosophy in relation to Dante is to suggest how it might be read otherwise than as a vain reduction to the self and the same. Seeing philosophy in a perspective that encompasses Dante's discovery of transcendental subjectivity as not itself absolute, but as a reflection of an *other* Self and Subject, can enable us to see a different intention and significance subtending the entire trajectory of modern philosophy. The search for self can be an indirect way of feeling out its border with otherness. The meaning and purport of philosophy cannot be contained by the self-enclosure of the self-reflecting subject. The very achievement of closure of sense in comprehension opens an abyss beyond and beneath itself.[27] Such closure sets up the moment of deconstruction, which cannot take place without the previously constructed structure of self-reflection. Hegel and other modern philosophers show up in a very different light when read in this perspective that can be elicited most readily from Dante's thought, which is not yet so encumbered by typical modern assumptions of self-sufficient self-centeredness.

Philosophy read this way, as exposing an inherent negativity of human self-consciousness, proves necessary to the sort of quasi-religious insight into which philosophy as deconstruction eventually opens itself. Following hard on Hegel's heels, this moment of comeuppance is anticipated already by Kierkegaard.[28] Today this dialectical reflection is being developed with

---

[26] The spell Hegel still casts over our postmodern age owing to his opening subjectivity to an infinity inherent within it can be gauged, for example, from Slavoj Žižek, Clayton Crockett, and Creston Davis, eds., *Hegel and the Infinite: Religion, Politics, and Dialectic* (New York: Columbia University Press, 2011).

[27] Emmanuel Levinas's thought, defining itself in *Autrement qu'être ou au-delà de l'essence* (Paris: Martinus Nijhoff, 1974) as the attempt to speak transcendence ("la tentative de dire la transcendence," 37), aims to recuperate a sense of "transcendence" in its analysis of "subjectivity" that is helpful for understanding Dante's. Levinas tirelessly asserts the claims to transcendence of subjectivity against its reduction to Being by Hegel and Heidegger. See, further, Excursus VI.

[28] Powerfully revealing of this negative or "apophatic" valence of subject-centered philosophy is Peter Kline, *Passion for Nothing: Kierkegaard's Apophatic Theology* (Minneapolis: Fortress Press, 2017).

reference to phenomenological tradition by the so-called New Phenomenology arising in the wake of the "theological turn" in phenomenology among a number of Christian-inspired religious thinkers including Michel Henry, Jean-Yves Lacoste, and Jean-Louis Chrétien, who carry on from Levinas's legacy.[29] Most pertinently to the present project, this movement has been extended to a phenomenology of Scripture in a specifically apophatic key.[30] This is one indicator of why Dante, as theological visionary, has again become so topical and compelling for us.

An amorphous school of "theological" criticism of Dante, emanating especially from English-speaking universities in the UK and the USA, brings out how the medieval theological insight embedded in Dante's texts can transform our understanding of the very nature of theology.[31] Evidencing the cohesion of this understanding of Dante with modern thought, and using it to develop modern thought beyond itself, is one goal of the present contribution.

---

[29] Dominique Janicaud, et al., *Phenomenology and the "Theological Turn": The French Debate* (New York: Fordham University Press, 2000). For a lucid overview and analysis, see J. Aaron Simmons and Bruce Ellis Benson, *The New Phenomenology: A Philosophical Introduction* (London: Bloomsbuy, 2013).

[30] Adam Y. Wells, *The Manifest and the Revealed: A Phenomenology of Kenosis* (Albany: SUNY Press, 2018), with a forward by Kevin Hart. Otherwise pertinent is *Dante and the Other: A Phenomenology of Love*, ed. Aaron B. Daniels (New York: Routledge, 2021).

[31] Among its landmarks, a manifesto text is Vittorio Montemaggi and Matthew Treherne, eds., *Dante's Commedia: Theology as Poetry* (Notre Dame: University of Notre Dame Press, 2010). Among its follow-ups is Claire E. Honess and Matthew Treherne, eds., *Reviewing Dante's Theology*, 2 vols. (Bern: Peter Lang, 2018). I outline this movement in "Religion and Representation: Dante Studies after the Theological Turn," in *The Year's Work in Critical and Cultural Theory* (Oxford: Oxford University Press, 2018), 86–105.

Unmanifest Wholeness of Sense: Language as Image of the Imageless

From Time to Eternity: The Whole of Sense

Dante's metaphors insist on our viewing the sentence excerpted from Scripture as the *speech* of God – and then also as a written transformation of "our speech." Nevertheless, I have stressed how Dante's resort to grammatical categories illustrates the transformation of language as a spoken stream into a visual field. So far as the language in which his vision speaks is concerned, Dante is working from a text, the Book of Wisdom, and his presentation of this text throws into relief its visual form, exploiting the spatial and pictorial qualities of the written word and its characters to a maximum. This visual materialization allows for and sets up the Word's apparent dismemberment and dispersion in the form of the combustion of sparks.

Dante fully embraces and emphasizes the breakdown into mutually defined parts entailed, in the grammatical outlook, by his vision's writtenness. Yet he also aims to turn this apparent disintegration back into a powerful new vision of divine revelation in its wholeness and immediacy. He not only represents the immediacy of speech as a transparent medium continuous with thought: he also presents this speaking as a reified visual immediacy. The scene's visionary vocabulary of writing illustrates language's mysterious capability of uprooting everything from time. In virtue of the wholeness of its sense or meaning, language is capable of originating and preserving a unified sense through its own simultaneous system of reciprocally differentiated significances.

In a visual synthesis, all parts are simultaneously present and are seen all together at once. This synoptic vision, encompassing all component elements simultaneously, will be achieved consummately in the vision of the celestial rose in which all Paradise is embraced as the sum total of the blessed who experience it. In exactly this regard, the final vision is anticipated in a most spectacular and analytically reflective way in the vision of writing in the Heaven of Jupiter.

Converted into a celestial spectacle, writing presents a visual immediacy and is therewith a fit metaphor for the transcendence of time through language. Thus en*vision*ed, writing has a significance opposite to that of *écriture* for Derrida. In this visual synthesis, it becomes possible in principle to transcend time, or at least to symbolize doing so, by transposition of the temporality of language and of the serial mode of hearing into the *totum simul* mode of existence in visual space. Of course, as Merleau-Ponty reminds us, any form of perception is possible only thanks to movement and specifically to the ceaseless motility of the body (*L'œil et l'esprit*, 78–79). Even the idea of transcending successiveness in *totum simul* perception itself builds on successive movements of perception. Such perception reaches out toward a theological ideal that can only be imagined and cannot as such be seen. The divine per se is hypothetically projected and cannot be totalized as an object of sight, yet the Scriptural writing in Jove presents the divine vision as if it could be.

In a first movement, Dante spatializes language spectacularly and realizes with all radicality its character as written. He nevertheless maintains the relation of writing to speech: Holy Writ, as divine Word, is understood as expressing the Mind of God. What is more, Dante enframes the space of the divine writing within the time of its being humanly comprehended. In fact, as Dante reads the phrase from Wisdom, the *spacing* of the letters on the page of Scripture is transformed into their *temporalization* in his perception of them appearing consecutively. They are without spatial relation to one another, since each letter disappears before the next one appears rather than remaining as successive letters are added to the sequence. The sequence that we see displayed on the page of Dante's text as a row of contiguous letters never appears as such in the *vision* all at once. The unity of the letters as a complete ensemble is realized only through the succession of letters and their synthesis in Dante's mind and memory once the series is complete. The different letters spelled out to Dante's mind are but parts of the whole, and Dante "notes" them as they are "dictated" to him (". . . e io notai / le parti sì, come mi parver dette," XVIII. 89–90). The simultaneous existence of the letters together as a whole is thus Dante's own mental and textual construction, even though, of course, he does not create the phrase itself, which is already familiar to all from the book of Wisdom. The phrase exists in its integrity as God's own Word. To this extent, it is only reconstituted and re-presented by Dante's mind and text.

For all the carnivalesque reveling in the energetic dispersion of graphic
elements across the externality of celestial space in Dante's vision, its
language cannot be accounted for without considering the temporality of
its particularized appearance in a sequence of component units, and this
entails also consideration of its sense for its speaking and hearing subjects.
In general, time remains indispensable to all of Dante's descriptions in
language of his experience in Paradise, despite the theoretical absence of
time from Paradise proper (the Empyrean), which is symmetrical with
time's elimination from the *Inferno*. Dante is concerned here with the time
of the realization of his representations of Paradise rather than with the
timeless present of this realm as such.

Indeed, it is language in its very temporality as event that becomes the
revelation of the eternity of heaven proper, the Empyrean, where all the
souls actually reside. Language reveals a whole sense that is prior to all its
parts, and it reveals all Creation and history as products of such a whole
Logos. Yet this Logos is unsayable and can only be envisaged as writing, as
an interplay of signifiers and their divergent signifyings, not as any unitary
signified object. The apparently unitary objects in this heaven are letters,
mere *pieces* of writing, and Dante breaks them up further into masses of
sparks, splintering them into fragments that *project* a meaning, one that
cannot as such appear whole.

In this manner, even the grammatical breakdown of language, by virtue
of its reference to meaning, seems to suggest the wholeness of eternity that
transcends time. The wholeness of eternity is intimated in the deconstruction of language and, finally, also of time as its medium. The thematization
of language as medium ultimately dissolves it into the time in which it
transpires as an image of the eternity of which time is all only a mediation.
Indeed, time is *intelligible* only in terms of a synthesis that is not itself
temporal. Dante follows Augustine in understanding this articulation
between time and eternity on the model of language and thereby in
terms of mediation (Excursus III).

What is at stake in the decomposition of language by grammar and in its
reintegration in a reflexive act of the subject is the ability of language to
convey the wholeness of sense and thereby to transcend time and reflect an
image of the eternal (Excursus IV). This is how Dante achieves his vision of
Paradise and realizes it as a theophany in the very writing of his poem. The
negation of the temporal mediation of language by turning it into an image
can complete its sense and thereby intimate an eternal reality. This suggests
why the experience of language, such as Dante's *Paradiso* pursues it, is the
privileged locus of his vision of God. The inextricablity of vision and

discourse conjugated to allude to a world beyond both motivates his fascination especially with ekphrasis.

Ekphrasis, or Writing in Images: Between Saying and Showing

Dante's vision in Jove overcomes the discursive temporality of speech through the synoptic simultaneity of vision. Making speech vision lends it a visionary wholeness and unity such as are expressed by Dante's referring metaphorically to "the whole painting" ("tutto 'l dipinto," 92). "Visible speech," that is, "visibile parlare," already familiar from *Purgatorio* X. 95, appears in this case not as sculptures on the wall of Purgatory but as writing in the sky of Jupiter. Not only textual "speaking out" (*ek-phrasis*) of pictures, with words appearing typically in embedded scrolls or cartouches, but also pictured text, like *DILIGITE*, etc., can qualify as ekphrasis. The intricate issues concerning ekphrasis that arise directly in relation to *Purgatorio* X are also obliquely pertinent to the display of letters as a kind of speaking painting in *Paradiso* XVIII.

The display in Jupiter can be defined, furthermore, in rhetorical terms as a "notional ekphrasis," since the full visual composition is formed only in Dante's mind.[1] The bi-dimensionality (verbal and visual) of ekphrasis opens a gap in which an unmanifest wholeness can be signified as transcending positive representation in whatever concrete medium. What particularly interests us here is how verbal and visual means are used in ekphrasis to supplement each other for purposes of triangulating on an, in principle, incommunicable sense that neither medium alone can render adequately.

Basically, ekphrasis makes images, which are ordinarily silent, speak. But it can also do the reverse and turn speaking into a visionary presence of the transcendent – as in Dante's scene. The verbal is transcended into the visionary. There is in art theory (especially in interart theory) a vast and variegated discourse surrounding ekphrasis as a way of lending speech to the speechless, of saying the unsayable by a showing that reveals all in simultaneity. In the ekphrasis of Dante's vision of Scripture, a text becomes itself a speaking picture, and in this particular case the transcendent Word is made into a visible object. Such ekphrasis is about crossing the threshold from the speaking to the speechless and even to the unspeakable.

Theorists of ekphrasis probe this threshold from various angles. Georges Didi-Huberman exploits, with speculative penetration, the apophatic

---

[1] John Hollander, "The Poetics of Ekphrasis," *Word & Image* 4 (1988): 209–19.

potential of ekphrasis in interpreting especially religious painting as presenting an image opening to infinity.[2] Douglas Hedley reads "iconology"
as religiously inspired and as aiming at a reality beyond the reach of
discourse.[3] W. J. T. Mitchell argues that ekphrasis serves to give access to
what is otherwise verbally inaccessible and to make the invisibile visible.[4]
This specific focus on representing the unrepresentable is superbly illus-
trated by Dante's Scriptural icon DILIGITE, etc. Dante is made to see
otherwise incomprehensible and humanly inexplicable divine Justice.

   This "apophatic" problematic tends to be central to contemporary
theory's diverse and thoroughly cross-disciplinary explorations of the inter-
animations between verbal and visual modes of expression.[5] Often, however, contemporary criticism has been anticipated by medieval intuitions
rendering – and reflecting on – such intermedial interactions. Andrea
Mirabile's history of ekphrastic theory indicates that, ever since Greek
and Roman antiquity, claims to completeness and immediacy in showing
all, with elegance and heightened energy, have been attributed to the
ekphrastic image.[6] Mirabile also highlights, however, the *impasses* to the
translation between words and images as constitutive of the genre. Its
constitutive aporias confer on this genre its special capacity and adapted-
ness for probing unrepresentable divinities (*Raccontare immagini*, 25 and
passim). Especially obstacles to vision open a dimension of the invisible that
ignites imagination and incites writing.[7] Such writing proliferates as representation of the unrepresentable. Other senses besides vision, too, are
brought in by synaesthesia, particularly to compensate where there is some
visual block or lack.

   In the Heaven of Jove, Dante is displaying and staging this dynamic
potential for interaction between these diverse media and modalities of
conveying sense. By making Scriptural revelation pictorial, Dante is

---

[2] Georges Didi-Huberman, *L'image ouverte: Motifs de l'incarnation dans les arts visuels* (Paris: Gallimard, 2007).
[3] Douglas Hedley, *The Iconic Imagination* (London: Bloomsbury Academic, 2016).
[4] W. J. T. Mitchell, "Ekphrasis and the Other," in *Picture Theory: Essays on Visual and Verbal Representation* (Chicago: University of Chicago Press, 1993), chapter 3.
[5] Particularly probing on this topic are Murray Krieger, *Ekphrasis: The Illusion of the Natural Sign* (Baltimore: Johns Hopkins University Press, 1991) and James Heffernan, *Museum of Words: The Poetics of Ekphrasis from Homer to Ashbery* (Chicago: University of Chicago Press, 1993). Also Peter Wagner, ed., *Icons – Texts – Iconotexts: Essays on Ekphrasis and Intermediality* (Berlin: De Gruyter, 1996) comprises a variety of suggestive approaches.
[6] Andrea Mirabile, *Raccontare immagini: Teorie dall'antichità al presente* (Milan: Editrice Bibliografica, 2019), 7–10.
[7] Andrea Mirabile, *Piaceri invisibili: Retorica della cecità in D'Annunzio, Pasolini, Calvino* (Rome: Carocci, 2017), 30–34 and 119–47 on "Rhetoric of Blindness."

contemplating how divine revelation does not abide within the boundaries of a verbal modality but has a propulsion to spill over into the kind of revelation specific to visual modes. Inversely, the objects of his vision translate ekphrastically into written signs or verbal communication. Dante's scene, by switching back and forth between diverse sensory and intellectual modalities, is apt to suggest how certain gaps in conversion and translation between different media can be exploited for the purpose of highlighting the ultimate unrepresentability of a transcendent divine reality.

Olivier Boulnois, in his "visual archeology of the Middle Ages," appropriately gives priority to the invisible and silent dimensions that must underlie visual representations or revelations of divinity in the medieval perspective.[8] Leveraging Greek Orthodox spirituality, Natalie Carnes emphasizes the negative capability of images as instrumental to their ability to convey a sense of presence.[9] Dante's skywriting, in fact, works by negative means to suggest what does not and cannot appear as a finite, determinate object – *viz.*, the presence of divinity. We are catapulted beyond, by the analogical suggestions of what appears, to a level higher than that of mere appearing. This is one place where the purportedly *anagogical* level of the meaning of the poem, referring to another world beyond or "up from" (*ana*) the visible one, can be distinctly felt and verified.

Iconography reaches beyond the aesthetic register not only to intimate a mystical-religious realm, but also to engage the social and political issues that ultimately animate Dante's heaven of justice. Claire Barbetti stresses that "the ekphrastic artifact can provide an ideological map of values given to the particular artistic media it employs in any given era."[10] Certainly, Dante's ekphrastic representation of Scripture is ideological in tenor: it provides a totalized representation of Justice in the universe. Its heraldic eagle projects from the heaven of justice Dante's idealized history of the Roman Empire, detailed most fully in *Paradiso* VI.

Our main interest here, which will be pursued in the next section, is in the philosophical understanding of language as a kind of tying or binding together

---

[8] Olivier Boulnois, *Au-delà de l'image: Une archéologie du visuel au Moyen Âge (Vᵉ–XVIᵉ siècle)* (Paris: Seuil, 2008).
[9] Natalie Carnes, *Image and Presence: A Christological Reflection on Iconoclasm and Iconophilia* (Stanford: Stanford University Press, 2017).
[10] Claire Barbetti, *Ekphrastic Medieval Visions: A New Discussion in Interarts Theory* (Basingstoke: Palgrave Macmillan, 2011), 3. This area of research has been dominated especially by David Freedberg, *The Power of Images: Studies in the History and Theory of Response* (Chicago: University of Chicago Press, 1989).

that enables the holistic view resourced by Dante to envision the invisible (divinity) as everywhere present. Before taking up this issue, however, I wish to note that recent Dante criticism has made some important headway in areas of research relating intricately to the theory of ekphrasis.

Commonly considered under the rubric of "ekphrasis" are also certain ways of using different sensory modalities in conjunction with each other in order to expand perception and open to more holistic types of awareness. Ekphrasis is significant for seeing things whole and in whole contexts. It can effect a kind of synaesthetic perception. Such multi-channeled perception in one way or another enfolds a story designed to expound images and is attuned particularly to their expressiveness. Ekphrasis can even reverse the vector of communication, endowing images with an uncanny empathic capacity to address the reader/viewer and interrogate us.[11] This reversal can blur, and even call into question, the conventional subject–object divide.

Manuele Gragnolati and Sara Fortuna bring out an ambiguous reversibility of subject and object through reference to Wittgenstein's theory of *Aspekt* in language and perception.[12] Aspect, in this sense, refuses the division between objective and subjective perspectives. Envisaging a more global view, the word "aspetto" in the *Convivio* and the *Commedia* comprises an "enantiosemic" sense in which it encompasses both the subject's gaze and the object's appearance indivisibly. Such a view centrally concerns the perception of physiognomies and their meanings – for example, the look of the Mona Lisa – but also the gazes of the blessed on one another's faces in Paradise. Dante's ekphrasis in *Paradiso* XVIII, where what is seen is speaking and vice versa, shows up in this light as another way to lend face and voice to God.

Specifically theological implications and applications of ekphrasis push it to the frontiers of the perceptible. Matthew Treherne stresses ekphrasis's engendering wonder at the incomprehensible through "a complex interaction of clarity and confusion."[13] Ekphrasis proves, thereby, to be like the Eucharist in inducing humility in the face of what is rationally impossible to comprehend. Crucial to the argument of the present book (especially

---

[11] David Freedberg and Vittorio Gallese, "Motion, Emotion, and Empathy in Esthetic Experience," *Trends in Cognitive Sciences* 11/5 (2007): 197–203.

[12] Sara Fortuna and Manuele Gragnolati, "Dante after Wittgenstein: 'Aspetto', Language, and Subjectivity from *Convivio* to *Paradiso*," in *Dante's Plurilingualism: Authority, Knowledge, Subjectivity*, eds. Sara Fortuna, Manuele Gragnolati, and Jürgen Trabant (Oxford: Legenda, 2010), 223–47.

[13] Matthew Treherne, "Ekphrasis and Eucharist: The Poetics of Seeing God's Art in *Purgatorio* X," *The Italianist* 26 (2006): 177–96. Quotation 180.

Chapter 5) is recognizing such a dimension of transcendence that can be discerned by activating the "inter" between different sense modalities. Through intensely realized visuality in the painting metaphor, Dante makes a show of language in the heaven of Jupiter and, in effect, thematizes the character of language, and more specifically of writing, as a "showing," even though it is a showing that points and reaches beyond the manifest.

The Logos, the word, although inevitably understood as discursive, is based more fundamentally on an intuitive "showing" or *disclosing* of how things really are that is presupposed by any "saying."[14] This seminal Heideggerian insight into *aletheia* will be expounded shortly. However, this turn to the apparently visual mode of showing actually leads to apophatic contemplation of the unmanifest. Hence, it requires the terms of the invisible and non-appearing as employed by the new approach to phenomenology after the "theological turn," which was introduced in the penultimate paragraph of the preceeding Excursus (IV).

Language as Logos – Binding Together as Manifestation of Being

According to Saint Augustine's theory of language and meaning, which is homologous to and interconnected with his theory of the relation of time and eternity, it is precisely from the conclusion, the last word and letter of a phrase, that the whole of it can be understood or "gathered" ("coligere") into a unified meaning (Excursus III). Heidegger's theory of language, too, is based on the phenomenon of gathering or binding together into unity ("legein"). However, for Heidegger and the (post)modern age, there is no stable end-point from which this gathering proceeds, but only the structural openness of time turned toward the future.[15] The disclosure of reality in language has a wholeness to it that is not fully completed and realized but is rather latent in the intertwinings of language. In language, each element is bound to the others from which it must be differentiated even in order to have or participate in meaning. Dante certainly subscribed to the Augustinan view of language as grounded in an eternal Word. The whole sense of the Scriptural verse in the Heaven of Jove as God's eternal Logos pre-exists its performance in Dante's text. And yet his representation of language presents it as essentially a *tie* in which the sense of the whole is constructed out of the bonds between one letter and the others. Dante

---

[14] John Sallis, "Towards the Showing of Language," in *Thinking about Being: Aspects of Heidegger's Thought* ed. Robert W. Shahan and J. N. Mohanty (Norman: University of Oklahoma Press, 1984), 75–83.

[15] Tony O'Connor, "Heidegger and the Limits of Language," *Man and World* 14/1 (1981): 3–13.

experiences revelation demonstrably through a synthetic linguistic operation of his own. (The exact terms of Dante's theory of language will be
elaborated further in the concluding section of this Excursus.)

It is as a phenomenon of tying things together into unity that language
functions in its capacity to reveal. Nonetheless, language also appears,
thanks to its grammatical anatomization, as the analytic tool that introduces differentiation into the continuous flux of existence. But when
language itself shows up as the object of analysis, or more profoundly as
what calls for contemplation or thinking, as in Heidegger's language
philosophy and in Dante's poetic vision in this heaven, then language
reveals its essence as a revealment of unity in difference and as a showing
that synthesizes.

The medium apprehended as immediate presence or revelation in the
vision of Jove is an imaginative representation of language in the deeper
philosophical and theological significance that has been attributed to it in
Western thought ever since Heraclitus. Language is what holds the world
together in the very event of disclosing it. Language reveals the connecting
tissue of the marvelously intricate order of things. Such an understanding
of language constitutes the underlying condition for Dante's representations of language in this heaven. His poem presents language as revelation
in the theological sense and, at the very same time, as a transcendent order
that orders the entire world according to the supreme principle of Justice.
This involves "ordering" especially in the sense of demanding or commanding. The deep structure of language revealed in Dante's text is not
"merely" a linguistic order but rather the essence of order itself. In its most
important dimensions, which include the ethical and political, the order
reflected in language is Justice. And justice makes an imperative demand
on us.

Hegel has been recognized, particularly by French thinkers and critics,
as the leading philosopher of Logos as total system. Much of French
thought in the postmodern era has been aimed at unraveling Hegel's
System by subjecting it to critique as consisting not purely in thought,
but also in writing.[16] In *De la grammatologie*, Derrida recognizes Hegel as
the "last philosopher of the book and the first thinker of writing" ("dernier
philosophe du livre et premier penseur de l'écriture," 41). When Logos is
deconstructed as writing by contemporary French thought, it disintegrates
into an effect without grounding in any final presence or *parousia*. Yet,
even in its disintegration into infinite mediation, the synthetic power of

---

[16] Derrida's *Glas* (Paris: Galilée, 1974) is a salient example.

language demonstrates itself compellingly. Language or Logos is not only subject to deconstruction as writing: it is also the place of synthesis of the whole edifice of the universe. Dante's demonstration of the absolute unity and oneness of all in God is based fundamentally on the revelation of language as a tying and binding of things together into unity – of the whole universe into "one volume" ("un volume," XXXIII. 86–87).

Dante has graphically embodied the deconstructive dynamic of language as writing in his anatomized vision of Scripture and indeed throughout his vision of Paradise. Yet the upshot of this, paradoxically, is a vision of total order and providential oversight of the universe. It is an order that transcends all orders immanent within the world. The link between the natural and the divine is the Logos in its ability to transcend all wordly order of which it is the Creator. All immanent order is contingent, and precisely the demonstration of its contingency points towards a transcendent principle of synthesis that is, in effect, produced as if without ground, as merely contingent. Not merely is there something rather than nothing (Leibniz's mystery), but *what* there is has a marvelous organization and an order beyond our comprehension. This order consists in the "legame" ("bond") that binds things to one another. All that is is bound together in this order. And this makes it all essentially language – a system of infinite referrals.

Dante's medieval vision is, in crucial regards, a pansemiosis. The interconnectedness of all is the condition of any revelation or disclosure of an order of beings. Things are revealed in and through and with one another, and this makes them essentially into "language" as constituted by their mutual *relations*. This aspect of language enables us to perceive how Dante's vision prefigures not only the insights of French structuralist and deconstructive thinkers into language as *langue* and *écriture*, but also the thought of logos as *legein* developed by German hermeneutic thinkers on the basis of Greek precedents.

Legare Parole or Logos as λέγειν – Heidegger and Heraclitus

Phenomenological analysis, in the wake of Husserl and as practiced by Heidegger and Gadamer, begins by taking whole structures of experience as primordial. Experiences are given as wholes before their various elements are individuated and separated out. Differentiation among perceptions is a secondary moment – and even the differentiation of perceptions from things themselves in the immediacy of their presence comes as a reflective afterthought. Language, accordingly, lends itself to phenomenological treatment because it is a conspicuously whole structure in which all elements depend on one another. This mutual interdependence is especially evident in the whole of sense – the unity of meaning – that a sequence of linguistic signs dispersed over a continuum of time and/or space takes on in a whole sentence or whole discourse.

All the elements in language are tied together by the mutual differentiations that first give rise to phonetic and semantic values alike (Excursus II). The whole sentence that Dante sees revealed in the heaven of Jove and as realized with the appearance of the final letter binds all the letters, $5 \times 7 = 35$, together into the meaning that, taken together, they spell out. This binding together of the letters takes place in Dante's and in his readers' minds and requires their use of their memories.

The link between language as a tying or binding together and language as revelation belongs to the earliest reflections about λόγος in Western thought. Heidegger demonstrates this particularly in his 1951 reading of Heraclitus's Logos fragment (50).[17] Some very basic and supremely important aspects of Dante's intuitive sense of language as revelation, which he projects poetically in the visions of the Heaven of Jove, can be illuminated by Heraclitus's apprehension of the Logos as a revelation of Being – especially as refracted through Heidegger's philosophical reflection on language as disclosure (*aletheia*).[18] In whichever perspective, Heraclitus's or Heidegger's, it is precisely the radical difference of historical situation that will help to make stand out in relief the fundamental theoretical presuppositions about language as phenomenological revelation that are being represented in Dante's vision.

Heidegger profoundly interprets the primordial meaning of λόγος (discourse), λέγειν (to speak) in ancient Greek, from which its familiar meanings of "saying" and "reasoning" essentially spring. The root sense of Logos, says Heidegger, is that of "laying," of the "gathering laying" ("ὁ λόγος ist: die lesende Lege und nur dieses," 216), or more exactly: "the laying-down and laying-before which gathers itself and others" ("das sich und anderes sammelnde Nieder- und Vor-legen," 208). Heidegger interprets language in this sense as "letting lie together before in unconcealment." Saying, as the action by which language performs its work of disclosure, is similarly defined out of the primordial sense of λόγος as

---

[17] Martin Heidegger, "Logos Fragment" in *Vorträge und Aufsätze* (Pfullingen: Neske, 1954), 207–29, trans. David Farrell Krell and Frank A. Capuzzi in Martin Heidegger, *Early Greek Thinking* (New York: Harper & Row, 1975), 59–78.

[18] Complementary here is Heidegger's 1954 reading of Heraclitus's Aletheia fragment (16), also in *Early Greek Thinking* and *Vorträge und Aufsätze*.

a laying out that brings things to presence: "Saying and speaking occur essentially as the letting-lie-together-before of all that which, laid in unconcealment, comes to presence" ("Sagen und Reden wesen als das beisammen-vor-liegen-Lassen alles dessen, was, in der Unverborgenheit gelegen, anwest," 212). And this presencing of what is present is what Heidegger calls "the Being of beings" ("das Sein des Seienden," 212). Being is disclosed only in and as the essential order of Being in language that lets things lie together. Being thereby, insofar as it is disclosed, is one with language. Gadamer adopts this insight and makes it formulaic: "Being which can be understood is language" ("Sein, das verstanden werden kann, ist Sprache").[19]

Heidegger, reading Heraclitus, determines the original sense of λόγος from the verb λέγειν as that of binding together in order to underwrite his theory of being as disclosure (*aletheia*) through language. Discourse in language is what reveals the world, bringing it forward for notice, articulating its being, and this disclosure comes about through linkings or bindings of one thing to another, whereby all are revealed *as* what they are. Any individual thing is revealed only in and through its relations to other things. And this disclosedness through articulation of relations is the essence of language as it comes to be expressed in individual languages such as Greek. Language is thought by Heidegger essentially as unconcealment. It is only by things being linked and gathered together and "laid down before" one that anything at all can be disclosed. Unconcealment for Heidegger is necessarily unconcealment of things together. In and by virtue of Heraclitus's λόγος, in truth, "all is one": ἓν πάντα εἶναι. The λόγος (logos) is ἓν πάντα (one in all).

Heidegger notes the link of the Greek λόγος (logos) and its cognates with the Latin forms that we find more directly built into the thought of Dante and his Italian vernacular. He explains particularly the link between "*select*ing" or "gathering" and "reading" (in Italian *leggere*) also in terms of "laying together" (*legen*). "In *legen* a 'bringing together' prevails, the Latin *legere* understood as *lesen*, in the sense of gathering and bringing together" ("Darin [in 'legen'] waltet das Zusammenbringen, das lateinische legere als lesen im Sinne von einholen und zusammenbringen," 208). In Latin *lego, -ere* and in German *lesen* alike, words meaning primordially laying together or binding and gathering become words for reading. This constitutes the historical semantic background for Dante's concept of the reader's reading and for reading's own synthesizing, binding function. As reader, Dante

---

[19] Hans-Georg Gadamer, *Wahrheit und Methode* (Tübingen: Mohr, 1960), 478.

dramatically performs the gathering, binding function of language in the script that flashes across the sky of Jove.

The same is essentially true of Dante's act as writer, according to his theory of the poet as a "lieur" tying words together. In *Convivio* IV. vi. 3–4, Dante analyzes the word "autore" (author) as deriving from words for binding together into unity. The poet is one who ties or binds words ("legare parole") and thereby reveals the binding that ties the universe together in a unified order. "Author" derives also from "Authority," or being "worthy of faith and obedience" (IV. vi. 5), but the notion in any case is based on figuring the image of a bond ("a figurare imagine di legame"). The essential being of things, like that of words in a poem, is thus found in their relational tying and mutual ordering to one another, not in their stuff (as encapsulated also by Saussure's diacritical insight concerning language discussed in Excursus II).

Central to especially the later Heidegger's thought is the idea of language as the disclosure of being. But Heidegger thinks disclosure as bound up together with concealment, thereby placing the moment of the ineffable – what denies itself to language – within the heart of the phenomenon of language itself.[20] In this sense, Heidegger's thought on language illuminates the moment or "point" of ineffability around which the discourse of the *Paradiso* pivots ("al punto che mi vinse," XXX. 11). But a feature of λέγειν in Heraclitus/Heidegger that is yet more telling for Dante's presentation of language is the fact that what is disclosed by the linkages of beings – their mutual relations and significant ordering – is disclosed through human discourse as an order and a binding or gatheredness that exists already in the nature of things. It is not just that language imposes order on the material of the world, which is otherwise chaos. Language reveals an order intrinsic to things. This is the "justice" that Heraclitus thematizes as Δίκη (*dikê*).

By virtue of Δίκη we speak according to how things really are. Heraclitus's terms are interpreted by Heidegger to mean that human discourse is a way of corresponding to things as they are. Human "conforming" or ὁμολέγειν (*homologein*) is a corresponding to an always already antecedent binding and gatheredness (λέγειν) intrinsic to the event of unconcealment itself. Heidegger thereby delineates the movement of transcending the subjective human activity of speaking and being appropriated into language as the event (*Ereignis*) of the logos (λόγος).

---

[20] See Martin Heidegger, "Das Wort," in *Unterwegs zur Sprache* (Pfullingen: Neske, 1959), 219–38. English translation in my *On What Cannot Be Said*, vol. 2, 185–201.

Heidegger emphasizes the initiative taken by language in its own self-disclosure. This gives language a quasi-mythical, suprahuman dimension that corresponds to how Dante experiences language written in the Heaven of Jove. Heidegger writes, "In experiences which we undergo *with* language, language itself brings itself to language" ("In Erfahrungen, die wir *mit* der Sprache machen, bringt sich die Sprache selbst zur Sprache," *Unterwegs zur Sprache*, 161). Fundamentally, not humans, but language speaks ("die Sprache spricht"). This point of view on language also emphasizes its eventhood, which we saw to be an equally vital aspect of Dante's poetic experience of language beyond the structural analysis embedded in his deployment of grammatical sign theory.

The German verb "lesen" for reading, according to this interpretation, belongs to the constellation of words based on λόγος in the sense of binding or λέγειν. Therefore, the reading of the reader too, as a synthesis and binding together, a "reading," of the various materials se*lect*ed and read, demands to be understood as an unconcealing. The *Paradiso* conspicuously witnesses to the transumption and binding of the reader into the *legere* (Latin: to read), λέγειν (Greek: to speak) of language. At this primordial level, language is the poem of the universe, which is itself "tied together with love in one volume" ("legato con amore in un volume"). Human participation in language is understood by Dante, as by Heidegger, essentially, in terms of an activity of λέγειν – of binding and, more outwardly, of reading. Yet Dante, every bit as much as Heidegger, is aware that in language he is up against what masters all human mastery. Language is not an instrument in his hands except only secondarily and derivatively. Essentially, it precedes and dominates him – and calls and commands us. It is his God revealed, the Logos, revealing him to himself.

In language, the order of the universe, and even the being of God (at least in the form of an image), is revealed to Dante. For, in language, there is a prior gathering of all into one, an ideal wholeness, which contains within itself all possibilities of revelation within the world and history. Heidegger stresses the λέγειν (binding) of language that transcends and precedes all human ὁμολέγειν (corresponding), while for Dante the Logos (Λόγος) or Verbum is prior as itself divine, specifically as the second person of the Trinity.

In his *Beiträge zur Philosophie* (*Contributions to Philosophy*), subtitled *Vom Ereignis* ("Of the Event"), Heidegger thinks the event of be-ing as an "enowning" (Er-eignis) by which human being comes to belong to the event of truth in language. For Heidegger, the initiative for this event comes not from us but from "be-ing" ("Seyn") – and possibly from "God" if we allow metaphysical poetic imagination to think it. In any case, Scholastic tradition understood thinking about God to be God's own thinking in the first instance and ours (humans') only participatively. This is the direction thought takes still in Nicholas of Cusa's *On the Vision of God* (*De visione Dei*, 1453). This is why I speak of the "transcendentality of language" in a sense (not Heidegger's) that will be developed in the next and final Excursus (VI).

In *Paradiso* XVIII, Dante invents through imagination – and thereby discovers – language as λέγειν, as a gathering–laying together, binding and tying. Even in letting the elements of language violently disperse and disintegrate, Dante nonetheless discovers in language a laying together in order that is revealed as anterior to any human linguistic activity. This is the togetherness, the lying together of things, which it is the function of language to reveal. Language reveals this arrangement as transcendent and eternal – the negative of our perception of language's contingency. Language is parceled out into individual letters, yet the linguistic whole that the letters together compose is pre-existent in the Word of God, in Scripture: this Whole is manifest as the first sentence of the Book of Wisdom. Dante's own mental act of synthesizing the sequence only aims to recover the original unity of the Word as it exists perfected in Scripture. Both the order of language and the ideal order of the world – that is, Justice – are revealed as preceding and grounding the human activity of reading–tying–binding together.

Dante's Theory of Poetry as Tying and Binding Together

Dante's understanding of language in its essential character as a binding ("legare") is expressed not only in the poetry of the *Paradiso* but also, in explicit terms, in his theoretical writings on poetry and lyric. Dante defines the *canzone* as essentially an art of composition of elements into a whole. Macroscopically, starting at the level of the stanza, a *canzone* is a "coniugatio stantiarum," a "marriage" or melding together of "stanzas," literally "rooms" (*De vulgari eloquentia* II. ix. 1). At a more minute level, and most importantly, the binding in which poetic language's being consists begins with letters and particularly with the vowels that function in order to bind letters together.

Dante derives the word for author ("autore") etymologically from an archaic verb – *auieo* – comprising the sequence of the five vowels strung together in a single word, and he gives it the significance of tying or binding words together ("legare parole"). Vowels, as Dante conceives of them, are the ties of words that bind them together. This word "auieo," at the root of "autore" ("author"), Dante says, "is made only of the liaisons of words, that is, of only the five vowels, which are the soul and bond of every word" ("Solo di legame di parole è fatto, cioè di sole cinque vocali, che sono anima e legame d'ogni parola," *Convivio* IV. vi. 3). Dante points out that Italian "autore" drops the "c" from the Latin "auctor," thereby moving closer to the archaic "auieo," which consists in nothing but vowels or "ties." Corroborating the *Convivio* in its understanding of the function of the author or poet as consisting essentially in the binding or tying of language, *De vulgari eloquentia* II. i. I likewise images poets as "avientibus" or "binders," evidently following the widely diffused etymology of Uguccione da Pisa: "*avieo, -es,* idest ligo –as, et indi *autor,* idest ligator."[21]

The word "auieo," moreover, is composed out of the vowels arrayed in an "enveloping mode," making it the "image or figure of a tie or bond" ("e composto d'esse per modo volubile, a figurare imagine di legame"). The word itself performs a turning motion in which all the vowels are enveloped and linked together to form the image of a liaison: "Since beginning from the A, it turns itself back to the U and comes directly through I to the E, then turns itself back and turns to the O; such that it truly images this figure: A, E, I, O, U, which is a figure of binding" ("Ché, comminciando da l'A, ne l'U quindi si rivolve, e viene diritto per I ne l'E, quindi si rivolve e torna ne l'O; sì che veramente imagina questa figura: A, E, I, O, U, la quale è figura di legame," *Convivio* IV. vi. 4). The rounding into a circle, of course, is an image of an all-encompassing whole, and thus connotes completeness.[22] The trajectory of Dante's description, moreover, moves from A to O, from alpha to omega (Revelation 1:8; 21:6; 22:13), thereby suggesting the analogy between the author and God.

In the first book of the *Convivio*, Dante had already connected this concept of language, specifically his vernacular language, as a tying or binding ("legare"), with the staying power of language, its vocation to make itself – and thereby all that is said in it – endure. "Everything strives naturally towards its own preservation: whence, if the vernacular were itself capable of striving, it would strive for that; and that would be to establish for itself greater stability, and greater stability could be obtained only by binding itself with meter and rime" ("Ciascuna cosa studia naturalmente a la sua conservazione: onde, se lo volgare per sé studiare potesse,

---

[21] Cited from Paget Toynbee, "Dante's Obligations to the *Magnae Derivationes* of Uguccione da Pisa," *Romania* 26 (1897): 541. See, further, *Magnae Derivationes*, eds. Enzo Cecchini et al., 2 vols. (Florence: Galluzzo, 2004) under the voce: *Augeo, -ges.*

[22] For probing interpretation of this verbal geometry, see Roger Dragonetti, "Le sens du cercle et le poète," *Romanica Gandensia* IX (1961): 81.

studierebbe a quella; e quella sarebbe acconciare sé a più stabilitade, e più stabilitade non potrebbe avere che in legar sé con numero e con rime," I. xiii. 6).

The transcendency of this poetic language bound together by the eternal Word, even in the transiency of its appearance to Dante, is what the theophany in *Paradiso* XVIII places on display in its presentation of Holy Scripture. Yet, in the *Paradiso*, the emphasis falls on the *in*stability of the phenomenal display as opening up a path beyond all phenomenal appearing. Ultimate stability is not, and cannot be, directly realized by the tying into unity of language. It can only be *signified* by means of a dialectic of all finite and phenomenal forms of language, in their inevitable instability, with divine simplicity – which must in itself, however, remain formless because it is *pure* form that contains *all* forms but is identical with none. This is why Ineffability becomes explicitly the central organizing principle of Dante's vision. The ineffable has no content and is no object, yet it serves as the overarching framework and limit for any representation of the universal such as Dante aspires to deliver.

As theorized in the *Convivio*, poetic language accedes to a metaphysical dimension in which it can introduce a factor of resistance into the unrelenting flux of the physical world. Dante hails and acclaims such a poetically perfected vernacular language. In *De vulgari eloquentia*, he goes hunting for it but finds it nowhere among the languages actually spoken on the Italian peninsula (I. xi. 1 – I. xv. 8). It can be plausibly found only in the inexhaustible creativity of language in the best poetry (I. xix. 1). In the *Convivio*, Dante envisions this language arising as a new sun in the place of the old sun that is setting. It rises as a light of truth and divinity lighting the way to salvation: "This will be new light, a new sun, which will rise where the old one sets and will give light to those in tenebrous obscurity because of the old sun that does not illuminate them" ("Questo sarà luce nuova, sole nuovo, lo quale surgerà là dove l'usato tramonterà, e darà lume a coloro che sono in tenebre e in oscuritade per lo usato sole che a loro non luce," I. xiii. 12).

This is language as gospel in the sense of good news. For language – and in particular Dante's illustrious vernacular ("vulgare illustre") – can bring about the new, which is actually the breaking-in of the eternal. The phrase "those who dwell in shadows and darkness" ("coloro che sono in tenebre e in oscuritade") most readily recalls the *Benedictus*, with its annunciation of the birth of John the Baptist, the one who "prepares the way" for the Savior. This Savior is the one who in person *is* the Gospel: he is the salvation "whereby the dayspring from on high hath visited us, / To give

light to those who sit in darkness and in the shadow of death" (Luke
1:78–79).

The God-given language that breaks into the firmament of Jove
("LOVE JUSTICE, YOU WHO RULE THE EARTH") is, in fact,
a word of tradition, indeed the Word as handed down in the Bible. But
it happens in Dante's text as new and as a call for the renewal of the world:
Let the entire order of the world be renewed in love of and obedience to
Justice. Dante realizes the newness of the eternal Word by his recreation of
it in a poetic language of his own invention. It is thus that this Word
achieves its stability – not by abiding statically identical with itself but by
entering into history with its peremptory ordering force, therewith effect-
ing renewal.

The myth of language that Dante sketches in *De vulgari eloquentia* is
realized in another form, poetically (the only way it could be), in the
Commedia. In the earlier theoretical work, Dante's myth of language as
the *vulgare illustre*, which figured as a "perfumed panther" (I. xvi. 1), is at
the same time a metaphor or figure for Christ, the Logos, the ultimate
ground of reintegration out of fragmented and alienated disunity
(Excursus III). In *De vulgari eloquentia*, Dante insists on stylistic homo-
geneity for his *vulgare illustre*. However, leaving the treatise unfinished, he
breaks off the project in favor of his multilingual, stylistically heteroge-
neous "comedía."[23]

Unity is not achieved in style, nor superficially at the level of the
signifier, but only at a transcendent level of the signified, which, in this
case, more exactly, is the unsignifiable (God). This positioning of unity
beyond our reach – though it still conditions us from beyond our control –
is key to Dante's opening the door to multiplicity, interruption, discon-
tinuity, and heterogeneity, without ever giving up his ideal of unity. Thus
appears, on our horizon, the "transcendentality of language," which
remains before us as the last height to be scaled in pursuit of Dante's
vision. If God is revealed in Dante's vision essentially in and *as* language,
this is in virtue of language's function of tying and binding everything
together. However, this gatheredness and bondedness of things in their
givenness is not self-explanatory. Instead, it alludes to a power beyond and
preceding language's own. Our access to this "beyond" passes through
ethical relation to the Other and, concretely, to other persons.

---

[23] On this crucial aspect of Dante's cultural project, see S. Fortuna, M. Gragnolati, and J. Trabant,
   eds., *Dante's Plurilingualism, Authority, Knowledge, Subjectivity* (Oxford: Legenda, 2010), as well as
   Jacqueline Risset, *Dante écrivain*, 79, 80.

Transcendentality of Language and the Language of the Other

Language makes thought historical and brings it to pass as event. Yet, presupposed in language is always some already gathered Gathering that conditions the possibility of history and event in their radical possibility as disclosure (Excursus V). The language of "condition of possibility" is used here advisedly to raise, in the technical vocabulary of Kant, the issue of the "transcendentality" of language.[1] A transcendent ground (such as God, the soul, or here language as such, or as a whole) can be known only indirectly as a transcendental condition of the possibility of knowing. But Dante, nevertheless, imaginatively displays such conditions poetically with vivid, visionary concreteness.

Walter Benjamin, via his speculations on "pure language," similarly approaches, through vivid metaphors, what Dante apprehends as the transcendent reality of language as such. Benjamin imagines an original language that is whole and total – and perfectly adequate to name everything that is or exists – as a vase that was shattered. Left behind, in the wake of its shattering, as its shards, are our historical languages. Benjamin's notion of "pure language" ("die reine Sprache"), as elicited and released by translation of literary classics, witnesses, furthermore, to a condition of the relatedness of all languages to one another. One perfect and universal language is projected by dint of their "kinship" ("Verwandtschaft") as it is revealed through translation.[2]

Dante reflects along comparable lines in *De vulgari eloquentia*, Book I, where he tries to reconstruct the "illustrious vernacular" ("vulgare illustre")

---

[1] Pertinent philosophical background here is gathered by Erich Heintel, *Einführung in die Sprachphilosophie*, 4th ed. (Darmstadt: Wissenschaftliche Buchgesellschaft, 1991 [1972]), in particular chapter 11: "Transzendentale und hermeneutische Sprachphilosophie, transzendentale Sprachgeschichte," 147–68.

[2] Walter Benjamin, "Die Aufgabe des Übersetzers," in *Gesammelte Schriften*, vol. IV/1 (Frankfurt am Main: Suhrkamp, 1972), 9–21, trans. Harry Zohn, "The Task of the Translator," in *Illuminations: Essays and Reflections*, ed. Hannah Arendt (New York: Schocken, 1968), 69–82. Benjamin's essay was originally published in 1923 as the preface to his translations of Baudelaire's "Tableaux parisiens."

as the ideal language for poetry after the original, God-given language in Eden has been lost through the shattering of the linguistic unity of humankind at Babel. Dante speculates on the process of change by which one and the same language became many ("de unius et eiusdemque a principio ydiomatis variatione secuta," I. ix. 1). The traces of the original unity are visible in the concordances of many words across related languages. In Dante's own Latinate family of languages, this is most evident in the word "love," *amor* ("maxime in hoc vocabulo quod est amor," I. ix. 3), with its obviously assimilable variants in French *amour*, Italian *amore*, and Spanish *amor*.

These traces of a common origin might be understood as alluding to an ideal language that haunts historical languages as a virtual, but elusive and disappearing, presence. Dante hunts for it as a panther ("pantherem") that leaves its scent everywhere, in each of the dialects of Italy, yet is to be actually seen in none of them ("redolentem ubique et necubi apparentem," I. xvi. 1). Instead, Dante must rationally reconstruct his ideal vernacular as a *poetic* language suited to an only hypothetical, inexistent and utopian, imperial court (*aula*) and tribunal of justice (*curia*). Both venues are instances of centralized power and consort with authority that is administrative or "*cardinale*" – the other institutional term Dante uses to qualify this "illustrious" (*illustre*) language. He summarizes in concluding Book I: "Now this vernacular, which has been shown to be illustrious, cardinal, aulic, and curial, is that which is called the Italian vernacular" ("Hoc autem vulgare quod illustre, cardinale, aulicum et curiale ostensum est, dicimus esse illud quod vulgare latium appellatur," I. xix. 1; cf. I. xvi. 6).

In the transition from Book I to Book II of *De vulgari eloquentia*, Dante's search for the original or ideal language shifts from an anthropological into a literary key. Consistent with this shift, Dante's interest in uncovering the Ur-language of humankind by a kind of archeological investigation mutates into an attempt to construct the ideal poetic language by attention to compositional technique in a perspective of comparative poetics. Just as for Benjamin, speculation about origins turns out here to be guided by an eschatological vision of the ends of language and of the language arts. For Benjamin, the literary classic is unveiled by the art of translation as belonging to world literature – and as releasing "pure language" into historical languages. Both Dante and Benjamin envisage a normative language that transcends – even while it grants and fosters – cultural multiplicity and historical variation. Both employ a speculative method in which their accounts of origins and ends mirror their own projects – a cultural poetics of translation, for Benjamin, and a comprehensive literary art, for Dante, which he eventually calls "comedía."

Dante also represents the transcendence of language throughout the *Paradiso* by practically identifying it with divinity. In fact, it is exactly the transcendence of language that makes it an apt metaphor for God. Language is the transcendent that can be perceived, the meaning that becomes material, the ineffable that is nevertheless said. Hence it is the revelation of God – theophany. However, it is especially the vulgar tongue – evolving within history and difficult to separate from regional dialects – that reveals God historically and within Dante's poem. Dante examines language as the transcendental condition of his theophany at the same time as he recognizes its symbolizing divine transcendence made accessible in and through its temporal materialization. It is because God becomes Word and can become manifest poetically in words, and thereby enter into the sphere of our knowing, that a true access to the real is possible for us in the first place. In this medieval view, a theological miracle of revelation is necessary first to enable knowledge.

Yet, taken without theological presuppositions, this transcendence signifies a certain *excess* to all definitive historical determination, an excess that lives and dwells in the event of language. The language of our understanding is never completely circumscribed by historical language. Dante has explored the virtues and virtualities inherent in language through a transcendental investigation – in effect, an experiment in representation. In Dante's prophetic representations, language emerges as the condition of the very possibility of history in its occurrence as a meaningful structure of events. Language transcends the knowledge of history in the limitative sense that would determine all knowing as objectively "historical." In some sense, accordingly, time is transcended always already in discursive knowing. When knowing through the word in the full sense occurs, any determination of consciousness as historically objective is burst open or suspended by the infinity that characterizes precisely language as the medium of knowledge. This infinity is possible not by the exclusion – but rather only on the basis – of finitude.

The discovery of the historicality of all knowledge (Hegel) and of thought as intrinsically linguistic (Humboldt), as assimilated by the early Heidegger, leads to the recognition in the late Heidegger (*Unterwegs zur Sprache*, 1959) that being reveals itself historically in language, while language itself remains unconcealed, unrevealed. This is thus a negative transcendence consisting not in the positive positing of language as transcendent: it is transcendence experienced, rather, in the implosion of finite being, its collapsing from within and breaking open to exposure to an uncircumscribable Other. The *in*finite emerges through negation – as in the linguistic impotence of Dante's negative poetics of divine ineffability.

Heidegger meditated much of his life long on the "last god" or the "coming god" and came to believe in the end that "only a god can save us" ("nur noch ein Gott kann uns retten").[3] This view was formulated incipiently after *Being and Time* (*Sein und Zeit*, 1927) and after the interpretations of Hölderlin (1934–35) and the *Introduction to Metaphysics* (1935), in Heidegger's thinking of the history of being (*seynsgeschichtliches Denken*) in *Beiträge zur Philosophie* (1938). Granted, human, historical speaking is always eventual, occasional, and finite. Still, this occasional, contingent event of human speech nevertheless expresses a totality of meaning ("ein Ganzes von Sinn") that can never be fully articulated. Dante's *Ineffabile* is such a Whole approached via the vernacular throughout the *Paradiso*. Such a paradoxical conjunction of finitude and infinity is thought poetically in Heidegger's philosophy of language. It is stated explicitly by Gadamer: "All human speaking is finite in such a way that there is laid up within it an infinity of meaning to be explicated and laid out" (*Truth and Method*, 458). Like the incarnate God, language realizes its infinity historically.

The Infinity of Language in Its Historicality

The λέγειν or tying–binding that is the essence of language also for Dante (*Convivio* IV. vi. 3–4), as discussed in Excursus V, is revealed through the historicality of language as something transcending, commanding, and mastering all possible human acts. Heidegger ingeniously shows the transcendence of λέγεῖν with regard to all human mental, linguistic functions, which are only ὁμολογεῖν or "corresponding" to a norm or logos. And this is already the sense of Heraclitus's contrast between listening to *him* and listening to the *logos*: οὐκ ἐμοῦ ἀλλὰ τοῦ λόγου ἀκούσαντας / ὁμολογεῖν σοφόν ἐστιν Ἓν Πάντα ("Listening not to me but to the Logos, it is wise to agree that all is one").[4] The Logos is normative and imperative and speaks with a higher authority than that of any mere mortal.

---

[3] Heidegger, interview in *Der Spiegel*, no. 23 (May 31, 1976): 193–219; reprinted in Heidegger, *Gesamtausgabe*, vol. 16, *Reden und andere Zeugnisse eines Lebensweges* (Frankfurt am Main: Klostermann, 1975), pp. 652–83. The interview, conducted in 1966, was withheld from publication until shortly after his death, as stipulated by Heidegger.

[4] Heraclitus, Fragment 50. Cited by Heidegger in "Logos Fragment," in *Vorträge und Aufsätze*. The essay was translated by Jacques Lacan in *La psychanalyse* 1 (1956): 59–79.

The divine Logos already contains the ties between things (λέγειν) invisibly prior to its revelation through the binding action of poetic language (Excursus V). Dante affirms this proleptic state of the intrinsic order of being as existing already in the letter (Excursus I). Heidegger emphasizes the *givenness* of this order, its heteronomy, even in affirming the immanence of the event or *Ereignis*, literally "En-owning," to the history of finite, mortal *Dasein* or human existence as being (*sein*) there (*da*). The entering into a gathering that discloses time and everything temporal and historical indeed occurs through a submitting to determination by history rather than by turning away from it towards supposedly eternal ideals. Dante's poem, even in its affirmation of theological transcendence, is remarkable for its showing language to be emergent in and from historical realities. This is evident even in its specifically linguistic features, quite apart from its historical content. The processual element of the poem's language hangs together with its being bound and gathered into a totality ("legato con amore in un volume") that is not itself given *by* history, even while it is given its perceptible shape *from* history.

Dante invokes the divine Artist whose just governance of the universe serves as model for princes and whose justice is referred to as producing the display of letters that he sees. Dante thereby reveals the phrase "Diligite iustitiam . . ." to be of the nature of what Heidegger calls a "sending" ("Geschick"). The phrase commands humans, specifically princes, to do justice, but they cannot do it simply on their own: to do justice, they can only conform to God's preordained norm. They must allow themselves to become instruments of a justice that hails from heaven and is not just their own doing.

What Heidegger especially emphasizes in interpreting the Heraclitus fragment is that λόγος among humans, as human language, always presupposes an antecedent gathering together and laying before on the part of Language, which no human can master. The connectedness and disclosedness of things in a world, their lying-together-before, is not produced by human activity or *techné*: it is, instead, discovered as unaccountably given. Hence also the astoundingly organized order of the letters that Dante sees spontaneously sparking – as if contingently – into recognizable and even portentous shapes. Heidegger's thinking (*Denken*) is the effort to think just that givenness ("Es gibt"), the astonishing fact that it *is* and that all that is is gathered and bound together in it. The phrase that Dante sees in the Heaven of Jove is a whole sentence: it is made such especially by its last word and letter, which syntactically close the series. The phrase, in which all elements are simultaneous, is itself timeless – not in the sense that it is impervious to particular contexts in which it comes to be understood, but by virtue of its having an integrity of its own that impinges a priori on those contexts and proactively shapes all times and occurences.

The whole thrust of Heidegger's thought, seen one way, is to open the dimension of transcendence from within – yet also from beyond – the human. His *Letter on Humanism* (*Brief über den Humanismus*, 1947) is his programmatic critique of modern reductions to the human and its measure of being (*Sein*), which is disclosed by language. He dwells on ways that humans do not master language as their instrument, but just the opposite. The later Heidegger's thought on Language opens this horizon for the linguistic ontology that forms the culmination of Gadamer's hermeneutic theory in the third and final part of *Truth and Method* – "The Ontological Turn of Hermeneutics Guided by Language" ("Ontologische Wendung der Hermeneutik am Leitfaden der Sprache").

Gadamer makes it clear that such a philosophical hermeneutics receives its most penetrating understanding of λόγος, its most far-reaching impulse, not from the Greeks, but rather from the biblical Logos tradition. He emphasizes the "inner word," the *Verbum mentis* of Christian theology, as the key to hermeneutic reflection on language. "There is, however, an idea that is not Greek which does more justice to the being of language, and so prevented the forgetfulness of language in Western thought from being complete. This is the Christian idea of incarnation" (*Truth and Method*, 418). Gadamer recognizes the doctrine of the Incarnation and, inseparably, that of the Trinity as the bearers of a hermeneutically superior thinking on the question of language. The phenomenon of language, with its mysterious unity produced by and consisting in differences, and particularly its union of sense or purely intellectual meaning with sensuous form or matter, reflects the same mysteries of being and revelation as do Christian theological doctrines.

Gadamer's linguistic ontology is based on the premise that "the mystery of unity [between God the Father and God the Son] is reflected in the phenomenon of language" (*Truth and Method*, 419). How can material marks or sounds be the bearers of, and even be identical with, something of an entirely different order, that of thought? How can the successive manifestations of marks ever attain to the wholeness of a word with a unified meaning? As Gadamer writes, "The greater miracle of language lies not in the fact that the Word becomes flesh and emerges in external being, but that that which emerges and externalizes itself in utterance is always already a word" (*Truth and Method*, 420). Like the divine Word, Christ, who fully expresses the Being of the Father, Godhead's infinity, in

the finite form of human flesh, so also "the word is a process in which the
unity of what is meant is fully expressed" (*Truth and Method*, 434). This is
the miraculous unity that astonishes Dante when it is revealed from the
midst of the apparent chaos of writing and its disintegrating elements in
the Heaven of Jupiter. Yet Dante also stresses that he can perceive this
unity only through its brokenness – and through an ethical relation to what
wholly transcends him as Other.

Levinas: Language as "Relation" and as "Religion"

As Gadamer well recognized, the word of the Hebrew prophets introduces
a momentous new type of linguistic reality that revolutionizes the possibilities of revelation in language. This reality is a word with a claim to divine
authority as the Word of God. Its philosophical assimilation has often been
submerged, and sometimes perhaps even unconscious, but it is nonetheless
a motivating force behind the thinking of Jewish philosophers and critical
theorists such as Adorno, Horkheimer, and Benjamin, no less than
Levinas. The prophetic Word of the Bible gave the impetus to fundamental innovations in philosophical thinking as based traditionally on the
Greek Logos by introducing a historical reality to be verified not by
universal intellect but rather as a singular word of truth addressed to the
heart of individual persons. No longer reserved for an intellectual elite in
esoteric schools of antiquity, the truth proclaimed by Christianity was *for
all*, women and slaves included: for all who would open their hearts to
receive it as a word of salvation. Nevertheless, while within the reach of all,
what actually happens in this event is scarcely fathomable by anyone. The
intellectual and spiritual revelation thereby engendered remains elusively
ungraspable and invites, in its turn, to subtle and even sublime philosophical analysis.

   In this vein, the most essential feature of the written language seen in
Dante's theophany – the feature that I am calling its "transcendentality" –
can be more deeply probed through reference to a theory of language as
revelation developed by the French phenomenologist and Jewish philosopher Emmanuel Levinas. Levinas thinks within a matrix impregnated by
reflection on the biblical tradition, particularly revelation in the Hebrew
Bible and its injunction to justice among humans on earth[5] – whence the

---

[5] This background is masked in Levinas's philosophical works but is openly expressed in his declaredly
   Jewish writings such as *L'Au-delà du verset: Lectures et discours Talmudiques* (Paris: Minuit, 1982). My
   On What Cannot Be Said, vol. 2, 406–26, situates Levinas in this lineage of apophatic thought.

theme-text of Dante's vision also derives, albeit via Hellenistic mediation. One of the most revealing ways to point up the starkly innovative intellectual maneuver enacted by Dante's text and its ultimately quite revolutionary consequences is to juxtapose it to this particular counterpart in modern philosophy and critical theory that illuminates the implications of a negative theology of representation along some strikingly parallel lines.[6]

Dante proposes language – the letters of his vision and of his poem – as revelation, as, in effect, the Face of the Other, or of God, in a sense that Levinas elucidates with remarkable penetration and aptness, given their disparate contexts and coordinates. In spite of the cultural–historical distances, the essence of language investigated at this most radical level shows itself with a certain transhistorical consistency. Language shows itself as consisting basically in exposure to the other person. For Dante and Levinas alike, beyond the differentiated senses of words, this bald fact of addressing another person constitutes the transcendental *signifyingness* of language.

Levinas relentlessly emphasizes that signification originates not in the assignment of sense (*Sinngebung*, borrowing Husserl's phenomenological vocabulary) by "the Same" ("le Même"), that is, by a self-identical subjectivity, but rather in the face of the Other ("l'Autre"). A statement's having a sense depends on "the presence of the Other in the proposition" ("la présence de l'Autre dans la proposition," *Totalité et infini*, 98). Assuming that "sense" inheres in propositions, a miraculous abundance and inexhaustible surplus attends this amplification of sense through its relation to an irreducible externality, an Other. This relation, furthermore, makes all language essentially "teaching" ("enseignement"), a form of "communication" from an Other.

It is the inexhaustible surplus of meaning gained through relation to someone external that makes language as such, for Levinas, equivalent to a form of "teaching." Dante's intensively didactic poem, too, can present language in its most essential use as teaching. In the *Paradiso*, Dante displays the didacticism or "teaching" inherent in language writ large in the Heaven of Jove. Here, explicitly, the lesson is to love justice: the ethical

---

[6] I offer such a comparison from a different angle of approach in "The Ethical Vision of Dante's *Paradiso* in Light of Levinas," *Comparative Literature* 59/3 (2007): 209–27, reprised in the epilogue to *Dante and the Sense of Transgression: "The Trespass of the Sign"* (London: Bloomsbury, 2012). That discussion was based on Levinas's culminating work *Autrement qu'être ou au-delà de l'essence* (Dordrecht: Kluwer, 1990 [1974]), whereas the present reflection works from his earlier *magnum opus*, his ground-breaking *Totalité et infini: Essai sur l'extériorité* (Dordrecht: Kluwer, 1992 [1961]). The latter work is the reference throughout this Excursus for all Levinas quotations not otherwise attributed.

injunction to love justice is the express content of the teaching that constitutes language and, therewith, the ethical relation to the Other. This relation entails relation to the infinite and its never exhaustible demand for justice – our infinite obligation to others.

The "teaching" that Levinas has in mind attends specifically to the infinite in its presence through signs and signifying. The infinite can never be thematized, yet it speaks: it is Face. Although not thematizable, the infinite is thema*tizing*. This *Who* signifies things linguistically, gives them their identities, and thereby speaks or, equivalently, shows its Face.

> The infinite, in which every definition is cut out, does not define itself, does not offer itself to our regard, but signals itself; not as a theme, but as thematizing, as the one from *whom* everything can be fixed in its identity; but also it signals in attending to the work that signals it; it does not merely signal itself, but speaks: it is face.
>
> (L'infini où toute définition se découpe, ne se définit pas, ne s'offre pas au regard, mais se signale; non pas comme thème, mais comme thématisant, comme celui à partir de *qui* toute chose peut se fixer identiquement; mais aussi il signale en assistant à l'œuvre qui le signale; il ne se signal pas seulement, mais parle, est visage, 101).

In Levinas's terms, the signs Dante displays are not entirely cut off from their Emitter, but are rather his showing of himself, his Face. This is what makes even the divine letters in Dante's imagination essentially oral, a word spoken or "dictated" ("dette"). Levinas similarly considers "oral discourse" to be "the plenitude of discourse" ("Le discours oral est la plenitude du discours," 98) and the spoken word to be "the origin of all signification" ("La parole est ainsi, l'origine de toute signification," 100). The meaning of signs is always infinitely exceeded by the meaning of the one who emits them, namely, the speaker, who can bring help or "succor" to them (Levinas recalls here the argument of Plato's *Phaedrus*) and by virtue of whose presence the word promises to elucidate itself. Such is the specific form of the fact that "signification" takes on meaning as communication of the Infinite that, in itself, remains unknowable.

Language, as a relation to the absolutely Other, interrupts the "apparition" of a phenomenal world in a speaking presence which disenchants ("désensorcelle") the world. Otherwise, the world is bewitched. But language pierces its appearing with a revelation of significance: "in language is accomplished the uninterrupted influx of a presence that tears the inevitable veil of its own appearing, which is malleable in form like every appearing" ("dans le langage s'accomplit l'afflux ininterrompu d'une présence qui déchire le voile inévitable de sa propre apparition, plastique comme toute apparition," 100). The phenomenon becomes speech and specifically teaching, in which the Teacher is present. This presence, however, remains external to the consciousness of the separate being of the subject (or learner). In language, the phenomenon of appearing is discontinuous with the infinity of the Other who speaks in language yet is not contained in any subject's thought. This transcendence of his own subjective capacity in the face of the Other (God, Beatrice, saints) lies at the core of Dante's experience, too, and he likewise understands it, deeply considered, as an experience of language.

The Language of the Other

Language moves into center stage as a theme for Dante partly because, beyond the sense assigned it through the intentions of its users, language as manifestation of their existence has a sense all its own – albeit one conferred from beyond and above. Dante's thematization and dramatization of language and its component letters lends itself to suggesting a probe that scrutinizes the sense of language as such. Language speaks to him in the Heaven of Jove directly; it becomes not just an instrument or means, but also in itself immediately a revelation. Heidegger's philosophy, similarly, culminated in an attunement to what language as such says, for "language speaks" ("die Sprache spricht").

More concretely and pregnantly, on the face of it, Levinas understands language *per se* in the biblical and particularly the prophetic tradition as bearing an ethical sense: it mediates a relationship to the Other as immediate and non-integratable, but as imperiously demanding. "The immediate is interpellation, and interpellation, if one may say so, is the imperative of language" ("L'immédiat est l'interpellation et, si l'on peut dire, l'impératif du langage," 44). The imperative here is justice – the ethical imperative vis-à-vis the Other. It is remarkable, in light of Levinas, that Dante, too, represents language – when it is displayed to him directly as divine revelation in the Heaven of Jove – as a revelation of Justice. And this revelation comes in the form of an injunction that is (like Levinas's) a peremptory imperative.

Certainly, the sense of Dante's language in the poem as a whole is ethical in nature. This is stated explicitly in the Letter to Can Grande: "The genus of philosophy under which the work as a whole and in part is comprehended is that of moral or ethical matters; for it is conceived in whole and in part not for speculation but for action" ("Genus vero phylosophie sub quo hic in toto et parte proceditur, est morale negotium, sive ethica; quia non ad speculandum, sed ad opus inventum est totum et pars," xvi. 40). But the poem's epic action is ethical also in a sense deeper than that of any determinate acting or knowing. Most basically, ethics consists in facing and deferring to the Other. Heightened to the religious level, this means a constitutive relation to the divine Other. Dante's poem is a linguistic journey to the divine Other. The route, however gnoseological it appears, in the end consists essentially in an ethical relation that surpasses the limits of knowing.

Somewhat like Martin Buber, Levinas opposes the knowing of the Being of beings to the ethical I–Thou relation. The two are opposed, finally, as are liberty and justice for Levinas (see *Totalité et infini*, 80–83: "La liberté mise en question"). The two are not contradictory for Dante because he does not subscribe to the modern absolutization of the individual. For Dante, liberty can be achieved only through justice. But the modern self, in its treating everything as the same as itself, as a resource to use for its own free self-realization and self-enhancement, is confronted by another person and therewith is faced with an incommensurable type of imperative: the demand for justice. Language, as a means of communication, immediately reveals this unmediatable, inappropriable otherness. The Other is not available for me and my purposes: the Other is not a material for mediation by me, but rather the immediate presence of another person before me – a Face. For Levinas, language is this Face of the Other, and for Dante, too, in the mystical sense attributed to his linguistic means in the *Paradiso*, language becomes the Face of God.

As for Dante, so also for Levinas, God as such is invisible and unrepresentable. For Levinas, God can be approached only through the demand to pursue justice in the face-to-face encounter with human beings. Theology, as a discourse directly about God, is replaced by – or translated into – an ethical discourse pivoting on human encounter. An ethical demand is verbalized in terms of "uprightness" in both Dante ("rettitudine") and Levinas ("droiture"), a coincidence that expresses their sense of human dignity in discovering a relation with the transcendent that leaves the human being free and responsible in itself, and yet still inextricably in relation to what is beyond it as irreducibly other.[7] This irreducible Otherness is imaginable as divine.

---

[7] Merold Westphal, *In Praise of Heteronomy: Making Room for Revelation* (Bloomington: Indiana University Press, 2017) defends the epistemic legitimacy of such theological belief against the critiques of modern philosophy (eminently by Spinoza, Kant, and Hegel) through showing that reason itself is always conditioned by heteronomous norms; it is never "a view from nowhere."

Work of justice is necessary – the uprightness of the face-to-face – in order to produce the puncture that leads to God – and "vision" coincides here with this work of justice.

(Il faut œuvre de justice – la droiture du face à face – pour que se produise la trouée qui mène à Dieu – et la "vision" coincide ici avec cette œuvre de justice. *Totalité et infini*, 77).

Such righteousness, therefore, makes the individual human being ethically responsible to an imperative from beyond all human use and purpose, even as this imperative is realized paradoxically on the human plane – and without the mystifications that would mix supposedly spiritual pretences into purely secular issues of justice. The paradox is that everything depends on an instance that humans do not have at their disposal and have no means of their own to fathom but that nevertheless remains an unsurpassable standard and exigency for them – an irrecusable ethical call.

Ethics as Revelation in Language

Levinas conceives of a revelation through metaphysical desire that is prior to all human knowing. He proposes that "The idea of the infinite *reveals itself* in the strong sense of the term" ("L'idée de l'Infini *se révèle*, au sens fort du terme," 56). We must remember, however, that this idea of the infinite is an object not of knowledge but of desire. And it is not a matter of need arising from lack; it is rather an aspiration born of the infinite itself as desirable. Levinas understands this situation as "language" ("telle situation est langage," 56). Without fusion or even ontological participation, there is inherent within language an address and even an imperative. Simply by being there, being present in the Face, the Other and Infinite speaks and addresses and ethically commands – and also "teaches."

This teaching, too, is realized grandly in the precept "Love justice" from the Book of Wisdom. It is accomplished, however, more than by any principle that is enunciated, rather through the immediate presence of the Voice speaking from the height that Dante imagines as heaven. This Saying, for Levinas, is equivalent to the face-to-face encounter. Paradoxically, he analyzes this encounter as the essential nature of language, which is to let revelation and revealer coincide in the face. In Levinas's terms, "the essential in language is the coincidence of revealer and revealed in the face, which is accomplished in situating itself at a height with respect to us – by teaching" ("l'essential du language: la coincidence de révélateur et révélé dans le visage, qui s'accomplit en se situant en hauteur par rapport à nous – en enseignant," 62).

This sense of language as such, however, as depending on an infinite otherness that it cannot grasp, remains necessarily indeterminate in terms of language. Dante shows all his carefully and richly articulated determinations to have their sense finally in this "beyond" of language, in an otherness that language cannot comprehend but that it runs up against at its own limit or frontier. Hence Dante's constant recourse to the ineffability topos. The breakdown of language into letters and component lights in the scene in Jupiter enables another sense to emerge from the chaos at the core of language. This sense transcends any finite, determinate senses that might be assigned to language in its specific propositional uses.

The randomness that Dante finds in the formation of the letters and the sentence featured in *Paradiso* XVIII is simply the denial of any determinate sense in order that the sense of language per se, beyond the order and significance imposed on it by finite, human speakers, might emerge. Now Dante does, of course, postulate that the Creator is in control of language, as of everything else produced in the universe – from the instinctive flight patterns of birds to the combustion of particles in a firebrand. But this ultimate instance of Intention is unknowable, or at least transcends all our possible positive determinations, as Cantos XIX–XX, immediately following upon the Vision of Scripture in XVIII. 70–117, emphatically and elaborately confirm.

All the minutely articulated determinations of the poem, particularly in these cantos, gesture toward a significance that is indeterminate, one that finds no stable figure and yet is the significance of language as such. It is necessarily indeterminate because its significance belongs to the Other – the one who can never be apprehended in our own terms without being reduced to the Same. The *Paradiso*'s search for the Other lends its language a strangeness that adheres to it in virtue of no longer emanating from anything known, nor from anything determinable as human. The sign itself speaks beyond human intention and determination of an otherness that language cannot comprehend, one that language can only evoke. Dante uses all his powers as poet to evoke this uncanny strangeness.

Levinas develops this connection between language and uncanny alterity at length in the subsection "Séparation et Discours" (45–79) of the first part, "The Same and the Other" ("Le Même et l'Autre") of his chef-d'œuvre, *Totalité et infini*. Testimony to this absolute otherness can be found exclusively in language, according to Levinas, which helps to illuminate why Dante's poem, the *Paradiso*, is also so essentially an exploration of language. The sense of language is revealed as an otherness that is, with all possible metaphorical embellishment, perhaps the only determination of divinity possible for philosophy.

Levinas postulates in us a metaphysical desire for the absolutely other ("Le désir métaphysique tend vers *tout autre chose*, vers *l'absolument autre*," *Totalité et infini*, 21). However, according to Levinas, it is language alone that expresses and actually constitutes metaphysical desire in the relation to the absolutely Other: "the *relation* of the Same to the Other … is language" ("le *rapport* du Même et de l'Autre … est le langage," 28). This metaphysical relation is beyond the reach of representation and cannot be adequately articulated by language, yet language as such "signifies" it (27). In order to reach the Other in a way that does not reduce it to the Same and the self, with its representations of everything, the rupture of totality is necessary together with a transcendence toward what the Same cannot comprehend. This is what discourse does by facing an Other and breaking its own inevitable circuits of thinking, finding itself with an Other *en face*. This is what makes language the key to opening up the dimension of the religious. "Instead of constituting with [the Other], as an object, a total, *thought consists in speaking*. We propose to call religion the tie that is established between the Same and the Other without constituting a totality" ("Au lieu de constituer avec lui, comme un objet, un total, *la pensée consiste à parler*. Nous proposons d'appeler religion le lien qui s'établit entre le Même et l'Autre sans constituer une totalité," 30).

We heard previously from Heidegger that "language speaks" ("Die Sprache spricht"). We learn now from Levinas that language speaks by revealing the absolute otherness of the Other that is irreducible to the Same. Language reveals the demand for justice toward fellow humans speaking to us in the Face of the Other that is at least ambiguously divine. This face of the Other, for example, the other human being in need – "the widow, the orphan, and the stranger within your gates," in the language of the biblical prophets – addresses us and commands us with all the authority of God. Such is the ethical imperative that Levinas reads directly in the phenomenon of language as such.

Such language is, in fact, what Dante's *Paradiso* displays as the agent of revelation in the heaven of Justice and as the privileged object of his paradisiacal vision. He faces it most acutely, however, already in *Purgatorio* XXX–XXXI, in his being attacked and humiliated by *Beatrice loquax*. Dante's ladylove is not the docile object of a courtly male discourse of adoration. She comes on the scene as a storm of language hurled at him and melting him down in shame and abjection.[8] However, this assault is also what breaks him open to the absolute alterity in which alone he can (and does) encounter the divine Other. This encounter takes place, finally, in language projecting itself even beyond all figures of impersonation.

One of the features peculiar to the *Paradiso* is its giving voice to pure form and structure. Language as sign and signification is the poem's formal object most conspicuously in the Heaven of Jupiter. The blessed image – "bella image" or "benedetta imagine" (XIX. 2, 95) – of the Eagle, also called "that sign" ("quel segno," 37), does the talking. In general, the *Paradiso* does not excel in the verisimilar, in mimetic imitation of the human. The great realistic human portraits come earlier, in the first two canticles of the poem. What speaks in the *Paradiso* is more eerie than that, more redolent of an unearthly world. In spite of the extent to which the poem still reverts to images drawn from the earth, Dante wishes to lend voice to something transcendent, something that at least previously has "never been voiced nor written" nor even imagined or "comprehended by fantasy" ("E quel che mi convien ritrar testeso, / non portò voce mai, né scrisse incostro, / né fu per fantasia già mai compreso . . ." (XIX. 7–9).

Something radically other is enabled to speak in the *Paradiso*. In order to represent this otherness, all significances of language determined by human intentions must be neutralized. Language's significance must be determined from beyond anything known or the same as anything known. There is an insistence in the imagery of the Heaven of Jove on destroying transparency between language and the intentions that are ascribed to it by its users. Language, in this heaven, is depicted as resting on an apparently random combination of elements that miraculously take on sense. Of course, this sense is ascribed, in the end, to the intention of the divine Author, but such sense appears to us as if engendered wholly by chance – as beyond any possibility of calculating and controlling the translation of linguistic form into sense. As far as we can tell, this sense arises from indeterminate play of mindless material elements. We cannot comprehend the divine Mind or the intention behind it.

The sense of the language of the *Paradiso*, nevertheless, is determined by the appeal it makes in the name of Justice. And, necessarily, the sense of that appeal remains structurally open to determination by human responses. This is the express meaning of the vision in Jupiter, as stated plainly by the imperative sentence that is displayed ("Love justice," etc.)

---

[8] Heather Webb, *Dante's Persons: An Ethics of the Transhuman* (Oxford: Oxford University Press, 2016), 172–75, brings this out effectively.

and by all the thematic material of these cantos that surrounds it. This sense is reinforced by the vituperations against the unholy popes with which Canto XVIII ends (verses 118–36) and against lawless princes at the end of Canto XIX (verses 115–48). Finally, Canto XX concludes the heaven by ending on the note of the inscrutability of Providence:

> O predestinazion, quanto remota
> è la radice tua da quelli aspetti
> che la prima cagion non veggion tota!
>
> (XX. 130–32)

> (O predestination, how remote
> is your root from those regards
> which do not see the first cause whole!)

Dante, like Job, receives a lesson concerning the human incapacity to question divine justice as a remedy for his myopia:

> Così da quella imagine divina,
> per farmi chiara la mia corta vista,
> data mi fu soave medicina.
>
> (XX. 139–41)

> Thus from that divine image,
> in order to make me clear about my short sight,
> sweet medicine was dispensed to me.

Recognizing its aim and intent as beyond our fathoming is the deeper ethical sense of Dante's making of Scripture into a poetic spectacle.

Thus, even after these visionary gymnastics, the sense of God's unrepresentability has only been reinforced. No phenomenal presentation could be even remotely proportionate to his Being. The insistence on manifestation and presence proves, in the end, to be futile. At this point, not just form, but also content, needs to be considered. Beyond all its pyrotechnics, the central message of the vision is conveyed in an injunction to justice. This is succinctly expressed in the theme-text of the vision and of the entire heaven in which it takes place: "Love justice, you who rule the earth" ("Diligite iustitiam qui iudicatis terram").

In effect, justice is an ethical obligation that precedes every image and idea. Levinas has apprehended this principle in a different vocabulary and cultural predicament but in ways that are nevertheless poignantly pertinent to Dante. My obligation to my neighbor is not dependent on images that anyone receives, and it cannot be measured by any of its possible representations. "The obligation raised by the proximity of the neighbor is not measured by the images it delivers; it concerns me antecedently or otherwise. Such is the sense of the non-phenomenality of the face" ("L'obligation suscitée par la proximité du prochain n'est pas à la mesure des images qu'il délivre, me concerne avant ou autrement. Tel est le sens de la non-phénoménalité du visage").[9] The face of the Other shows me my timeless, immemorial openness to my neighbor, and this is, in essence, what Dante "sees" in envisioning God's presence in his Word as an imperative to do justice towards others on earth.

Levinas and the Face of the Other as Revelation and Theophany – Im/mediacy

We have just seen that in a philosophical vein, but still in the biblical tradition of receptiveness to revelation, Levinas has theorized the Face of the Other in its sheer externality as an immediacy in which the Other is made present beyond all means of access available to thought and representation. The immediacy of the Face telling me that I stand in the presence of an Other before me reveals this Other to me in "its" otherwise unattainable otherness. The Scriptural letters in Dante's Heaven of Jove present the divine Visage in a similarly immediate, and yet ungraspable, way. The concepts of "presence," "otherness," and "divinity" are all inadequate and serve only as allegories for what necessarily escapes conceptualization in the presentation of the letters as an unmediated presence of what Dante represents as divine vision ("visio Dei"). Dante is enabled, by envisioning the letters, to evoke a moment of presence, or of a kind of contact, with the Unrepresentable. He then elaborates on this experience allegorically. That the experience is an experience of divinity remains an article of faith. It cannot be logically proved, yet it can be persuasively presented in poetry, and it can instill desire for truth beyond any and all assurances of proof by argument.

Levinas's description of "the notion of the immediate" ("la notion de l'immédiat") stresses how only language and its imperative, in effect, the interpellation that it issues, can achieve immediacy: "The immediate is interpellation and, as it were, the imperative of language" ("L'immédiat est l'interpellation et, si l'on peut dire, l'impératif du langage," *Totalité et infini*, 44). Levinas *defines* the immediacy of the Other as the interpellation or imperative of language. Consequently, and very surprisingly, it is only in

---

[9] Levinas, *Autrement qu'être*, 142.

and indeed as the *medium* of language that the face-to-face relation with the Other can be realized. Any other form of contact is always already mediation and thus "we are never with a being as such, directly" ("nous ne sommes jamais avec l'étant comme tel, directement," 44). The unthematizable face-to-face of language, in contrast, realizes immediacy. This very closely resembles the paradox of the immediacy of mediation that we have elicited since the outset, and throughout this book, from Dante's vision of Scripture. Language, the medium, like writing, becomes im/mediate presence, or Face. The Levinasian face speaks the ineffable presence of the Other in a kind of ek-phrasis in which speech is broken off and lets its outside, the Other, break into presence and so "speak" beyond words and representation.

Levinas sees language as the privileged, indeed the unique, locus of revelation, and it is specifically language as im-mediate contact with the other in "signification" that necessarily stands beyond representation. For the wholly other to be revealed, it is necessary to undergo a relation with someone genuinely external to oneself. This must be an im-mediate encounter because any mediation would falsify or efface the otherness of the Other. For Levinas, the immediate presence of the external is the revelation of an otherness that remains inaccessible to thought and representation.

It is precisely, and only, by saying or *expressing itself* that being can be revealed as it really is in itself (καθ'αὐτό) rather than only as a modification of *our* faculties and projects of knowing. "Manifestation καθ'αὐτό consists in being's saying and *expressing itself* to us independently of any position taken by us in its regard" ("La manifestation καθ'αὐτό consiste pour l'être à se dire à nous, indépendament de toute position que nous aurions prise à son égard, *à s'exprimer*," 60–61). In language, and in language alone, for Levinas, and also for Dante in his Heaven of Jove, the absolute Other or divinity presents itself *as itself*. Instead of showing up as an object inscribed into the purview of an apprehending consciousness, divinity is *literally* present as directing or guiding this self-expression.

Appearing as a phenomenon, Being or the Absolute is never simply itself, but always *for* the one to whom it appears, for there is never any contact with a being that is not mediated by Being as the horizon in which beings appear, the ambit in which alone they can be what they are. Immediacy, as interpellation, is possible only in the medium and via the imperative of language – not an appearing within a prescribed horizon, but only in a direct address from . . . one cannot say whom.

The coincidence of the expressed and the one who expresses it is what
Levinas calls the face, a face that is manifest in, though not identical with,
visible form. For being a face entails a continual countering or undoing of
the form ("Il défait à tout instant la forme qu'il offre," 61) so as to avoid its
freezing into a formed image by which the one revealed is made manifest.
The faces of the blessed in Dante's *Paradiso* (starting from III. 10–16) are
similarly impossible to fix in any traceable outline. In line with this,
Levinas calls the face a living presence and expression ("Le visage est une
présence vivante, il est expression," 61). In this sense, the face speaks ("Le
visage parle"), and "the manifestation [of presence] in the face is already
discourse" ("la manifestation du visage est déjà discours," 61). The essential
thing in language is the coincidence of revealer and revealed in the face
("l'essentiel du langage: la coincidence du révélateur et du révélé dans le
visage," 62). Only language speaking in the face of the interlocutor can be
experienced in this pure sense that enables "the Other to enter into
relation, even while remaining what it is in itself (καθ'αὐτό)" ("Seul
l'interlocuteur est le terme d'une expérience pure où autrui entre en
relation, tout en demeurant καθ'αὐτό," 62).

For Levinas, language is the element of separation from the Other as
infinite, as beyond every possible totalization of knowledge: "the truth
arises where a being separated from the other is not engulfed by but
rather speaks to the other" ("la vérité surgit là où un être séparé de l'autre
ne s'abîme pas en lui, mais lui parle," 56). Truth emerges in the search in
and through Language for the Other who is external to the self or the
subject. The Beatrice of Dante's *Paradiso* is present as such an inaccessible Other through a series of superlatively demanding *discourses*. The
Other is an absolutely separate being that can address and be invoked by
the self, who is created from nothing. In the guise of the idea of the
Infinite, this Other is experienced not as an object of knowledge but as
desirable (so Beatrice). There is a knowledge implied here, but it is
a knowledge that is purely revelation "without a priori," and it is speech.
"The idea of the Infinite *reveals itself* in the full sense in the word"
("L'idée de l'Infini *se révèle*, au sens fort du terme," 56). This is not to be
mistaken for "disclosure" or ἀλήθεια in the sense Heidegger rediscovered
and refurbished, for it is not an impersonal event but rather a personal
self-expression. Levinas criticizes Heidegger's understanding of being as
"neutral" ("neutre"). For him, the "who" or "someone" of the Other is
irreducible to any being.

Levinas theorizes speaking as a presenting of oneself by signifying ("Se
présenter en signifiant, c'est parler," 61), where signification is "the

presence of exteriority" ("la présence de l'exteriorité," 61), that is, of the irreducibly Other. Discourse is par excellence "an original relation with exterior being" and is thereby opposed to all the ways of knowing by "modification of one's own sensibility or intellect" ("Le discours n'est pas simplement une modification de l'intuition [ou de la pensée], mais une relation originelle avec l'être extérieur," 61). Discourse, to be precise, is ethical relation ("discours se précise comme relation éthique," 78), which is infinite and transcendent. Beatrice is simply an other person, but she opens to Dante the infinite dimension of the Transcendent.

Even more specifically, for Levinas true discourse, that of the face of the Other, is justice. Rhetoric, for Levinas, is injustice and violence. In a certain sense, the whole show of letters in *Paradiso* XVIII reduces to artificial fireworks, a rhetorical show, but this is where the content rather than just the form of the phrase comes into play. The show of letters vanishes: what remains is an ethical injunction, addressed to the rulers of the earth, to love (and consequently do) justice. If the divine vision that Dante has imagined solidifies into a poetic rhetoric, however unique and original, as to its form, it becomes counterproductive. It must produce, rather, the content of its ethical injunction through its effects in actual life and history. The revelation of God is ultimately a realization of justice.

For Levinas, there can be no direct "intellection of God," no "intellectual participation in the divine life" ("L'intelligence de Dieu comme participation à sa vie sacrée, intelligence prétendument directe, est impossible," 76). Instead, access to God comes through justice and its claim on us. All spiritual experience is at bottom ethical: "The invisible God does not signify only an unimaginable God, but a God accessible through justice. Ethics is a spiritual optics" ("Dieu invisible, cela ne signifie pas seulement un Dieu inimaginable, mais un Dieu accessible dans la justice. L'éthique est l'optique spirituelle," 76). This implies that there is no knowledge or experience of God except via relations with human beings ("Il ne peut y avoir, séparée de la relation avec les hommes, aucune 'connaissance' de Dieu," 77).

In spite of his writing in the mystical tradition of the *visio Dei*, Dante similarly holds that we have no intellectual intuition of God. *Convivio* III. iv. 9 bases this conviction on the inability of our imaginative faculty (*fantasia*), as a physical power (*virtù organica*), to give us intuitions of immaterial substances. In the *Paradiso*, Dante does not relinquish the contemplative tradition and its claim to intellectual union with the divine essence as consummated at the end of the poem (XXXIII. 46–145). Still, his vision of God is, in essence, ethical. We have already noted the Letter to

Can Grande's explicit statement to this effect (*Epistole* XIII. xvi. 40). And the vision of God presented in the *Paradiso* is inseparable from and totally fused with a vision of relations of justice among humans. The poem is a constant cry of protest against the injustices perpetrated by the powerful, especially by popes and princes. But beyond this, Dante's vision is emphatically a *written* vision – achieved through the mediation of language and poetic rhetoric rather than by the supposedly unmediated intellection of divinity.

The doctrine of purely intellectual intuition of the divine essence is still present in Dante's poem all the way to its final, impossible *visio* realized nevertheless by a lightning strike on Dante's mind ("la mia mente fu percossa / da un fulgore in che sua voglia venne," XXXIII. 140–41). And, according to the Letter to Can Grande, "We see by intellect many things for which verbal signs are lacking" ("Multa namque per intellectum videmus quibus signa vocalia desunt," XIII. 29. 84). We see them rather as mythologized by writing and so as becoming motifs within a literary journey and vision. Does not Dante, too, in effect, seek God in the openness of "communication," as Levinas employs this notion, and in desire? Dante in his poetical ascent is willing to lose the certainty of a known presence in order to explore, instead, the significance or "signify-ingness" of language when divested of any apodictically known term. Revelation in language *à la* Levinas as im-mediate encounter with an absolute Other is, in fact, the ethical substance of Dante's poem, to which its dogmatic contents and framework serve as a mythological scaffolding.

In ways illuminated by Levinas's philosophical speculations, Dante's theophantic vision in Jove represents language as the face of the Other. The written signs displayed in the heaven are not dead and cut off from their Emitter, nor are they merely objects in a spectacle. They constitute, instead, God's self-showing. They are, in Levinas's sense, God's "Face." Dante underwrites this image in a Levinasian sense by his injunction to ethical relation.

Encountering or *facing* the Other in the persons of other human beings is what theology boils down to in the *Commedia* as interpreted also by Vittorio Montemaggi.[10] Dante's poem presents its theology, above all, in the form of Dante's encounters with other human beings, and this

---

[10] Vittorio Montemaggi, *Reading Dante's Commedia as Theology: Divinity Realized in Human Encounter* (Oxford: Oxford University Press, 2016).

procedure makes theology for him a matter primarily of justice and truthfulness and of love among *persons*. This interpersonal axis is enacted preeminently in his face-to-face gazing on Beatrice as mediating his experience of divinity in the *Paradiso*. This is the vein in which also Heather Webb, in *Dante's Persons: An Ethics of the Transhuman*, probes the transcendent ethical implications of personhood in Dante.

Beyond: Dante, Levinas, and the Imperative of Justice

For modern, secular individuals, the world becomes an object and so is no longer bewitched as a speaking phenomenon or apparition. This disenchantment is achieved chiefly through language. My relation to the Other in language is an association essentially ethical in nature. As a result, "truth is founded on my relation with the Other or justice" ("la vérité se fonde sur mon rapport avec l'Autre ou la justice," *Totalité et infini*, 101). The phrase is deeply resonant with Dante because his poem is not just an unveiling to solitary vision and contemplation: it is a solicitation to just action and worldly engagement. Revelation, unlike "disclosure," cannot be reduced to any merely neutral point of view: it remains free, undetermined by the given objectivity of any object. Revelation is rather a "presenting" of the strange or "the foreign" to "me" ("Ce qui se présente comme indépendant de tout mouvement subjectif, c'est l'interlocuteur dont la *manière* consiste à partir de soi, à être étranger et, cependent, à se présenter à moi," 63). This makes "revelation" in relation to the "call of the Other" ("l'appel d'Autrui," 63) fundamentally different from objectivizing modes of knowing and their disclosures, which are based on an ontological relation to being in general rather than on an ethical relation to someone other (63).

In a Levinasian optics, God cannot appear except as justice, and his justice cannot be present as an achieved fact but only as an imperative enjoined upon humans, precisely as in the banner phrase of Dante's vision, in which its whole significance is concentrated: "Love justice! You who rule the earth." Immediate revelation of God in language is inseparable from his revelation in and as justice. There is no more complete or final revelation of the divine essence in itself – even though the whole poem is directed towards such a revelation and is built on assuming such a possibility as its hypothesis. All these themes woven inextricably into Dante's vision are also worked out in their necessary interpenetration by Levinas's religiously inspired philosophical thinking.

Dante has deeply contemplated the necessary "externality" or heteronomy of any encounter with otherness, such as our encounter with a transcendent divinity can only be, and he has understood this possibility in terms of language. This brings him astonishingly near to Levinas, in spite of enormous historical and cultural distances. Yet it is not completely incredible, if we consider that both are moved by and concentrate on the ethical vision at the heart of Scriptural revelation in the divine Word and on translating this into their respective philosophic and poetic idioms. This, on the face of it, arbitrary and anachronistic juxtaposition in the end bears powerful witness to the nearness or affinity of Dante's late medieval culture to our own postmodern age – or at least to the ability of the two ages to communicate with one another transhistorically.

Dante does not offer an intimate mysticism of communion with sweet Jesus, nor even an indulgently impressionistic expression of absorption in and fusion with the Godhead. His is a secularized mysticism turned toward the world and human encounters and the ethical demand for justice that emanates from history and life in society. His filtering this more exterior view through a linguistic optics makes for some striking accords with the philosophical, secularly religious outlook of Levinas.

In the postwar period, Levinas revolutionized continental philosophy and phenomenology by turning it in an ethical direction – towards ethical relation as the indispensable basis for any kind of philosophical or human truth. Largely in his wake, phenomenological philosophy took a theological turn, as was previously outlined in concluding Excursus IV. This new phenomenology of the invisible or non-phenomenal is still all about how to deal with otherness. The other person is a pivot point from which a relation opens to an otherness that can hardly be delimited because it enfolds a relation to the Infinite.

It bears remarking that this imperative mood is also the drift of postmodern theologies such as those of John Caputo and Richard Kearney. The former pivots on the infinite *appeal* to justice incumbent upon the individual to enact rather than on metaphysical assurances about the order of the world.[11] In the latter, the imperative modulates into an optative mood: God concerns what *may be* – *if* we make it happen.[12] These kinds of wide-ranging and distant connections suggest ways in which Dante,

---

[11] John Caputo, *The Weakness of God: A Theology of the Event* (Bloomington: Indiana University Press, 2006) and *The Insistence of God: A Theology of Perhaps* (Bloomington: Indiana University Press, 2013).

[12] Richard Kearney, *The God Who May Be: A Hermeneutics of Religion* (Bloomington: Indiana University Press, 2001).

through his treatment in the Heaven of Jupiter of divine revelation transpiring essentially in and through writing, raises questions of the nature of experiencing God that remain pertinent, in the highest degree, for our postmodern era. These connections afford valuable resources for theological and a/theological reflection in the excruciating dilemmas of our present cultural predicament.

Paradiso XVIII. 70–136

⁷⁰Io vidi in quella giovïal facella
⁷¹lo sfavillar de l'amor che lì era
⁷²segnare a li occhi miei nostra favella.

I saw in that jovial torch
the sparkling of the love that was there
signify to my eyes our speech.

⁷³E come augelli surti di rivera,
⁷⁴quasi congratulando a lor pasture,
⁷⁵fanno di sé or tonda or altra schiera,

And even as birds risen up from banks,
as if congratulating themselves on their good fare,
make of themselves a round or other-shaped swarm,

⁷⁶sì dentro ai lumi sante creature
⁷⁷volitando cantavano, e faciensi
⁷⁸or *D*, or *I*, or *L* in sue figure.

so, within the holy lights, creatures
flying sang and made themselves
now D, now I, now L in its figures.

⁷⁹Prima, cantando, a sua nota moviensi;
⁸⁰poi, diventando l'un di questi segni,
⁸¹un poco s'arrestavano e taciensi.

First, singing, they moved to its note,
then, becoming one of these signs,
they paused for a little and kept silent.

⁸²O diva Pegasëa che li 'ngegni
⁸³fai glorïosi e rendili longevi,
⁸⁴ed essi teco le cittadi e ' regni,

O divine Pegasea, you who make wits
glorious and render them long-lived,
just as they, with you, do cities and realms,

⁸⁵illustrami di te, sì ch'io rilevi
⁸⁶le lor figure com' io l'ho concette:
⁸⁷paia tua possa in questi versi brevi!

illuminate me with yourself, so that I may exalt
the letters' figures even as I conceived them:
let your power appear in these brief verses!

⁸⁸Mostrarsi dunque in cinque volte sette
⁸⁹vocali e consonanti; e io notai
⁹⁰le parti sì, come mi parver dette.

So, then, five times seven vowels and consonants
showed themselves; and I noted
the parts just as they appeared dictated to me.

⁹¹*"DILIGITE IUSTITIAM"*, primai
⁹²fur verbo e nome di tutto 'l dipinto;
⁹³*"QUI IUDICATIS TERRAM"*, fur sezzai.

"DILIGITE IUSTITIAM," were first,
the verb and noun of the whole painting;
"QUI IUDICATIS TERRAM," were last.

⁹⁴Poscia ne l'emme del vocabol quinto
⁹⁵rimasero ordinate; sì che Giove
⁹⁶pareva argento lì d'oro distinto.

Then in the M of the fifth word
the souls remained arranged; so that Jove
appeared there to be silver chased with gold.

⁹⁷E vidi scendere altre luci dove
⁹⁸era il colmo de l'emme, e lì quetarsi
⁹⁹cantando, credo, il ben ch'a sé le move.

And I saw other lights descend to where
the M culminated and settle there singing,
I believe, the good that moved them to
  itself.

¹⁰⁰Poi, come nel percuoter d'i ciocchi
  arsi
¹⁰¹surgono innumerabili faville,
¹⁰²onde li stolti sogliono agurarsi,

Then, as in the beating of burnt brands,
numberless sparks spring up,
from which fools are wont to discern
  omens,

¹⁰³resurger parver quindi più di mille
¹⁰⁴luci e salir, qual assai e qual poco,
¹⁰⁵sì come 'l sol che l'accende sortille;

more than a thousand lights seemed
to surge and rise, some much and some
  little,
as the Sun that ignites them alots;

¹⁰⁶e quïetata ciascuna in suo loco,
¹⁰⁷la testa e 'l collo d'un'aguglia vidi
¹⁰⁸rappresentare a quel distinto foco.

and when each one was quiet in its place,
I saw the head and neck of an eagle
represented in that distinct fire.

¹⁰⁹Quei che dipinge lì, non ha chi 'l
  guidi;
¹¹⁰ma esso guida, e da lui si rammenta
¹¹¹quella virtù ch'è forma per li nidi.

He who paints there has no one to
  guide him;
he guides, rather, and the power which is
  the formal principle of being in nests
puts us in mind of him.

¹¹²L'altra bëatitudo, che contenta
¹¹³pareva prima d'ingigliarsi a l'emme,
¹¹⁴con poco moto seguitò la 'mprenta.

The other beatitude, which appeared
  content
at first to form a lily in the M,
with a little motion filled out the design.

¹¹⁵O dolce stella, quali e quante gemme
¹¹⁶mi dimostraro che nostra giustizia
¹¹⁷effetto sia del ciel che tu ingemme!

O sweet star, what gems, and in what
  numbers,
demonstrated to me that our justice
is the effect of the heaven that you bejewel!

¹¹⁸Per ch'io prego la mente in che s'inizia
¹¹⁹tuo moto e tua virtute, che rimiri
¹²⁰ond' esce il fummo che 'l tuo raggio
  vizia;

For which I pray to the mind in which your
motion and virtue originate that you
  look down
to whence issues the smoke that vitiates
  your ray;

¹²¹sì ch'un'altra fïata omai s'adiri
¹²²del comperare e vender dentro al
  templo
¹²³che si murò di segni e di martìri.

so that once again you now grow wroth
against the buying and selling within the
  temple
that was built through martyrs and
  miracles.

¹²⁴O milizia del ciel cu' io contemplo,
¹²⁵adora per color che sono in terra
¹²⁶tutti svïati dietro al malo essemplo!

O militia of the heaven that I contemplate,
pray for those who are on earth,
led all astray by that bad example!

¹²⁷Già si solea con le spade far guerra;
¹²⁸ma or si fa togliendo or qui or quivi
¹²⁹lo pan che 'l pïo Padre a nessun serra.

Once it was customary to make war with swords;
but now it is waged by taking away here and there
the bread that the loving Father denies to none.

¹³⁰Ma tu che sol per cancellare scrivi,
¹³¹pensa che Pietro e Paulo, che moriro
¹³²per la vigna che guasti, ancor son vivi.

But you who write only in order to erase,
remember that Peter and Paul, who died
for the vine that you ruin, are still alive.

¹³³Ben puoi tu dire: "I' ho fermo 'l disiro
¹³⁴sì a colui che volle viver solo
¹³⁵e che per salti fu tratto al martiro,

You can well say: "'I' have my desire steady set on him who willed to live alone
and who for a dance was dragged to martyrdom,

¹³⁶ch'io non conosco il pescator né Polo."

since I know neither the fisherman nor Pol [Paul]."

Index

Ingram Content Group UK Ltd.
Milton Keynes UK
UKHW020617190723
425395UK00033B/573